Orthodoxy and Heresy
in Early Christian Contexts

Orthodoxy and Heresy
in Early Christian Contexts

Reconsidering the Bauer Thesis

EDITED BY

PAUL A. HARTOG

PICKWICK *Publications* · Eugene, Oregon

ORTHODOXY AND HERESY IN EARLY CHRISTIAN CONTEXTS
Reconsidering the Bauer Thesis

Pickwick Publications
An Imprint of Wipf and Stock Publishers
199 W. 8th Ave., Suite 3
Eugene, OR 97401

www.wipfandstock.com

ISBN 13: 978-1-61097-504-9

Cataloguing-in-Publication Data

Orthodoxy and heresy in early Christian contexts : reconsidering the Bauer thesis / edited by Paul A. Hartog.

X + Y p. ; 23 cm. Includes bibliographical references.

ISBN 13: 978-1-61097-504-9

1. Christian heresies—History—Early church, ca. 30–600. 2. Church history—Primitive and early church, ca. 30–600. 3. Bauer, Walter, 1877–1960. I. Title.

BR166 O66 2015

Manufactured in the U.S.A.   01/26/2015

Dedicated to the memory of Rod Decker (1953–2014),
contributor and colleague

gloriosa in conspectu Domini mors sanctorum eius

Contents

Preface

I ESPECIALLY THANK MY parents, John and Martha Hartog, for their support of this project. I wish to acknowledge Allison Brady's help with the bibliography. Amy Kramer's assistance with interlibrary loans was indispensable, as always. I thank all the contributors for their patience in seeing this extended project through to completion. My utmost gratitude is offered to my sweetheart Alne and to our three blessings (Ethan, Anastacia, and Isaiah), for their continual love and support. Abbreviations throughout conform to *The SBL Handbook of Style*, edited by Patrick H. Alexander (Peabody, MA: Hendrickson, 1999).

List of Contributors

David C. Alexander (PhD, University of Edinburgh) is Adjunct Professor of Church History at Liberty University, and he is the author of *Augustine's Early Theology of the Church* (2008).

Rex D. Butler (PhD, Southwestern Baptist Theological Seminary) is Professor of Church History and Patristics at New Orleans Baptist Theological Seminary, and he is the author of *The New Prophecy and "New Visions"* (2006).

Rodney J. Decker (ThD, Central Baptist Theological Seminary) was Professor of Greek and New Testament at Baptist Bible Seminary, and he authored *Temporal Deixis of the Greek Verb in the Gospel of Mark with Reference to Verbal Aspect* (2001); *Koine Greek Reader* (2007); *Reading Koine Greek* (2014); and *Mark: A Handbook on the Greek Text* (2014).

Paul A. Hartog (PhD, Loyola University Chicago) is Professor of New Testament and Early Christian Studies at Faith Baptist Seminary, and he is the author of *Polycarp and the New Testament* (2002) and *Polycarp's Epistle to the Philippians and the Martyrdom of Polycarp* (2013), and the editor of *The Contemporary Church and the Early Church* (Pickwick, 2010).

Bryan M. Litfin (PhD, University of Virginia) is Professor of Theology at Moody Bible Institute, and his works include *Getting to Know the Church Fathers* (2007), *Early Christian Martyr Stories* (2014), and *After Acts: Exploring the Lives and Legends of the Apostles* (2015).

W. Brian Shelton (PhD, Saint Louis University) is Vice President for Academic Affairs and Professor of Theology and Church History at Toccoa Falls College, and his works include *Martyrdom from Exegesis in Hippolytus* (2008).

Carl B. Smith (PhD, Miami University) is a Department Chair and Program Director at South University, and he is the author of *No Longer Jews: The Search for Gnostic Origins* (2004).

Edward L. Smither (PhD, University of Wales—Trinity Saint David; PhD, University of Pretoria) is Professor of Intercultural Studies at Columbia International University, and he is the author of *Augustine as Mentor* (2009), *Brazilian Evangelical Missions in the Arab World* (Pickwick, 2012), *Mission in the Early Church* (Cascade, 2014), the editor of *Rethinking Constantine* (Pickwick, 2014), and the translator of *Early Christianity in North Africa* (Cascade, 2009).

Glen L. Thompson (PhD, Columbia University) is Academic Dean and Professor of Historical Theology and New Testament at Asia Lutheran Seminary (Hong Kong), and he is the author of *The Correspondence of Pope Julius I* (2014).

William Varner (EdD, Temple University) is Professor of Bible and Greek at The Master's College, and he is the author of many books, including *Ancient Jewish-Christian Dialogues* (2005); *The Didache: The First Christian Handbook* (2007); and *The Book of James: A New Perspective* (2011).

Introduction

Paul A. Hartog

WALTER BAUER (1877–1960) WAS an influential German professor, a skilled linguist of classical languages, a biblical commentator, and a historian of early Christianity.[1] He enjoyed a prolonged academic career at the universities of Marburg, Strasburg, and Berlin. Theological students around the world still acknowledge the enduring standard of his lexical work, now known (in the most recent edition) as "BDAG," the Bauer-Danker-Arndt-Gingrich *Greek-English Lexicon of the New Testament and Other Early Christian Literature*.[2]

Bauer's major work that re-oriented the underlying foundations of New Testament scholarship, however, was his 1934 study entitled *Rechtgläubigkeit und Ketzerei im ältesten Christentum* (second German edition, 1964).[3] This year (2014) marks the golden anniversary (semicentennial) of the second German edition and the eightieth anniversary of the first German edition. The 1971 Fortress edition of *Orthodoxy and Heresy in Earliest Christianity* catapulted his influence upon English scholarship. As a testament to its enduring importance, Bauer's volume is still readily available in print in French as well as in English.[4]

---

1. See Fascher, "Walter Bauer als Kommentator"; Gingrich, "Walter Bauer"; Schneemelcher, "Walter Bauer als Kirchenhistoriker"; Strecker, "Walter Bauer"; Baird, *History of New Testament Research*, vol. 2, 451–55.

2. See Baird, *History of New Testament Research*, vol. 2, 415–17.

3. Bauer, *Rechtgläubigkeit und Ketzerei*; Bauer and Strecker, *Rechtgläubigkeit und Ketzerei*.

4. Bauer, *Orthodoxie et hérésie*; Bauer, *Orthodoxy and Heresy*.

Bauer's work questioned basic assumptions of New Testament and early Christian scholarship. He specifically challenged the traditional view of Christian origins, which privileged the primacy of "orthodoxy."[5] He argued: 1) In many geographical regions, what came to be deemed as "heresy" was the original form of Christianity. 2) In many locales, the "heretical" adherents often outnumbered the "orthodox" adherents. 3) As one form of Christianity among many, "orthodoxy" suppressed "heretical" competitors, often through ecclesiastical machinations and coercive tactics, and especially through the powerful influence of the Roman church. 4) The "orthodox" parties then revised the church's collective memory by claiming that their views had always been the accepted norm. Hans Lietzmann praised the final product as "A splendid book . . . a frontal attack on the usual approach to church history, vigorously carried out with solid erudition, penetrating criticism, and balanced organization."[6]

Although first published eighty years ago, and although criticized in specific details, the *general* thrust of the Bauer Thesis enormously influences early Christian studies even in the present.[7] Bart Ehrman has called Bauer's study "the most important book on the history of early Christianity to appear in the twentieth century"[8] and "possibly the most significant book on early Christianity written in modern times."[9] Bauer's work widened the horizons of New Testament scholarship by bringing the question of "unity and diversity" to the forefront.[10] Prodigées of the

---

5. As Bart Ehrman explains regarding Bauer's employment of "orthodoxy" and "heresy," "He uses the terms descriptively to refer to social groups, namely, the party that eventually established dominance over the rest of Christendom (orthodoxy) and the individuals and groups that expressed alternative theological views (heresies). In doing so, he implies no value judgment (one group was right, the others were wrong) and does not embrace the traditional notion that one of the groups (orthodoxy) could claim historical priority and numerical superiority over the others" (Ehrman, *Orthodox Corruption*, 8). Thus "heretical" simply refers to "forms subsequently condemned by the victorious party" (ibid.). Ehrman agrees that "the labels *can* retain their usefulness as descriptions of social and political realities, quite apart from their theological connotations" (ibid., 13).

6. As found in Bauer, *Orthodoxy and Heresy*, 287.

7. Besides the famous names that follow in the paragraph above, see also Dart, *Jesus of Heresy and History*; Riley, *One Jesus, Many Christs*.

8. Ehrman, *Lost Christianities*, 173.

9. Ehrman, *Orthodox Corruption*, 7.

10. See Dunn, *Unity and Diversity in the New Testament*; Carson, "Unity and Diversity in the New Testament"; Smalley, "Diversity and Development in John"; Martin, "Some Reflections"; Köstenberger, "Diversity and Unity."

Bauer Thesis (in revised forms) include such famous and accomplished scholars as Karen King (Harvard University), Helmut Koester (Harvard University), Gerd Lüdemann (University of Göttingen), Elaine Pagels (Princeton University), James Robinson (Claremont Graduate University), and the late Marvin Meyer (Chapman University).[11] Perhaps the most celebrated contemporary disseminator of Bauer's basic approach is Bart Ehrman, a prolific author who has written or edited around thirty volumes, including four books on the *New York Times* bestseller list.[12]

These scholars, following in the footsteps of Bauer, emphasize the diversity of "early Christianities,"[13] sometimes denying any theological strand or core that could claim normative continuity with apostolic tradition. As a result, substantially diverse movements become more or less equally valid forms of Christianity, and ancient "heresies" can be recovered as rehabilitated "lost Christianities."[14] The Bauer Thesis has become "the now-familiar story of the tremendous diversity of early Christianity and its eventual suppression by a powerful 'proto-orthodox' faction."[15] As Ehrman explains, the group eventually tagged as "orthodox," which possessed "a kind of spirited intolerance of contrary views," achieved social dominance through such power ploys as "social ostracism, economic pressures, and political machinations."[16] "Only when one social group had exerted itself sufficiently over the rest of Christendom did a 'majority' opinion emerge; only then did the 'right belief' represent the view

---

11. For the intervening period between Bauer and these contemporaries, Köstenberger and Kruger highlight the work of Rudolf Bultmann (Köstenberger and Kruger, *Heresy of Orthodoxy*, 27–28).

12. Ehrman, *Misquoting Jesus*; Ehrman, *God's Problem*; Ehrman, *Jesus Interrupted*; and Ehrman, *Forged*. One would imagine that Ehrman's recently published *How Jesus Became God* will enjoy similar popularity.

13. "Evidence for this view has been steadily mounting throughout the present century: we know of the widespread diversity of early Christianity from both primary and secondary accounts, and can sometimes pinpoint this diversity with considerable accuracy" (Ehrman, *Orthodox Corruption*, 4).

14. See Ehrman, *Lost Christianities*.

15. See Koester, "Gnomai Diaphoroi." Cf. Henry, "Why is Contemporary Scholarship So Enamored of Ancient Heresies?"

16. Ehrman, *Orthodox Corruption*, 13, 17. "Looked at in sociohistorical terms, orthodoxy and heresy are concerned as much with struggles over power as with debates over ideas" (ibid., 14).

of the Christian church at large."[17] But this was due to "the 'accident' of their preservation."[18]

The last eighty years have proven that the Bauer Thesis was a bold, provocative understanding of Christian origins. On the one hand, even Bauer's critics acknowledge his fascinating suggestions and erudite contentions, as well as his dismantling of simplistic, ahistorical views of "monolithic dogma." By examining data from specific geographical locations with careful attention to localized details, he rightfully persuaded other scholars to mistrust sweeping generalizations.[19] He motivated theologians to consider the role of sociological and political forces within theological debates. Furthermore, he helped to renew interest in forgotten movements that had been swept away by history. On the other hand, Bauer overlooked, ignored, or manipulated historical data, and he often resorted to unfounded conjectures, special pleading, or arguments from silence.

On any view, the Bauer Thesis has greatly influenced New Testament studies, although his original work purposely targeted only second- and third-century Christianity. In this sense, the word *earliest* in the title of his work (*Orthodoxy and Heresy in Earliest Christianity*) can be a misleading descriptor.[20] Ironically, Bauer dismissed the New Testament as "both too unproductive and too much disputed to be able to serve as a point of departure."[21] Most critical assessments of Bauer's work, however, have come from the pens of New Testament scholars, even to this day (most recently, Andreas Köstenberger and Michael Kruger, *The Heresy of Orthodoxy*, 2010).

The reconstruction of equally valid forms of Christianity without a normative center continues to be a "live" topic. The present volume forms a unique contribution through its comprehensive analysis, including critical evaluations by a range of New Testament and especially Patristic scholars. The Patristic focus reflects the second- and third-century emphasis of Bauer himself. Moreover, the interdisciplinary approach guarantees that the compilation will be a valuable resource in both the New Testament and Patristic fields. The essayists have re-examined the Bauer Thesis by taking a fresh look at orthodoxy and heresy, unity and

17. Ibid., 8.

18. Ibid.

19. See Gero, "With Walter Bauer on the Tigris."

20. Marshall, "Orthodoxy and Heresy in Earlier Christianity"; Staten, "Was There Unity in the Sub-Apostolic Church?"

21. Bauer, *Orthodoxy and Heresy*, xxv.

diversity, theology and ideology, and rhetoric and polemic within early Christian contexts. They have updated the discussion through investigations of post-Bauer evidence concerning Gnosticism and Jewish Christianity, and they have examined a region of early Christianity completely overlooked by Bauer—the North African churches. All contributors have authored previous publications in their respective topics.

These focused essays, supplemented by post-Bauer discoveries and refined by post-Bauer scholarship, reveal new insights through careful attention to historical detail and geographical particularity, even as Bauer himself demanded.[22] Although recognizing the importance of Bauer's innovative methodologies, fruitful suggestions, and legitimate criticisms of traditional views, the contributors also expose Bauer's numerous claims that fall short of the historical evidence. The contributors' desire is that this fresh examination of Bauer's paradigm may serve as a launching point to a richer and deeper understanding of the unity and diversity (and even normativity) found in the variegated early Christian movement.

---

22. The majority of these essays were presented at an invited session of the Patristics and Medieval History Section of the Evangelical Theological Society. As chairperson of the section, I was tasked with editing this volume. As always, the particular views expressed remain those of each individual contributor alone.

1

The Bauer Thesis: An Overview

Rodney J. Decker

CONTROVERSIES REGARDING JESUS AND the early Jesus movement are certainly not new, dating back now several centuries.[1] Philip Jenkins summarizes an often-forgotten history of the proposals which have been "a perennial phenomenon within Western culture since the Enlightenment."[2] The primary impetus for the recent outbreak of speculation has not been the discovery of new data very different from what we have known for a long time. Rather it is, claims Jenkins, a philosophical/ideological shift in Western culture: the rise of postmodernism and its entailments.[3]

One of the current writers in the media spotlight is Bart Ehrman. He is not the first nor only voice advocating a radical overhaul of our conception of early Christianity.[4] He has been, however, one of the more

---

1. For an overview of the various "Jesus Quests," see Bock, *Studying the Historical Jesus*; Boyd, *Cynic Sage or Son of God?*; Johnson, *Real Jesus*; Schweitzer, *Von Reimarus zu Wrede*; later titled *Geschichte der Leben-Jesu-Forschung*, 2nd German ed., ET, *The Quest of the Historical Jesus*, 2nd English ed.; Wilkins and Moreland, *Jesus Under Fire*; Witherington *Jesus Quest*, 2nd ed.; and Witherington, *What Have They Done with Jesus?*; and, on a broader scale, Baird, *History of New Testament Research*, 3 vols.

2. Jenkins, *Hidden Gospels*, 15; see his summary on pp. 13–15.

3. Ibid., 15–20, 124–47, 169–77. I have not attempted to track all the reasons for the contemporary speculation, being content with noting only the most significant issues.

4. For similar literature, see Riley, *One Jesus, Many Christs*; Lüdemann, *Heretics*; Hopkins, *World Full of Gods*; Pagels, *Gnostic Gospels*; Dart, *Jesus of Heresy and History*;

visible and influential voices.[5] This is due to several factors. First, he is a first-rate scholar in a significant discipline, New Testament textual criticism. In this regard he has justifiably benefited from his association with the "dean" of that field, Bruce Metzger.[6] He is also a good writer and effective communicator. In addition, he has achieved broad media exposure for his popularization of more scholarly work.[7] His major publications relevant to the history of early Christianity include the following:

- *Orthodox Corruption of Scripture: The Effect of Early Christological Controversies on the Text of the New Testament* (1993)

- *Lost Christianities: The Battle for Scripture and the Faiths We Never Knew* (2003)

- *Lost Scriptures: Books That Did Not Make It into the New Testament* (2003)

- *Misquoting Jesus: The Story Behind Who Changed the Bible and Why* (2005)

- *Jesus Interrupted: Revealing the Hidden Contradictions in the Bible (and Why We Don't Know about Them)* (2009)

- *Forged: Writing in the Name of God, Why the Bible's Authors Are Not Who We Think They Are* (2011)

- *How Jesus Became God: The Exaltation of a Jewish Preacher from Galilee* (2014)

The thesis which Ehrman proposes runs as follows, in his own words. After listing a wide range of phenomena in the diverse groups comprising "Christendom"[8]—including everything from Roman Catholic mis-

Funk, *Honest to Jesus*; and Ruether, *Women and Redemption*.

5. The real issues are not in Ehrman, though he builds on them; he is only the most recent popularizer of much older ideas. Perhaps this record of my explorations (and excavations!) in the piles that have accumulated in my study of late will be of help in orienting others to the issues which Ehrman's writings have raised.

6. Ehrman was one of Metzger's last two PhD students in textual criticism at Princeton (the other being Michael Holmes) and he was selected to prepare the most recent revision of Metzger's standard textbook, *Text of the New Testament*, 4th ed.

7. Ehrman has been featured on National Public Radio, has served as a consultant for major media specials on related topics (e.g., the Gospel of Judas), and has achieved significant rankings on bestseller lists.

8. The use of "Christendom" is my term, intended to be understood as a very broad cover term for any and all groups that profess any form of allegiance to Jesus and/or

sionaries, snake handlers, Greek Orthodoxy, fundamentalists, mainline churches, to David Koresh—Ehrman writes,

> All this diversity of belief and practice, and the intolerance that occasionally results, makes it difficult to know whether we should think of Christianity as one thing or lots of things, whether we should speak of Christianity or Christianities.
>
> What could be more diverse than this variegated phenomenon, Christianity in the modern world? In fact, there may be an answer: Christianity in the ancient world. . . .
>
> Most of these ancient forms of Christianity are unknown to people in the world today, since they eventually came to be reformed or stamped out. As a result, the sacred texts that some ancient Christians used to support their religious perspectives came to be proscribed, destroyed, or forgotten—in one way or another lost. . . .
>
> Virtually all forms of modern Christianity . . . go back to *one* form of Christianity that emerged as victorious from the conflicts of the second and third centuries. This one form of Christianity decided what was the "correct" Christian perspective; it decided who could exercise authority over Christian belief and practice; and it determined what forms of Christianity would be marginalized, set aside, destroyed. It also decided which books to canonize into Scripture and which books to set aside as "heretical," teaching false ideas.
>
> And then, as a coup de grâce, this victorious party rewrote the history of the controversy, making it appear that there had not been much of a conflict at all, claiming that its own views had always been those of the majority of Christians at all times, back to the time of Jesus and his apostles, that its perspective, in effect, had always been "orthodox" (i.e., the "right belief") and that its opponents in the conflict, with their other scriptural texts, had always represented small splinter groups invested in deceiving people into "heresy."
>
> It is striking that, for centuries, virtually everyone who studied the history of early Christianity simply accepted the version of the early conflicts written by the orthodox victors. This all began to change in a significant way in the nineteenth century as some scholars began to question the "objectivity" of such early Christian writers as the fourth-century orthodox writer Eusebius, the so-called Father of Church History, who reproduced

---

the term *Christian*. Ehrman calls it simply "Christianity"—without delineation as to how that ought to be defined.

for us the earliest account of the conflict. This initial query into Eusebius's accuracy eventually became, in some circles, a virtual onslaught on his character, as twentieth-century scholars began to subject his work to an ideological critique that exposed his biases and their role in his presentation. This reevaluation of Eusebius was prompted, in part, by the discovery of additional ancient books . . . other Gospels, for example, that also claimed to be written in the names of apostles.[9]

Ehrman is quite right that this is not the traditional portrait of early Christianity. But it is by no means original with him, though he has done as much to popularize it as anyone in recent years. The real credit for this view of history belongs to Walter Bauer, so we will fittingly commence with the fountain and by first examining Bauer's influential thesis.[10]

Bauer's *Orthodoxy and Heresy* (1934)

Brilliant, profound, extremely well read, indefatigable—these are all accurate descriptions of the German scholar to whom we owe much.[11] Although taking sharp issue with Bauer's thesis under consideration, I have a great respect for his lexical work.[12] No serious work in New Testament

---

9. Ehrman, *Lost Christianities*, 1, 4, 5.

10. It is possible that the core of Bauer's ideas are much older; Harold O. J. Brown refers to Johann Semler's contention that "the present canon is arbitrary and represents the victory of the Roman see in the ecclesiastical politics of the early church" (Brown, *Heresies*, 71; citing Semler, *Abhandlung von freier Untersuchung des Canons*, but no page reference is given; I have not had access to Semler's work to see if the idea is developed further).

There are definitely other contributing factors, most of which are closer at hand than Semler's eighteenth-century work. Michel Desjardins comments that Bauer's "study was a natural extension of a preceding century's scholarly work," listing the Tübingen school (F. C. Baur), the *Religionsgeschichtliche Schule*, and Harnack's work on heresy and the gnostics as direct contributors to the thesis of Bauer's *Orthodoxy and Heresy* (Desjardins, "Bauer and Beyond," 67–68). See also Robinson, *Bauer Thesis Examined*, 15–18, who qualifies the nature of the relationship between Tübingen/F. C. Baur and Walter Bauer's argument.

11. In this section references to the English translation of Bauer's *Orthodoxy and Heresy* are given parenthetically (as is also the case in other summaries that follow). The sketch given here cannot be complete due to limitations of space, but the main lines of Bauer's argument are traced, though without much of his supporting evidence. I have tried to make the summary just that and refrain from critique at this point. When unavoidable, I have added my comments in a footnote.

12. My extensive tributes (and corrections) to BDAG may be found at www.

exegesis is possible without reference to his lexicon, whether the third English edition[13] or the sixth German edition.[14] But before the professor from Göttingen turned his attention to lexicography[15] Walter Bauer (1877–1960) published several works on the history of the early church, including a 1903 study of the Syrian canon of the epistles in the fourth and fifth centuries[16] and another in 1909 of Jesus in the apocrypha.[17] Bauer published a major work in 1934 which has had major influence in its field over the last eighty years: *Rechtgläubigkeit und Ketzerei im ältesten Christentum*[18]—a "paradigm-shaping book."[19] Although widely discussed on the Continent and in England,[20] it was not until the release of an English translation almost forty years later that its impact was noticeably felt in America.[21] Since that time it has influenced almost every discussion of the topic.[22] *Orthodoxy and Heresy* is not a full statement of Bauer's ideas

ntresources.com/blog/?s=bdag. It should be noted that Danker's contributions to the English edition are at least equally valuable with Bauer's original work.

13. Edited by Frederick Danker. The first English translation, known as "BAG," appeared in 1957, based on the 4th German edition. The second English edition of 1979 ("BAGD") was based on the fifth edition of the German work.

14. Aland, Aland, and Reichmann, *Griechisch-Deutsches Wöterbuch*, 6th ed. The third English edition is known as BDAG (Bauer and Danker, *Greek-English Lexicon*). See Decker, "Using BDAG."

15. Bauer was the editor for the 1928, second edition of Preuschen's lexicon with the third edition of 1937 bearing Bauer's name alone. The fourth edition in 1949–1952 was the most significant revision, followed by a fifth edition, the last edited by Bauer, in 1957–1958; a sixth edition of the German work appeared in 1988 For a more detailed history of BDAG, see Decker, "Using BDAG." Jerry Flora's dissertation provides a broad review of Bauer's life and scholarly career (Flora, "Critical Analysis of Walter Bauer's Theory," 23–35).

16. Bauer, *Der Apostolos der Syrer.*

17. Bauer, *Das Leben Jesu.*

18. Bauer, *Rechtgläubigkeit und Ketzerei im ältesten Christentum.* The text of the two editions is essentially the same with only typographical corrections; the major difference is the addition of two essays by Strecker in the second edition.

19. Bingham, "Development and Diversity," 50.

20. See Strecker, "Reception of the Book," 286–316 for a listing of reviews and an extensive discussion of reactions to Bauer's German work.

21. Bauer, *Orthodoxy and Heresy.*

22. A surprising exception is the 500-page work on heresy by H. O. J. Brown (*Heresies*). I can find no citation of Bauer in the footnotes and he is not listed in the index. Although one chapter bibliography lists the title (chap. 2, p. 22), there is no interaction with Bauer in the chapter.

regarding the origins of "orthodoxy" and "heresy," but this limited essay does not allow a broader discussion of Bauer's other writings.[23]

Bauer's *Orthodoxy and Heresy* argues that we cannot merely assume that orthodoxy came first and that heresy is a later deviation, for in doing so we "simply agree with the judgment of the anti-heretical fathers for the post-New Testament period" (xxi). This is neither scientific nor fair since we are listening to only one voice—that of the winners; we do not allow the losers to speak for themselves. "Perhaps . . . certain manifestations of Christian life that the authors of the church renounce as 'heresies' originally had not been such at all, but, at least here and there, were the only form of the new religion—that is, for those regions they were simply 'Christianity.' The possibility also exists that their adherents constituted the majority" (xxii).

This is the hypothesis that Bauer proposes to test, though Bauer's professed neutral critical method too frequently slips into the role of defense lawyer or apologist for the heretics rather than impartial judge of the evidence.[24] The evidence he examines in subsequent chapters is considered geographically, area by area, to determine the evidence for what form/s of Christianity are attested in the earliest discernible period. Bauer begins with Edessa and follows with Egypt, Antioch, Asia Minor, and Rome.

Syrian Edessa, located on a tributary of the Euphrates just north of the present north-central border of Turkey and Syria, is the focus of Bauer's first chapter. After discrediting all traditional accounts of the origins of Christianity in Edessa, Bauer argues that the original form of Christianity there was Marcionite (and that not until mid-second century, followed by Bardesanes and his followers shortly afterwards). It was not until the end of the second century that there is any trace of what came later to be known as "orthodoxy," which remained a small minority through the fourth century. Only in the fifth century is orthodoxy finally imposed on Edessa by the "rather coarse methods" of Bishop Rabbula, the "tyrant of Edessa" (27). The "beginnings for the history of Christianity in Edessa" rest on "an unmistakably heretical basis" (43).

---

23. For a survey of the relevant material from Bauer's previous books and articles, see Betz, "Orthodoxy and Heresy in Primitive Christianity," 299–311.

24. I have read similar statements several times and do not know who originated the analogy. For two representative instances, see Moffat, "Review," 475 ("he tends to take the position of the barrister rather than of the judge"); and Desjardins, "Bauer and Beyond," 68n9 ("his professed impartiality shifts at times to an apologist on behalf of the 'heretics'").

Egypt next receives attention. Bauer declines to be discouraged by the silence of the sources regarding the early history of Christianity in Egypt since Edessan history establishes the pattern. Why would the churchmen have been "silent about the origins of Christianity in such an important center as Alexandria if there had been something favorable to report?" (45). The answer, though conjectural, is clear: Egyptian Christianity was, like Edessa, heretical in origin. The earliest form of the faith was gnostic no later than the beginning of the second century. Not until the end of that century does "orthodoxy" appear and "even into the third century, no separation between orthodoxy and heresy was accomplished" (59).

Bauer then turns to Antioch, which, though seeming to the reader of the New Testament to be a bastion of normative Christianity,[25] had long been heavily influenced by heretical movements. Since the time of Paul's defeat there (Gal 2), Antioch "played no significant role in the history of the church" (63)—that is the proto-orthodox church. Instead there was a syncretistic mixture of "Jewish Christianity," Gentile Christianity [i.e., what was left of Paul's influence], and Gnosticism. Not until the "frantic concern" (63) of Ignatius in the early second century is there a renewed attempt to reestablish "orthodoxy." Ignatius, however, is not a reliable source since his exuberance causes him to lose "all sense of proportion . . . [so] one must be especially careful in evaluating the accuracy of his statements" (61). His attempt to impose a powerful monarchical bishop structure on the church is a political move by someone in a minority position attempting to gain power and control (62).

Asia Minor also shows unmistakable gnostic influence, and that *within* the churches, as reflected in the Johannine literature.[26] Ignatius's letters to churches in Asia Minor are also relevant in this regard, since they reflect the limit of his influence. He can expect to be heard in only a few churches, and even then he is attempting to "stretch the circle of his influence as widely as possible" (79). It is significant that four of the churches in the region which had earlier been addressed in the Apocalypse are not included in Ignatius's list. Since these are the churches most

25. Bauer declines to consider New Testament evidence since it "seems to be both too unproductive and too much disputed to be able to serve as a point of departure" (Bauer, *Orthodoxy and Heresy,* xxv).

26. John the "apocalyptic seer" is not very useful for the current question according to Bauer since his "extremely confused religious outlook that peculiarly mixes Jewish, Christian, and mythological elements and ends up in chiliasm . . . [a] stormy outburst, seething with hate" marks him, not as an intellectual or spiritual leader of influence, but only as a proponent of "wishful thinking" (Bauer, *Orthodoxy and Heresy,* 77–78).

severely rebuked by John, it is evident that they moved into full-blown heresy by the time of Ignatius (78–79). That Hierapolis and Colossae are "bypassed in icy silence by both John and Ignatius" (80) further reflects the lack of influence of orthodoxy in this area. Peter likewise is very selective in his address to the churches of Asia Minor (1 Pet 1:1), leaving large "blank spots on the map" of Asian orthodoxy: "there simply was nothing to be gained for 'ecclesiastically' oriented Christianity in that area at that time" (82). Even Ephesus, often perceived as the bastion of Pauline orthodoxy, has been lost to that cause by the end of the first century, perhaps to the extent that Paul's foundational labors there had been forgotten. Paul "lost the contest in Ephesus" (85), something that was becoming evident even during his lifetime. "Orthodoxy" was only reorganized much later when the apostle John became their patron, likely due to the arrival of Jewish Christians (including John and Philip) from Jerusalem following the war with Rome. Yet even this did not result in an "orthodox" victory since the Pastorals still reflect a major problem with Gnosticism in the second century (89).

Next Bauer considers the Roman church and its tactics in establishing their particular brand of Christianity as the dominant form worldwide. The initial foray in this direction is Bauer's study of *1 Clement*, the letter from the church of Rome to the Corinthian church written near the end of the first century. We cannot trust the direct statements of this biased letter, says Bauer, but must read between the lines to reconstruct the actual situation which prompted the letter and decipher the real motivation for Rome's letter. "Rome takes action not when it is overflowing with love or when the great concerns of the faith are really in jeopardy, but when there is at least the opportunity of enlarging its own sphere of influence" (97–98).

The first evidence we have of this Roman strategy is in relation to the church at Corinth, reflected in the letter of *1 Clement*. In that situation "internal discord greatly reduced the power of resistance of the Corinthian church, so that it seemed to be easy prey" (98). The specifics there involve the usurpation of the existing church leaders by younger ones; Rome writes in an effort to reinstate the older leaders who were more favorable to the Roman position. The conflict goes all the way back to Paul. Those rebuked by him as "the strong" were gnostics who, though silenced at the time, had gradually increased in number (their position was more attractive to the community than Paul's approach), though they chafed under the repressive leadership of the church. By the time of *1 Clement* they had become strong enough to oust the leaders (which by this time were a coalition of the Paul and Cephas parties) and to take over the church (100–101), perhaps even imposing an "energetic bishop" on the previously plural presbyterate (112). "Rome succeeded in imposing its will on Corinth" to the extent that a half century later the Corinthian church still accepted Roman authority and read *1 Clement* in their services (104). And so began the Roman movement to consolidate her authority one church at a time, culminating in the exclusive establishment of Rome's brand of Christianity, now branded as "orthodoxy," in the fourth century.

The Roman juggernaut evidenced itself in later claims of apostolic succession used in the fight against heresy, not only in Rome but elsewhere under Roman influence. Rome also extended her influence through teaching Christians in other places and also through generous financial gifts—and "such gifts were not the least reason why their opponents emerged victorious" (122, seeming to imply that Rome's opponents were "bought"). Bauer cites Eusebius's (much later) comment as reflective of a practice that had been operative earlier as well:

> The encomium of Eusebius upon the Emperor Constantine (3.58) teaches us that Rome viewed it as an altogether legitimate practice in religious controversy to tip the scales with golden weights: "In his beneficent concern that as many as possible be won for the teaching of the gospel, the emperor also made rich donations there [in Phoenician Heliopolis] for the support of the poor, with the aim of rousing them even in this way to the acceptance of saving truth (123).[27]

The following two chapters trace the rhetoric in the orthodoxy-heresy debate, as well as the use of literature. Both parties used written documents, and each used whatever means possible to discredit their opponents, to the extent of falsifying and/or destroying documents (160) and even modifying their own source documents to more clearly make their case (160, supported with several pages of illustration from the *Odyssey*!). The various polemical writings employed cannot be trusted to represent accurately the opponents' position, and since the "orthodox" came to hold the privileged position, we have little from the heretics' own pens even though they were the more prolific writers (194). The most extensive "orthodox" writer, Eusebius, is not to be trusted; his "serious

---

27. Bracketed material is original in Bauer.

misuse of the superlative" (and other problems), says Bauer, "is sufficient to remove any inclination I might have to take such assertions seriously" (192). Other than his citations from other writers, little is useful; "we cannot establish any firm foothold on the basis of what Eusebius himself contributes" (192).

Traditional literature is treated next: the use of the Old Testament as well as divergent gospels. "At that point there probably was no version of Christianity worthy of note that did not have at its disposal at least *one* written gospel, in which Jesus appears as the bearer and guarantor of that particular view" (203). Though the other gospels were accepted fairly early (especially Mark and Matthew), John's gospel was viewed with suspicion in orthodox Rome almost from the start (208). It was rather the preferred gospel of the gnostics and other heretics. "When the gospel canon was defined, which was to be valid for the entire church, Rome found itself overruled, to put it rather crudely" (212).[28]

When we come to the epistles, Paul is nearly irrelevant to early Roman orthodoxy, being the darling of many of the heretics (215–25). Bauer's summary is worth citing.

> Perhaps, as the situation developed, some would have preferred henceforth to exclude Paul completely. . . . But it was already too late for that. Rome (together with the "church," which it led) had already accepted too much from the Apostle to the Gentiles, had appealed to him too often, suddenly to recognize him no longer. . . . 1 Corinthians had proved itself to be extremely productive for purposes of church politics in the hands of Rome. . . .
>
> . . . I am inclined to see the pastoral Epistles as an attempt on the part of the church unambiguously to enlist Paul as part of its anti-heretical front and to eliminate the lack of confidence in him in ecclesiastical circles. . . . The church raised up the Paul of orthodoxy by using [pseudonymous] means. . . .
>
> The price the Apostle of the Gentiles had to pay to be allowed to remain in the church was the complete surrender of his personality and historical particularity. . . . Whenever the "church" becomes powerful, the bottom drops out from under him and he must immediately give way to the celebrities from the circle of the twelve apostles. . . . To some extent Paul becomes influential only as part of the holy scriptures acknowledged in the church—not the personality of the Apostle to the Gentiles

---

28. This is a rather ironic statement in Bauer regarding the church which otherwise exercised such authoritarian power!

and his proclamation, but the *word* of Paul . . . whenever it is useful for the development and preservation of ecclesiastical teaching. . . . The introduction of the pastoral Epistles actually made the collection of Paul's letters ecclesiastically viable for the very first time (225–28 *passim*).

Paul seems to fare quite poorly in the hands of Bauer's early "orthodoxy." This is largely because of what Bauer perceives to be Paul's "as yet quite rudimentary organization of thought patterns" (234), but even more because of his plasticity and tolerance. Not only could he be used by so many diverse groups, he "scarcely knows what a heretic might be" (234). He knows that a lot of other Christians disagree with him—and that is fine with him. It is only the "most serious moral deviation" (235) that gets him upset. Even when he felt opposing positions to be "defective, he still did not detest and condemn them as heretical" (237).[29]

What we have known since the fourth century as "orthodoxy" was originally the dominant form of Christianity only in Rome. Through generous financial "gifts" and persuasive correspondence, "Rome confidently extends itself eastward, tries to break down resistance and stretches out a helping hand to those who are like-minded, drawing everything within reach into the well-knit structures of ecclesiastical organization" (231). Rome is thus the winner who vanquishes heresy by superior ability, backed by financial and political resources.

Bauer concludes by reflecting that "it is indeed a curious quirk of history that western Rome was destined to begin to exert the determinative influence upon a religion which had its cradle in the Orient, so as to give it that form in which it was to achieve worldwide recognition" (240). None of the heretical forms of Christianity, be they gnostic, Marcionite, or Montanist, "could have achieved such recognition" (240).

The essence, then, of Bauer's thesis is two-fold: in the beginning there were many varieties of Christianity (i.e., not a single, unified set of beliefs that later became what we know as "orthodoxy"), and second, it

---

29. In regard to passages that seem to contradict this portrait of Paul, Bauer adds a footnote: "The thrust of the polemic in Phil. 3 and in Rom. 16.17–20 is not entirely clear—or in any event, can be interpreted in different ways—and may be left aside at this point" (Bauer, *Orthodoxy and Heresy*, 236n11). In other words, he ignored what was not convenient for his theory! For a careful consideration of Paul's influence vis-à-vis Bauer, though in this case in the context of Philippi, see Hartog, *Polycarp and the New Testament*, 216–22. For Paul's influence on Polycarp, see Berding, *Polycarp and Paul.*

was the victory of one party, the church of Rome, which established the
official dogma, suppressing all other competing views.[30]

Responses to Bauer

In an essay of this restricted length it is obviously impossible to respond
fully to a substantial book like Bauer's. Rather I will summarize some of
the key responses that have been posed in some detail by others, both as
a direction for further reading and as a focused summary of the critical
verdicts that have accumulated since *Rechtgläubigkeit und Ketzerei im ältesten Christentum* was first published in 1934.[31] In one sense, this survey
of literature may seem rather tendentious or superfluous. It is justified,
however, by the fact that contemporary scholars such as Ehrman seem to
assume the validity of Bauer's general thesis.[32] For our purposes, the most
significant critiques of Bauer, in historical order, include the following.[33]

30. See the similar summary in Ehrman, *Lost Christianities,* 176 (172–75 in greater
detail); McCue, "Orthodoxy and Heresy," 119–20; and Bock, *Missing Gospels,* 49–50.

31. I give, for the most part, only the conclusions and do not attempt to detail
all the supporting evidence in these critiques. Also note that I have included only
reviews that are critical of some aspect of Bauer's thesis. Since I am persuaded that
most of Bauer's work is misguided, and that the studies discussed here demonstrate
that quite clearly, it is not necessary to list the areas in which I agree with his analysis or note other scholars who do the same. For an extended discussion of (largely
positive) responses, see Georg Strecker's appendix in the English translation of Bauer
(Strecker, "Reception of the Book"). These are, of course, only the earlier responses
to the German edition. Most reviews have included positive elements of appreciation
(see Köstenberger and Kruger, *Heresy of Orthodoxy,* 33).

32. See Ehrman, *Lost Christianities,* 172–75.

33. For broad-ranging surveys of reviews published since 1934, see the articles by
Harrington, "Reception," 289–98; Flora, "Critical Analysis," 37–88; and Desjardins,
"Bauer and Beyond," 65–82. For a review of earlier responses to the German edition,
see Strecker, "Reception of the Book." Another work that is sometimes listed as a critique of Bauer is Hultgren's *Rise of Normative Christianity,* but though disagreeing with
Bauer, it is not a particularly focused critique—and a number of Hultgren's proposals,
building on Robinson and Koester, *Trajectories through Early Christianity,* are themselves problematic. For a brief summary of Hultgren's approach, see Köstenberger and
Kruger, *Heresy of Orthodoxy,* 37.

Turner, *The Pattern of Christian Truth* (1954)

The first major critique of Bauer was H. E. W. Turner's *The Pattern of Christian Truth*[34]—the Bampton Lectures for 1954. The 500+ pages of this study offer Turner's "equivalent" of Bauer's work, but chapter two is an explicit critique of Bauer. His analysis follows Bauer's geographical outline. In regards to Edessa he concludes that "the evidence is too scanty and in many respects too flimsy to support any theory so trenchant and clear-cut as Bauer proposes" and "his skepticism on many points of detail appears excessive" (45). Turning to Egypt he proposes that there is more literary evidence than Bauer has acknowledged (some of it unknown in Bauer's day, but not all). "Most of the new discoveries have the effect of moving what we know of Alexandrine Christianity further to the right" (i.e., toward a more "orthodox" view). The greater probability is that the evidence Bauer examined is to be understood as representative of "splinter groups on the fringe of the Church" (57). All told, there is less evidence for Bauer's thesis from Alexandria than from Edessa (59). Likewise in Asia Minor there is nothing which "supports the more daring features of Bauer's reconstruction" (63). The picture Bauer draws of Corinth, Rome, and *1 Clement* "is at best non-proven" (67). As will others who follow, Turner charges Bauer with a "misuse of the argument from silence. If we have no evidence for the fact, we can hardly offer any profitable conjecture about its alleged cause" (67). Turner's final verdict is that Bauer's "fatal weakness appears to be a persistent tendency to over-simplify problems, combined with the ruthless treatment of such evidence as fails to support his case" (79).

Betz, "Orthodoxy and Heresy in Primitive Christianity" (1965)

Although basically in agreement with Bauer's approach, Hans Dieter Betz pointed out two significant problems. First, on Egypt, Bauer got it wrong: there was a strong gnostic presence, but that is not the only form of Christianity seen there. Second, he ignored the New Testament evidence; in particular, he "clearly underestimates Paul's fight against his opponents. Bauer overlooks the fact that Paul claims to be 'orthodox.' Wherever Paul

---

34. Turner, *Pattern of Christian Truth*.

argues in his letters, he does it to prove that his theological understanding is in accordance with the kerygma itself."[35]

Chapman, "Some Theological Reflections on Walter Bauer's *Rechtgläubigkeit und Ketzerei im ältesten Christentum*: A Review Article" (1970)

G. Clarke Chapman's review article was published prior to the release of the English translation of Bauer.[36] Chapman targets two major tactics: Bauer's numerous arguments from silence ("habitually sees many gaps in our records as significant or ominous"), and his "habitually coercing ambiguous pieces of evidence" to fit a preconceived theory (567). According to Chapman, Bauer is also overly skeptical of Eusebius and other Fathers who defend the traditional view, yet "gives immediate and weighty credence to the slightest reference by the church fathers to widespread or predominating heresy" (567).[37] Chapman also rejects Bauer's portrait of "power politics and sociological pressures" emanating from Rome, suggesting instead that we ought to consider the possibility that the victory of orthodoxy is related to providence: "certain broad lines of interpretation may have triumphed because of their theological adequacy" (572), though he realizes that "historians" have trouble dealing with such theological categories.

Flora, "A Critical Analysis of Walter Bauer's Theory of Early Christian Orthodoxy and Heresy" (1972)

One of the first full-length critics of Bauer from an American writer was the dissertation presented at The Southern Baptist Seminary in 1972 by Jerry Flora.[38] Flora leveled some stiff criticism against Bauer's thesis, which he viewed as a one-sided over-reaction to the traditional, Eusebian view of heresy. As a result, Flora argued that Bauer's conclusions need to be substantially modified (though not rejected out of hand).

35. Betz, "Orthodoxy and Heresy," 306–8 (direct quote from 308).
36. Chapman, "Some Theological Reflections," 564–74.
37. Chapman later used the phrase "Eusebius demythologized" (ibid., 569).
38. Flora, "Critical Analysis of Walter Bauer's Theory."

There were four major criticisms. First, Bauer's view of Paul is misguided. Rather than a "tolerant" apostle who became "all things to all men" and "did not know what a heretic might be" (105), Paul claimed to be orthodox in contradistinction to others whom he pronounced quite decidedly to be wrong (106). "He plainly conceived himself to be an authorized apostle and his doctrine to be correct, as over against that of his unnamed opponents" (107). Second, Bauer was selective in the evidence cited and in the areas of the early church discussed: Edessa and Egypt are crucial, followed in importance by second-century Antioch and western Asia Minor. But, Flora asks, "what of the origin and development of Christianity in Judea (Jerusalem), in western Syria (Antioch), in Gaul (Lyons), in Africa (Carthage), and in Italy (Rome)? Here are other regions important to the life of the church by the close of the second century, but he did not analyze their origins, nor did he say why he chose not to" (113).[39] Though Bauer may have been able to offer a plausible argument for the priority of heresy in some areas, he conveniently ignored those areas not compatible with his thesis. Third, to argue that orthodoxy only gradually developed later after a long struggle with prior heresy is an over-simplified picture (115–24). Fourth, that Rome imposed its brand of Christianity on other churches assumes that the church in Rome was unified in the second century, but this flies in the face of the evidence for considerable diversity in Rome (125–30). Many of the early heretics were associated with Rome, including Simon Magus, Valentinus, Marcion, Apelles, Praxes, Theodotus, and Sabellius (131). "Prior to the time of Irenaeus and Victor, Rome was scarcely the juggernaut that Bauer described. It was a divided community, trying to find its way into an uncertain future. . . . The doctrine of Rome could not alone and automatically guarantee orthodoxy" (138).

Flora also develops an argument regarding the evidence for continuity between the first-century church, and particularly the apostolic church, and the second-century church:

> To maintain that orthodoxy was a late development which triumphed only with great difficulty seems to be saying too much. While it may have emerged *in strength* comparatively late and not without struggle, orthodoxy existed in continuity with the commitment and purpose of the first two generations of the

---

39. In the two overlaps in his lists (Antioch and Rome), Flora intends the second list to refer to the *origin* of these churches in the first century. Bauer discusses both cities/churches, but only in the second century and later.

Christian movement. That apostolic witness with its historical perspective became the foundation on which Catholicism
built and at the same time the stumbling block over which the
heresies fell (149).

Heron, "The Interpretation of I Clement in Walter Bauer's *Rechtgläubigkeit und Ketzerei im ältesten Christentum*" (1973)

Rather than addressing the entire scope of Bauer's thesis, most subsequent studies have focused on individual aspects of it. One of the first of
these was A. I. C. Heron's examination of Bauer's use of *1 Clement* within
Rechtgläubigkeit und Ketzerei im ältesten Christentum.[40] A crucial aspect
of Bauer's thesis is the influence of Rome—the early orthodox "power
broker" who forced her way into a dominant position over weaker
churches and alternate interpretations of Christianity. It is this argument
that Heron examines in considerable detail. He acknowledges that it appears "extremely attractive" due especially to it being clear, direct, and
comprehensive. But this attractiveness is itself problematic:

> Precisely because the whole interpretation is so plausible, one
> must immediately wonder whether its virtues of simplicity
> and comprehensiveness are to be attributed to Bauer's discov-
> ery of the real significance of the events and developments he
> describes, or whether rather they reflect a desire to impose on
> the complexity of history an over-simplified pattern. Is the plau-
> sibility and attractiveness of the whole theory based upon its
> coherence with the available evidence, or is it rather based upon
> the power of Bauer's synthesizing imagination?[41]

Heron will conclude that the latter is, unfortunately, the case. His
first major criticism is that Bauer's interpretation of *1 Clement* is *not* based
on *1 Clement*. It is based, rather, on evidence drawn from elsewhere and
from attempting to read between the lines in *1 Clement*, assuming that
the letter itself is in part designed to hide Rome's true message and motive
(526). "He has explained—indeed, explained away—all those elements in
I Clement which might seem to weigh against his interpretation, which

---

40. Heron, "Interpretation of I Clement," 517–45.
41. Ibid., 525.

he opposes to the meaning which Clement prefers to suggest" (i.e., what a plain reading of the text of *1 Clement* itself would seem to say).

In more specific terms, Heron argues that there is no evidence that Rome succeeded in imposing a monarchical bishop on Corinth, nor that they bribed the leaders of the opposition in Corinth. Even more seriously, Bauer's assumption that Rome's motive is not love and concern (as *1 Clement* seems to suggest), but a power move to extend orthodoxy is unsupported; Bauer can only adduce this by reading back evidence from a century or more later (529–30). Nor will Bauer's hypothesis stand that the real issue in Corinth is that of an "orthodox" minority being ousted by a gnosticizing majority. Although an appealing and plausible suggestion, "the evidence which is given to show that it is in fact what *did* happen is remarkably tenuous, and is drawn almost exclusively not only from evidence other than that of I Clement, but from evidence which relates to events and developments which all took place in places or at times more or less remote from Corinth 95–96" (530). Bauer's suggestions that second-century writers who refer to *1 Clement* understand that letter to relate to the question of "orthodoxy" versus "heresy" is likewise "exceedingly doubtful" (536; see 533–36).

Heron concludes that,

> Bauer's whole interpretation of I Clement is . . . rather less satisfactorily buttressed by convincing evidence than one might wish. . . . It need hardly be said that when all the components of an argument are as weak as those we have to deal with here, the argument as a whole, however plausible or attractive in itself it may appear, cannot be taken very seriously. . . .
>
> . . . The theory as a whole indeed depends more on his powers of imagination than on the facts available to us.[42]

After then devoting the following eight pages to a positive study of the relevant issues in *1 Clement*, Heron reiterates that "attractive, and in itself plausible as [Bauer's] interpretation of I Clement is, it cannot be regarded as anything more than an interesting but improbable speculation" (545).

---

42. Ibid., 536–37.

Norris, "Ignatius, Polycarp, and I Clement: Walter Bauer Reconsidered" (1976)

Although Frederick Norris accepts Bauer's negative thesis (his critique of the traditional, orthodox theory of the origin of heresy), he argues that Bauer's positive theses are not defensible; that is, his reconstruction of how things *did* happen in the second century. Bauer's explanations of the events related to Ignatius, Polycarp, and 1 *Clement* are invalid. Much of this failure is Bauer's frequent argument from silence, but

> his basic error is in reading history backwards, either by de-manding that the fullest or even 'ideal' stage of a development must be present at its beginning in order for it to exist, or by imposing later events on earlier ones to support his interpreta-tions. Frankly, he misreads the texts. One should be cautious in following his lead in places where there are few texts and much silence, when it can be demonstrated that he does not proceed on good grounds with the existent texts.[43]

Roberts, *Manuscript, Society, and Belief in Early Egypt* (1977)

One of the most detailed studies of Egyptian Christianity, particularly the strange silence regarding it prior to AD 200, is Colin H. Roberts's *Manuscript, Society and Belief in Early Christian Egypt*.[44] His purpose is not primarily a critique of Bauer; that is a secondary outcome in the second half of the book. In contrast to Bauer's query as to where the evidence is for orthodoxy in the second century, Roberts asks why there is no trace of *either* orthodoxy *or* heresy; there are hardly any traces of Christianity in any form. But there is some and Roberts proceeds to sort through the available evidence, beginning with the papyri and evidence within vari-ous documents (such as *nomina sacra*). His conclusion is that the silence has little to do with the prevalence of Gnosticism, but rather that Egyptian (and in particular Alexandrian) Christianity originally remained more tightly connected to the Jewish community in Alexandria than it had in other parts of the empire, and apparently on better terms with their

43. Norris, "Ignatius, Polycarp, and I Clement," 43.

44. Roberts, *Manuscript, Society, and Belief.*

non-Christian Jewish neighbors. Few Gentiles apparently became part of the church there, so it retained a strongly Jewish flavor, even after AD 70. Only when the Jewish community in Egypt was nearly exterminated during the Jewish revolt there (AD 115–117) does Christianity begin to evidence itself distinctly.

> We may surmise that for much of the second century it was a church with no strong central authority and little organization; one of the directions in which it developed was certainly Gnosticism, but a Gnosticism not initially separated from the rest of the Church. It was the teaching and personality of the two Gnostic leaders, Basilides and Valentinius, that impressed the Christian world outside Egypt and were remembered, but this is not the whole story. . . . [eventually] the line between Gnostic and Catholic Christianity was more sharply drawn; but in Egypt, as can be seen in Clement and Origen, the process was slow and distinctions sometimes remained blurred.[45]

McCue, "Orthodoxy and Heresy: Walter Bauer and the Valentinians" (1979)

Related to Roberts's study of Egyptian Christianity, James McCue, in his article "Orthodoxy and Heresy: Walter Bauer and the Valentinians," debated Bauer's handling of the Valentinian gnostic data.[46] He argues that "Bauer is simply wrong" (119) since he overlooks three key points regarding Valentinianism:

> 1) The orthodox play a role in Valentinian thought such that they seem to be part of the Valentinian self-understanding. 2) This reference often suggests that the orthodox are the main body, and at several points explicitly and clearly identifies the orthodox as the many over against the small number of Valentinians. 3) The Valentinians of the decades prior to Irenaeus and Clement of Alexandria use the books of the orthodox New Testament in a manner that is best accounted for by supposing that Valentinianism developed within a mid-second century matrix (120).

45. Ibid., 71–72. The description of the church there as de-centralized and less organized can be confirmed and documented in some detail from Pearson, *Gnosticism and Christianity*, 18–20, who depends on Jakab, *Ecclesia Alexandria*, 176–77.

46. McCue, "Orthodoxy and Heresy," 118–30.

McCue's subsequent discussion documents these three points from the Valentinians' own statements. Points one and two, in particular, validate Edwin Yamauchi's claim that "Gnosticism always appears as a parasite. . . . 'it is always built on earlier, pre-existing religions or on their traditions.'"[47]

Robinson, *The Bauer Thesis Examined* (1988)

By far the most detailed analysis of Bauer's work is Thomas A. Robinson's *The Bauer Thesis Examined*.[48] This carefully argued work proposes that "Bauer's understanding of orthodoxy and heresy does not provide the kind of insight into the character of earliest Christianity that is widely attributed to it" (27). In contrast to Bauer's thesis that heresy was early and dominant, Robinson concludes that "it is the catholic community, not the gnostic, that represents the character of the majority in western Asia Minor in the early period" (203). To support this conclusion, he first sketches the history of the debate (chap. 1). Robinson addresses one of the unique features of Bauer's approach: the geographical treatment of the question of heresy in the early church. Bauer's choice to begin with Edessa was deliberate since there he could make his strongest case. Robinson evaluates the evidence available from various areas, concluding that only Asia Minor can form an adequate basis for evaluating the orthodoxy-heresy debate—"no other area is remotely comparable" (41). The criteria for this judgment is two-fold: extensive literature, including literature that addresses the question of heresy. On this basis Bauer is faulted for placing the greatest weight on two areas, Edessa and Egypt, that have neither feature—the evidence there is scanty and ambiguous, to say nothing of the fact that neither was a primary center of the early church (42). The other potential areas (Jerusalem, Antioch, Corinth, and Rome) are not satisfactory either.[49]

---

47. Yamauchi, *Pre-Christian Gnosticism*, 185, citing in part, Drijvers, "Origins of Gnosticism," 331.

48. Robinson, *Bauer Thesis Examined*; originally, Robinson, "Orthodoxy and Heresy."

49. Edessa, in particular, is problematic in that "our information is too ambiguous or mute to allow us confident reconstructions of Christianity in this area" (Robinson, *Bauer Thesis Examined*, 58). Egypt, likewise: "the scarcity of the materials from Egypt results in suspicious gaps in the logic of these various reconstructions" (64). Corinth may sound more promising, but beyond 1 and 2 Corinthians, we have only

Robinson then turns to the one area which provides the primary data unavailable elsewhere—Asia Minor. After examining the importance and character of Ephesus and western Asia Minor (chap. 3), he turns to a detailed evaluation of Bauer (chaps. 4 and 5). "Bauer's detective work—never dull, sometimes ingenious, occasionally brilliant—suffers from defects more serious than the sporadic overstatements and tendentious claims . . . . Far more fundamental and less easily corrigible, the defects of Bauer's argument are structural" (129). These structural defects include: "(1) the hypothetical alliance of 'ecclesiastically oriented' Paulinists with Palestinian immigrants against Gnosticizing Paulinists; (2) the alleged strength of heresy in the area; and (3) the proposed cause for the rise of the monarchical episcopate (129–30)."

The final verdict is that,

> Bauer's reconstruction of the history of the early church in western Asia Minor is faulty—not just in minor details—but at critical junctures. For one thing, the thesis does not adequately explain the alliance between Palestinian immigrants and anti-gnostic Paulinists; for another, it does not recognize the early consciousness of orthodoxy that might be indicated by such a shift. Further, it has failed to explain how a browbeaten orthodox minority could have so radically altered the structure of power in their favour. Finally, and most significantly, it has not demonstrated that heresy was as widespread and strong as Bauer had contended. In light of these weaknesses, Bauer's reconstruction of primitive Christianity in western Asia Minor must, to a large measure, be set aside.
>
> But the setting aside of Bauer's reconstruction of the early church in western Asia Minor points to something more seriously flawed about the Bauer Thesis. The failure of the Bauer Thesis in western Asia Minor is not merely one flaw in an otherwise coherent reconstruction. The failure of the thesis in the only area where it can be adequately tested casts suspicion on the other areas of Bauer's investigation. Extreme caution should be exercised in granting to the Bauer Thesis insight into those areas for which

---

one document for late first and early second century: *1 Clement*, which is "a less detailed and considerably more ambiguous momentary glimpse of that church from a person who seems not to have had first-hand acquaintance with the church there. That makes for inventive, untestable, and not necessarily accurate hypotheses" (77). Rome is unfruitful since we have too little information to determine the original form of Christianity there (81), and the literary evidence is meager as it relates to Rome itself and none of it addresses the question of heresy (81–84). We have no literary evidence for either Jerusalem or Antioch in the relevant period (84–87, 88–91).

inventive theses appear credible only because evidence is either too scarce or too mute to put anything to the test (204).

Desjardins, "Bauer and Beyond: On Recent Scholarly Discussions of Αἵρεσις in the Early Christian Era" (1991)

A helpful, synthetic response to Bauer's work is Michel Desjardins's article, "Bauer and Beyond."[50] Much of the article consists of digesting and evaluating the work of others, but in so doing he synthesizes these other studies in a helpful way. He approves Robinson's arguments "on the whole" as being "well-taken and well-argued," concluding that Robinson has added "another row of nails to the coffin enclosing Bauer's thesis."[51] Desjardins's primary contribution relates to the meaning of αἵρεσις. He suggests that Bauer has asked the wrong question. Instead of asking whether orthodoxy or heresy came first (Bauer's question), one should ask "what αἵρεσις actually meant for first and second-century writers."[52] He seems to endorse Cohen's suggestion that heresy was not a category invented by early orthodoxy as Bauer assumes, but arises from the church's Jewish heritage, reflecting similar categories as the rabbis. The "common use of scripture and belief in one God possibly led [the Jewish rabbis and the early church] independently to notions of unity, oneness, and exclusivity."[53] This has obvious implications in support of a more traditional view in which "orthodoxy" is original and "heresy" later and derivative.

Pearson, *Gnosticism and Christianity in Roman and Coptic Egypt* (2004)

Although not formally a critique of Bauer's work, Birger A. Pearson's study examines in considerable detail one of the key geographical areas on which Bauer's thesis is founded. I do not accept some of Pearson's dates or interpretations, but he has provided a very helpful survey of the

50. Desjardins, "Bauer and Beyond," 65–82.

51. Ibid., 72.

52. Ibid., 72; see also 78.

53. Ibid., 77.

documentary evidence for Christianity in second- and third-century Egypt. He clearly demonstrates that there was diversity present, yet he rejects Bauer's explanation that heresy was original and dominant. He cites in particular *The Preaching of Peter,* an early second-century pseude-pigraphal writing that reflects traditional, "orthodox" Christianity. Since this is the earliest such documentary evidence available, it carries consid-erable weight in the discussion. Pearson comments that "Bauer ignores this important work, which would have been detrimental to his theory."[54]

Davidson, *The Birth of the Church* (2004)

A more recent critique of Bauer comes in Ivor J. Davidson's history of the early church. He concludes that Bauer has ignored the evidence of theological diversity with the Roman church itself, and that Rome's "po-litical" influence over other churches only developed slowly; they were surely not in a position to repress their peers when Christianity was still an illegal religion (as it was until the fourth century). Nor does Bauer give sufficient credit to the influence of the Jerusalem church as the "mother church" which specified key matters of doctrine and practice (158).

> Above all, however, Bauer's theory overlooks the degree to which there clearly was from the beginning a certain set of convictions about Jesus that bound a majority of believers together, and it underestimates the intrinsic impetus that existed within these convictions to work out the logical parameters within which the gospel and its advocates could be said to exist. The process of discerning truth and falsehood that evolved in the late first and second centuries was implicitly grounded in the attempts by the first followers of Jesus to think through the consequences of their newfound faith with regard to personal salvation and practical living.[55]

---

54. Pearson, *Gnosticism and Christianity,* 16n18. This work is described as lying "on a trajectory leading to the mainline Christianity of Clement" (16; see also 44).

55. Davidson, *Birth of the Church,* 158.

Trebilco, "Christian Communities in Western Asia Minor into the Early Second Century: Ignatius and Others as Witnesses against Bauer" (2006)

One of the plenary addresses at the 2005 annual meeting of the Evangelical Theological Society directly addressed a key portion of Bauer's arguments.[56] Paul Trebilco made four points regarding Bauer's use of the Ignatian evidence with regard to Asia Minor. 1) The evidence shows that the earliest form of Christianity in western Asia Minor was orthodox and that the heresies that Ignatius opposed were later, derivative forms, especially in regard to Docetism. 2) Bauer's inference (based on Ignatius and John *not* writing a letter to them) that Colossae and Hieropolis were heretical churches is ill-founded; several other explanations are much more probable than Bauer's argument from silence. 3) Bauer's contention that disagreement with the bishop was evidence of theological differences (i.e., heresy) is overstated; many of the differences that Ignatius discusses were organizational and structural. And 4) contrary to Bauer's conclusion that any Pauline memory or influence has been completely lost in Ephesus (because the church there had been heretical for so long), there is evidence of Pauline influence in western Asia Minor at the time of Ignatius.

Trebilco has some specific comments regarding the existence of "orthodoxy" in the geographical area covered by his study. "So in the literature from Western Asia Minor we find a strong sense of applying criteria by which to judge whether, in the opinion of the author and his community, a certain belief or practice is in keeping with the tradition. This trend is consonant with the sense of "the tradition," "sound teaching," or "the truth" that we find in these documents" (42). "Thus the roots of later 'orthodoxy' are to be found here. 'Orthodoxy' is not to be seen as a later victory by those in power, or something determined by politics. It goes back to and is an organic development from the much earlier period. . . . [There is] a strong sense of doctrinal self-consciousness on the part of the canonical authors. . . . This sense of a limit, self-consciously adopted, is a very significant feature of Western Asia Minor" (43).

The conclusion of Trebilco's article is that "Bauer's thesis does not stand up to scrutiny with regard to the situation in Western Asia Minor. Where we can investigate the matter, what Bauer calls 'heresy' is neither the earliest form of Christian faith, nor is it in the majority" (43).

56. Trebilco, "Christian Communities," 17–44.

Köstenberger and Kruger, *The Heresy of Orthodoxy* (2010)

A recent critique of the Bauer Thesis appears in Andreas Köstenberger and Michael Kruger, *The Heresy of Orthodoxy: How Contemporary Culture's Fascination with Diversity Has Reshaped Our Understanding of Early Christianity*. If Thomas Robinson's work solidified the label of the Bauer Thesis in the secondary literature, Köstenberger and Kruger have contributed the compounded tag of the "Bauer-Ehrman Thesis." Although a critique of the "Bauer-Ehrman Thesis" was "not the main purpose" of the book (233), the topic fills up the initial one hundred pages, as the entire first section of the book examines the "Bauer-Ehrman Thesis" in some detail. Köstenberger and Kruger explain,

> In chapter 1, we will look at the origin and influence of the Bauer-Ehrman thesis, including its appropriation and critique by others. Chapter 2 examines Bauer's geographical argument for the precedence of early diversity in the Christian movement and considers patristic evidence for early orthodoxy and heresy, and chapter 3 turns to an area of investigation that Bauer surprisingly neglected—the New Testament data itself. How diverse was early Christianity, and did heresy in fact precede orthodoxy? These are the questions that will occupy us in the first part of the book as we explore the larger paradigmatic questions raised by the Bauer-Ehrman proposal (17).[57]

In chapter one, Köstenberger and Kruger argue, "One main reason for Bauer's surprising impact is that his views have found a fertile soil in the contemporary cultural climate" (23). The authors highlight the postmodern context, which praises subjective experience, diversity, pluralism, and an inclusivity that repudiates exclusive truth claims as ideological power ploys.[58] Therefore, "Bauer's thesis has received a new lease

---

57. Part 2 applies their insights to "Picking the Books: Tracing the Development of the New Testament Canon." And Part 3 examines "Changing the Story: Manuscripts, Scribes, and Textual Transmission." For Michael Kruger's further canonical studies, see Kruger, *Canon Revisited*; and Kruger, *Question of Canon*.

58. "And thus the tables are turned—diversity becomes the last remaining orthodoxy, and orthodoxy becomes heresy, because it violates the new orthodoxy: the gospel of diversity" (Köstenberger and Kruger, *Heresy of Orthodoxy*, 234); cf. Blaising, "Faithfulness."

on life through the emergence of postmodernism, the belief that truth is inherently subjective and a function of power" (39).

The opening chapter also summarizes early critiques found in initial reviews of Bauer's work:[59]

> First, Bauer's conclusions were unduly conjectural in light of the limited nature of the available evidence and in some cases arguments from silence altogether.
>
> Second, Bauer unduly neglected the New Testament evidence and anachronistically used second-century data to describe the nature of "earliest" (first-century) Christianity. . . .
>
> Third, Bauer grossly oversimplified the first-century picture, which was considerably more complex than Bauer's portrayal suggested. . . .
>
> Fourth, Bauer neglected existing theological standards in the early church.

The first chapter also reviews the "later critiques" of Turner, Marshall, Martin, McCue, Robinson, and Hultgren (33–38).

Chapter two retraces Bauer's steps by investigating the rise of Christianity in various locales, arguing that the earliest Christianity in these places was orthodox in form rather than heretical. The authors survey the evidence available for (1) Asia Minor, (2) Alexandria, (3) Edessa, and (4) Rome.[60] Köstenberger and Kruger conclude that "in all the major urban centers investigated by Bauer, orthodoxy most likely preceded heresy or the second-century data by itself is inconclusive" (52). The second chapter further argues that apostolic Christianity was more unified than many scholars allow and that Gnosticism was less organized than many acknowledge (59–60). "In light of the available first-century evidence, any assessment that concludes that Gnosticism was organized earlier than the second century is ultimately an argument from silence" (61).

Chapter three of *The Heresy of Orthodoxy* focuses upon materials in the New Testament. As others have done, Köstenberger and Kruger note the irony of Bauer's *Orthodoxy and Heresy in Earliest Christianity* not actually examining *earliest* Christianity.[61] "This explains, at least in part, why Bauer found early Christianity to be diverse and orthodoxy late—

---

59. They also acknowledged that "most reviews were appreciative" to varying degrees (Köstenberger and Kruger, *Heresy of Orthodoxy*, 33).

60. Bauer also focused investigations upon Antioch, Macedonia, and Cyprus.

61. A similar point is made in Marshall, "Orthodoxy and Heresy in Earlier Christianity."

he failed to consult the New Testament message regarding Jesus and his apostles" (69). Köstenberger and Kruger distinguish between "legitimate diversity" (which they find in the New Testament) and "illegitimate diversity, striking at the core of the earliest Christological affirmations" (100). "Bauer and his followers also fail to do justice to the massive Old Testament substructure of New Testament theology and vastly underestimate the pivotal significance of Jesus (who was both the primary subject and object of the gospel message) in linking Old Testament messianic prophecy organically with the gospel of the early Christians" (100–101).

Conclusion

Following his own survey of previous studies, Daniel Harrington concludes that "Bauer's reconstruction of how orthodoxy triumphed remains questionable."[62] It would seem that a stronger statement is justified. Larry Hurtado's judgment is correct:

> Over the years . . . important studies have rather consistently found Bauer's thesis seriously incorrect. . . . In fact, about all that remains unrefuted of Bauer's argument is the observation, and a rather banal one at that, that earliest Christianity was characterized by diversity, including serious differences of belief. Those who laud Bauer's book, however, obviously prefer to proceed as if much more of his thesis is sustainable. Unfortunately, for this preference, Bauer's claims have not stood well the test of time and critical examination.[63]

Or, as Darrell Bock asks, "if the two central Bauerian positions are flawed [diverse origins and Roman influence], why does the overall thesis stand?"[64] We might rather conclude with Hans-Dietrich Altendorf that Bauer has posed, at times, a "konstruktive Phantasie" or an "elegant ausgearbeitete Fiktion."[65] Nevertheless, this "constructive" and "elegantly

---

62. Harrington, "Reception," 297–98.

63. Hurtado, *Lord Jesus Christ*, 520–21.

64. Bock, *Missing Gospels*, 47.

65. "A constructive fantasy" and "an elegantly assembled fiction" (Altendorf, "Zum Stichwort," 64, cited by Bock, *Missing Gospels*, 50). Altendorf's article has not been accessible to me; according to Bock, the first description relates to Bauer's arguments from silence, and the second refers to his view of the Roman church's relation to Corinth in *1 Clement*.

assembled" work of scholarly speculation continues to wield substantial (though disputed) sway over the discipline.[66]

66. An earlier version of this essay appeared in *Journal of Ministry and Theology* 13 (2009) 30–63. It has been adapted and updated here.

2

Walter Bauer and the Apostolic Fathers

Paul A. Hartog

WALTER BAUER OPPOSED RECONSTRUCTIONS in which orthodoxy was an original, consistent form of Christianity and heresy was a subsequent deviation.[1] His work included some basic theses.[2] First, in many locations, what was later deemed as "heresy" was often earlier and more dominant than an "orthodox" counterpart. Second, the triumph of "orthodoxy" was largely due to the role of Rome. Bauer's work was engaging and provocative, and its pioneering ideas served to advance scholarship by stirring the pot for followers and opponents alike. As Robert Wilken later remarked, Bauer had created "a new paradigm."[3]

Bauer's work remains "impressive."[4] Bart Ehrman has called Bauer's work "possibly the most significant book on early Christianity written in modern times."[5] Ehrman maintains, "Probably most scholars today

---

1. Bauer, *Orthodoxy and Heresy*, 90. Bauer recognized, of course, the difficulties in using the collective terms "orthodoxy" and "heresy" (Bauer, *Orthodoxy and Heresy*, 77).

2. See Bingham, "Development and Diversity," 52.

3. Wilken, "Diversity and Unity," 103.

4. Norris, "Ignatius, Polycarp, and I Clement," 23.

5. Ehrman, *Orthodox Corruption of Scripture* , 7. Koester, "Häretiker im Urchristentum," 17–21 listed various works influenced by Bauer up to that time. For a review

think that Bauer underestimated the extent of proto-orthodoxy throughout the empire and overestimated the influence of the Roman church on
the course of the conflicts." [6] Nevertheless, concludes Ehrman, "Bauer's
intuitions were right."[7] While Ehrman has limited the role of Rome in the
triumph of orthodoxy, he has gone beyond Bauer by maintaining that
"the extent of proto-orthodoxy in the second and third centuries was
even less than Bauer had estimated" and "early Christianity was even less
tidy and more diversified than he [Bauer] realized."[8]

Bauer began with a geographical approach. After investigating
Edessa and Egypt, he turned his sights upon Asia Minor and Macedonia,
with a special focus upon Ignatius and Polycarp. Chapter three of *Orthodoxy and Heresy in Earliest Christianity* was entitled "Ignatius of Antioch and Polycarp of Smyrna; Macedonia and Crete." And chapter four
was entitled, "Asia Minor Prior to Ignatius."[9] Bauer suggested that "all"
of Ignatius's letters to the Asiatic Christians "bear eloquent testimony to
this acute danger of heresy."[10] Bauer declared that Ignatius's own position
in Antioch was "not as secure" as those bishops in Ephesus, Magnesia,
Tralles, and Philadelphia, and "the same [insecurity] can be said of his
friend Polycarp."[11] Bauer raised good and fascinating questions, including the state of the churches of Pergamum, Thyatira, Sardis, and Laodicea.[12] These churches seem to have faced strife or disarray when the Book
of Revelation was composed, and they are unmentioned in the Ignatian
and Polycarpian extant correspondence.

Paul Trebilco's recent article appropriately entitled "Christian
Communities in Western Asia Minor into the Early Second Century:
Ignatius and Others as Witnesses against Bauer," focused upon Western

of the book's influence throughout the 1970s, see Harrington, "Reception of Walter
Bauer's *Orthodoxy and Heresy.*"

6. Ehrman, *Lost Christianities*, 176. Bingham surmises that Ehrman has rather
emphasized the role of literary polemics. Bauer maintained that "a far more extensive
literary activity had developed" in heretical than in ecclesiastical circles. "And thereby
a new foothold is established to substantiate the view that the heretics considerably
outnumbered the orthodox" (Bauer, *Orthodoxy and Heresy*, 194).

7. Ehrman, *Lost Christianities*, 176.

8. Ibid.

9. For a response, see Robinson, "Orthodoxy and Heresy"; Robinson, *Bauer Thesis
Examined.*

10. Bauer, *Orthodoxy and Heresy*, 65.

11. Ibid., 69.

12. Ibid., 79.

Asia Minor and "particularly on Ignatius."[13] Trebilco emphasized four "significant points": 1) The nature of Ignatius's opponents: They were not Judaizing Gnostics as Bauer supposed, but rather two separate groups.[14] Judaizers were deemed a threat in Magnesia and Philadelphia, and docetists were deemed a threat in Tralles and Smyrna, and were also warned against in Ephesus.[15] 2) The absence of a given church among the seven churches in Revelation 2–3 or the seven church recipients in the Ignatian corpus do not necessarily reflect "heretical" takeovers. 3) Some disagreements with the bishop were related to church structure rather than theology. 4) Both Pauline and Johannine influence thrived in Western Asia Minor throughout the first half of the second century, even though Bauer maintained that Paul's influence had faded in Ephesus and vanished from Western Asia Minor.[16] "This ongoing chain of *both* Pauline and Johannine tradition in Western Asia Minor strongly counters Bauer's thesis."[17]

As Thomas Robinson has noted, we have "both in quantity of material and in content of that material, a situation for Western Asia Minor unmatched by any other area to which we may address the questions of the orthodoxy/heresy debate."[18] While Trebilco has recently focused upon Ignatius, I wish to focus rather upon *1 Clement* and Polycarp's *Letter to the Philippians* (*Pol. Phil.*) by addressing thirteen issues in the limited space available here.[19] In keeping with the number thirteen, these matters may prove to be unlucky omens for Bauer's reconstructions—a baker's dozen of inconvenient difficulties. The discussion of thirteen top-

13. Trebilco, "Christian Communities," 19.

14. The number and nature of Ignatius's opponents have been debated. See Molland, "Heretics Combatted by Ignatius of Antioch"; Barnard, "Background of St. Ignatius of Antioch"; Saliba, "Bishop of Antioch and the Heretics."

15. For a different tactic in response, see Robinson, *Bauer Thesis Examined*, 134–36. The nature of Ignatius's opponents continues to be debated, of course. Bauer theorized that Jewish Christians and anti-gnostic Pauline Christians joined to form a unified front against the heretics. The nature of Pol. Phil., including its limited use of the Hebrew Scriptures, does not fit this reconstruction. See also Robinson, *Bauer Thesis Examined*, 132–39.

16. See also Trebilco, "Christians in the Lycus Valley," 196–202.

17. Trebilco, "Christian Communities," 40.

18. Robinson, *Bauer Thesis Examined*, 107.

19. Representative of his general neglect of Jewish Christian sources, Bauer did not examine the *Didache* in *Rechtgläubigkeit und Ketzerei*. And he considered the *Epistle of Barnabas* to be a gnostic and perhaps docetic work (Bauer, "Orthodoxy and Heresy," 47–48).

ics will begin with Polycarp and then move on to "Clement," concluding with further thoughts on normativity and authority in these two authors.

Bauer and Polycarp

1. Bauer argued that the Thessalonian church had been overtaken by heresy, by noting that we have a Polycarpian letter to Philippi but not one to Thessalonica, which was also along the Egnatian way and presumably along Ignatius's journey to martyrdom.[20] Bauer noted that "Polycarp never wrote to Thessalonica in spite of the fact that in addition to his letter to the Philippians he seems also to have sent letters containing instructions to other communities."[21] Bauer declared, "Were I not fearful of misusing the argument from silence, I would now have to raise the question as to why we hear nothing at all about the community in neighboring Thessalonica in this connection."[22]

Within a paragraph, Bauer quickly abandoned his professed fear of arguments from silence. He queried, "Could it be that what we suspected in Philippi obtained to an even greater degree in Thessalonica and thus explains this reticence of Ignatius and silence of Polycarp?"[23] Bauer acknowledged, "To be sure, this is only a conjecture and nothing more!"[24] But as often happens in his volume, Bauer immediately went on to treat his conjecture as a given. He suspected that "heretical" teaching was so prevalent in Thessalonica that there was no possibility of gaining a hearing there.[25] He concluded, "Accordingly, I would also include post-Pauline Macedonia among those districts reached by Christianity in which 'heresy' predominated, along with Edessa and Egypt from their very earliest Christian beginnings, and Syria-Antioch from almost the outset."[26]

According to Irenaeus, Polycarp's aversion to heresy was evident in "his letters which he sent either to the neighboring churches, strengthening them, or to some of the brethren, exhorting and warning them"

---

20. See Schoedel, *Ignatius of Antioch*, 11–12.

21. Bauer, *Orthodoxy and Heresy*, 74.

22. Ibid.

23. Ibid., 74–75.

24. Ibid., 74.

25. Ibid.

26. Ibid.

(Eusebius, *Hist. eccl.* V.20.8).[27] But since these letters mentioned by Eusebius are no longer extant, we have no way of knowing that one of them was *not* written to Thessalonica. The Eusebian evidence and arguments from silence actually cut both ways. More basically, however, Polycarp himself states in 3.1 that he wrote to the Philippians at their request. If the Thessalonians did not make a similar request, the lack of an epistle addressed to Thessalonica becomes rather intelligible.[28]

2. Bauer underscored the embattled position of Polycarp within the Smyrnaean church.[29] Polycarp's inscription describes the epistolary sender as *Polykarpos kai hoi syn autōi presbyteroi* ("Polycarp and the elders with him"). Bauer interpreted "the elders with him" as a contrast to elders who might have been "against him" (docetic opponents).[30] Thus, in Bauer's reconstruction, the inscription portrayed an embattled Smyrnaean bishop with the elders on his side standing opposed by a gnostic anti-bishop and his followers.[31] Nevertheless, the text simply implies a level of collaboration or association between Polycarp and the elders "with him" (cf. Gal 1:1–2, where Paul speaks of "the brethren who are with me").[32] The Greek (behind the extant Latin) of the reference to Ignatius in Pol. *Phil.* 14 may have been similar: "And concerning Ignatius himself and concerning those with him, report whatever you may have learned more definitely."[33] The Greek does not require Bauer's interpretation—the inscription may merely imply that Polycarp's position was *primus inter pares* ("first among equals").[34]

---

27. ET from Lake, *Eusebius*, 499.

28. Contra Bauer, *Orthodoxy and Heresy*, 74.

29. Bauer's work accentuates a "majority" role of heresy in various locations, although gnostics themselves implied that they were in the minority (see McCue, "Bauer's *Rechtgläubikeit und Ketzerei*," 402). For a summary of the debate concerning whether gnostics saw themselves as spiritual "elite" ones, see Karen, *What is Gnosticism?*, 331n56; cf. 26–27, 169.

30. Bauer, *Orthodoxy and Heresy*, 70.

31. Ibid., 69–70. In his earlier *Handbuch*, Bauer had simply translated the phrase as "Polycarp and the presbyters with him," but then retracted this translation (see Bauer, *Orthodoxy and Heresy*, 70). Cf. *Martyrdom of Polycarp* 12.3

32. The argument here comes from Hartog, *Polycarp's Epistle to the Philippians*, 97.

33. ET from ibid., 95.

34. Schoedel, *Polycarp*, 7; Paulsen, *Die Briefe des Ignatius*, 113. See, however, Bauer, *Die Polykarpbriefe*, 33. Kleist's translation (Kleist, *Didache*, 75), "Polycarp and his assistants, the presbyters," goes beyond the Greek text. Lightfoot also over-reached by asserting, "Polycarp evidently writes here as a bishop (ἐπίσκοπος) in the latter and

Bauer reasoned that Polycarp did not have a secure position in Smyrna. To support his contention, Bauer cited Ignatius, *Epistle to the Smyrnaeans* 6.1: "Do not let a high position make anyone proud, for faith and love are everything."[35] Bauer assumed that the use of *topos* here was the office of bishop.[36] He noted that *topos* was used of Polycarp in Ignatius, *Epistle to Polycarp* 1.2: "Do justice to your office (*topos*) with constant care for both physical and spiritual concerns."[37] Bauer then concluded that there was "something like a gnostic anti-bishop in Smyrna."[38] But the term *topos* could be used of various positions. Ignatius himself makes no implication of a second bishop in Smyrna in Ignatius, *Epistle to the Smyrnaeans* 9.1. Recent studies, such as those of Allen Brent, have questioned how much of Ignatius's portrayal of Polycarp as bishop is Ignatius's projection and how much reflects the reality of the situation.[39] In any case, the details do not warrant the assumption that Polycarp and his supporters comprised a minority in Smyrna, or that Polycarp's position was in immediate jeopardy.

3. Bauer noted that the letter opening of Pol. *Phil.* does not address a bishop in Philippi, and he therefore assumed that the city was home to a gnostic anti-bishop.[40] The inscription is addressed *tē ekkēsia tou Theou tē paroikousē Philippous* ("to the church of God sojourning at Philippi"), without mention of a bishop. The absence of address to a bishop, according to Bauer, "suggests the presence of a heretical community leader."[41]

Other options remain, however. Perhaps there was no monarchical bishop in Philippi at all or perhaps the position was vacant. Perhaps Valens was the elder-bishop, but he had fallen into avarice (as reflected in Pol. *Phil.* 11.1). Perhaps "elder" and "bishop" were equivalent terms in Philippi, and the congregation was led by a plurality of elders. One notes that Paul's Philippians 1:1 refers to the "bishop and deacons" in Philippi, but not elders.

fuller sense of the title, surrounded by his council of presbyters" (Lightfoot, *Apostolic Fathers* vol. II.3, 321).

35. ET from Holmes, *Apostolic Fathers*, 253

36. Bauer, *Orthodoxy and Heresy*, 69.

37. ET from Holmes, *Apostolic Fathers*, 263.

38. Bauer, *Orthodoxy and Heresy*, 69.

39. Brent, *Ignatius of Antioch*, 11–13. Bauer himself notes, "In this respect, his letters bear witness to his fervent desire, but not to existing reality" (Bauer, *Orthodoxy and Heresy*, 70).

40. Bauer, *Orthodoxy and Heresy*, 69.

41. Ibid., 93.

Bauer further noted that Polycarp's collection of *Gemeindetafeln* in Pol. *Phil.* 4–6 never addresses the office of bishop. "In this he also is in sharp contrast to Ignatius, whom he regarded most highly along with his letters (Pol. *Phil.* 13.2). Neither does Polycarp prescribe the office of bishop as a remedy to the problems at Philippi, nor does he advise them to organize along monarchial lines. And yet it is precisely in this city that such an overseer would have been appropriate for more reasons than one."[42] Bauer thus contended that the *presence* of an Ignatian emphasis upon the bishop was proof that "orthodoxy" was embattled in Antioch and Smyrna.[43] Notwithstanding, he also argued that the *absence* of the term bishop in Pol. *Phil.* is proof that "orthodoxy" was embattled in Philippi. Either way, presence or absence, Bauer's presumptions won out in Bauer's reconstructions.

Nevertheless, because Polycarp addresses wives, widows, deacons, and elders, one might assume that "elder" and "bishop" are proximate terms in Polycarp's mind, similar to Titus 1:5–9.[44] Andrew Selby has recently argued for the "continuity" of a plurality of leadership ("a tradition") at Philippi between Paul and Polycarp.[45] Selby uses Philippians 1:1 and Pol. *Phil.* as evidence of a "blurring" between *episkopoi* and *presbyteroi*.

4. Bauer emphasized the "majority" nature of the heretics in Polycarp's epistle. Pol. *Phil.* 2.1 warns against the "meaningless talk and the error of the crowd (*tōn pollōn*)."[46] And Pol. *Phil.* 7.2 exhorts, "Therefore, forsaking the folly of the many (*tōn pollōn*) and their false teachings, let us return to the word entrusted to us from the beginning."[47] Bauer emphasized that Polycarp opposed the *hoi polloi*, which he took as a statistical enumeration of "the great majority" or "the great mass," an "admission which certainly can be trusted that the majority rejects the ecclesiastical faith."[48] To the German scholar, this was proof that "heretics" were the majority in Philippi and even Smyrna—those Bauer labeled as the *massa perditionis*.[49]

---

42. Ibid., 73.

43. Ibid., 62–63.

44. Cf. Acts 20:17, 28; 1 Pet 5:1–3.

45. Selby, "Bishops, Elders, and Deacons."

46. ET from Holmes, *Apostolic Fathers*, 283.

47. ET from Hartog, *Polycarp's Epistle to the Philippians*, 89.

48. Bauer, *Orthodoxy and Heresy*, 72–73.

49. Cf. Tit 1:10.

In this specific case, Bauer's argumentation could be informed by contemporary rhetorical studies that have examined the castigation of the *hoi polloi*, going back to Greek philosophical polemics.[50] For example, heightened rhetoric may have reflected the level of perceived danger more than the statistical accounting of opponents.[51] Bauer recognizes the use of *hoi polloi* as exaggeration or hyperbole when it fits his own purposes.[52] Thus *hoi polloi* was often more pejorative than statistical.[53] Elsewhere, Bauer is forced to downplay the "many," as when Irenaeus reports that Polycarp won over "many" Valentinians, Marcionites, and other "heretics" (Irenaeus, *Haer.* 3.3.4). Moreover, Bauer dismisses Celsus's description of the "great church" against the heretics, where the former are "those of the multitude" (Origen, *Cels.* 5.59).[54]

5. Bauer read an anti-heretical emphasis into Polycarp's *Philippians*. Yet Pol. *Phil.* 3 provides a purpose statement for the epistle: "Brethren, I do not write to you concerning this righteousness on my own initiative, but because you invited me. For neither I nor another like me is able to emulate the wisdom of the blessed and glorious Paul, who being among you in the presence of the people back then diligently and firmly taught concerning the word of truth, who also being absent wrote letters to you. If you examine them, you will be able to build yourselves up in the faith given to you."[55]

A theme of the letter is "righteousness," as seen in this statement of purpose in Pol. *Phil.* 3.1.[56] Although Polycarp praises the wisdom of the "blessed and glorious Paul" in the context, in some aspects, Polycarp's understanding of "righteousness" seems rather to resemble that of both Matthew and *1 Clement*.[57] The concept of patient endurance ties into

50. Though see Bauer, *Orthodoxy and Heresy*, 73.

51. Köstenberger and Kruger, *Heresy of Orthodoxy*, 62.

52. A critique hammered home by Völker, "Walter Bauer's *Rechtgläubigkeit und Ketzerei*," 403. Note the use of "some" (*tines*) in Ign. *Philad.* 7; Ign. *Trall.* 10.1; Ign. *Magn.* 4, 9.1; Ign. *Eph.* 7.1.

53. Hartog, *Polycarp and the New Testament*, 104.

54. Bauer, *Orthodoxy and Heresy*, 216. Cf. Burke, "Walter Bauer and Celsus"; Burke, "Celsus and Late Second-Century Christianity."

55. ET from Hartog, *Polycarp's Epistle to the Philippians*, 83.

56. Steinmetz, "Polykarp von Smyrna über die Gerechtigkeit."

57. Steinmetz, "Polykarp von Smyrna über die Gerechtigkeit"; Köhler, *Die Rezeption*, 103–4; Ritter, *De Polycarpe à Clement*, 154–55; Theobald, "Paulus und Polykarp," 375–82; Holmes compares Polycarp's understanding of "righteousness" to Matthew, James, and 1 Peter (Holmes, "Paul," 68). Dehandschutter situates Pol. *Phil.*'s understanding of "righteousness" between the New Testament writings and *2 Clement*

righteousness in 8.1, and endurance reappears elsewhere throughout Pol. *Phil.* Jesus often serves as an example of such endurance in suffering (comparable in approach to 1 Peter), and Paul and the other apostles similarly function in the *paradeigmata* of 9.1–2. Ignatius and his companions are mentioned in chapter 9 as well.

Moreover, the letter frequently warns against avarice and calls for self-control and forgiveness. The warnings against avarice build from widows to deacons to elders, perhaps in preparation for the case of Valens, an elder who fell into greed, as discussed in 11.1. In sum, Pol. *Phil.* regularly emphasizes moral paraenesis.[58]

6. Bauer believed that the Pastoral Epistles were composed after Pol. *Phil.*, perhaps written against Marcion.[59] However, Pol. *Phil.* 4.1 states, "But avarice is the beginning of all difficulties. Knowing therefore that we brought nothing into the world but neither have we anything to carry out, let us arm ourselves with weapons of righteousness and let us teach ourselves first to follow in the commandment of the Lord."[60] The phrase "avarice [the love of money] is the beginning of all difficulties" is conceptually similar to 1 Timothy 6:10: "For the love of money is a root of all sorts of evil (NASB)." Polycarp's wording differs from 1 Timothy in that he refers to the "beginning" (*arxē*) rather than the "root" (*riza*), and his choice of *xalepōn* differs from *kakōn*.[61]

Nevertheless, because the following phrase parallels 1 Timothy 6:7, it seems likely that Polycarp is dependent upon 1 Timothy.[62] Polycarp continued, "Knowing therefore that we brought nothing into the world but neither have we anything to carry out."[63] The wording is "virtually identical" with 1 Timothy 6:7, although Pol. *Phil.* exchanges *alla* for the

(Dehandschutter, "Polycarp's Epistle," 170; cf. Bovon-Thurneysen, "Ethik und Eschatologie," 256; Jefford, *Apostolic Fathers: An Essential Guide*, 66; Lohmann, *Drohung und Verheißung*, 180).

58. Hartog, "Relationship between *Paraenesis* and Polemic"; Hartog, *Polycarp and the New Testament*, 121–34.

59. Bauer, *Orthodoxy and Heresy*, 84.

60. ET from Hartog, *Polycarp's Epistle to the Philippians*, 85.

61. As explained in ibid., 116. Polycarp already referred to the *riza* of the Philippians' faith in Pol. *Phil.* 1.2.

62. This argument comes from Hartog, *Polycarp's Epistle to the Philippians*, 116. See also Oxford Society of Historical Theology, *New Testament in the Apostolic Fathers*, 95; Berding, *Polycarp and Paul*, 67; Hartog, *Polycarp and the New Testament*, 178–79.

63. ET from Hartog, *Polycarp's Epistle to the Philippians*, 85.

"very difficult" *hoti*.[64] Polycarp's use of the introductory formula "knowing that" points to the use of a source.[65] Rensberger postulates, "The most natural explanation would seem to be that Polycarp repeated a version of the old saw about φιλαργυρία [greed], and that this called to mind its connection with the other saying in 1 Timothy 6, which he then also cited, using his favorite introductory formula."[66]

Bauer theorized that the Pastorals were derivative, that their author was dependent upon Polycarp.[67] In fact, Bauer believed that 1 Timothy 6:20 is a reference to Marcion's *Antitheses*.[68] But one should consider the pastiche-like nature of Pol. *Phil.*, pointing to the secondary nature of Polycarp's letter in comparison with the Pastorals. In this regard, one is reminded of Kenneth Berding's examination of the clustering of Pauline sources in Pol. *Phil.*, including materials from the Pastorals.[69]

7. Bauer claimed that prior to Irenaeus, "sure traces of Galatians are lacking while the uncertain traces are sharply limited to Polycarp."[70] Pol. *Phil.* 5.1 states, "Knowing therefore that God is not mocked."[71] The material is similar to Galatians 6:7, and could be termed as an almost certain reference. Polycarp introduced this material using the formulaic, "Knowing that." Moreover, the verb "mocked" (*myktērizetai*) is found only in Galatians 6:7 within the New Testament, causing Berding to assert that literary dependence is "beyond any reasonable doubt."[72] While Michael Holmes postulates that both Paul and Polycarp may have made use of "a familiar saying" (thus giving it a "c" rating), he acknowledges that "the

---

64. Holmes, "Polycarp's *Letter*," 216. Johannes Baptist Bauer discusses more remote parallels as well, including Job 1:21 (Bauer, *Die Polykarpbriefe*, 50).

65. Berding, *Polycarp and Paul*, 68; Hartog, *Polycarp and the New Testament*, 231; Hartog, *Polycarp's Epistle to the Philippians*, 64, 116.

66. Rensberger, "As the Apostle Teaches," 125. See also Schoedel, *Polycarp*, 16; Lindemann, *Paulus im ältesten Christentum*, 223.

67. Bauer, *Orthodoxy and Heresy*, 224.

68. Bauer mentioned that he had changed his mind to this view (Bauer, *Orthodoxy and Heresy*, 223, 226).

69. Berding, *Polycarp and Paul*, 142–55; Berding, "Polycarp of Smyrna's View." Without this external *terminus ad quem* for the composition of the Pastorals, Bauer is left with the first attestation of them being found in Irenaeus.

70. Bauer, *Orthodoxy and Heresy*, 222.

71. ET from Hartog, *Polycarp's Epistle to the Philippians*, 85.

72. Berding, *Polycarp and Paul*, 73. The 1904 Oxford Society cited "a very Pauline context" for Pol. *Phil.* 6.1 (Oxford Society of Historical Theology, *New Testament in the Apostolic Fathers*, 92).

saying does not appear to be otherwise attested in antiquity."[73] This fact tilts the evidence toward dependence upon Galatians.[74] Pol. *Phil.* 5.3 continues with materials similar to Galatians 5:19–21 as well as 1 Corinthians 6:9. While the 1904 Oxford Society of Historical Theology classified use of Galatians with a "b" rating, Holmes has downgraded it to a "c" rating, and Berding has upgraded the categorization to "almost certain."[75]

8. Bauer emphasized the anti-heretical materials in Pol. *Phil.* 7.1, where Polycarp opposed false teachers: "For everyone who does not confess that Jesus Christ has come in [the] flesh is an antichrist. And whoever does not confess the testimony of the cross is of the Devil. And whoever distorts the sayings of the Lord for his own desires and alleges [there is] neither a resurrection nor a judgment, this one is a firstborn of Satan."[76]

Pol. *Phil.* 7.1 seems rather stereotyped.[77] It borrows from the anti-secessionist sentiments of 1 John.[78] Various scholars, including both Peter Steinmetz and Michael Holmes have argued that Pol. *Phil.* serves more as a warning against possible infiltration than as a reflection of heretical dominance.[79]

Scholars have debated the relationship between avarice and heresy in the letter. On a level of certainty, the letter addresses the topic of "righteousness" (3.1) and discusses the fall of Valens, an elder at Philippi, into avarice (11.1). In a possible reading, the community may have been tempted toward retaliation rather than forgiveness.[80] In this context, Polycarp highlighted the future judgment. But the false teachers he warned against denied such judgment, and therefore undermined his

73. Holmes, "Polycarp's *Letter*," 208–9.

74. This argument comes from Hartog, *Polycarp's Epistle to the Philippians*, 119.

75. Oxford Society of Historical Theology, *New Testament in the Apostolic Fathers*, 92; Holmes, "Polycarp's *Letter*," 210. Berding, *Polycarp and Paul*, 200. Cf. Hartog, *Polycarp and the New Testament*, 177; Hartog, *Polycarp's Epistle to the Philippians*, 122. Berding contrasts the "thin" reading of Holmes, the tempered "thin" reading of Hartog, the "thick" reading of Harrison and Hill, and his own "middle approach" (Berding, "Polycarp's Use," 131). See also Hernando, "Irenaeus and the Apostolic Fathers," 348–49.

76. ET from Hartog, *Polycarp's Epistle to the Philippians*, 87.

77. Hartog, "Opponents in Polycarp."

78. Bauer recognized that Polycarp's use of 1 John "is certain" (Bauer, *Orthodoxy and Heresy*, 207). See Hartog, "Opponents in Polycarp"; Wilhite, "Polycarp's Reception."

79. Holmes, "Polycarp of Smyrna," 936; Steinmetz, "Polykarp von Smyrna," 73; Headlam, "Epistle of Polycarp," 9.

80. Hartog, *Polycarp and the New Testament*, 139–42.

moral paraenesis. Thus Polycarp's concern with heresy was secondary to his paraenesis.[81] One notices the flow of Pol. *Phil.* 6.2–7.1, with its exhortation against avarice (6.1); call to forgiveness (6.2); reference to the judgment seat of Christ (6.2); call to reverent service as espoused by the prophets, Lord, and apostles (6.3); warning against false teachers (6.3); and condemnation of the denial of the incarnation, future resurrection, and judgment by "antichrist" figures (7.1).

9. Bauer argued that the return of "peace" to the Antiochene church was not the cessation of external persecution but the cessation of internal fighting. Much of modern scholarship has followed Bauer's view, and it has much to commend it. Pol. *Phil.* 13.1 speaks of representatives being sent to Syria, which is tied to the congratulations sent to the Antiochene church upon the return of peace (Ign. *Philad.* 10, Ign. *Smyrn.* 11, Ign. *Polyc.* 7). Yet assuming the validity of Bauer's interpretation, the point of sending congratulations to Antioch is that such "peace" has returned,[82] which actually softens Bauer's portrayal of the dire straits in Antioch that led to Ignatius's "frantic efforts" and "frantic concern."[83] Moreover, even granting that the return of peace was the cessation of internal fighting, various other causes beyond heresy may have played a part in the dissension.

Bauer seems to overplay the desperation of the situation in Antioch. Citing Pol. *Phil.* 13.1, he insisted, "Polycarp is to exert influence upon those Asian churches which Ignatius himself had been unable to reach. And the necessity of such a task was impressed upon Polycarp to such an extent that, regardless of the precarious position of orthodoxy in Smyrna itself, he would have preferred to undertake the journey to Antioch in person."[84] But is this the tenor of Pol. *Phil.* 13.1? Polycarp stated, "You wrote to me, both you and Ignatius, that if anyone travels to Syria, he should also take along your letter. This I will do, if I get a suitable opportunity, whether I myself or one whom I will send [as] representative on your behalf as well."[85] The tenor of "if I get a suitable opportunity" does not reflect desperation. "Those are not the words of a man who saw the survival of the Antiochian church endangered or one who was so worried about the state of

---

81. Hartog, "Relationship between *Paraenesis* and Polemic."

82. Ign. *Philad.* 10; Ign. *Smyrn.* 11; Ign. *Polyc.* 7–8.

83. Bauer, *Orthodoxy and Heresy*, 63–64.

84. Ibid., 64.

85. ET from Hartog, *Polycarp's Epistle to the Philippians*, 95.

things in Smyrna that he could not leave the city."[86] Frederick Norris has even reasoned that Polycarp was "unimpressed" with the undertaking of the task.[87] Furthermore, Bauer believed that the churches between Smyrna and Antioch were a lost cause. But Ignatius, *Epistle to the Philadelphians* 10.2 affirms that "the neighboring churches" sent bishop or presbyters and deacons to congratulate the return of peace to Antioch.

10. Bauer reasoned that the orthodox contingency at Philippi "had requested the letters of Ignatius as a weapon in its struggle against Docetism."[88] Nevertheless, Polycarp discusses the fuller nature of Ignatius's letters in Pol. *Phil.* 13.2: "We send to you the letters of Ignatius that were sent to us by him, and as many others as we had with us—just as you directed. They are attached to this letter, [and] you will be able to derive great benefit from them. For they contain faith and endurance and every edification that pertains to our Lord."[89]

One notes that Polycarp characterizes the letters through his own lens of not only faith but also endurance, a Polycarpian theme as discussed above. And he described the Ignatian correspondence as profitable to "every edification." Polycarp does not pigeonhole the Ignatian correspondence as anti-heretical alone. Furthermore, Polycarp explains why he attached the letters he did: they were as many as the Smyrnaeans had with them. Bauer made an issue of Ignatius's addressing the Ephesians, Philadelphians, and Smyrnaeans, similar to Revelation 2–3, but not Pergamum, Thyatira, Sardis, or Laodicea. True to form, Bauer assumes that these churches (along with Colossae) had been abandoned to "heretical" opponents. Robinson responds, "Bauer depended much too heavily on his assumption that churches were omitted by the Apocalyptist and by Ignatius mainly because of the rampant heresy within those churches."[90]

This passage in Polycarp reminds us not only of the occasional nature of epistolary composition, but also of the contingencies of letter collection.[91] One cannot build a stable structure upon a foundation of arguments from silence. It is noteworthy that Ignatius's *Epistle to the*

86. Norris, "Ignatius, Polycarp, and I Clement," 28.
87. Ibid.
88. Bauer, *Orthodoxy and Heresy*, 175.
89. ET from Hartog, *Polycarp's Epistle to the Philippians*, 95.
90. Robinson, *Bauer Thesis Examined*, 150.
91. See Robinson, *Bauer Thesis Examined*, 151–61.

Romans has a different textual history than the other letters.[92] Ignatius's *Romans* was sent from Troas, and Polycarp may not have obtained a copy of the epistle.[93] Pol. *Phil.* 13 implies a compilation of Ignatian materials, a fascinating example of how one collection of particular, early Christian letters may have been assembled.[94] Various scholars have proposed that Ignatius's *Romans* had a different textual history precisely because it was not forwarded by Polycarp to Philippi, unlike the other six letters of the Ignatian middle recension.[95]

Bauer and *1 Clement*

Bauer ended chapter 4 by referencing *1 Clement*: "I am of he [sic] opinion that this famous letter of the Roman community to Corinth can only be understood correctly if it is considered in this sort of context," alluding to an embattled orthodoxy threatened by the overwhelming force of heresy. Fittingly, chapters 5 and 6 go on to address the role of Rome, and Bauer took *1 Clement* as his "starting point for determining the position of Rome in the struggle between these outlooks."[96] Bauer sought to paint a powerful Roman church, imposing its singular will upon others. He acknowledged, however, "By the middle of the second century Rome had made an attempt to impose its will upon Asia, but held back from taking the final steps when the elderly Polycarp came to Rome in person."[97]

11. Bauer depicted *1 Clement* as primarily serving as an anti-heretical missive, opposing a gnostic threat in Corinth. First, Bauer argued that the letter appeals to the same "unshakable foundation of tradition" as found in other anti-heretical texts: God, Christ, the apostles, and the leaders of the church.[98] Second, Bauer noted that the schisms in the Corinthian church in Paul's own time included facets of false teaching as

92. "It is interesting to notice that the one epistle which neither Polycarp nor the Philippians could easily obtain . . . seems to have had a different textual history from that of the other six" (Lake, *Apostolic Fathers*, vol. 1, 280–81).

93. This is a different reading of the evidence than Robinson, *Bauer Thesis Examined*, 157.

94. Thus the scenario perhaps illustrates how other early Christian collections (including a Pauline collection) may have been gathered.

95. Lake, *Apostolic Fathers*, vol. 1, 280–81; Brent, *Ignatius of Antioch*, 146.

96. Bauer, *Orthodoxy and Heresy*, 95.

97. Ibid., 97.

98. Ibid., 99.

well.[99] Bauer recognized that gnostic heresy was not an explicit concern in *1 Clement* but reasoned that he could not find "a more satisfactory answer" than his reconstruction "based on the history of Christianity in Corinth."[100] He also believed that it would be strange for "Clement" to write so long a letter if there was no grave heretical threat. A. I. C. Heron counters that it would make no sense to write such a long letter targeting heresy while never discussing what would have been "the real issues."[101] According to Bauer, *1 Clement* is not at all concerned with the Pauline gospel, and therefore borrows heavily from 1 Corinthians but was not at all concerned with Romans.[102] He interpreted *1 Clement*'s references to the resurrection as anti-heretical, although Heron's rhetorical study of the instances points otherwise.[103] Bauer also argued that "Even the predilection of *1 Clement* for God the creator appears to us to have an anti-heretical thrust."[104] Although *1 Clement*'s use of the Old Testament could reflect arguments of continuity against heretics, perhaps the author of *1 Clement* himself simply assumed that arguments based upon such biblical texts would serve as arguments from authority that would appeal to the epistle's recipients.[105]

---

99. Ibid., 99–102. See also Schmithals, *Gnosticism in Corinth*, which swims against the scholarly tide by finding Gnosticism behind 1 Corinthians. For tracing developments between 1 Corinthians and *1 Clement*, see Horrell, *Social Ethos*.

100. Bauer, *Orthodoxy and Heresy*, 102. A. I. C. Heron responds, "To put the alternatives in this pointed way is not to imply any denigration of Bauer: any historian must engage in reconstruction, and must use his imagination . . . but we are not thereby absolved from the responsibility of asking whether any particular historical construction rests so heavily on imagination and so little on evidence that it can only be regarded as an interesting speculation, but not as a valid or probable interpretation or history" (Heron, "Interpretation of I Clement," 525; cf. 530, 537).

101. Heron, "Interpretation of I Clement," 543.

102. Bauer notes that *1 Clem.* 35.5–6 follows Rom 1:29–32, and *1 Clem.* 33.1 follows Rom 6:1. Nevertheless, *1 Clement* uses Romans "only for the purpose of moral admonition" (Bauer, *Orthodoxy and Heresy*, 220n41). Of course, this begs the question of *1 Clement* using 1 Corinthians for anti-heretical purposes and not for moral paraenesis. *1 Clement*'s concern with "the Pauline gospel" leads into wider interpretive matters, which I cannot address fully here.

103. Heron, "Interpretation of I Clement" 531–32.

104. Bauer, *Orthodoxy and Heresy*, 148.

105. *1 Clement* at least demonstrates that the author and his ilk in Rome were "in exceptionally close contact with the Old Testament" (Bauer, *Orthodoxy and Heresy*, 240).

Bauer also pointed to the early users and interpreters of *1 Clement*. He argued that Polycarp was "thoroughly familiar with *1 Clement*" and found "its main fulfillment in the struggle against the heretics."[106] The claim that Polycarp finds the "main fulfillment" of *1 Clement* within anti-heretical objectives faces the hurdle that Polycarp's *Philippians* is a letter filled with paraenesis that draws from Synoptic-like materials, the Pastorals, *1 Clement*, and 1 Peter for paraenetic purposes.[107] And while it is true that Irenaeus highlighted *1 Clement*'s frequent use of the Old Testament and its remarks upon "the almighty creator God" for anti-heretical ends, one must not confuse the later use of material with the original purpose of that material's composition.[108] *1 Clement* was emphasizing continuity with biblical material, which Irenaeus then used for his own anti-Marcionite purposes.

Bauer also summoned Dionysius of Corinth and Hegesippus, who remarked, "The church of the Corinthians continued in the true doctrine up to the time when Primus was bishop of Corinth. When I traveled by ship to Rome I stayed with them, and had conversations with them for several days during which we rejoiced together over the true doctrine."[109] Bauer concluded, "Here *1 Clement* is interpreted as a call to orthodoxy with which the Corinthians complied for a long time."[110] But this type of material is a common rhetorical device in early Christian literature—to praise the continuing faithfulness of a church or individual (cf. Pol. *Phil.* 1.2; *1 Clem.* 47.6).[111]

---

106. Bauer, *Orthodoxy and Heresy*, 103. On Polycarp's knowledge of *1 Clement*, see Berding, "Polycarp's Use of *1 Clement*." On Polycarp as a heresiologist, see Hill, *From the Lost Teaching*, 80–82.

107. Hartog, *Polycarp and the New Testament*, 194. On *1 Clement* as paraenesis, see Bowe, *Church in Crisis*. See Heron's blunt critique of Bauer's argument from Polycarp: "The fact that Polycarp shows massive dependence on the thought of Clement, and was himself a notable opponent of heresy in Asia Minor through the first half of the second century prove—that Polycarp was massively dependent on the thought of Clement and was himself a notable opponent of heresy in Asia Minor through the first half of the second century. But we are in no way justified in concluding that Clement faced in Corinth at the end of the first century the kind of situation which faced Polycarp in Asia Minor through the first part of the second" (Heron, "Interpretation of I Clement," 533).

108. Heron, "Interpretation of I Clement," 534; Hartog, "Opponents in Polycarp," 390.

109. Bauer, *Orthodoxy and Heresy*, 103; cf. Eusebius, *Hist. eccl.* 4.22.1; 4.23.11.

110. Bauer, *Orthodoxy and Heresy*, 103.

111. See Hartog, "Implications of Paul."

Bauer claimed that Hegesippus was acquainted with *1 Clement* but not 1 Corinthians. The basis of his argument is that Hegesippus declares, "Blessed are your eyes, since they see, and your ears, since they hear." Bauer contrasts this with 1 Corinthians 2:9 and its mention of "Things which eye has not seen and ear has not heard" (NASB). Nevertheless, Bauer failed to quote the next verse of 1 Corinthians: "For to us God revealed them through the Spirit" (NASB).[112] His insistence that Hegesippus was not acquainted with 1 Corinthians is based upon an argument from silence.

A foundational problem is Bauer's desire to read *1 Clement* in an anti-gnostic manner.[113] But a scholarly consensus views the epistle as a letter addressing disunity (and disorder) without explicit reference to heresy.[114] *1 Clement* 47.6 simply states, "It is disgraceful, dear friends, yes, utterly disgraceful and unworthy of your conduct in Christ, that it should be reported that the well-established and ancient church of the Corinthians, because of one or two persons, is rebelling against its presbyters."[115] *1 Clement* 54 refers to "rebellion and strife and schisms."[116] The underlying causes of the disunity at Corinth are not discussed, allowing scholars to posit a variety of options. Horacio Lona lists some of them: tensions between Jewish and Gentile Christians; debates over Christian teaching; tensions between "spirit" (charisma) and office (structure); and relational or personality power struggles.[117] L. L. Welborn adds the further possibility of monetary struggles or tensions.[118] As H. E. W. Turner noted, Bauer's "reconstruction of the events which led up to the letter of St.

---

112. See Hartog, "1 Corinthians 2:9."

113. Heron critiques Bauer for trying to fit *1 Clement* into his pre-constructed theory and for reading between the lines, as if heresy were the key issue although left unmentioned. Heron argues that "on Bauer's hypothesis, the writing of the letter makes practically no sense at all—what possible point could there have been in writing at such length—to the Church in Corinth and not discussing the real issues?" (Heron, "Interpretation of I Clement," 543).

114. See Grant, *Apostolic Fathers*, vol. 1, 100–101; Bakke, "Concord and Peace." This point was already reflected in the *Muratorian Canon* (see Heron, "Interpretation of I Clement," 541n15).

115. ET from Holmes, *Apostolic Fathers*, 109.

116. ET from ibid., 117. On "schism" in *1 Clement*, see Rohde, "Häresie und Schisma."

117. Lona, *Der erste Clemensbrief*, 79–80. On "spirit" vs. office, see Camphenhausen, *Kirchliches Amt*.

118. Welborn, "Clement," 1059.

Clement is at best non-proven," and the traditional interpretation of the epistle is more probable.[119]

12. Bauer's interpretation of *1 Clement* serves a wider purpose—the role of the Roman church as an intrusive guardian of orthodoxy.[120] Bauer portrays *1 Clement* as an imposed ruling from Rome rather than as an attempt to persuade.[121] "In any event," argued Bauer, "Rome's intervention had a decisive effect. Rome succeeded in imposing its will on Corinth."[122] Rome had completely "cast its spell over the capital of Achaia."[123] This fits with Bauer's wider reconstruction of the role of Rome, which "was from the very beginning the center and chief source of power for the 'orthodox' movement within Christianity."[124] Roman control was not immediate. "The undoubted Roman success was surely achieved by the employment of tactics which *1 Clement* rather more conceals from us than reveals."[125]

In post-Reformation debates, traditionalist Roman Catholic theologians have maintained that *1 Clement* reflects the primacy of the bishop of Rome.[126] According to John Lawson, the internal evidence of the letter itself demonstrates that "though there was as yet in the Church no accepted and permanent visible administrative machinery of central government, yet the sentiment of corporate cohesion was strong."[127] Nevertheless, "it is evident that the letter did not aim to impose a theological position onto the Corinthian church but to persuade the Christians there to accept it."[128] Andrew Gregory writes, "Thus the church at Rome shows concern for the

119. Turner, "Relation between Orthodoxy and Heresy," 69–71.

120. See Heron, "Interpretation of I Clement," 520. For discussions of *1 Clement* situated within the broader history of Roman Christianity, see Brown and Meier, *Antioch and Rome*, 159–83; Jeffers, *Conflict at Rome*; Gregory, "Disturbing Trajectories."

121. Heron, "Interpretation of I Clement," 520; Bock, *Missing Gospels*, 50

122. Bauer, *Orthodoxy and Heresy*, 104.

123. Ibid.

124. Ibid., 229. Heron points out that Bauer's view of Roman intervention implies his understanding of diversity, but not vice versa (Heron, "Interpretation of I Clement," 518–19).

125. Bauer, *Orthodoxy and Heresy*, 111.

126. Kleist, *Epistles of St. Clement of Rome*, 4. Cf. Altaner, "Der 1. Clemensbrief"; Fuellenbach, *Ecclesiastical Office*. For past studies on *1 Clement* and so-called "early catholicism," see Beyschlag, *Clemens Romanus*; Opitz, *Ursprünge frühkatholischer Pneumatologie*; Räisänen, "'Werkgerechtichkeit.'" On the influence of *1 Clement* upon later ecclesiastical thought, see Gerke, *Die Stellung*.

127. Lawson, *Theological and Historical Introduction*, 23.

128. Köstenberger and Kruger, *Heresy of Orthodoxy*, 50–51.

situation in Corinth, but makes no claim of authority over the Christians there. . . . The church at Rome writes to the church at Corinth of its own free will, but the form in which it does so makes clear that it could not take for granted that its counsel would be either welcome or in any way binding at Corinth."[129] That the Corinthian church eventually sided with the perspective of *1 Clement* seems to be implied by the fact that the epistle was read in assembly during the time of Dionysius of Corinth.[130]

Bauer interpreted *1 Clement* through the lens of late second-century interventions.[131] But 1 Peter (from the first century) seems to have been written from Rome, and it addressed Christians in Pontus, Galatia, Cappadocia, Asia, and Bithynia. Moreover, Roman leaders were not alone in such interventions, and Bauer did not do justice to parallels not involving Rome. The Book of Revelation instructs seven churches in Asia Minor. Polycarp counseled the Philippian congregation, and Ignatius exhorted various Asian churches. Ignatius, as a leader from Antioch, even instructed the Roman church. According to Norris, "The literature of this period shows a pattern of territorial intervention or interpenetration from many Christian centers."[132] In fact, declares Rowan Williams, early Christian congregations manifested "an almost obsessional mutual interest and interchange" among themselves.[133] Bauer painted these other examples in a weak manner when compared with his depiction of the strong intervention of *1 Clement*. Furthermore, although Bauer maintained that the Roman church foisted a hierarchical structure upon others, monepiscopacy is not in evidence in Rome at the beginning of the second century (nor in

---

129. Gregory, "*1 Clement*," 25–27. Heron maintains, "Where Clement speaks in an authoritarian fashion to or about the leaders of the revolt, he speaks not as a Roman to a Corinthian, but as a churchman to a group who have brought about division in the Church, where he speaks to the Corinthian Church, he speaks to his brothers" (Heron, "Interpretation of I Clement," 539).

130. Eusebius, *Hist. eccl.* 4.23.11; cf. Kleist, *Epistles of St. Clement of Rome*, 5.

131. Heron, "Interpretation of I Clement," 529. For six specific critiques of Bauer's understanding of the Roman church's authoritative intervention reflected in *1 Clement*, see Bock, *Missing Gospels*, 51; cf. Köstenberger and Kruger, *Heresy of Orthodoxy*, 51–52. On *1 Clement* as ecclesiastical intervention, see Van Cauwelaert, "L'intervention de l'église de Rome."

132. Norris, "Ignatius, Polycarp, and I Clement," 38.

133. Williams, "Does It Make Sense," 11–12. See also Thompson, "Holy Internet."

1 Clement in particular).[134] And our earliest extant liturgical texts come from Syria and not Rome.[135]

Pol. *Phil.* 3.1 affirms that the letter was written because the Philippian assembly had requested advice from Polycarp of Smyrna. This passage alone demonstrates that other churches beyond Rome played key, influential roles in the webbing of second-century Christianity. Polycarp's influence is further attested by his visit to Anicetus in Rome, when he was invited to participate in the celebration of the Eucharist.[136] Norris reasoned, "Since this was Roman territory, the stronger argument most probably came from Polycarp and the Asia Minor contingent."[137] One also recalls Irenaeus's *Letter to Victor*, in which Polycarp's representation of Asia Minor counterbalanced Roman leadership.[138] Turner fittingly described the "collateral" "rather than derivative" influence of Asia Minor in comparison with Rome.[139] Norris concluded that Bauer "pushed Roman centrality back to a point in history where it did not exist" and "underrated the strength and influence" of ecclesiastical centers outside of Rome.[140] "When the strength and contributions of these centers to the development of orthodoxy is recognized, it is impossible to see Rome as the dominant center of 'orthodoxy' at the beginning of the second century."[141] Ehrman concurs that "The regnant view now is that Bauer probably overestimated the influence of the Roman church."[142]

Normativity and Authority

13. As we near conclusion, let us move beyond these twelve specific discussion points to the framing subject of normativity and authority, as

134. Norris, "Ignatius, Polycarp, and I Clement," 38; Lampe, *From Paul to Valentinus*; Ziegler, *Successio*; Heron, "Interpretation of I Clement," 527.

135. Bock, *Missing Gospels*, 51.

136. Eusebius, *Historia ecclesiastica* 5.24.16–17.

137. Norris, "Ignatius, Polycarp, and I Clement," 40.

138. See Lohse, *Das Passafest der Quartadecimaner*, 122–27.

139. Turner, *Pattern of Christian Truth*, 73–79.

140. Norris, "Ignatius, Polycarp, and I Clement," 41.

141. Ibid., 42. See also Thomassen, "Orthodoxy and Heresy in Second-Century Rome." Bauer has seemingly read the power of the fourth-century Roman church (buttressed by political means of influence) upon second-century Rome (see Köstenberger and Kruger, *Heresy of Orthodoxy*, 61).

142. Ehrman, *Orthodox Corruption*, 9.

one can make a two-fold argument from Pol. *Phil.* (with *1 Clement* in corroboration).[143]

First, Polycarp's letter serves as witness to the integration of multiple streams of authority within the early second century.[144] Polycarp directly mentions Paul on four occasions, in Pol. *Phil.* 3.2, 9.1, and twice in 11.2–3.[145] Polycarp uses introductory formulae to introduce materials from Ephesians in Pol *Phil.* 1.3, 1 Timothy in Pol. *Phil.* 4.1, and Galatians in Pol. *Phil.* 5.1. Materials in Pol. *Phil.* 5.3 and 6.2 clearly resemble Pauline texts as well.[146] Furthermore, Pol. *Phil.* 12 seems to apply the term "scripture" to the New Testament book of Ephesians.[147]

The influence of 1 John is ably demonstrated by Pol. *Phil.* 7.1.[148] Other early Christian sources (apart from the *Vita Polycarpi*) tie Polycarp into Quartodecimanism, which would seem to be another argument for Johannine influence (at least broadly construed) upon the Smyrnaean leader, even if indirectly.[149] Moreover, the use of 1 Peter is immediately apparent as well (a fact already noted by Eusebius). Patent examples appear in Pol. *Phil.* 1.3, 8.1–8.2. Polycarp's epistle seems to stand out as an important, early witness to 1 Peter.[150]

143. On theological norms in Ignatius, see Schoedel, "Theological Norms"; Saliba, "Bishop of Antioch and the Heretics."

144. See Dehandschutter, "Polycarp's Epistle to the Philippians."

145. Bauer erroneously states that Polycarp refers to "Paul" three times, overlooking the fact that "Paul" is mentioned twice in 11.2–3 alone (Bauer, *Orthodoxy and Heresy*, 218).

146. Hartog, *Polycarp and the New Testament*, 177–79.

147. See Hartog, "Polycarp, Ephesians," which did not interact with Stroker, "Formation of Secondary Sayings of Jesus," 132–45. But see Hartog, *Polycarp's Epistle to the Philippians*, 152–53. Andreas Köstenberger and Michael Kruger have recently cited and adopted my study (Köstenberger and Kruger, *Heresy of Orthodoxy*, 142–43). Beyond the support that I have marshaled, they note that Lee McDonald concurs with the interpretation (McDonald, *Biblical Canon*, 276). Bauer seems to take the mention of "scripture" in Pol. *Phil.* 12.1 as a reference to Old Testament materials alone (Bauer, *Orthodoxy and Heresy*, 200).

148. Hartog, "Opponents of Polycarp"; Wilhite, "Polycarp's Reception."

149. See Irenaeus, *Haer.* 3.3.4; Eusebius, *Hist. eccl.* 5.24; Hartog, *Polycarp's Epistle to the Philippians*, 13–15; Trebilco, *Early Christians in Ephesus*, 241–63. Polycarp cannot be used as positive evidence for "orthodox" Johannophobia, to borrow Charles Hill's term (see Wilhite, "Polycarp's Reception"). Cf. Hill, *Johannine Corpus in the Early Church*; Chapa, "Fortunes and Misfortunes of the Gospel of John."

150. Hartog, *Polycarp and the New Testament*, 189, 195. This claim holds true if Papias wrote after Polycarp. See Hill, *Johannine Corpus*, 383–84; Yarbrough, "Date of Papias"; Körtner, *Papias von Hierapolis*.

Bauer himself acknowledged that Polycarp's letter interacts with Pauline materials, 1 Peter, and 1 John.[151] In a recent article, Berding concludes that "Polycarp is not *merely* in a stream of any *one* apostle or another. He is willing to draw from any of a number of different streams of God-given authority, including a Pauline stream, a Petrine stream, a Johannine stream, the words of the Lord (both in oral and written form), and the Old Testament Scriptures. His writings clearly demonstrate that he understands himself to be in continuity with these authorities, not opposed to any of them."[152]

These final words of Berding's essay—including the reference to "the words of the Lord (both in oral and written form)"—cite a matter that is only briefly developed in his article.[153] When Polycarp relates these dominical materials, he sometimes seems to be influenced by "Synoptic" (or "Synoptic-like") traditions, causing a number of scholars to conclude that he was probably influenced by Matthew (and possibly by Luke as well).[154] Berding himself fully discusses this semblance to "Synoptic" traditions in his monograph on Polycarp. He classifies Polycarp's use of Matthew as "almost certain," his use of Luke as "probable," and his use of Mark as "possible."[155] Perhaps these classifications could be lowered a notch.[156] In any case, the best arguments for a direct Synoptic role can be made for Matthean influence upon Pol. *Phil.* 2.3 and/or 7.2.[157]

The image that emerges from Pol. *Phil.* is of a writer who borrowed from Pauline, Petrine, and Johannine traditions, while at the same time emphasizing paraenetic materials credited to "the Lord" (teachings often resembling Synoptic materials and thus "Synoptic-like" at least).[158] All the while, Polycarp conscientiously highlighted his own alignment with

151. Bauer, *Orthodoxy and Heresy*, 217. Yet he declared, "I cannot free myself from doubts concerning the Pastoral Epistles" (contrast the discussion above).

152. Berding, "John or Paul?" 143; italics original.

153. Although this matter is fully developed in Berding's monograph.

154. See Hartog, *Polycarp and the New Testament*, 180–85. But see Young, *Jesus Tradition*.

155. Berding, *Polycarp and Paul*, 185.

156. See Hartog, *Polycarp's Epistle to the Philippians*, 55–56.

157. See Hartog, *Polycarp and the New Testament*, 183–84; Berding, *Polycarp and Paul*, 92–94; Metzger, *Canon of the New Testament*, 61.

158. *1 Clement* demonstrates the use of fewer books now in the New Testament than does Polycarp. See Gregory, "*1 Clement* and the Writings"; cf. Oxford Society for Historical Theology, *New Testament in the Apostolic Fathers*, 37–62; Hagner, *Use of the Old and New Testaments*, 135–71.

Pauline traditions (a purposeful self-portrait and self-interpretation, likely due to the Pauline recipients of the letter).[159]

Second, Polycarp emphasizes a threefold strand of authority (and therefore normativity) in Pol. *Phil.* 6.3, as discussed in some detail by Berding.[160] Polycarp affirms, "So therefore let us serve him with fear and all reverence, even as he himself commanded, and the apostles who preached the good news to us and the prophets who foretold the coming of our Lord."[161] The prophets foretold the Lord's coming, and the apostles proclaimed the good news about the Lord. At the center of this threefold sense of normativity stands the Lord. Pol. *Phil.* highlights the commandments (2.2; 4.1; 6.3), teachings (2.3), and words and sayings (2.3; 7.1; 7.2) of the Lord.[162] Farkasfalsvy compares Polycarp's "tryptichon" (the prophets and apostles combined through Christ) with materials found in Romans 1:1–2; 2 Peter 3:2; and Ignatius, *Philadelphians* 5.2.[163] One could also compare the *Epistle to Diognetus* 11.5–7; and 2 *Clement* 14.2

What is interesting about these passages is the moral, paraenetic focus of Pol. *Phil.* 2.2–2.3, 4.1, and 6.3. Even the anti-heretical passage of 7.1–2 merges into paraenesis (as discussed above).[164] While Bauer depicted Pol. *Phil.* as a work of anti-heretical desperation, the basic purpose of the work is moral paraenesis.[165] Valens, the one identified Philippian leader, had fallen into avarice (along with his wife) and not into heresy.[166] For this reason, Polycarp prays for true repentance and restoration. Bauer not only got the details of Pol. *Phil.* wrong, he misconstrued the general impetus and multiple purposes of the letter as well.

Thus Polycarp's letter serves as witness to a sense of "apostolic normativity" in the early second century. Trebilco concluded as follows:

159. Berding, *Polycarp and Paul*, 126–41.

160. Ibid., 158–62.

161. ET from Hartog, *Polycarp's Epistle to the Philippians*, 87.

162. On the authority of "the words of the Lord" in the Apostolic Fathers, see Metzger, *Canon of the New Testament*, 39–73.

163. Farkasfalvy, "'Prophets and Apostles,'" 122–23. For a chart of Ignatius's use of "prophets" and "apostles," see Hill, "Ignatius," 284–85.

164. See also Hartog, "Relationship between *Paraenesis* and Polemic."

165. Hartog, *Polycarp's Epistle to the Philippians*, 45–53.

166. As recognized by Bauer: "There was a presbyter by the name of Valens, who apparently was unassailable doctrinally, but who, with his wife, had gone astray in a serious ethical matter and because of their conduct had severely damaged the cause of their party (11.1–4)" (Bauer, *Orthodoxy and Heresy*, 73–74).

"By contrast, in the period from around AD 65 to 135, we can argue that there were strong and influential voices which stood for what later became 'orthodoxy', notably voices in both the Pauline and Johannine traditions."[167] While Ignatius's use of the term "catholic" seems to reflect a sense of "universal" rather than "orthodox," Ignatius does have a notion of normativity focused upon received apostolicity.[168] "Further," argues Trebilco, "in the documents bearing witness to these traditions, we find a strong concern to discern what the authors regarded as acceptable belief and practice—which is in continuity with what later became orthodoxy. The situation in Western Asia Minor in the early second century thus supports a quite different scenario from that proposed by Bauer."[169]

When one moves beyond Trebilco's focus upon Ignatius to a correlative focus upon Polycarp, an even fuller picture appears. And the portrait further buttresses Trebilco's critiques of the Bauer Thesis. Norris claimed, "Bauer is probably correct in asserting that no clear separation between 'orthodoxy' and 'heresy' can be constructed from the Ignatian and Polycarpian letters."[170] William Schoedel suggested (and Robinson agreed) that Ignatius was the one "who drew the lines more sharply and censored any activity not under the strict control of the bishop.[171]

While the term "heresy" in Ignatius may mean *Sekte* rather than *Ketzerei*, there is still a strong distinction of ideation between what Ignatius and Polycarp considered apostolic and aberrant teaching, even without a locative separation of worship. Ignatius's strong language of "atheists," "unbelievers," "mad dogs," and "wild beasts" heightens this distinction of ideation.[172] Moreover, Ignatius only recognized the validity of baptism and the Eucharist performed under the auspices of recognized

167. Trebilco, "Christian Communities," 44.

168. See Staats, "Die Katholische Kirche des Ignatius von Antiochien." Norris maintained, "Although the phrase 'catholic church' was used for the first time in ecclesiastical history by Ignatius, it was employed in an inclusive sense rather than the exclusive sense in which it was to appear in the Muratorian Canon at the end of the second century" (Norris, "Ignatius, Polycarp, and I Clement," 29; cf. 30). Norris overlooks the use of the phrase "catholic church" in *Mart. Pol.*

169. Trebilco, "Christian Communities," 44. Bauer examines the trifold authority in *Orthodoxy and Heresy*, 212.

170. Norris, "Ignatius, Polycarp, and I Clement," 30.

171. See Norris, "Ignatius, Polycarp, and I Clement," 92.

172. 1 John 2:18–19 already speaks of secessionists separating from the congregation (Norris, "Ignatius, Polycarp, and I Clement," 31; Smith, "Epistles of John," 382).

bishops.[173] At the same time, the antagonists seem not to have been fully excommunicated or excluded in some of the congregations addressed. "There is still time for the offenders to return to soberness and repent. . . . Ignatius' overall attempt appears to be to preserve unity, rather than to exclude impurity."[174]

Norris concluded, "Bauer's inability to grasp the difference between the beginning of a process and its fullest development led him to emphasize the lack of separation in Ignatius and Polycarp and to miss the attempts at distinction."[175] Norris opposed Bauer's "tendency to use peculiar definitions of important terms, employing them with these meanings in such a fashion as to apparently strengthen his argumentation."[176] For Norris, such terms included "orthodoxy," "heresy," and "monepiscopacy."[177] "Bauer has been unable to demonstrate that what he terms 'heresy' was prior to and/or stronger than 'orthodoxy' in Antioch and Asia Minor."[178]

By adding *1 Clement* back into the mix, one finds further materials relevant to the propagation of received tradition (*1 Clem.* 5; 7.2; 42; cf. Ign. *Magn.* 13.1; Ign. *Phld.* 9; Ign. *Smyrn.* 7.2). As Heron remarks, "Clement" expected "the *entire* Corinthian congregation to respect the memory of the Apostles, and to be impressed by his appeal to their example and to their institution of the office in the Church."[179] *1 Clement* repeatedly quotes or alludes to the Old Testament scriptures and explicitly mentions the words of the Lord Jesus. Furthermore, "The apostles received the gos-

---

173. Norris, "Ignatius, Polycarp, and I Clement," 32.

174. Ibid., 33. Cf. Ign. *Polyc.* 1.2: "Do justice to your office with constant care for both physical and spiritual concerns. Focus on unity, for there is nothing better" (ET from Holmes, *Apostolic Fathers*, 263). In his discussions of unity, Ignatius borrowed from the rhetoric of political imagery. See also Maier, "Politics and Rhetoric."

175. Norris, "Ignatius, Polycarp, and I Clement," 34.

176. Ibid., 35.

177. For other studies of "heresy," see Betz, "Orthodoxy and Heresy in Primitive Christianity"; Desjardins, "Bauer and Beyond"; Le Boulluec, *La notion d'hérésie*; Simon, "From Greek *Hairesis* to Christian Heresy."

178. Norris, "Ignatius, Polycarp, and I Clement," 36; cf. 43. Norris added, "At the same time he [Bauer] has also been unable to establish that monepiscopacy did not exist in these regions." According to Clayton Jefford, "It is much more likely, however, that the fervent emphasis of Ignatius on this hierarchy of offices resulted from his desire to establish such a structure among the numerous competing forms of church order that existed throughout Syria, Anatolia, and Greece" (Jefford, *Reading the Apostolic Fathers*, 53). For one take on the development of monepiscopacy, see Brent, *Ignatius of Antioch*.

179. Heron, "Interpretation of I Clement," 541.

pel for us from the Lord Jesus Christ" (*1 Clem.* 42.1).[180] More specifically, the author brings up the figures of both Peter and Paul by name (*1 Clem.* 5). Irenaeus later claimed that Clement handed on apostolic tradition (Irenaeus, *Haer.* 3.3.3).[181] Like Polycarp's *Philippians*, the text and nature of *1 Clement* further corroborate Trebilco's work on compounded strands of authority within the Ignatian correspondence.

Conclusion

When viewed through the lens of the Apostolic Fathers, the particular details of Bauer's thesis do not fare well. While scholars can appreciate the new vistas opened up by Bauer's work, many of his specific arguments cannot stand in the face of the extant evidence. The Apostolic Fathers—*1 Clement* and Polycarp as well as Ignatius—cannot serve as validating witnesses for Bauer's tenuous reconstructions. These authors do, however, evidence a sense of normativity that drew from multiple streams and centered upon the trifold authority of the prophets, the Lord, and the apostles.

---

180. ET from Holmes, *Apostolic Fathers*, 101.
181. See Hartog, "Peter in Paul's Churches."

3

Post-Bauer Scholarship on Gnosticism(s): The Current State of Our "Knowledge"

Carl B. Smith

IF MODERN SCHOLARSHIP CAN agree on anything regarding Walter Bauer's challenging reconstruction, it is the fact that there was a variety of expressions in early Christianity. That consensus breaks down, however, when it comes to questions of the degree and nature of that variety and determining how early it occurred and to what extent Jesus and his immediate disciples represented, created, or inspired that diversity. Central in these concerns is the topic of Gnosticism,[1] which held a crucial position in Bauer's reconstruction. Essentially, it was the heresy which preceded

1. While the definition and origin of Gnosticism are major discussions later in this paper, the working definition is: a religious impulse in the early Christian era which came to fruition in a variety of forms and which was characterized by: (1) an anti-cosmic dualism between good and evil; (2) an oppositional relationship between a higher and lower god with the latter responsible for creation and frequently identified with the God of the Jews; (3) human beings' possession of a "spark of divinity," which is suppressed by ignorance caused by material existence and the rule of the archons; (4) the elevation of knowledge of one's identity, origin, and destiny as a basis for enlightenment or salvation; and (5) the identification of a revealer figure who is sent by the highest god to enlighten humans to their identity and who often is identified as a docetic Christ or another Biblical figure (e.g., Seth). All of these features are matters of scholarly debate.

orthodoxy. Yet, in no area of his study is Bauer more worthy of correction than in his treatment of Gnosticism, if such a term is even allowed today.[2] Following generally the lead of the heresiological defenders and definers of early orthodoxy, Bauer categorized groups with docetic, libertine, or anti-Judaism tendencies, who claimed "gnosis" or who believed in a spiritualized resurrection, as gnostic.[3] Although there are good reasons for this imprecision,[4] such gratuitous categorization is unwarranted and unacceptable today. Subsequent to the publication of *Orthodoxy and Heresy in Earliest Christianity*, significant primary gnostic documents have been discovered, and modern scholarship on Gnosticism has been born and matured. Thus, many of Bauer's conclusions on Gnosticism must be rejected; others need to be nuanced; still others remain valid concerns with which contemporary scholarship must grapple.[5]

While there is much that could be discussed regarding gnostic studies in the post-Bauer era, this essay considers the major discoveries of the intervening decades, the various scholarly discussions generated by the new finds, and the problems of origins and definitions which condition the current state of gnostic research. These considerations are followed by recommendations for contemporary scholarship.

Gnostic Discoveries

Bauer was a scholar of the first rate and was fully acquainted with the resources which were then available, including literary materials from the ancient world, Greek and Roman histories, as well as contemporary archaeological discoveries. However, when he wrote his seminal work, the primary materials for gnostic research were quite limited. If it were not for

2. "Gnosticism" as a meaningful category in the ancient world has been challenged in recent decades, first by Williams, *Rethinking "Gnosticism,"* followed by King, *What is Gnosticism?* These works have caused intense discussion and yielded a paradigm shift in gnostic studies.

3. The following page references are to Bauer's *Orthodoxy and Heresy*: Docetism (in *Barnabas*, 48–49; Polycarp's opponents, 72; Johannine letters and Ignatius's opponents, 93–96); libertinism (in Corinth, 100–101; in Polycarp and Ignatius, 200); anti-Judaism (in *Barnabas*, 47–48); "gnosis" (in Corinth, 100–101; in *Barnabas*, 47–48); and spiritualized resurrection (in Corinth, 100–101).

4. This is largely due to the paucity of primary evidence available in Bauer's time and the imprecision of second-century heresiologists, to be discussed below.

5. For critical reviews of Bauer's thesis, see Robinson, *Bauer Thesis*, and more recently, Köstenberger and Kruger, *Heresy of Orthodoxy*.

the works of the heresiologists (church fathers who opposed the gnostics) as well as other orthodox writings, Bauer's understanding of Gnosticism would be paltry. Yet, even with these accounts, the representation of the gnostics and their beliefs needed to be read with caution as the authors often resorted to rhetoric and caricature, as Bauer was well aware.

Bauer had at his disposal the heresiological accounts of Justin Martyr, Irenaeus, Tertullian, Clement of Alexandria, Hippolytus, Origen, and Epiphanius, along with the historical work of Eusebius of Caesarea.[6] Bauer also utilized pagan works which provided critical assessments of Christianity, including Celsus's *True Doctrine,* preserved in part in Origen's *Against Celsus,* and Porphyry's *Life of Plotinus.* Plotinus's *Enneads* was also available and pertinent, especially book 2.9 which warned his followers against the gnostics' rejection of this world and its creator. Beyond these secondary materials,[7] Bauer had at his disposal some primary gnostic materials, particularly *Pistis Sophia* and fragments of a dominical statement of Jesus from P. Oxy. 654, which we now know is from *The Gospel of Thomas* (logion 3). He was aware of apocryphal sources such as *The Gospel of the Hebrews* and *The Gospel of the Egyptians,* which he related to Jewish Christians and Gentile Christians respectively, each of which he contended was influenced by gnostic syncretism. In sum, he had practically no direct access to the primary sources of Gnosticism or any "heresy" for that matter. Essentially, Bauer was working from the "under-side" of heresiological sources, a tenuous enterprise with the potential for unwarranted caricatures and misunderstandings.

Thus, it is with a certain degree of empathy and understanding that Bauer's claims about gnostics and Gnosticism can be assessed.[8] Contemporary scholarship, however, which should have advanced over the eight decades since Bauer first published his thesis, is less entitled to such empathy. Further, working with a broad definition of the term, Bauer saw

---

6. See the analysis of Shelton in this volume, which argues that Bauer treated Eusebius's history as a heresiological work and served as his primary interlocutor.

7. While these works are primary texts for the study of early Christianity, they are in reality secondary accounts of Gnosticism since they were not written by proponents. I term this phenomenon "secondarity."

8. While this essay reflects the enormous impact of the Bauer Thesis, it is not specifically Bauer's understanding of gnosis or Gnosticism that has given his thesis its enduring influence. Rather, it is the theory that there was greater diversity in the ancient world than was previously admitted, and that heretical movements were equally prominent and may have preceded and exceeded the orthodox in various arenas of the Mediterranean world.

Gnosticism as a major concern in many New Testament books, including 1 Corinthians, the Pastorals, Johannine literature, Jude, and 2 Peter, and he categorized as gnostic *The Epistle of Barnabas*. Each of these designations is either rejected or highly disputed today.

The Nag Hammadi Codices

Arguably the most important discovery of the twentieth century for early Christian studies was not made near Qumran where the Dead Sea Scrolls were found,[9] but rather in Egypt, near the village of Nag Hammadi. The details of the discovery of these documents and their survival are quite dramatic, involving poor Egyptian peasant laborers searching for fertilizer, fear of demons, a blood feud, two murders, the mutilation and burning of a portion of at least one codex,[10] and a long trail of clandestine bartering and bargaining until the final deposition of the documents with Egyptian authorities in the Coptic Museum in Cairo.[11] However, even more dramatic is the content of the find: in thirteen codices, fifty-two individual tractates were copied, most of which were entirely unknown or known only by title or brief excerpt.[12] Though there were several duplications of tractates in the collection, forty-six separate works were found, including forty previously unknown texts.

The discovery at Nag Hammadi has been commonly labeled the "Nag Hammadi Library" and the "Coptic Gnostic Codices." Both of these titles require points of clarification. While the nearest village was Nag Hammadi, the location of the find was more accurately Jabal al-Tarif, a prominent cliff near the Nile River. Although all thirteen codices were

---

9. Though the discovery of the Dead Sea Scrolls offers important information about the Jewish context of early Christianity, it sheds no direct light on Christian origins or development, contrary to the sensational claims of some scholars. For introductory matters, see Fitzmyer, *Dead Sea Scrolls*. The Nag Hammadi documents were discovered in 1945, two years prior to the Dead Sea Scrolls.

10. A codex is a bound book, a new technology developed in the early Christian world. On the Christian origin and significance of the codex, see Roberts, *Manuscript, Society, and Belief*.

11. For a full account of the discovery, see Robinson, "Introduction," in *Nag Hammadi Library in English*, 1–26 (hereafter, *NHLE*); and Meyer, *Gnostic Discoveries*, 13–31.

12. The thirteenth codex had the cover removed and its surviving pages were preserved inside Codex VI.

found in a single storage jar, it may be a stretch to call them a "library."[13] The tractates were written in Coptic, a late Egyptian language developed in the early Christian era; however, there is good reason to believe that most of these texts were translations of Greek originals. Calling the entire collection "gnostic" evades the fact that some tractates could not possibly fit under that rubric, particularly a portion of Plato's *Republic* (NHC VI,5), *The Teachings of Silvanus* (NHC VII,4), and *The Sentences of Sextus* (NHC XII,1), along with three examples of Hermetic literature,[14] *The Discourse on the Eighth and Ninth* (NHC VI,6), *The Prayer of Thanksgiving* (NHC VI,7), and *Asclepius 21–29* (NHC VI,8).

What do we really know about the Nag Hammadi Library? It is clear from the cartonnage of the codices that the collection itself was produced in the mid-fourth century. The clue to this fact is that some of the paper fragments which made up the covers were discarded records and scribal notes very possibly from a nearby Pachomian monastery at Chenoboskia.[15] Some of these materials had dates near the mid-fourth century. Whereas this fact defines with relative precision the provenance of the thirteen codices and their *terminus ad quem*, it does not shed any light on the reason they were discarded or the original date and place of composition of the individual tractates. It has been suggested that the historical context of their deposition was the attempt by archbishop Athanasius of Alexandria in AD 367 to bring Egypt under his brand of orthodox by defining acceptable and unacceptable literature to be used in churches and monasteries.[16] As the Pachomian monasteries were under

13. As a case in point, James Robinson argues for the inclusion of *The Gospel of Mary* and *The Acts of Peter*, tractates 1 and 4 respectively of P.Berol. 8502, in the Nag Hammadi Library. The basis of his argument is that since these documents were found in a codex that also included two tractates which were found at Nag Hammadi—*The Apocryphon of John* (P.Berol. 8502,2; NHC II,1; III,1; IV,1) and *The Sophia of Jesus Christ* (P.Berol. 8502,3; NHC III,4)—these documents belong to the same world of ancient literature. See Robinson, "From *The Nag Hammadi Codices*."

14. Hermetic literature consisted of speculative pagan writings that originated in the second or third centuries AD. For the primary materials, see Nock and Festugière, *Corpus Hermeticum*. For a review of its relationship with Gnosticism, see Yamauchi, "Hermetic Literature," 408; Filoramo, *History*, 8–9; and Mahé, "Hermetic Religion," 795–98.

15. See Barns et al., *Nag Hammadi Codices*, esp. 11, and Scholer, "Gnosis, Gnosticism," 408.

16. See Athanasius's famous Paschal letter, Letter 39 in NPNF 2.4 (series II, volume 4). Available online at http://www.ccel.org/ccel/schaff/npnf204.xxv.iii.iii.xxv.html. Both J. Robinson (*NHLE*, 10–22) and Pearson ("Nag Hammadi Codices," 984–91)

his hegemony, it makes sense that the monks would have purged their library of questionable apocryphal works. The fact that they buried rather than destroyed them may indicate a level of reverence for the texts as well as the possible intent to retrieve them at a later time.

Publication of the Nag Hammadi Library[17]

As dramatic as the discovery was, research on the Nag Hammadi Library was limited without direct access to the documents. As is sadly the case with various discoveries, scholarly rivalries and regional difficulties hindered progress. A couple of individual tractates were published early (e.g., *The Gospel of Truth* in 1955 and *The Gospel of Thomas* in 1959),[18] but the remainder of the codices were inaccessible for decades following the discovery. In 1966, The Coptic Gnostic Library Project was created under the auspices of the Institute for Antiquity and Christianity, Claremont, California. In 1970, the Ministry of Culture of the Arab Republic of Egypt and UNESCO formed an international team of scholars and funded the project to ensure the timely publication of photographic facsimiles, which was accomplished between 1972 and 1977. In 1977, E. J. Brill and Harper & Row published the first edition of *The Nag Hammadi Library in English*, with James M. Robinson serving as general editor. With the publication of these volumes, research into the interpretation and implications of the Nag Hammadi codices was in full stride.

Other Gnostic Discoveries

Before turning to scholarship related to Nag Hammadi and Gnosticism, it is important to note three other modern gnostic discoveries. While none has been as dramatic as that at Nag Hammadi, gnostic documents have continued to be uncovered and published through the persistent work of archaeologists and scholars as well as fortune-hunters.[19] Further

---

support this hypothesis.

17. The following is a brief summary of Richard Smith's "Preface" to Robinson, *Nag Hammadi Library in English*.

18. Respectively, Unnik, "*Gospel of Truth*," 79–129; and Guillaumont et al., *Gospel According to Thomas*.

19. A Coptic fragment that came to light in 2012 was given the sensational title, *The Gospel of Jesus' Wife* (*GJW*). Scholars are still evaluating this recently published

discoveries should be expected as professional, fiscal, and sensational motivations run strong.

Gospel of Mary. Although a fragmentary copy of *The Gospel of Mary* was among the four tractates contained in P.Berol. 8502, discovered in 1896,[20] due to a number of unfortunate circumstances it was not accessible to the public until it was ultimately published in 1955 and, later, included in the *Nag Hammadi Library in English.*[21] The text has come into recent focus by the publication of several scholarly works which analyze the import of the document for earliest Christianity.[22] Karen King, for example, argues for a branch of early Christianity that was egalitarian and focused upon spiritual perfection through gnosis quite apart from Jesus's death and resurrection.

Secret Gospel of Mark. In 1973, Morton Smith of Columbia University announced his discovery of an early edition of Mark's gospel with the publication of both a scholarly and popular work on the subject.[23] Smith alleged *The Secret Gospel of Mark* preceded the canonical gospel of Mark and intimated that Jesus himself was a gnostic teacher who initiated converts into his cult through a nocturnal ritual involving homoerotic overtones. Mystery surrounds Smith's discovery at the Greek Orthodox Monastery at Mar Saba, Israel, and the subsequent loss of the text, such that many scholars remain skeptical of the gospel's authenticity.[24] Still some scholars consider *Secret Mark* an important text in the transmission of Mark's gospel.[25]

---

fragment, which does address concerns found in other gnostic texts. Even if an authentic document, it likely says more about the diverse Christian currents of subsequent centuries than it does about Jesus's actual marital status. See King, "Jesus said to them"; Pattengale, "How the 'Jesus' Wife' Hoax Fell Apart."

20. Even earlier, Greek fragments were found, but they are more fragmentary duplicates of the Coptic text of P.Berol. 8502.

21. While not discovered at Nag Hammadi, it was included in the publication of the *NHLE* by its editor. See footnote 13 above.

22. Pagels was among the first to draw attention to this gospel in *Gnostic Gospels.* More recently, the *Gospel of Mary* has received further attention, beginning with Leloup, *Gospel of Mary Magdalene,* followed by King, *Gospel of Mary of Magdala.*

23. Smith, *Clement* and Smith, *Secret Gospel,* respectively.

24. Two recent works charge Morton Smith with forgery: Carlson, *Gospel Hoax,* and Jefferey, *Secret Gospel.*

25. E.g., Koester, "History and Development," 35–58, and Koester, *From Jesus,* 50–53.

Gospel of Judas. More recently, the restoration, translation, and publication of *The Gospel of Judas* in 2006 created quite a stir in the academy as well as the public square.[26] Discovered in the late 1970s in a codex with three other works (*Letter of Peter to Philip, The [First] Apocalypse of James,* and the *Book of Allogenes*), the immense popularity of *The Gospel of Judas* was largely due to its publication by *National Geographic* magazine. This may also be seen as an indication of the widespread public interest in Gnosticism and early Christianity, particularly when long-held assumptions are challenged. *The Gospel of Judas* features Judas as the possessor of secret knowledge and co-conspirator with Jesus in the latter's death, even as the other eleven disciples remain unenlightened. Numerous monographs have been published on *The Gospel of Judas,*[27] sometimes identified as the Tchacos Codex after its modern owner, including the proceedings from the Codex Judas Congress held in 2008 at Rice University.[28]

Research on Nag Hammadi and Gnosticism

The discovery and publication of the Nag Hammadi codices and subsequent finds have generated an enormous amount of publications. The late Professor David Scholer of Fuller Seminary served the academy by providing an exhaustive bibliography of research related to Nag Hammadi and Gnosticism which was published annually (with minor exceptions) in *Novum Testamentum* from 1971 to 2008. These bibliographies on three occasions were collated into volumes and published by Brill.[29] Besides interpretive works on specific tractates in the Nag Hammadi Library and other gnostic texts, the bibliography includes general works on Gnosticism, special focus on gnostic schools and leaders, as well as various studies on the New Testament and Gnosticism. Over the forty-one years of Scholer's service, 11,579 items were catalogued.[30]

---

26. Kasser et al., *Gospel of Judas*; Kasser et al, *The Gospel of Judas, Critical Edition.*

27. Ehrman, *Lost Gospel*; Pagels and King, *Reading Judas*; and DeConick, *Thirteenth Apostle.*

28. DeConick, *Codex Judas Papers.*

29. Scholer, *Nag Hammadi Bibliography 1948–1969, Nag Hammadi Bibliography 1970–1994,* and *Nag Hammadi Bibliography 1995–2006.*

30. The materials include primarily monographs, articles, and book reviews. The final number is from the last entry in volume three from 2006.

The modern study of Gnosticism is truly an international phenomenon, involving scholars and universities across the globe. California's Claremont Graduate University has had an important place in gnostic studies, as James Robinson directed The Coptic Gnostic Library Project which produced *The Coptic Gnostic Library* and *The Nag Hammadi Library in English*. The Berliner Arbeitskreis für koptisch-gnostische Schriften at Humboldt University, Germany, and the Institut d'études anciennes and the Faculté de théologie et de sciences religieuses of the Université Laval in Quebec, Canada, have produced the *Nag Hammadi Deutsch* and the *Écrits gnostiques* respectively. Beyond these centers of focused research, numerous scholars have built distinguished careers in gnostic studies. The revival of Coptic studies in the modern academy was inspired largely by the discovery of the Nag Hammadi codices.[31]

E. J. Brill Publishers, in Leiden, Netherlands, has had significant involvement in the publication of scholarly monographs and resources related to the Nag Hammadi texts and Gnosticism. The *Nag Hammadi Studies* series was initiated in 1971 and continues under a new title, *Nag Hammadi and Manichaean Studies*. The Université Laval of Quebec, Canada, has been an important center for Nag Hammadi and gnostic research and is responsible for the publication of the series *Bibliothèque copte de Nag Hammadi*. Beyond these serials, a significant number of monographs and edited volumes have been devoted to gnostic subjects, and issues related to Gnosticism are frequently found in journals devoted to biblical studies, ancient philosophy, as well as early Christian studies.

Specific Areas of Study Related to the Nag Hammadi Library

Nearly every document and topic with reference to the Nag Hammadi Library has been studied and published; however, several areas of concentrated research should be mentioned. Each of these illustrates the far-reaching impact of the library as well as the intense polarization which Bauer's reconstruction, in part, inspired.

Gospel of Thomas (NHC II,2). No document in the Nag Hammadi Library has received greater scholarly and popular attention than

31. The International Association for Coptic Studies was founded on the occasion of the First International Congress of Coptology in Cairo: Colloquium on the Future of Coptic Studies, December 11–17, 1976.

the *Gospel of Thomas*. This unique gospel containing 114 sayings attributed to the living Jesus was known only by title from three early church fathers who considered it suspect (Hippolytus, Origen, and Eusebius). Three Greek papyrus fragments from Oxyrhynchus (*P. Oxy.* 1, 654, and 655) were discovered and published in the late 1800s, but without titles, no one knew these sayings were from the *Gospel of Thomas*. Thus, the Nag Hammadi text of the *Gospel of Thomas* was the first occasion that the document was known in its entirety in the modern world. Since its original publication in English in 1959, nearly every feature of the *Gospel of Thomas* has been the subject of intense debate, including authorship, provenance, date, original language, audience, theological perspective, as well as its import for Christian origins and history. It has even become the subject of a full-length commentary.[32]

Many scholars have touted the radical impact of the *Gospel of Thomas* upon early Christian history, including our understanding of Jesus;[33] yet, there is definite reason for pause in this assessment.[34] While there are still scholars who call for an early dating of the *Gospel of Thomas*, some even prior to the canonical gospels,[35] most scholars hold that the gospel was composed or edited in the early to mid-second century, without denying that some sayings may derive from an earlier period, perhaps even from Jesus himself. One of the major detractors from this opinion is Nicholas Perrin, who argues for a Syriac original for the *Gospel of Thomas* and dates it subsequent to the publication of Tatian's *Diatessaron*, which he maintains influenced its composition (perhaps around AD 180).[36] Quite amazingly, the range of proposed dates for this gospel spans over 130 years.

32. DeConick, *Original Gospel.*

33. On a popular level, see Pagels, *Gnostic Gospels* and Pagels, *Beyond Belief.* See also Meyer, *Gospel of Thomas*; Meyer, *Gnostic Gospels*; Davies, *Gospel of Thomas*; and Miller, *Complete Gospels.*

34. Roukema, author of *Gnosis and Faith*, has recently published a sequel comparing textual perspectives on Jesus's teachings and deeds among several gospel and early Christian traditions, including the *Gospel of Thomas*. See *Jesus, Gnosis & Dogma.* On pages 9–14, Roukema responds to Pagels's claims of a Thomas-John debate in their gospel writings.

35. The *Gospel of Thomas* provides an actual example of a sayings collection much like sources which scholars had proposed to underlie the canonical Gospels (e.g., Q). On this basis, Koester (*Ancient Christian Gospels*, 75–128, and *From Jesus*, esp. 277–84) and Crossan (*Four Other Gospels*) have argued that it pre-dates the canonical Gospels. Koester argues that its sayings are more primitive and thus earlier than canonical parallels.

36. Perrin's compelling thesis argues for a unity to the gospel based upon the use of

Equally contested is the gnostic character of the *Gospel of Thomas*. Though reconstructions presupposing a gnostic myth are quite persuasive,[37] other scholars are more hesitant based upon the absence of characteristic gnostic elements, such as a creation myth, a fallen Sophia, or an ignorant demiurge. Yet the *Gospel of Thomas* does possess several features in line with clearly gnostic works, including secret teachings, a docetic Christ, anti-cosmic dualism, anti-Judaism, self-knowledge as a basis of salvation, the bridal chamber, androgyny, and asceticism. Caution is warranted, however, since some of these latter features were characteristics of Thomasine Christianity of Eastern Syria, especially Edessa, which was not essentially gnostic.[38] While the jury is still out on the actual provenance and gnostic proclivities of the *Gospel of Thomas*, its import for understanding second-century Christianity is well established.

Sethian Gnosticism. Although scholars have struggled to identify an overarching rubric which captures the purpose of the varied tractates in the Nag Hammadi Library,[39] there has been relative success in identifying a sub-grouping of documents which have been classified as Sethian Gnosticism or simply Sethianism.[40] The title itself is derived from the fact that several heresiologists identified individuals or texts with Seth, and the name is prominent among several documents in the Nag Hammadi Library. In this material, Seth is portrayed as the progenitor of an

key Syriac terms in succeeding sayings. See Perrin, *Thomas*.

37. See Ehrman's rendering in *Lost Christianities*, esp. 59–65.

38. See Uro, *Thomas*; Pearson, *Ancient Gnosticism*, 256–72; and Meyer, "Thomas Christianity," 779–83.

39. This is likely a failed enterprise, given the diversity of the tractates and that the only definite unity to the collection is its burial in a single storage jar. Though I find Wisse's and Scholer's suggestion of asceticism compelling (Wisse, "Nag Hammadi Library," 205–23; Scholer, "Gnosis, Gnosticism," 402), Williams's appeal to liturgy and worship interesting (*Rethinking "Gnosticism,"* 235–62), and other claims of an anti-heretical catalogue unpersuasive (why Plato's *Republic*, three Hermetic tractates, and multiple copies of several tractates?), the answer may simply be that these were works that interested the copyists. It should be noted that the strong and consistent strain of asceticism in the NHL was one of its most surprising features, considering the charges of libertinism by the heresiologists.

40. Although some scholars remain skeptical that such a grouping of texts is possible, a relative consensus has accepted the claim. Leading detractors include Wisse, "Stalking," 563–76, and van den Broek, "Present State," 55. Williams also challenges the categorization in *Rethinking "Gnosticism,"* 91–93. What follows is a summary of my analysis of Sethian Gnosticism in Smith, *No Longer Jews*, 216–27, while engaging recent publications.

"immovable race," a redeemer figure, and/or revealer of gnostic truth. The grouping is also quite important given that several approaches to analyzing the Nag Hammadi collection have yielded a similar set of documents as representing a specific group of gnostics or perhaps even the entire category of Gnosticism itself.[41] Some scholars even identify Sethianism as "Classical Gnosticism,"[42] seemingly implying that it is its original or earliest form.

The identification and classification of Sethian Gnosticism and its "canon" is credited to Hans-Martin Schenke.[43] The works that allegedly represent the Sethian system are as follows:[44]

- The teachings opposed in Irenaeus, *Haer.* 1.29 ("Barbeloite")

- The teachings opposed in Epiphanius, *Panarion* 26, 39–40 ("Sethians" and "Archontics")

- The teachings opposed in Pseudo-Tertullian, *Haer.* 2

- The teachings opposed in Filastrius, *Haer.* 3

- The Untitled Text from the Bruce Codex

- *The Apocryphon of John* (NHC II,1; III,1; IV,1; BG 8502,2)

- *The Hypostasis of the Archons* (NHC II,4)

- *The Gospel of the Egyptians*, a.k.a., *The Holy Book of the Great Invisible Spirit* (NHC III,2; IV,2)

- *The Apocalypse of Adam* (NHC V,5)

- *The Three Steles of Seth* (NHC VII,5)

- *Zostrianos* (NHC VIII,1)

41. For example, Brakke argues that when *gnostikos* or *gnostikoi* is treated as a social category in the heresiological texts (esp. Irenaeus), it yields a group which shares a similar myth as well as crucial texts in distinction from other groups, which, though perhaps derived from or related to the Sethians or gnostics, formed their own religious systems and communities in this dynamic period. See Brakke, *Gnostics*, and further discussion below.

42. Pearson, *Ancient Gnosticism*, 51–100, though he holds to an early origin of Gnosticism.

43. See Schenke, "Das sethianische System," 165–74; and idem, "Phenomenon and Significance," in Layton, *Rediscovery*, 2:588–616. The entire second volume of Layton's work is devoted to Sethian Gnosticism.

44. Although there are some variations in this list among scholars, it is relatively static. Brakke's list adds the recently discovered *Gospel of Judas*. Brakke, *Gnostics*, 50–51.

- *Melchizedek* (NHC XI,1)

- *The Thought of Norea* (NHC IX,2)

- *Marsanes* (NHC X,1)

- *Allogenes* (NHC XI,3)

- *The Trimorphic Protennoia* (NHC XIII,1)

Much debate has arisen regarding the nature and dating of the Sethian system, though its unity as a legitimate trajectory in early Gnosticism has generally been upheld.[45] Though much could be said regarding this tradition, it is highly significant that it encompasses one-quarter of the Nag Hammadi Library, and, arguably, some of its most important texts.

The Sethian tradition is deeply rooted in Jewish literature and traditions, particularly related to Wisdom (Sophia), Yaldabaoth (creator), Adam, Eve (Pronoia), and various biblical events. Those factors which are defined as central to the Sethian system were summarized into six major themes by Schenke: "(1) The Gnostics' self-understanding as the seed of Seth; (2) Seth as the saviour of his seed; (3) four illuminators of the Autogenes; (4) a trinity of Father, Mother (Barbelo), and Son (Autogenes/Anthropos); (5) the evil demiurge Yaldabaoth; and (6) the division of history into three ages with the appearance of a saviour in each age."[46] Although other gnostic traditions may share elements in this list, these features are quite standard in Sethian literature.

John D. Turner, in his *Sethian Gnosticism and the Platonic Tradition*, offers a thorough review of Sethianism and its literary, theological, philosophical, and social history. What is quite significant is that this early gnostic system is posited by Turner to have developed in its original form in the first half of the second century.

---

45. A great deal of commentary has been written on the Sethians. Some of the most important works include Klijn, *Seth*; Turner, "Sethian Gnosticism," 55–86; Turner, "Sethian School," 784–89; Stroumsa, *Another Seed*; Pearson, "Figure of Seth," 52–83; Pearson, "Jewish Elements," 124–35; Pearson, *Ancient Gnosticism*, 51–100; MacRae, "Seth," 17–24; and Attridge, "Valentinian and Sethian Apocalyptic Traditions," 173–211. Turner has developed a complete history of Sethian traditions and texts in engagement with Platonism in *Sethian Gnosticism*. See also the essays in Corrigan, *Gnosticism* and the recent reconstruction of the history of Sethianism in Burns, *Apocalypse of the Alien God*.

46. As listed in Yamauchi, *Pre-Christian Gnosticism*, 223.

Social History of Gnostics and Gnosticism

The current focus on Sethian Gnosticism is part of a recent trend to move the spotlight off the impasse regarding gnostic definitions and origins to the social histories of gnostic individuals and groups. Renewed attention is given to issues of myth, liturgy, ritual, and polemics, as well as social relationships and literary interdependence. Beyond the Sethians, scholars have distinguished several further groupings of gnostic texts which may be connected to specific teachers and/or schools of gnostic thought.

Basilides and Basilideans. While no historical figure is correlated with Sethian Gnosticism, several movements associated with Gnosticism are identified by founding teachers. One of the most significant early figures is Basilides of Egypt, and his son Isidore. Eusebius provides several important facts about Basilides in his *Chronicle* of the sixteenth year of Hadrian (i.e., AD 132): "Basilides the heresiarch was living in Alexandria; from him derive the Gnostics."[47] Our knowledge of Basilides comes primarily from the conflicting accounts found in Irenaeus and Hippolytus and from fragments of Basilides's writings provided by Clement of Alexandria. Other church fathers reference his work and teachings, but much of what they wrote was dependent upon earlier works or more reflective of Basilides's followers. Although it is possible that he may have spent time in Antioch where he met Menander and Saturninus, the bulk of his life was in Egypt where he developed the unique features of his system, which include concepts based upon exegesis of certain New Testament texts, creator-angels (the chief of which is the God of the Jews), salvation of the soul only, reincarnation, the descent of the heavenly Christ on the human Jesus (adoptionism?), and the value of human suffering. Birger Pearson identifies him as a Christian gnostic, the first Christian philosopher, and the first exegete of a New Testament text.[48] His son, Isidore, was his disciple and author of three texts: *On the Grown Soul, Ethics,* and *Expositions of the Prophet Parchor.* Little is known of the content of these non-extant sources.

Valentinus and Valentinians. According to some scholars, Valentinus may have known Basilides, who flourished in Alexandria before Valentinus's departure to Rome around AD 140.[49] Irenaeus's *Against All Heresies,*

47. For Eusebius's quote and a discussion of this text and Basilides's life and teachings, see Pearson, "Basilides," 1–31. Eusebius's claims are disputed.

48. Pearson, "Basilides," 28.

49. Pearson, "Basilides," 28. In the same volume, see Dunderberg, "School," 64–99.

which addresses heresies generally, is most decidedly and immediately focused upon Valentinus and his followers. Several tractates from the Nag Hammadi collection are identified with Valentinus and his school: *Prayer of the Apostle Paul* (NHC I,1), *The Gospel of Truth* (NHC I,3; allegedly authored by Valentinus), *Tripartite Tractate* (NHC I,5), *Treatise on the Resurrection* (also known as *Letter to Rheginus*; NHC I,4), *Gospel of Philip* (NHC II,3) *(First) Apocalypse of James* (NHC V,3), *Interpretation of Knowledge* (NHC XI,1), and *A Valentinian Exposition* (NHC IX,2).

Scholars question the gnostic nature of Valentinus and the Valentinians, noting their shared confessions with other Christians, participation in churches, usage of the New Testament in their writings, as well as the fact that no Valentinian was excommunicated from churches in the second century.[50] While Irenaeus emphasized their attribution of the creation to the demiurge (the God of the Jews), their tripartite division of humanity into pneumatic, psychic, and material groupings, and possibly a docetic Christology,[51] the primary works do not necessarily confirm these features. Some scholars see in Valentinus a rejection of extreme gnostic views and a "rehabilitation of Judaism."[52] The fact that he was considered a candidate for bishop at Rome may be an indication of his moderation. Valentinian followers are generally divided into two schools based upon information from Hippolytus: an Italian school featuring Ptolemy, Flora, and Heracleon, and an Eastern school with Theodotus and Marcus (Marcosians). While Valentinus was quite assuredly a gnostic, some of his followers may have become more extreme than their teacher.[53]

Sociological Concerns. Although other gnostic traditions and texts do not lend themselves to natural groupings, a number of individual tractates have special features which indicate sociological concerns. Several Nag Hammadi texts indicate ritualistic elements, particularly *The Gospel of Philip* (NHC II,3), which tells of five mysteries: baptism, chrism,

50. Dunderberg emphasizes this point in contrast to Marcion, Valentinus's contemporary (Dunderberg, "School," 72). Marcion's teachings shared the anti-Judaism character of Gnosticism, though most scholars do not include him among the gnostics and, thus, no separate treatment is warranted here. See Räisänen, "Marcion," 100–24, esp. 107.

51. Valentinus held to Jesus's divinity. Irenaeus, *Haer.* 3.22.2, indicates that Valentinus held that Jesus both ate and drank; however, he was not subject to corruption, so he did not eliminate waste.

52. Pétrement, *Separate God*, 351–86, and Markschies, *Valentinus Gnosticus?*

53. For further study, one of the most significant scholarly works on Valentinianism is Thomassen, *Spiritual Seed*.

Eucharist, redemption, and the bridal chamber. *The Apocalypse of Peter* (NHC VII,3) manifests separation and perhaps persecution through polemical statements against "bishop and deacons," who are "dry canals." Whereas gnostic works are often lauded for their egalitarian attitudes toward women, some scholars question the validity of this reading.[54]

Gnostic Pre-History. Given the conflicted nature of the accounts regarding the clearly historical persons alleged to be gnostics, both among the church fathers and between their accounts and primary sources, figures identified with the pre-history of Gnosticism are even more vaporous and suspect. Heresiological accounts identify Simon Magus (of Acts 8), Menander (Simon's alleged disciple), Cerinthus,[55] and Saturninus as predecessors in the lineage of gnostic teachers. Not only are accounts of these figures sparse in detail, they are often widely divergent in description.[56] Further, the identifying marks of Gnosticism are rather meager in their so-called "systems." Perhaps the most that can be stated with certainty is that particular features which later were incorporated into second-century gnostic schools were characteristic of earlier teachers; however, none exhibit the full range of features which distinguish one as gnostic. This question brings into relief the essential issues of the definition and origin of Gnosticism.

Questions, Origins, and Definitions of Gnosticism[57]

Bauer's thesis and recent discoveries have been catalytic in terms of research and publications; however, they have not necessarily yielded greater clarity in terms of the origin and definition of Gnosticism. In fact, these elements may have generated more polarization than consensus even beyond gnostic studies, most particularly in the academic study of

54. For example, see Hoffman's assessment of Pagels's views in *Status of Women*.

55. Of names in this list, perhaps the most is known about Cerinthus. See Myllykoski, "Cerinthus," 213–46.

56. See my review of alleged gnostic teachers in *No Longer Jews*, 113–49. Cf., Markschies, *Gnosis*, 73–83.

57. Although it may seem strange that the question of Gnosticism's origins and definitions is reserved for the end of this discussion, it has been primarily within the last two decades that the issue of origins and definitions has reached a high pitch, with a paradigm shift in the discipline. The publication of Williams's *Rethinking "Gnosticism"* in 1996 followed the celebration of the fiftieth anniversary of the discovery of the Nag Hammadi Codices at a conference at Haverford College, PA, in November 1995.

Christian origins itself. The following questions remain at the forefront of contemporary discussions:[58]

- Is Gnosticism a religion in its own right (Jonas, Pearson), was it an attitude or a religious spirit or perspective which transcended other religions and times (Rudolph, Couliano), or was it a religious phenomenon which attached itself to other religio-philosophical entities in a parasitic manner (Pearson)?

- Did Gnosticism emerge before Christianity, whether in Hellenistic, Eastern or Jewish contexts (history of religions school, Robinson, Koester), did it arise concurrently with Christianity either within Judaism (Jonas, Pearson, Scholer) or along with other types of Christianity (Rudolph, Filoramo, Perkins) in the first century, or was Gnosticism a post-Christian phenomenon deviating from apostolic teaching as the heresiologists contended (Pétrement, Yamauchi, Logan, C. Smith)?

- Are gnostic documents which possess no or very little Christian verbiage evidence for a non-Christian Gnosticism which may have preexisted or developed concurrently with earliest Christianity? Is the absence of Christian verbiage in texts which are focused on cosmogony a clear indication of their non-Christian status?

- What is the major generator of gnostic ideas – Hellenism (church fathers, Harnack), oriental religion (history of religions school, Bousset, Reitzenstein), Hellenistic Judaism (Pearson, Scholer, C. Smith[b]), or Christianity (Pétrement, C. Smith [a])?

- Should Gnosticism be understood as a Christian heresy or as one of several alternative forms of Christianity which equally vied for existence and dominance as various followers of Christ sought to interpret the verities of Jesus's existence, life, death, and resurrection in the early Christian centuries (Bauer)?[59]

---

58. The bibliography related to these questions is extensive, so only the names of movements or last names of central scholars are mentioned in parentheses, for the benefit of those desiring to pursue matters further.

59. One of the main issues of this question is the development of the concept of "heresy," which is a term that displays power and dominance. This is a major discussion in early Christian studies. For two approaches, see Evans, *Brief History*, as well as Iricinschi and Zellentin, *Heresy and Identity*.

- Was Gnosticism caused by a crisis of faith and/or history in which a variety of traditions were appealed to in the formation of an innovative religious impulse (Grant, Yamauchi, C. Smith; contra Williams)?

- Given the abundance of new gospel literature and the possibility that some may represent actual sayings of Jesus, how much of the gnostic impulse can be traced to the Master himself? In other words, was Jesus a gnostic?[60]

- Did Jesus have "secret" teachings which he reserved for his inner circle of followers which they continued to conceal and reveal only to those who became their disciples?

- Should the works that were canonized in the New Testament in the fourth century be given privileged status in the discussion of Christian origins, or should there be a level playing field for the various gospels, letters, apocalypses, sermons, and acts-accounts of early Christian leaders regardless of having "made the list"?

These questions loom large in contemporary scholarship, and the answers given often are determined by the definition one holds for Gnosticism.

The issues of the origin and definition of Gnosticism are fundamentally connected.[61] One's approach to these issues greatly determines the questions one asks, where one looks for answers, and what evidences are considered. When Bauer wrote *Orthodoxy and Heresy*, the dominant German view was that of the history of religions school which postulated that Gnosticism was essentially the product of Eastern oriental influence which had deeply impacted the Hellenistic world and the later writings of the Old Testament and Judaism, as well as those of the New Testament and early Christianity.[62] While some scholars see the gnostic impulse as transcending religious partitions to reflect a more global human experience of alienation and meaning-making,[63] a rising majority focuses upon

60. On this topic, see Bock, *Missing Gospels*, and Roukema, *Jesus*.

61. For a review of the widely diverse proposals, see Smith, *No Longer Jews*, esp. 7–71.

62. The record of the rising and waning of the history of religions school project is well-known and need not be retold here. See the overview of Yamauchi, "History-of-Religions School," 308–9, and Robinson, *Bauer Thesis*, 15–23. For a positive assessment of the movement, see Koester, *From Jesus*, 105–21.

63. For example, Couliano, *Tree of Gnosis*.

this religious phenomenon within its historical context of the early centuries AD.

Over the decades since the discovery at Nag Hammadi, scholars have consistently identified Middle Platonism and Hellenistic Judaism as two main impulses for the various gnostic cosmogonies and myths. Though it may seem odd at first that a theology that posits the God of the Jews as a lower archon below the highest god and often characterizes him as evil and ignorant would originate from Judaism, it is undeniable that the Jewish Scriptures, Jewish theological concepts, and characters and events of Jewish history are woven deeply into the fabric of gnostic mythology and cosmogony.[64] This agreement breaks down, however, when the issues of the dating of gnostic myths and their relation to Christianity are considered.

The issues of the dating and Christian orientation of the gnostic myths are likewise fundamentally connected.[65] Numerous scholars argue for a non-Christian or parallel-with-Christianity origination for Gnosticism. These theses face the hurdle of the lack of direct evidence for them, since all of our extant primary sources for Gnosticism can be dated with confidence no earlier than the second century AD. For scholars who contend for a non-Christian Gnosticism (whether Hellenistic or Jewish) in the first century, a further difficulty is that there is no degree of certainty that a source which lacks clearly Christian verbiage is indeed non-Christian,[66] since Christianity shared so much with Judaism, especially in terms of basic theology of God, cosmogony, and anthropology, three crucial components of Gnosticism. Likewise, a number of sources exhibit only a minimal Christian character, leading to a debate over whether Christian influence was original to the texts or if the Christian veneer was added in a later period of the texts' transmission.[67] Further, the conundrum is compounded by the fact that scholars frequently claim Gnosticism where only shared terminology or components of the whole

---

64. A major proponent of the Jewish origins of Gnosticism is Pearson in "Friedländer Revisited," 10–28, and more recently, *Ancient Gnosticism*, 15–19.

65. The most focused analysis of this issue remains Yamauchi, *Pre-Christian Gnosticism*; and more recently, Yamauchi, "Issue of Pre-Christian Gnosticism," 72–88.

66. The exception to this may be the usage of the codex form which clearly distinguishes Christian from Jewish texts of Old Testament sources. See Roberts, *Manuscript, Society, and Belief*.

67. Particularly debated are *The Apocalypse of Adam* (NHC V,5), *The Paraphrase of Shem* (VII,1), and the *Trimorphic Protennoia* (NHC XIII,1).

are present.[68] Needless to say, this debate will continue unabated unless new evidences surface or greater precision is delineated in what constitutes Gnosticism—which leads to the issue of definition.

That the category "Gnosticism" is a modern scholarly construct is undisputable.[69] Its first usage is traced to Henry More (1614–1687), an English metaphysical theologian and a member of the Cambridge Platonist School, who devised the term in his study on the seven letters of the Apocalypse.[70] That a variety of religious groups existed in the ancient world who claimed to possess a special knowledge or "gnosis" is also undisputed; however, the term is so commonly used and in so widely diverse manners that it is not a helpful term to delineate any specific movement of antiquity. For example, "gnosis" first appears in Christian literature in 1 Timothy 6:20 as a term of derision against those who possess "knowledge falsely so-called."[71] However, the author of *The Epistle of Barnabas* and Clement of Alexandria both claimed to possess a "gnosis" that leads to truth and life, and each of these represents what is often termed "proto-orthodox" Christianity. Thus, the term requires specific modifiers (as in "Christian" or "gnostic") or clear parameters in order to carry precise meanings, thus defining a certain type of "gnosis."

Perhaps a term with greater utility is "gnostic" (*gnostikos*, pl., *gnostikoi*), a term which does appear in ancient Christian literature, particularly in the works of the heresiologists. Although the term was used in a pejorative sense by these authors, there are indications that the individuals or groups they sought to implicate as heretical may have generated the term as a self-applauding appellation.[72] However, the tenuous nature of this claim must be kept in mind, because no surviving primary text

68. Yamauchi calls this "part-for-the-whole" argumentation. See Yamauchi, *Pre-Christian Gnosticism*, 171–73.

69. Marjanen provides a helpful overview of the usage of the terms "gnosis," "gnostic," and "Gnosticism." See "What is Gnosticism?," his introduction to *Was There a Gnostic Religion?* 1–53. This volume, featuring keynote addresses from the 1999 International Society of Biblical Literature Meeting in Finland, includes excellent essays related to the gnostic phenomenon from Williams, Pearson, and King.

70. More introduced the term as a generic name for all heresies of the ancient world. See the discussion in Layton, "Prolegomena," 348–49. Many see More's usage as transcending time to posit the orthodox-gnostic conflict as a parallel to the Protestant-Catholic divide of the post-Reformation world. See King, "Origins," 116.

71. For a helpful discussion of this terminological development, see Markschies, *Gnosis*, 5–7.

72. See Brakke, *Gnostics*, 31–35; following Layton, *Gnostic Scriptures*, 163–69.

presents this term as a self-designation.[73] Yet, the question remains, what specifically is meant by this moniker? Has it been and can it be used with discipline and accuracy to portray a clear set of beliefs, behaviors, and/ or tendencies of particular individuals or groups in the ancient world?[74] Further, it should be asked if this attempt at group analysis bears any resemblance to real social groupings of individuals and texts in antiquity.

Since the discovery at Nag Hammadi and the research which it inspired, scholars have struggled to define terms which accurately reflect the dynamics of the ancient world without skewing the historic picture. In an attempt to remedy this situation, a conference was held in Messina, Sicily, in 1966.[75] An international team of scholars proposed a set of definitions of key terms which were approved by those present. "Gnosis" was defined as a broad construct which related to secret knowledge held by an elite group, and "Gnosticism" related more specifically to developed gnostic systems of second-century Christianity and beyond. Also proposed at the conference were the terms "pre-gnostic" and "proto-Gnosticism," which refer to rudimentary elements that were later included in Gnosticism and non-Christian or pre-Christian forms of Gnosticism respectively.

Unfortunately, the definitions established at Messina did not satisfy, and the academy has continued to struggle with matters of definition and terminological precision. Contemporary scholars seeking to find a way out of this definitional impasse tend to fall into four categories in their usage of the terms. First, in light of the variegated nature of the gnostic phenomenon, the confusing way that contemporary scholars have used the terminology, and the unfortunate negative stereotypes attached to the terms (e.g., anti-cosmic and parasitic), Michael Williams has proposed that "Gnosticism" be abandoned as a scholarly construct entirely and be replaced by more measurable phenomena such as "biblical demiurgy."[76] His critique has been received with great acclaim in the academy; how-

73. Scholer, "Gnosis, Gnosticism," 400.

74. For instance, Irenaeus used the term for a specific group in his first book of *Adversus haeresis*; however, he seems to devolve into a generic usage of the term in his second volume, bringing a wider constituency under this rubric. See Brakke, *Gnostics*, 31–35.

75. For an account of the proceedings and keynote lectures, see Bianchi, *Le origini dello Gnosticismo*.

76. Williams, *Rethinking "Gnosticism."* On "biblical demiurgy," see 51–53. More recently, see "Was There a Gnostic Religion?" (55–79), where Williams reflects upon his original proposal of "biblical demiurgy" and adds "preincarnational" traditions of the human soul/spirit as another subject for investigation.

ever, the seeming inability of scholars to put his proposal into practice has demonstrated how imbedded and persistent these terms are in our historical analysis of the gnostic phenomenon, especially considering the lack of any suitable terminological alternative.[77]

The second category includes those who consider Gnosticism a religion in its own right, originally proposed by Hans Jonas,[78] followed by Kurt Rudolph,[79] and most recently defended by Birger Pearson.[80] Using a typological model to describe the characteristics of the gnostic religion, they see Gnosticism as a dualistic religion of alienation, protest, and transcendence, which, though multifarious, adapted itself readily to other religious traditions, perhaps in a parasitic manner.[81]

Third, there are those who do not argue for Gnosticism as an independent religion with a common myth, but rather see the terms *gnosis*, *gnostic*, and *Gnosticism* as meaningful in the ancient world and seek to create typological constructs with precise characteristics that can be analyzed by modern scholars. In this way, various individuals and movements can be compared and contrasted in their own right. Christoph Markschies, for example, champions this approach and proposes a set of eight characteristics which include a distinction between higher and lower divinities, a notion of divine sparks in human beings, a sense of alienation, and a tendency toward anti-cosmic dualism. Comparing texts, individuals, and social groups with similar traits has the promise of determining historical connections and/or a common cultural climate.[82]

A fourth approach has recently been proposed by David Brakke, but follows closely the nominative model of his mentor, Bentley Layton.[83]

---

77. The precise difficulty is once the term "Gnosticism" is abandoned, what should take its place? This problem is illustrated by the enduring title of a study group which meets at the Society of Biblical Literature's annual meetings: "Nag Hammadi and Gnosticism."

78. For his mature thought, see Jonas, *Gnostic Religion*; and Jonas, "Delimitation," 90–108.

79. Rudolph, *Gnosis*.

80. Pearson, *Ancient Gnosticism*, 7–24; and Pearson, "Gnosticism," 81–101.

81. So Rudolph and Pearson. This negative metaphor has been derided by many. See Marjanen's discussion in *Was There a Gnostic Religion?* (esp. 57 and 87n24).

82. Markschies, *Gnosis*. See also Marjanen, "Gnosticism," 203–20, esp. 210–11, where he proposes two main features: an evil creator separated from a higher divinity and the divine origin of the human soul or spirit that can transcend this world and return to its place of origin.

83. Brakke, *Gnostics*, following Layton, *Gnostic Scriptures*; and Layton,

Brakke proposes that scholars isolate those individuals, groups, and texts in the ancient world which called themselves "gnostic" (*gnostikoi*), identified themselves as possessors of "gnosis," or were perceived by their contemporaries as making those claims. Grouping them together and analyzing their texts and systems has the potential of delineating self-defining social groupings in the ancient world and even identifying other related individuals and texts which share characteristics.

What is fascinating, in the final analysis, is that the latter three approaches are quite varied in their methods and presuppositions yet have yielded similar results. What emerges from each of these approaches is the identification of Sethianism as the primary category which encompasses the gnostic myth and provides the widest grouping of gnostic texts and teachers.[84] This is highly significant, in that similar conclusions generated by scholars using quite different methods have yielded results that largely coincide with ancient authors' categories, a testament to the historical veracity of the grouping. Similarly, a number of other groupings are also identified, including Basilides and the Basilideans, Valentinus and the Valentinians, and Thomas traditions, among others.[85] Further, several of the proponents of these approaches identify enduring movements which shared gnostic traits but continued to survive and develop beyond the first few centuries of the Christian era due to greater organizational cohesion (versus their gnostic progenitors): Manichaeanism and Mandaeism.[86] Thus, it appears obvious that an entirely skeptical approach to the study of Gnosticism is unwarranted, though research certainly must be nuanced by contemporary discussions.

As an example of this nuance, Karen King has concluded that the terminology is not ultimately the problem; rather, the problem lies with the purpose and motives behind scholarly categories and definitions.[87] Though King is by no means ambivalent regarding definitions and methods, she rightly argues that the way scholars create categories, define terms, shape questions, and approach data in many senses determines their outcomes.

"Prolegomena," 334–50.

84. Williams makes this same observation regarding Pearson and Layton in "Was There a Gnostic Religion?" 74.

85. These are essentially the groups which Layton defined in *Gnostic Scriptures* and which continue to be identified in more recent works. E.g., Meyer, "Epilogue," in *Nag Hammadi Scriptures,* 777–98.

86. So Markschies, *Gnosis,* 101–8, and Pearson, *Ancient Gnosticism,* 292–332.

87. King, *What Is Gnosticism?* and "Origins," 103–20.

She recommends that all scholars ask themselves the purposes behind their definitions. What stakes do scholars hold in their research? The general answer is, a great deal. While objectivity and neutrality are impossible, awareness of one's proclivities and commitments is crucial to historical analysis. King surmises that many scholars of ancient Gnosticism and Christian origins frame their questions in order to perpetuate their "ongoing project of defining and maintaining a normative Christianity."[88]

Admittedly, this is true, but it should be added that other scholars may reveal hidden motives in seeking to broaden the boundaries of contemporary Christianity by positing greater diversity in the early Christian movement and a late development of normative or "orthodox" Christianity, thereby redefining what they perceive to be original Christianity as pluralistic and inclusive.[89] What seems to be in evidence here is that our understanding and practice of Christianity has not progressed much beyond the polemics and caricatures of second-century debates, nor much beyond those generated by Bauer's provocative thesis over the last seventy years.

Conclusion: Is There a Way Forward?

It must be admitted that each of the scholars in the debate over the definition of Gnosticism makes valid points. Based upon their observations, I would like to propose some steps forward in order to bypass the current impasse in gnostic studies and address its implications for Christian origins.

1. With the advancement of our knowledge of ancient Gnosticism, it is no longer acceptable to perpetuate the misguided stereotypes that Michael Williams illustrates so clearly in *Rethinking "Gnosticism."* Scholars must speak with greater precision about the various movements that existed in the early Christian centuries without the polemical spirit or the broad generalizations of the early Christian heresiologists or the modern academy. This may require more focused studies and courses

88. King, "Origins," 116.

89. Though it is simply wrong to posit all scholarship on these two poles, scholars must be willing to do the hard work of self-critical introspection. Representing the quest for a pluralistic Christianity are Ehrman, most directly in *Lost Christianities* and *Lost Scriptures*, and Meyer, in numerous books with some sensational claims, including *Gnostic Discoveries* and *Gnostic Gospels*. These materials make clear that Bauer's thesis is still highly influential.

on Christian origins and developments in the early Christian centuries, with particular attention to the varieties of religious expression related to Christianity.[90] Further, since Gnosticism is having a resurgence in contemporary times corresponding with the discovery of texts and a shattering of boundaries by postmodern impulses,[91] graduates from seminaries need to understand its teachings and history as well as contemporary manifestations.[92]

2. Though the works of the Christian heresiologists must be analyzed with a critical eye, there is no warrant for complete skepticism regarding their accounts. It must be admitted that apart from their records, we would have very little capacity to create a history of second-century individuals and movements, largely due to the fact that most of the primary gnostic sources in our possession are almost completely lacking in historical data.[93] It is only through the accounts of the heresiologists, particularly Irenaeus, that we can definitively position the *Apocryphon of John*, the *Gospel of Truth*, or the *Gospel of Judas* as well as certain gnostic teachers in the second century.

3. King's call for scholars to examine their motives and purposes in the way they shape definitions and questions as well as approach data should not go unheeded. This call is not merely for those who seek to define and establish an early and continuous normative (or "orthodox") Christianity, but also for those who would recast the history of early Christianity as more pluralistic and hospitable. We must ask what purposes lie behind both of these efforts and how much these efforts lead us to skew evidences and overstate or understate conclusions.

4. What Williams and others seem to be calling for is a more focused analysis of particular phenomena in the ancient sources. Williams has proposed "biblical demiurgy" and "preincarnational" as two topics worthy of further study. Even as this proposal holds a certain degree of promise, special attention will need to be given to historical connections

90. Nicola Denzey Lewis recently published a textbook written specifically for the undergraduate classroom (*Introduction to "Gnosticism"*). A text more suitable to the seminary or graduate school student would be Pearson, *Ancient Gnosticism*.

91. For example, the website, www.gnosis.org, provides information related to The Gnostic Society and Ecclesia Gnostica, as well as primary and secondary sources on gnosis and Gnosticism.

92. Students should also learn of the resources that access gnostic texts and thought. For example, a particularly helpful resource for examining the intersection between the Bible and gnostic literature is Evans et al., *Nag Hammadi Texts*.

93. Brakke demonstrates a healthy balance in *Gnostics*, esp. 29–51.

and the possibility for artificial groupings, which, though informative, may have no actual historical or intellectual intersection.[94]

5. Added to this is the call for precise naming of those phenomena without resorting to anachronistic or "part-for-the-whole" renderings. For instance, Docetism is an important subject of study in earliest Christianity and its manifestation in Christian theology may be derived from a variety of impulses, mostly Jewish and/or Platonic. While these issues should be fully explored, casting Docetism as pre-gnostic or gnostic is misleading and does not reflect the multifarious nature of what became second-century Gnosticism.[95] There is no inevitability of progression from Docetism to Gnosticism, Jewish concepts of mediation to gnostic emanations, or Platonic concepts of demiurgy to the oppositional demiurge of Gnosticism. To call these phenomena "proto-gnostic," "pre-gnostic," or "incipient Gnosticism" is as misleading as categorizing all messianic movements prior to Jesus as pre-Christian, proto-Christian, or simply Christian. In each of these cases, the terms imply too much for the historical reality.

6. Further, the usage of similar terminology such as "proto-orthodox" or "pre-orthodox" for early "orthodox" teachers and authors is also anachronistic and misleading, as it seems to imply that earlier points in the trajectory were something less than "orthodox" theologically and less than a majority numerically. While this may be true in a historical sense when comparing fourth-century orthodoxy to what existed in earlier centuries, it is simply not correct when comparing the early apostolic movement with its contemporary interlocutors. In this case, the terminology implies too little, as if no essential core of historical and theological commitments defined Christianity in the earliest stages of the movement. Additionally, these terms are also inadequate in that they seem to imply a necessary or organic connection between Nicaea and earlier teachers and movements, as well as an inevitability of progress toward Nicaea.

Thus, more accurate and historical terminology for earliest Christianity is required. Alternative titles with greater historical validity and

---

94. For example, "biblical demiurgy" would include the ideas of mediation found in Jewish intertestamental literature. Although the sense of God's transcendence is parallel, most Jewish mediator figures are cooperative with the highest God and not oppositional as in some gnostic systems. See Smith, "Is the Maker," 25–63.

95. For example, Pearson demonstrates that some Nag Hammadi texts were gnostic but not docetic, even as others were docetic but not gnostic in "Anti-Heretical Warnings," 183–93. See also, Yamauchi, "Crucifixion," 1–20.

utility in the second century are Ignatius's "catholic church" (Ign. *Smyrn.* 8.2) or Celsus's "great church" or "the majority" (or "majority church").[96] Going a step further, one might be so bold as to appropriate "Christian" (Acts 11:26) or "Christianity" (Ign. *Magn.* 8.3) for those groups which held to Luke's "apostles' doctrine" (Acts 2:42) and/or "apostolic *kerygma*" (the preaching of Acts), Paul's "gospel" (1 Cor 15:1–4),[97] or the various early creeds and versions of the *regula fidei.*[98] Those not holding such core commitments fell outside the parameters of Christian faith, however they may have formulated a doctrine of Christ, expressed worship to Jesus, or claimed the title "Christian."[99] This obviously counters Ehrman's identification of alternative "Christianities" in the early church. However, if a "Christianity" that is historical, original, and apostolic can be identified, does this not serve as a definition or "norm" for the term, and would not other movements which arise or theological trajectories which run along parallel tracks or move away be called something other than "Christianity" versus other "Christianities"?[100] This is especially true if the trajectory takes on such theological commitments as Gnosticism does, which are fundamentally incongruous with Christianity's historic origins and formulations – rejecting the God of the Jews, separating Jesus not merely from Christ but from the God of the Jews, and locating salvation in knowledge of one's self-identity (as divine) versus a saving knowledge of Christ and faith in his atoning work. On the other hand, individuals and groups which retain the core but demonstrate diversity in non-crucial matters remain under the umbrella of "Christianity."[101]

96. As reflected in Celsus's *True Doctrine*. It seems significant that a non-Christian author who is removed from the internecine polemics within the Christian movement would identify a certain group as the majority church in this early period.

97. Ignatius of Antioch seems to have embraced Paul's concept of "gospel" and extended it to refer to the incarnation of Jesus Christ and the attending features of this doctrine, including Jesus's birth, life, sufferings, death, and resurrection. See Ign. *Phld.* 5, 9–10; Ign. *Smyrn.* 5.1, 7.2. What seems to be in evidence here is that these conceptions were enfolded into Irenaeus's Rule of Faith and the later creeds with historic continuity.

98. See Litfin's helpful analysis of these matters in this volume.

99. More analysis is necessary regarding the self-designation of various individuals and social groups in this era. Brakke's analysis and method in *Gnostics* is particularly insightful here.

100. This is essentially Ignatius's position in *Magn.* 8 mentioned above.

101. My ultimate question here is, how do we classify what is present without overstating or understating the evidence or prejudicing the evidence toward a certain answer? I am also seeking to resist the caricature that orthodoxy is a political versus a

7. Traditionalist scholars must be willing to embrace the fact that Christian theology and practice underwent development during the early centuries of its history, even as it continues to develop today. Much of that development came as it reckoned with new questions and cultures as well as diverse and divergent ideas. Anachronistically reading Nicene orthodoxy back into earlier centuries must be avoided, as it obscures the legitimate developments of this early period, veils early attempts at identity formation and boundary-marking, and seems to imply inevitable progression. For example, Paul's recasting of the Shema in 1 Corinthians 8:6 is an important stage in the early development of Trinitarian theology and Christology, as is Ignatius's clear statement of Christ's humanity and divinity in the early second century.[102] These developments should be recognized and at the same time distinguished from full-orbed Trinitarian theology or Nicene orthodoxy. It should also be recognized that some of these developments caused fragmentation within the early Christian movement.

8. All this requires a more honest approach to the history of our sources. For instance, the cache of documents discovered at Nag Hammadi offers great insights into the early history of Christianity and the religious impulses of that era; however, since no gnostic document from that collection can be definitively dated earlier than the second century, the conclusions which can be drawn from them have much more to say about Christianity in the second through the fourth centuries than they do about anything from the first century when Jesus and his apostles lived and taught and when the earliest Christian documents were composed. Developing theories of origins in the first century from these materials, though arguably an important exercise, should be attended with honesty and transparency regarding the tentative nature of such reconstructions.

9. Finally, an entirely skeptical approach toward the earliest Christian documents which were later canonized is unwarranted. King's challenge regarding definitions and scholarly motives and purposes has implications for all conversation partners and relates as much to the question of "What Is Christianity?" as it does to "What Is Gnosticism?" For instance, it must be affirmed that the canonical Gospels remain our primary sources for historical information regarding Jesus and his followers,[103] and motives for judging otherwise should be examined.

theological position, as Ehrman and others seem to argue.

102. Hurtado's historical approach in *Lord Jesus Christ* provides an excellent model of what is recommended here.

103. This is the admission of Ehrman in *Truth and Fiction*, 102. Ehrman is perhaps

And it is this criticism which is most devastating to Bauer's analysis in *Orthodoxy and Heresy in Earliest Christianity.* In dismissing New Testament evidences, Bauer set himself up to produce an anachronistic account of Christian origins and development which trampled on obvious historical realities of the first century. While claims regarding early orthodoxy in his day may have been overstated and under-supported, Bauer's questions and counterclaims have yielded a similar edifice without a solid foundation. Scholars in the past eight decades have continued to build upon this foundation using the newly discovered materials and creative analytical methods to make broad claims about Christian origins. As much as the Christian academy and church needed Bauer's push to reestablish its foundations and nuance its claims, it seems appropriate at this point in scholarship to offer some push back to correct the claims of the "new orthodoxy" that Bauer, at least in part, helped establish.

---

the most significant proponent of Bauer's ideas in modern culture.

4

Baur to Bauer and Beyond: Early Jewish Christianity and Modern Scholarship

William Varner

"They just don't fit very neatly. They never did."[1]

BURTON VISOTZKY'S BLUNT COMMENT about the historical manifestations of so-called "Jewish Christianity" points out the difficulty that such movements have experienced in "fitting" within the history of the "great church."[2] It also points out, however, the marginalization of Jewish Christianity among many writers on the early church. Church histories have often ended their comments on the development of "Jewish Christianity" with the destruction of Jerusalem in AD 70. Indeed, even Walter Bauer did not include any discussion of Jewish Christianity in his volume on orthodoxy and heresy. Only when the English translation of *Rechtgläubigkeit und Ketzerei im ältesten Christentum* appeared in 1971 was an appendix titled "On the Problem of Jewish Christianity" added by Georg Strecker, a scholar loyal to Bauer's general historical perspective.[3]

1. Visotzky, *Fathers of the World*, 129.

2. On the problem of "Jewish Christianity(ies)" and appropriate definition(s), see below.

3. Bauer, *Orthodoxy and Heresy*, 241–85.

Bauer and Strecker's hypothesis about the relation of orthodoxy and heresy relative to early Jewish Christianit(ies) has been taken up, however, in Bart Ehrman's more popular books.[4] Therefore, it is surprising that the first monograph-length response to the "Bauer-Ehrman Thesis" gives only scant mention to the role of the Nazarenes and the Ebionites.[5] This neglect is significant since the Nazarenes and the Ebionites and their Jewish Christian Gospels are mentioned by a number of significant church fathers,[6] particularly those heresiologists who are often the guilty parties in the Bauer-Strecker-Ehrman revisionist hypotheses.[7]

The purpose of this chapter is to compare and contrast the "traditional" treatment of early Jewish Christianity in its various forms with the newer approach represented by Strecker and Ehrman. Furthermore, we will survey what some other revisionist scholars have written about this neglected chapter of early church history, and some more traditional responses to them. Finally we will address the question of whether the interpretation of Jewish Christianity from "Baur to Bauer and Beyond" should cause us to rethink the traditional attitude toward the orthodoxy of Jewish Christianity in its earliest manifestations.

The Traditional Scholarly View of Jewish Christianity

From what sources can we summarize the traditional approach to handling early Jewish Christianity? In the introduction to one of the recent books that will be described later in this chapter, Matthew McCabe mentions only three serious works on Jewish Christianity that were written prior to the spate of books and articles addressing the subject in "recent years." Those three were *Judaistic Christianity* by F. J. A. Hort (1894); *The Theology of Jewish Christianity* by Jean Daniélou (English tr. 1964),

---

4. Ehrman, *Lost Christianities*, 99–103; *Lost Scriptures*, 9–16.

5. Köstenberger and Kruger, *Heresy of Orthodoxy*, 58, 222, 60n77. On the Ebionites and the Nazarenes, see Häkkinen, "Ebionites" and Luomanen, "Nazarenes."

6. On the Jewish Gospels, see Evans, "Jewish Christian Gospel Tradition"; Gregory, "Jewish Christian Gospels"; Gregory, "Hindrance or Help"; Henne, "L'Évangile des Ebionites."

7. See Batluck, "Ehrman and Irenaeus." For an overview of Jewish Christianity in Patristic Literature, see Kessler, "Writings of the Church Fathers." Cf. Verheyden, "Epiphanius and the Ebionites."

and *Jewish Christianity: Factional Disputes in the Early Church* by Hans Joachim Schoeps (English tr. 1969).[8]

As we seek to synthesize the points of agreement in these "traditional" treatments, I would add two other important, although neglected works. The first effort to write a history of this movement from the first century to the twentieth century was *The History of Jewish Christianity* by Hugh Schonfield.[9] The second is the published doctoral dissertation of Jacob Jocz, *The Jewish People and Jesus Christ*.[10] Each of these volumes also mentions other important monographs, especially in German and French, but the five works I have described can serve as "older" sources to construct the following simplified schema of early Jewish Christianity that can also serve as the model that is questioned by scholars writing from the "Bauer perspective."

The traditionally held historical and theological "chapters" in early Jewish Christianity are as follows:

1. The early church that emerges from the Book of Acts and the earliest New Testament epistles was overwhelmingly Jewish in its composition, and exclusively made up of Jewish believers in the mother church in Jerusalem. It is important to remember that early "New Testament" Christianity *was* Jewish Christianity. These Jewish followers referred to themselves simply as "believers" or "saints" who followed "the Way." Those outside the movement initially referred to them as "Nazarenes," while the term "Christians" seems to have been used of congregations drawn largely from the Gentiles.

2. James the Lord's brother was the leader of the Jerusalem believers and also exercised authority over the burgeoning movement as a whole. A group called the "elders," which probably included some of the original apostles, was associated with him in leadership, although the apostles appear to have served more in the realm of "missionaries" outside Jerusalem. These early Jewish believers were observant of the Mosaic law, although not insisting on its observance by the new believers from the Gentiles; at least in the formal view promulgated after Acts 15.

8. McCabe, *Jewish Christianity*, 1.

9. Schonfield, *History of Jewish Christianity*. Schonfield wrote sympathetically about his subject since he himself was a "Hebrew Christian" at the time. Schonfield eventually renounced his faith and wrote books proposing a radically alternative view of Christian origins, the most famous of which was the best-selling *Passover Plot*. For a recent study of Schonfield's life and thought, see Power, *Hugh Schonfield*.

10. Jocz, *Jewish People and Jesus Christ*.

Even when Luke sought to minimize the differences, he could not avoid mentioning that there were Jerusalem believers who felt that the law should have an even greater role in the lives of all believers. These seeds of varying views would sprout in later years. There is no reason to doubt, however, that early Jewish Christianity affirmed the full Lordship of Jesus the resurrected Messiah.[11]

3. James was executed by the Sanhedrin leadership in AD 62, which probably led to a renewed pressure on the thousands of Jewish believers in Jerusalem and Judea.[12] This led to the migration of nearly all of the Jerusalem church members to the region of Pella on the east side of the Jordan rift prior to the war with Rome (66–70). This relocation was under the leadership of James's successor, Simeon, who was also a relative of Jesus. A significant enough number returned after the war to renew the Jerusalem ministry, centered on Mt. Zion. Congregations of Jewish believers also existed in other areas of Judea and Galilee. Relatives of Jesus held a prominent role at least through the end of the first century. After Simeon's death the leadership of the prosperous Jerusalem church was in the hands of Jewish believers (bishops) until the Hadrianic War from AD 132–135.

4. Despite the silence of the Book of Acts for the period prior to AD 70, there is evidence of a successful Jewish Christian mission in the Galilee during the post-70 period. The movement centered around the relatives of Jesus known as the *desposynoi* ("related to the Master"—*despotēs*), and was based in such towns as Nazareth and Kokaba. This is based further on some admittedly disputed archaeological evidence at Galilean towns such as Capernaum, and illustrated by rabbinic stories about Jewish believers and their influence at such towns as Sikhnin and Sepphoris.

5. During the period from AD 70–100, the Jewish rabbis reorganized the surviving Jewish cause at Jamnia (Yavneh) under the surviving Pharisaic leadership. They responded to what they saw as the growing Messianic threat by enacting certain changes in the synagogue prayers and liturgy that would make it difficult for the Nazarenes to worship in the synagogues. These changes included the insertion of a nineteenth benediction in the *Shemoneh Esreh* prayers called the *birkhat*

---

11. For the summary of a proposal for a more diverse, four-fold group of Jewish-Gentile Christians during this period, see the excursus at the end of the chapter.

12. Craig Evans has recently argued effectively that the entire period from James to Justin was marked by a continual conflict between the family of Jesus and the family of Annas (Evans, *From Jesus to the Church*, 1–50).

haminim.[13] These changes were part of the process known as the "parting of the ways" between "Messianic" Jewish congregations and rabbinic Jewish congregations.[14]

6. During the Bar Kochba Rebellion (AD 132–135), Simon ben Kozeva (Bar Kochba) oppressed Jewish Christian believers, because of their non-support of his rebellion. The Nazarenes simply could not support a pseudo-Messiah when they already knew the true Messiah. In the traditional approach, this was the final stage of the "parting of the ways" between the Synagogue and the Nazarene believers. They had in effect been "expelled" from the rabbinic synagogues by the Jamnia decisions and now they were no longer welcomed as part of the Jewish communities because of the Bar Kochba decisions.

7. During the first half of the second century, two streams of Jewish believers emerged. Hort suggested the two-fold model of "Judaic Christians" and "Judaistic Christians" to distinguish between them. The *Judaic* group affirmed belief in the orthodox doctrines of Jesus's virginal conception, his pre-existence, his Messiahship and resurrection, and his full deity. They also affirmed a continuing role for the written Torah, although they did not insist on its observance by the Gentile believers. The *Judaistic* group denied the virgin birth and affirmed a sort of adoptionist view of the sonship of Jesus, as well as a rejection of the apostleship of Paul. The Torah was absolutely binding in order to please God. Justin Martyr is the first writer to describe the two different groups of Jewish Christians, mentioning one as acceptable to him and the other as considered heterodox.

8. These two strains of Jewish Christianity emerged in the second half of the second century as what could be called the Nazarenes and the Ebionites. From the end of the second century there appeared to be some confusion among the heresiologists about the nomenclature applied to these groups. This is because the term Ebionites was used by some writers for both the more orthodox and the more heterodox groups within Jewish Christianity. By the end of the century, the Nazarenes and Ebionites were

13. Is this a reference to the twelfth benediction concerning heretics? Scholars continue to debate the origin and purpose of the twelfth benediction. See Bobichon, "Persécutions, calomnies"; Ehrlich and Langer, "Earliest Texts of the Birkat ha-Minim"; Instone-Brewer, "Eighteen Benedictions and the Minim"; Katz, "Issues in the Separation of Judaism and Christianity"; Kimelman, "Birkat ha-Minim"; Marcus, "Birkat ha-Minim Revisited"; Mimouni, "Birkat ha-minim"; Van der Horst, "Birkat ha-Minim in Recent Research"; Teppler and Weingarten, *Birkat haMinim.*

14. For an introduction to this issue, see Martin, *House Divided.*

dwindling in number due to assimilation with the "great church" and because of suspicion about their orthodoxy. Hegessipus was a Jewish believer whose writings mentioned by Eusebius serve as a primary source for our knowledge of Jewish Christianity in its first full century of existence.

9. Groups of adherents to Jewish Christianity continued to exist primarily in the region of Syria and the lands to the east of the Jordan rift well into the third century and even the fourth century. Individual Christian leaders with a Jewish background such as Melito of Sardis, Joseph of Tiberias, and Epiphanius of Salamis continued to make contributions although not always in a specifically Nazarene context. Jerome referred to believing Jewish teachers in Palestine who influenced him. He also mentioned the continuing role of the *Gospel of the Hebrews* which he translated into Greek and Latin, although it survives now only in secondary quotations. Other Jewish Christian Gospels are mentioned such as the *Gospel of the Ebionites* and the *Gospel of the Nazarenes*. These two also survive only in partial references.

10. It is difficult to identify dogmatically the works of literature that emerged from the Jewish Christians during this later period. Most agree, however, that the Pseudo-Clementine literature emerged from a group of Jewish Christians, as well as three other "apocryphal" gospels and acts.

11. By the middle of the fifth century there is no discernible separate existence of anything that could be called Jewish Christianity that has left its mark in the literature. Jewish believers from this time onward were evidently absorbed into the "great church."

I fully recognize that the scholars previously mentioned may themselves differ on some of the specific details of my generalized interpretations of their data. Nevertheless, the above model of an orthodox original Jewish Christian "core" that later splintered into at least one or more heterodox groups still serves as the general view that is questioned by advocates of the Bauer-Ehrman reconstruction of early Christian and Jewish Christian history.

The Baur Before Bauer

Having explained the traditional view of the rise and fall of Jewish Christianity, we now inquire how the scholarship of the last one hundred and fifty years has sought to modify this traditional conception.

It is important to recognize that the theory of Christian origins expounded by Walter Bauer did not emerge in an intellectual vacuum. European scholars of early Christianity had been profoundly affected by the ideas of Ferdinand Christian Baur (d. 1860) and what came to be known as his "Tübingen Hypothesis." While the topic of early Jewish Christianity was not directly addressed by Walter Bauer, it lay at the very heart of Ferdinand Baur's hypothesis. In the opinion of the present writer, the Bauer Hypothesis is in some ways the natural implication of the earlier Baur Hypothesis, simply extended beyond the immediate worlds of Peter and Paul.

Baur maintained that early Jesus-faith was characterized by a conflict among Jewish believers, some of whom desired to maintain ties to Judaism and so maintain Christianity as a *particularist* religion, and Gentile believers (along with some Hellenistic Jewish Christians) who desired to sever ties with Judaism in order to make the new faith a *universalist* religion. The conflict was spearheaded by Peter, head of the Jewish-Christian faction, and by Paul, head of the Gentile/Hellenistic faction. In the end there was no clear winner, but what emerged was a historical compromise that melded into what became the early "catholic" church.

Baur sought to isolate the more Jewish-Christian books like the Apocalypse and the more Gentile books like the Pauline letters to Galatia and Rome. He even classified the *mediating* books that resulted from the conflict like Hebrews,[15] James, 1 Peter, and the Pastoral Epistles. At the same time he denied the traditional authorship of those books and placed them quite late in the process. But the ultimate mediating force between these warring factions was the second-century Book of Acts, which sought to smooth over the conflicts that can be seen in Galatians and Romans.[16]

Baur sought to further his hypothesis in one of his last works (1878).[17] His proposal was doomed to failure, however, because he could not adequately explain (in my estimation) why after the supposed synthesis leading to catholic Christianity there continued a viable, although at times struggling, Jewish Christianity well into the third century. He rather steered the discussion toward another Hegelian-like struggle

---

15. According to Baur, Hebrews was a product of Jewish Christianity that was broad enough to presuppose Paulinism as a foundation.

16. Readers alert to nineteenth-century European thought may perceive a Hegelian-like dialectic of thesis—antithesis—synthesis in this proposed model.

17. Baur, *Church History of the First Three Centuries*, 2 vols.

between the dogmatic thesis confronting the antitheses of Gnosticism and Montanism resulting in the synthesis of a Catholic Church.[18]

Despite the towering erudition of Baur, there are few today who follow his views. His shadow is still cast over the study of Christian history in its earliest period, however, particularly manifested in the continued skepticism toward the *tendential* bias of the Book of Acts.[19] There is another reigning paradigm at the present, and it consists of the application to Jewish Christianity of the opinions of another German with quite a similar name.

Bauer and Strecker/Ehrman

Walter Bauer became a household name in New Testament studies with the numerous editions of his masterful *Lexicon of the Greek New Testament and Early Christian Literature*.[20] As previously mentioned, Bauer did not directly apply his reading of early Christian history to Jewish Christianity, but this was remedied by Georg Strecker's appendix in the English translation of Bauer's work.[21] How does Strecker apply Bauer's hypothesis to the "problem" of the Jewish Christian sects that existed in the second and third centuries? And how does this re-reading differ from the standard treatment of Jewish Christianity briefly summarized earlier?

Strecker begins by expressing surprise at Bauer's glaring omission of Jewish Christianity in his book because Strecker firmly believed that it offered a very clear example of the Bauer hypothesis. One may wonder, however, how Bauer overlooked this clear example if it was so obvious!

---

18. Ibid., vol. 2. Cf. Evans, "Tübingen School." To be fair, Baur himself denied that he was a Hegelian in any sense (Baur, *Ausgewählte Werke in Einzelausgauben*, vol. 1, 313).

19. Harnack, *Mission and Expansion*, 401–3. To relegate Adolph Harnack to a footnote may appear to be an insult, but ironically that is basically what the great historian basically did with Jewish Christianity. Harnack believed that Christianity was destined to supersede Judaism and that Gentile Christianity did the same to Jewish Christianity. As ancient Judaism was destined to die, so did its Jewish Christian daughter, and quickly! After the nascent apostolic period, the best that Nazarenes and Ebionites could earn from Harnack was an extended footnote, describing their extinction.

20. See Bauer and Danker, *Greek-English Lexicon*.

21. Bauer, *Orthodoxy and Heresy*, 241–85. Since this chapter is part of a larger work that assumes an understanding of Bauer's hypothetical reading of early Christian history, I will not re-state here Bauer's proposals about the relationship of "orthodoxy" and "heresy."

Strecker bases most of his argument on two literary works that probably did arise out of a Jewish Christian context: (1) the early third-century *Didascalia Apostolorum* in Syria and (2) the early third-century *Kerygmata Petrou* source found in the *grundschrift* of the *Pseudo-Clementine* literature coming from "the dividing line of Greek and Edessan Syria."[22]

While most of our evaluative comments on the Bauer/Strecker/Ehrman reconstruction of orthodoxy and heresy will be reserved for the end of this chapter, a few observations about Strecker's appendix to Bauer will be offered here. Strecker is an acknowledged authority on Jewish Christianity who has contributed major works on the subject.[23] While acknowledging that contribution, it still remains quite difficult to follow the details of his argument that the *Didascalia Apostolorum* and *Kerygma Petrou* affirm the application of Bauer's hypothesis to Jewish Christianity.

The *Didascalia Apostolorum* is a church manual in the tradition of the earlier *Didache* and the later *Apostolic Constitutions.* It may have been written by a Jewish Christian who addressed concerns about Jewish practices and the problem in following them in the churches under his care. What is lacking in the document, however, is any clear indication about how this "church order" indicates that an aberrant form of Jewish Christianity in third century Syria can be traced back to the first century as an accepted form of the faith, along with or superior to that which emerged in the "great church." We are simply not able to portray the theological profile of the communities the author has in view—apart from the fact that there was some adherence to Jewish ritual and purity laws. No low Christology is mentioned and no awareness of a conflict with other believers in Jesus is made clear. It is even possible that the author is more concerned about the external influence of the non-believing Jewish communities on these Jewish believers—which was also the focus of Ignatius's concern in the early second century. It seems that Strecker is simply over-reading his source at this point to make it say something more than it allows.

Strecker's second source, the *Kerygmata Petrou*, is part of the larger *Pseudo-Clementine* literature. Some have maintained that this work (or the combination of sources) has engendered more controversy about its original structure and purpose than any other work from the early days of

---

22. Ibid., 260.

23. Strecker, *Das Judenchristentum in den Pseudoklementinen.*

Christianity.[24] This cannot be the place to discuss the relevant secondary literature. Nevertheless, the controversies surrounding the *Clementines* ought to give us pause about any dogmatic use of it to prove such an important point that Strecker is making. A reading of the earliest part of the literature, as it has been isolated and studied by scholars such as F. Stanley Jones, indicates that the *Clementines* simply cannot be used to argue that the "aberrant" form of Jewish Christianity expressed in them goes back to the first century. As a matter of fact, the theology that emerges from this literature sounds at times like a theology of the "great church" expressed in a Jewish Christian manner. Jesus is the prophet foretold by Moses in Deuteronomy 18 and through Jacob (Gen 49), who was the "eternal Christ" (Messiah). Baptism is even in the threefold divine name mentioned in Matthew—a Gospel that seems foremost in the author's mind. The author sees himself as an heir to the pre-70 Palestinian believing Jewish community, especially loyal to James as his original "bishop." There is no clear indication that he sees himself or his community as a rival to the rest of Gentile believers or in competition with them.

One aspect of the author's writing may still concern us. There appears to be a veiled although transparent character that certainly looks like Paul.[25] It is difficult to ignore the conclusion that the "evil man" who opposes the apostles is a reference to the apostle of the Gentiles. Richard Bauckham, however, points out that these references to Paul are describing his pre-conversion period, since at the end of the debate he sets off to Damascus to persecute the believers (cf. Acts 9). If this is the case, the so-called "anti-Paulism" of the text is severely blunted.[26]

Finally, if Jones's sustained argument that *Recognitions* 1:27–71 can be traced back to a Jewish believer in Jerusalem/Judea around AD 200 is valid, then the Syrian source of this type of Jewish Christianity dissolves. This does not preclude, however, its use in Syria and Trans-Jordan, which all agree was a major center for Jewish Christianity.

I conclude that Strecker, despite all of his evident scholarship, has allowed his sources to "prove" far more than they allow. Because of the labors of Jones and others on the Clementine literature, it is doubtful that it can serve as a lynchpin in the Bauer/Strecker hypothesis.

24. For a recent commentary, see Cambe, *Kerygma Petri.*

25. Cited in Jones, *Ancient Jewish Christian Source,* 106–9.

26. Bauckham, "Origin of the Ebionites," 169–71. On the figure of Paul in second-century Jewish Christianity, see Willitts, "Paul and Jewish Christianity." Cf. Langton, *Apostle Paul in the Jewish Imagination.*

Bart Ehrman's popular treatment of Jewish Christianity repeats the views of Strecker without directly acknowledging them. Ehrman's discussion also suffers from a tendential bias by labeling all of early Jewish Christianity as "Ebionism." This is a patent anachronism that attaches to *all* early Jewish Christians the name of a group of Jewish believers that held aberrant views from the Jewish Christians known as "Nazarenes." Ignoring the important contributions of Justin Martyr, Ehrman does not even mention the "Nazarenes" nor does he ever attempt to connect them with the pre-70 Jewish believers. By labeling them all as Ebionites, he prejudices the discussion to support his assumptions.[27]

Beyond Bauer

The final phase in the scholarly portrayal of early Jewish Christianity focuses on a survey of the literature that has emerged since the English publication of *Orthodoxy and Heresy*. The first group of works consists of those that continue in the general viewpoint of Bauer and Strecker, but also extend their ideas into areas of seeing even greater doctrinal diversity among the various Jewish Christian sects. The second group of works functions generally in the vein of affirming the "classic" viewpoint of Hort and authors up to the publication of Bauer in English. It will be seen, however, that these "traditional" works recognize the difficulty of maintaining a pristinely clean and uniform picture of the diversity revealed in the ancient texts.

Toward More Diversity and a Blurring of the Border Lines

The last twenty years have witnessed a flood of articles and collaborative volumes on "Jewish Christianity," or "Jewish Christianities" to use a phrase that is preferred by many authors. The articles have appeared in diverse journals of biblical, theological, and historical studies. Many of these articles and papers were originally delivered at conferences devoted to the subject, and were included as chapters in collected volumes arising from the conferences. A recurring theme in this literature is the problem of definition, as border lines that formerly were considered firm are now

---

27. Ehrman, *Lost Christianities*, 99–110.

recognized as blurred. Many of the recent articles seek to question old ideas like the historicity of the Pella tradition, the "parting of the ways" between synagogue and church, and the entire concept of "heresy" as applied to early "Jewish believers in Jesus."

As a survey of each of these volumes would unduly burden this chapter and its readers, the following titles will serve to illustrate the diversity of concerns among these multi-authored volumes, not all of whom could be called "revisionist." *Jews and Christians: The Parting of the Ways A.D. 70–135*;[28] *Tolerance and Diversity in Early Judaism and Christianity*;[29] *The Image of the Judaeo-Christians in Ancient Jewish and Christian Literature*;[30] *The Ways That Never Parted: Jews and Christians in Late Antiquity and the Middle Ages*;[31] *A Companion to Second-Century Christian "Heretics"*;[32] and some of the themed articles in both the *Anchor Bible Dictionary* and the *Cambridge History of Judaism*, volume 3. Important single-author monographs which ask the reader to rethink traditional readings are such works as *Heretics: The Other Side of Christianity*;[33] *Neither Jew nor Greek?: Constructing Early Christianity*;[34] and *Border Lines: The Partition of Judaeo-Christianity*.[35] Authors like Judith Lieu and Daniel Boyarin have certainly raised serious questions about the neat and clean lines of demarcation between Jews and Christians (and those belonging to both communities) that are often tacitly assumed by moderns reading, and sometimes not reading, these ancient texts.[36]

---

28. Dunn, *Jews and Christians*.

29. Stanton and Stroumsa, *Tolerance and Diversity*.

30. Tomson and Lambers-Petry, *Image of the Judaeo-Christians*.

31. Becker and Reed, *Ways that Never Parted*.

32. Marjanen and Luomanen, *Companion to Second-Century Christian "Heretics."*

33. Lüdemann, *Heretics*. See also his work on Paul: Lüdemann, *Opposition to Paul*, and his questioning of the Pella Tradition: Lüdemann, "Successors of Pre-70 Jerusalem Christianity."

34. Lieu, *Neither Jew nor Greek?*

35. Boyarin, *Border Lines?*

36. Although the ideas of Robert Eisenman have been largely ignored by the academic community, he deserves a better fate (Eisenman, *James the Brother of Jesus*). Even though his ideas are eccentric, they are erudite and closely argued. Eisenman identifies James with the Righteous Teacher of the Qumran community and interprets all of early Jamesian Jewish Christianity in that light. John Painter offers a critical evaluation of Eisenman's ideas in an excursus to his work on James (Painter, *Just James*, 277–88). Further critical evaluation can be found in Myllykoski, "James the Just." For a more positive appraisal, see Price, "Eisenman's Gospel of James the Just."

It is safe to conclude that no subject on the table of "Jewish Christianity," including even that two-word title, is exempt from being reconsidered and redefined in this recent literature. Occasionally there are voices that affirm with an informed scholarship some of the traditional ideas— Bauckham has been one such voice—but the generally prevailing trend has been toward an increased diversity and blurring of distinctions.[37]

One such volume that can serve as an example of the current handling of these issues is *Jewish Christianity Reconsidered*, edited by Matt Jackson-McCabe, a collection of papers delivered in the Society of Biblical Literature Section on Jewish Christianity. The editor's opening chapter, "What's In a Name?," exemplifies the pessimism that he and many other recent writers possess about clearly defined delineations in this area.[38] It is well known that the expression "Jewish Christianity" is a modern invention that was *not* used of these groups of "Jewish believers in Jesus" in the early period.[39] The confusion regarding the name extends to confusion in almost every subject related to them, according to McCabe. One wonders at times in reading this chapter whether any discussion about the issues is a futile effort in the end. My personal appraisal is that McCabe and some other writers have almost defined their subject out of existence by their overly pessimistic evaluations.

Fortunately, some of the contributors are a bit firmer in their conclusions as they survey such themes as "The Jerusalem Church" (Craig Hill); "Ebionites and Nazarenes" (Petri Luomanen); "The Religious Context of the Letter of James" (Patrick Hartin); and "The Pseudo-Clementines" (F. Stanley Jones). While it does not cover every topic related to these "Jewish believers," the volume can serve as a good introduction to the issues and as a work that includes varying perspectives on the subject.[40]

---

37. Thomas Robinson is another of those "voices" that have generally affirmed the traditional picture of the "parting of the ways." He has strongly criticized writers like Boyarin for neglecting the clear evidence of Ignatius, e.g., in their blurring of the boundaries between Judaism and Christianity in the emerging era of the second century (Robinson, *Ignatius of Antioch*, 203–41).

38. McCabe, *Jewish Christianity*, 7–37.

39. See Broadhead, *Jewish Ways of Following Jesus*.

40. The chapter by Lynn Cohick on "Jews and Christians" is a helpful survey of the literature but focuses more on external Jewish and Christian relations rather than the internal development of Jewish Christianity (Cohick, "Jews and Christians," 68–83).

Affirming the Traditional Understanding

Reference has been made to the occasional contributions of Richard Bauckham to these discussions. He has been an informed voice that generally affirms the traditional understanding of early Jewish Christianity in a number of scholarly articles.[41] It should not be concluded, however, that Bauckham affirms the traditional portrayal out of devotion to some "tradition." He rigorously examines all the texts but does not approach them with a bias against the early heresiologists, who seem to be the chief culprits among many of the recent revisionist writers that have been mentioned.[42] For example, Bauckham critically evaluates the tendency toward using the label "Jewish Christianities" for Jewish Christianity as falling into the same trap that entailed easily labeling the Judaism prior to AD 70 as consisting of many "Judaisms." Namely it assumes that every Jewish person, or Jewish believer for that matter, was a member of a denomination like a contemporary Presbyterian or Lutheran. Most Jews and Jewish believers probably did not self-consciously consider themselves "card carrying members" of some sect. Bauckham also thinks this tendency obscures the difference between legitimate variety and divisive schism.[43]

The only recent volume by a single author that attempts to provide a connected history of Jewish believers in Jesus from a non-revisionist viewpoint is the published doctoral dissertation at the Hebrew University by Ray A. Pritz, *Nazarene Jewish Christianity: From the End of the New Testament Period until Its Disappearance in the Fourth Century* (1992). Pritz attempts to narrate a continuous history of the Nazarenes from their first-century birth until their demise as a distinct sect in the fourth century. He affirms the continuity of the New Testament Jewish believers with the orthodox group described by Justin and Epiphanius by asserting and defending the historicity of the Pella flight, which becomes a foundational point in his entire construction of the history. The orthodox Nazarenes connect with the Jewish Christianity of the New Testament period through this flight to Pella and return to Judea. And there is no evidence of serious doctrinal aberration prior to the two Jewish wars (AD

---

41. Bauckham, "Jews and Jewish Christians," 228–38; "Why Were Christians Called Nazarenes?," 80–85; "Parting of the Ways," 175–92; "The Origin of the Ebionites," 162–81.

42. An invaluable source for studying the references to these groups in early Christian writers is Klijn, *Patristic Evidence for Jewish Christian Sects.*

43. Bauckham, "Parting of the Ways," 177–78.

70 and 135). While not directly addressing the Ebionites, the Symmachians, and the Elkasites (which was not his purpose), Pritz's work is the first effort by a single author since Schonfield to attempt such a task. He traces the flight of Jewish believers in Jesus, their return to Jerusalem, their struggles with Bar Kochba, their orthodoxy, and their harsh rejection by rabbinic Judaism and some later church fathers. It is undoubtedly a sympathetic treatment of its subject. But it cannot be accused of a blind sympathy that avoids the hard questions that such a history must face. He recognizes both the paucity of the sources and also the confusion of terminology by some of the heresiologists. It is an admirable work of scholarship that has served its generation well and has prepared the way for the following volume.

The entire discussion of all issues related to Jewish Christianity has been admirably served by the publication of *Jewish Believers in Jesus: The Early Centuries* (2007).[44] This massive work of 900 pages, consisting of twenty-three separate chapters by nearly twenty scholars, leaves virtually no stone unturned in its treatment of this controversial subject. Originally envisaged as a full history of Jewish Christianity,[45] the volume eventually adopted a more modest goal of tracing each of the themes related to Jewish believers in Jesus in the first four centuries of our era. To express it colloquially, it is as close as can be to a "one stop shop" for all things Jewish Christian in the first four centuries after Christ. From "James and the Jerusalem Community" (Bauckham) and the "Archaeological Evidence for Jewish Believers?" (James Strange) to the sects and divisions found in communities from Antioch to Rome, each subject is addressed by a published authority in that field. Each subject receives a thorough handling, with all views mentioned and addressed and with up-to-date literature on the subject. Much attention is given to the patristic references to Nazarenes (Wolfram Kinzig) and Ebionites (Oskar Skarsaune). The writings attributed to the Jewish believers themselves such as the Jewish Gospels (Craig Evans) and the Clementine Literature (Graham Stanton) also receive a full treatment. Bauer's work focused on geographical locations where he thought that he saw early variant forms of "Christianity." There are chapters, therefore, on evidence for Jewish believers in Jesus in Rome (Reidar Hvalvik), in Asia Minor (Peter Hirschberg), and in Syria (Sten Hidal).

---

44. Skarsaune and Hvalvik, *Jewish Believers*.

45. Ibid., xi.

The evidence for Jewish believers in Jesus in the rabbinic literature (Philip Alexander), in the Jewish-Christian Dialogues (Lawrence Lahey) and in the "Church Orders" (Anders Ekenberg) is thoroughly traced. There is a meticulous and critical treatment given to all the patristic references to Jewish believers in both Greek and Latin Fathers (Oskar Skarsaune). It is difficult to see any stone that has been left unturned in the book. It may be the closest thing to a *status quaestionis* on the subject from a more traditional perspective (although not all the authors would probably accept the label of "traditional").

The strength of this massive work, however, is also its only weakness. It is so thorough in its treatment of individual topics that it lacks an overall historical narration of its subject, although we should be reminded that such was not its purpose.[46] One of the editors, Oskar Skarsaune, admirably introduces the subject in chapter one: "Jewish Believers in Late Antiquity: Problems of Definition, Method, and Sources,"[47] and offers a good summary in chapter twenty-three: "The History of Jewish Believers: Perspectives and Framework."[48] Perhaps the best way to describe the overall thrust of this tome is to summarize Skarsaune's own attempted summary of the issues addressed in the book. Furthermore, this summary can also serve as my own final response to the Bauer-Strecker-Ehrman hypothesis about early Jewish Christianity.

Skarsaune asks and attempts to answer the following questions: 1. Is the Term "Jewish Believers" an Artificial Category? 2. How Close Were Jews and Christians in Antiquity? 3. Were Jewish Believers In Jesus to Be Found in Clearly Defined Sects? 4. Where Do We Find the Jewish Believers? 5. How Many Jewish Believers in Jesus Were There?[49]

The terms "Jewish Christian" and "Jewish Christianity" are neologisms. In the ancient sources that we possess no one is self-labeled as a "Jewish Christian."[50] The discussion centers around whether the term

---

46. Ibid., xii.

47. Ibid., 3–21.

48. Ibid., 745–82.

49. Ibid., 747–72. Rather than overly burdening the discussion of these questions with a plethora of footnote citations, it should be understood that the answers to these questions are all taken from the above section of *Jewish Believers*.

50. This is a point that is also effectively made by Carleton Paget in his excellent article in the *Cambridge History of Judaism*. Paget's article, because of its breadth of scholarship, fairness to all views, and succinctness is probably the best current, single-authored summary treatment of early Jewish Christianity (Paget, "Jewish Christianity," 731–75). Paget also contributed to *Jewish Believers in Jesus* (Paget, "Definition of

"Jewish" should be based on ethnicity (born a Jew), praxis (observes Jewish customs), or doctrine (believes in Jesus as the Jewish Messiah). While some recent authors have despaired of finding the most correct title to apply to these people, in the ancient sources a clear distinction is made between Jewish believers in Jesus and Gentile believers in Jesus. One gets the impression at times that some authors have almost defined the term out of existence with all the problems and defined nuances that they bring to the discussion. One thing should be clear: in antiquity Christians and Jews knew who the Jewish believers in Jesus were with the same degree of precision as they knew in general who was Jewish and who was not. Any one term such as "Nazarenes" or "Ebionites" cannot cover the entire group, and we cannot be sure that these believers even applied these titles to themselves or if they were labeled with these terms by outsiders. The most often-used expression was "those who believe *from the Jews*." In light of this, the title of this book is probably the best one to work with: "Jewish believers in Jesus."

There have been two extremes in addressing the question about how close Jews and Christians were in antiquity. One understanding of the traditional model is that after AD 70, and certainly after AD 135, direct contact ceased except for polemical witness and debate. On the other hand, authors like Boyarin and writers among "the ways that never parted" group affirm that the lines were blurred and that something like a "Judaic Christianity" was the norm for both communities until the Constantinian period. The first view certainly needs to be re-thought, because the evidence from both archaeology and the literary texts from the second through the fourth centuries indicates extensive interaction between Christians and Jews.[51] Even the existence of the *adversus Judaeos* literature implies that contacts were extensive enough for some church fathers to warn against contact with the Jews.[52] While Boyarin and others may have blurred the lines too severely, "the ways that never parted" paradigm may open a window to recognize a greater historical ambience of Jewish believers vis-à-vis their unbelieving Jewish neighbors.[53]

Terms," 22–52).

51. See also Horbury, *Jews and Christians in Contact and Controversy*.

52. For further implications of the *adversus Judaeos* "dialogue" literature as well as the first English translations of three of these dialogues, see Varner, *Ancient Jewish-Christian Dialogues*; and Varner, "In the Wake of Trypho."

53. Daniel Boyarin's most recent book (*Jewish Gospels*) argues that the Gospels are quite Jewish, even in their doctrinal teaching about the Messiah. By a fresh analysis of

Were Jewish believers always in defined sects? If we begin the search for an answer with the fourth-century Epiphanius, the answer is a resounding "yes." Research has shown, however, that the author of the *Panarion* was highly speculative in his definition of these mostly heretical groups whom he names either the Nazarenes, Ebionites, Cerinthians, Elchasites, or Sampseans. While it has become too easy and fashionable to bash the heresiologists as a whole, it is quite clear that Epiphanius wrote more out of hearsay than personal contact. From Irenaeus on, however, it appears that the Ebionites held to a purely human birth of Jesus. And from Justin to Jerome, the Nazarenes were viewed as doctrinally within the fold of what could be called "catholic Christianity."

Although this term for Jewish believers goes back to apostolic times (Acts 24:5), it eventually morphed into a term that describes all believers in the Nazarene, Jesus. This was the way it survived into the Muslim period and in Modern Hebrew today (*notzrim*). The term does appear to be limited to Jewish believers by others from the early second century. The silence of some authors about the Nazarenes may also imply that they were simply viewed as part of the "great church," although as a variety within it that sought to observe the non-cultic practices in the Torah. Skarsaune advises that we should leave behind the baggage-laden terminology of the heresiologists and simply call them "Jewish believers in Jesus."

And *where* were these Jewish believers to be found? A simple answer to that question is: Wherever Jews were to be found in any significant numbers. First of all, Jewish believers in Jesus were found in the Land of Israel—Jerusalem itself, the coastal plain, and Galilee with Transjordan east of the Sea of Galilee. Following the disastrous two wars with Rome, the rabbinic center of Judaism shifted, first to the coast and then to Galilee and probably Transjordan. This was likely true also for the Jewish believers in Jesus, and the story of the flight to Pella is consistent

---

pre-Christian Jewish documents like Dan 7, the Similitudes of Enoch, and 4 Ezra, he sets forth the idea that Jews anticipated a divine Son of Man who came to be identified with the Messianic Son of God. Judaism thus expected a divine redeemer who was to be a God-man. Furthermore, there was a history of faith in a suffering Messiah (i.e., Isa 53) before Jesus. The usual debate about whether Isa 53 concerns Israel or Messiah is a moot argument, because there is evidence in the Targums and other rabbinic material that Isaiah's "servant" was a description of a suffering Messiah. While such evidence has occasionally been pointed out before, the significance of this book is that it is written by an academic rabbi recognized as one of the world's leading Talmudists. Time will tell how other scholars, especially Jewish ones, will respond to Boyarin, but his evidence, while standing on its head many an assumption about the Jewish expectation of the Messiah, simply cannot be ignored.

with that. Eusebius's list of fifteen Jewish-Christian "bishops" in Jerusalem may have consisted of leaders in exile or resident leaders of a community mostly in exile. A writer like Aristo of Pella may represent the continuation of that community.[54]

The Jewish loss of Jerusalem after Bar Kochba became permanent, and a shift to the Galilee took place with the establishment of rabbinic academies in Usha and later in Sepphoris and Tiberias. This sets the scene also for Jewish believers in Galilee, and the bishop list of the Jerusalem church from this time consisting of Gentile names confirms this probable "migration."[55] Although the sources are scant, we do find Jewish believers living closely together with their Gentile neighbors in some instances. The only probable areas where Jewish believers connected with their Gentile brethren were in coastal locales like Caesarea or in the more Hellenistic inland cities like Scythopolis, and Origen is a witness to these contacts.[56]

The dramatic impact of the "Christianization" of the Holy Land in the fourth and fifth centuries must have had a serious impact on what remained of the Jewish believers at that time. Most of this impact I will briefly mention later, but the effect of it may have been the retreat of Jewish believers eastward, especially to the Golan. Epiphanius's vague mentionings of the "Nazoreans" whom he knows of in Syria appear to be references to these isolated communities. The continued references in the rabbinic literature to these "minim" also attest to their presence during this period.

In the Diaspora, there were two regions; the Roman/Byzantine west and the Persian east, although the latter has been often overlooked by many historians. In the West it was Antiochian Syria and Asia Minor that were dominant; the Book of Acts, not surprisingly, is an early witness to their presence there.[57] An overlooked area for Jewish Christianity in

54. One of the strongest arguments for the basic historicity of the Pella tradition is Pella itself—why would later writers falsely choose this unlikely city in the Decapolis? See also a defense of the Pella Tradition in Koester, "Origin and Significance."

55. See Eusebius, *Hist. eccl.* 5.5 for the list of Jewish Christian bishops until AD 135, "all of them from the Circumcision." For a list of the "Gentile" bishops in Jerusalem after 135, drawn from various sections of Eusebius, see the convenient chronological table of "Emperors and Bishops" in Louth, *Eusebius*, 428–30.

56. The testimonies from Origen about Jewish Christians are scattered through a number of his expository works. For a discussion of these passages as well as documentation for his contacts with Jews in general, see *Jewish Believers in Jesus*, 361–73; and Lange, *Origin and the Jews*.

57. Sadly our lack of information on the birth of Christianity in first-century (?) Egypt keeps us from dogmatically including it as a possible locale for Jewish

the West has been North Africa. Thanks now to the fresh research of Thomas Oden, we do well to recognize some thriving communities of Jewish believers in Jesus in the country we now call Libya, who traced their heritage to Simon of Cyrene.[58] For the East, such documents as the church orders—the *Didache* and the *Didascalia Apostolorum* with their heavy Jewish Christian character—are clear evidence of the presence and influence of Jewish believers in the East throughout the fourth century. Skarsaune mentions many more details of how that influence may have been felt in worship and lifestyle.[59]

But how many Jewish believers are we considering during this period? Skarsaune spends a good bit of time relating and evaluating Rodney Stark's sociological study of how Christianity grew, especially in its Jewish manifestation.[60] Despite Origen's rough estimate that Jewish believers would probably not equal the 144,000 in the Apocalypse, Skarsaune extrapolates a larger number. Referring to the thirty percent of names in the Roman epistle as Jewish, he offers the following educated guess: "If we make a bold extrapolation and take only 10 percent as a representative ratio, it would still mean that around AD 250 there would, within the limits of the Roman Empire, be 100,000 Jewish believers. Of a total Jewish population of five million, that would be two percent. There is nothing in this figure to strike one as unrealistic.[61]

Most scholars would consider Skarsaune's extrapolation as unlikely. It should be kept in mind, however, that the number of Jewish believers should be considered in light of the total population of Jewish people. Many ancient sources indicate that Jews constituted a rather large percentage of the population in the Roman Empire. Why should Skarsaune's extrapolation, therefore, be considered as absurd? Furthermore, not every one of these believers may have been identified as Torah observant, and many may have found their identity in the "great church."

All would agree, however, that in the East the population of Jewish believers would have been even more numerous than in the West. Syrian

---

Christianity. The large Jewish community in Alexandria, the role of a man like Apollos, and the Markan legends may allow one to conjecture a first-century Jewish Christian presence there. Of course the traumatic effects of the Trajanic War in 115–117 may have altered many matters.

58. Oden, *Early Libyan Christianity*, 76–85.

59. Skarsaune, "Perspectives and Framework," 763–67.

60. Stark, *Rise of Christianity*, 49–71.

61. Skarsaune, "Perspectives and Framework," 770.

Christianity strikes one as generally more Jewish than its counterpart in the Roman Diaspora. Furthermore, if the "Constantinian revolution" had a negative impact on the continuance of discernible Jewish Christian communities, and I would argue that it did, the absence of any similar "revolution" in the Persian Diaspora should be recognized.

Conclusions

The purpose of *Jewish Believers in Jesus* was not to criticize the Bauer-Strecker-Ehrman re-reading of orthodoxy and heresy in early Jewish Christianity. The results of its research, however, seriously call into question that a multi-variegated picture of Jewish Christian beliefs can be traced back to the years prior to AD 70. There was diversity to be sure, even during the New Testament period. But that diversity was held together by a common commitment to the essentials of the Gospel which have always formed the common kernel of Christian belief, whether it was reflected in a Jewish or a Gentile dominated faith—a high Christology that saw Jesus as the Messiah of Israel and God's Son, the risen Lord raised from the dead. Strecker and Ehrman have failed to connect later aberrations of this "Gospel" with the pre-70 Jerusalem community of believers. And failing to do that seriously blunts their underlying assumptions.

With all of this history, there remains one question that has concerned me for years and has been highlighted in my review of this research. Why did Jewish Christianity, or whatever one desires to call it, basically not survive as a distinct movement beyond the fourth century? Was Adolph Harnack correct in seeing its demise as evidence of an inevitable forward movement beyond Christianity's Jewish roots (almost a religious "survival of the fittest")?[62] Jerome's famous comment was to the effect that these "Nazarenes" wanted to be both Jews and Christians and ended up being neither. Perhaps the burden of attempting to live in two worlds simply became too heavy, and they were absorbed into the "great church."

There is another historical factor, however, and it was transpiring during that fateful fourth century. The Constantinian revolution, with its greater pressure on the Jews and limitation of their rights that had been granted so freely during the pagan period of the empire, must have had

---

62. According to Harnack, to conserve the Jewish Old Testament as a canonical text in Protestantism after the nineteenth century "was the result of a religious and ecclesiastical paralysis" (Harnack, *Marcion*, 248).

its effects on the Jewish believers as well. Previously it had not been a political embarrassment to be Jewish; many Jews were full Roman citizens. With the "new" Roman Empire, centered in that *Nova Roma* on the Bosporus, it was no longer politically acceptable to be Jewish. This new situation, with its effects on those who wanted to remain Jewish ethnically while still espousing the newly legalized faith, must have furthered the slow erosion of any loyalty to the first word of that designation, a *Jewish* believer in Jesus.[63]

Excursus: Early Jewish-Gentile Christianity and Raymond Brown

On the one hand, the binary polarity of "Jewish Christianity" and "Gentile Christianity" is too simplistic. On the other hand, labels remain heuristic devices that aid in mutual understanding and shared discourse. In a largely overlooked article that was reprinted as the "Introduction" to a book co-authored with John Meier, Raymond Brown divided what he called "Jewish-Gentile Christianity" into *four* groups that emerged from their pre-70 ethos.[64] Brown did not attempt to trace their development beyond that date. Nevertheless, his groupings might form a helpful starting point for generalist, middle paths that steer between unsophisticated discussions of "Jewish Christianity" without attention to detail and those sophisticated reconstructions that emphasize diversity to the dissolution of meaningful labels. Brown's four groups can basically be summarized as follows.

Group One, consisting of Jewish Christians and their Gentile converts, who insisted on *full observance of the Mosaic Law, including circumcision,* for those who believed in Jesus. In short, these ultraconservatives insisted that Gentiles had to become Jews to receive the messianic blessings brought by Jesus. Such a demand was advocated by those Jewish Christians at Jerusalem whom Acts calls "of the circumcision" (11:2) and describes as "of the sect *[hairesis]* of the Pharisees" (15:5), and whom Paul speaks of as "false brothers who slipped in to spy out our freedom" (Gal 2:4). Since these people were at Jerusalem and presumably were not enthusiastic about Gentile converts, many scholars have ignored their

---

63. I would like to thank Cliff Kvidahl and Tavis Bohlinger for their assistance with bibliographical and proof-reading tasks.

64. Brown, "Not Jewish Christianity and Gentile Christianity," as re-printed in Brown and Meier, *Antioch and Rome.*

views in speaking about the Christian mission to the Gentiles. However, the whole of Paul's letter to the Galatians shows that Jewish Christians of similar persuasion had made inroads among his Gentile converts in Galatia in distant Asia Minor. Chapter 3 of Philippians shows a fear of similar Jewish Christian inroads among Gentile converts in Greece, while 1:15–17 hints at such preaching where Paul is imprisoned (Rome? Ephesus?). Therefore, we must speak of a *mission* to the Gentiles that was quite antagonistic to Paul and resulted in the existence of a Jewish/Gentile Christianity of the strictest Law observance, not only in Palestine but in some of the cities of Asia Minor and Greece at the very least.

Group Two, consisting of Jewish Christians and their Gentile converts, who did *not* insist on circumcision but did require converted Gentiles to keep *some Jewish observances*. One may speak of this as a moderately conservative Jewish/Gentile Christianity. According to Acts 15 and Galatians 2, James (brother of the Lord and head of the Jerusalem church) and Peter (Cephas, the first among the Twelve), whom Paul describes as "so-called pillars" (Gal 2:9), agreed with Paul that circumcision was not to be imposed on Gentile converts. But according to Acts 15:20, James insisted on certain Jewish observances, particularly food laws; according to Galatians 2:12 "men from James" caused embarrassment at Antioch over the question of Jewish Christians eating with Gentiles and thus presumably not keeping the food laws. Acts 15:14–15, 19–21, and 22–29 indicate that, while such a demand associated with James was not originally Peter's idea, he went along with it peaceably as did other Jerusalem notables. But Galatians 2:11–14 may suggest that Peter's acquiescence was only under pressure.[65] The fact that "men of James" came to Antioch with demands about certain law observances (Gal 2:11–12) and that a letter embodying James's position was sent to Gentile Christians ("brethren") in "Antioch, Syria, and Cilicia" (Acts 15:23), suggests once again that we are dealing with a *missionary* thrust that produced another style of Jewish/Gentile Christianity, less rigid than that described in Group One above, but less liberal toward the Law than that in Group Three to be explained below. One can speak of this as a mediating view, inclined to see a value in openness (no demand of circumcision) but preserving some of the wealth of the Jewish Law as part of the Christian heritage. This Jewish/Gentile Christianity would have been particularly associated with the Jerusalem apostles. The Gospel of Matthew, which

65. One should also take into account the portrayal of Paul's role and tacit approval of the Jerusalem Assembly as found in Acts 15:22–29; 16:4.

speaks of a church founded on Peter, gives the eleven Apostles a mission to all nations (Matt 28:16–20; see also Acts 1:2, 8.) The *Didache,* close in many ways to Matthew, is titled: "The Teaching of the Lord to the Gentiles *through the Twelve Apostles.*"

Group Three, consisting of Jewish Christians and their Gentile converts, who did *not* insist on circumcision and did *not* require observance of the Jewish ("kosher") food laws. Despite the evidence in Acts 15:22 implying Paul's and Barnabas's acceptance of James's position, Galatians 2:11–14 explains that Paul vigorously resisted the views advocated by "certain men from James" in reference to the Gentiles, even while Barnabas yielded. In a nuanced way, Paul did not *require* Christians to abstain from food dedicated to idols (1 Cor 8),[66] a requirement imposed by James and the Jerusalem leaders according to Acts 15:20, 29.[67] While Paul is the main New Testament spokesman for this liberal attitude, we can assume that the Jewish Christians with whom he associated in missionary activities would have shared his views. Having opposed Cephas/Peter face to face (Gal 2:11), and having ceased to work with Barnabas (Gal 2:13; Acts 15:39) over this issue, Paul would scarcely have tolerated diversity about it among his missionary companions.[68] Thus, we may speak of a Pauline (and perhaps more widespread) type of Jewish/Gentile Christianity, more liberal than that of James and of Peter in regard to certain obligations of the Law.

Group Four, consisting of Jewish Christians and their Gentile converts, who did not insist on circumcision or observance of the Jewish food laws and who *saw no abiding significance in Jewish cult and feasts.* Brown believed that one can detect in the New Testament a body of Jewish Christians more radical in their attitudes toward Judaism than Paul (a group with whom his opponents in Acts 21:20–21 would associate him). The best explanation of the name "Hellenists" in Acts 6:1–6, who made Gentile converts (11:19–20) is that they were Jews (in this instance, Jews who believed in Jesus) who had been raised with heavy

66. At least not in all cases. Paul's reasoned responses to specific situations involving food dedicated to idols seems to vary based upon location, audience, and available knowledge. Above all, Paul seems interested in persuasion not coercion, all the while guiding the Corinthians in moral reasoning (see Garland, *1 Corinthians,* 353–62)

67. Again, however, one should note the references to Paul himself in Acts 15:22–29; 16:4. See also the relevant materials in Rev 2:14, 20.

68. Brown explains the Acts 15 rift between Paul and Barnabas through varying views on food consumption. But this issue is not explicitly cited as the cause of division in Acts 15:35–41 (rather, the text refers to differences over the accompaniment of John Mark).

Greek acculturation, perhaps often to the point of being able to speak only Greek, not a Semitic language. Stephen's speech indicates a disdain for the Temple where God does *not* dwell—an attitude quite unlike that attributed by Acts to Paul who is kept distinct from them.[69] The Epistle to the Hebrews sees Jesus as replacing the Jewish high priesthood and sacrifices, and places the Christian altar in heaven. There is every reason to think that John and Hebrews were written by Jewish Christians, and clearly John envisions Gentile converts (12:20–24). There is sufficient evidence in the New Testament of a Jewish/Gentile Christianity that had broken with Judaism in a radical way and so, in a sense, had become a new religion, fulfilling Jesus's saying in Mark 2:22 that new wine cannot be put into old wineskins since it causes them to burst.

Therefore, it is meaningless to speak of *the* Jewish Christianity or *the* Gentile Christianity without specifying which type or types of Jewish/ Gentile Christianity and without challenging the supposition that, because Paul visited a city, Pauline Christianity was always dominant there. While Raymond Brown's breakdown is not without its own difficulties,[70] it points to a helpful, middle approach. The numerous complexities, as demonstrated by the available extant evidence, challenge the simplicity of the "traditionalist" scheme as explained in the beginning of this essay.

---

69. But see 1 Kgs 8:27; 2 Chr 6:18.

70. As reflected, for example, in the footnotes above.

5

"Orthodoxy," "Heresy," and Complexity: Montanism as a Case Study

Rex D. Butler

WHICH CAME FIRST: ORTHODOXY or heresy? To some, this question may seem as simplistic as the riddle about the chicken or the egg, but to historians of Christianity during the past several decades, it has become increasingly significant and controversial. To a great extent, the controversy has been generated by Walter Bauer's seminal work, *Rechtgläubigkeit und Ketzerei im ältesten Christentum*, which was first published eighty years ago in 1934, was re-issued in a second edition in 1964, and then was translated into English in 1971, as *Orthodoxy and Heresy in Earliest Christianity*.[1]

Prior to Bauer, the traditionally held answer to our question was that orthodoxy came first. Jesus taught his apostles the true doctrine, which they preserved pure, untainted, and unified and then passed on to their disciples as they took the gospel throughout the world. After the deaths of the apostles, Christianity continued to spread, but the true doctrine, which became known as orthodoxy, began to be challenged in various places by false teachings, which became known as heresies. The Scriptures had prophesied the rise of heretics and, thus, confirmed

1. For a summary of Bauer, *Orthodoxy and Heresy*, see Decker's essay in this volume.

the primacy of orthodoxy. Orthodoxy was unified and universal, while heresies were diverse and limited geographically. Therefore, according to this traditional answer, orthodoxy preceded heresy.[2]

Bauer, however, often answered our question in favor of heresy, depending upon the specific geographical location. According to his thesis, "certain manifestations of Christian life that the authors of the church renounce as 'heresies' originally had not been such at all, but, at least here and there, were the only form of the new religion—that is, for those regions they were simply 'Christianity.' The possibility also exists that their adherents constituted the majority, and that they looked down with hatred and scorn on the orthodox, who for them were the false believers."[3] What became known as orthodoxy represented only one movement within Christianity, which was centered in Rome. The Roman Church, however, was able to gain ascendancy through its powerful hierarchy, wealth, and literary production. Ultimately, the orthodox not only established themselves as the dominant faction in Christendom but also were able to suppress what they determined to be heresy and rewrote history to claim primacy for their own views.[4] Bauer, therefore, reversed the traditional view of early Christianity with his thesis that heresy preceded orthodoxy (in many locations).

The simplistic manner in which I have worded these positions, however, belies the actual complexity of the issues involved.[5] First, the terms "orthodoxy" and "heresy" either appeared late, in the case of the former, or underwent narrowing and hardening over time, in the case of the latter. Second, in spite of the late development of the linguistic terminology, a sense of normative Christianity represented by apostolic

2. Bauer, *Orthodoxy and Heresy*, xxiii–xxiv. See summaries of the traditional view in Turner, *Pattern of Christian Truth*, 3–7; Bingham, "Development and Diversity," 48–49; Köstenberger and Kruger, *Heresy of Orthodoxy*, 24.

3. Bauer, *Orthodoxy and Heresy*, xxii.

4. Ibid., 229–40; Ehrman, *Lost Christianities*, 173; Köstenberger and Kruger, *Heresy of Orthodoxy*, 24.

5. In response to Bauer's thesis, two more nuanced approaches have been brought forth. Turner, *Pattern of Christian Truth*, 26, posited that both fixed and flexible elements interacted during the development of Christian theology. Robinson and Koester, *Trajectories through Early Christianity*, devised a trajectory-critical approach, which finds canonical and noncanonical, orthodox and heretical streams flowing simultaneously out of traditions from and about Jesus. Therefore, according to this approach, neither tradition claimed original authority over the other. For summaries of these two approaches, along with the traditional view and Bauer's thesis, see Hultgren, *Rise of Normative Christianity*, 7–18; and Bock, *Missing Gospels*, 54–55.

teaching and tradition appears in early Christian records even before the label "orthodox" is used to describe it. Third, many would differentiate between a "heresy" and a "schism."[6] Fourth, the divide between "orthodoxy" and "heresy" was not necessarily impermeable, as is evidenced by the movement known variously as Montanism, the Phrygian heresy, or the New Prophecy. Montanism began in the east but also thrived in the west, relating in a different way to the official church in every location where it existed. After a discussion of some of the issues involved in the relationship between orthodoxy and heresy, I will present Montanism as a case study of that complex relationship.

"Orthodoxy," "Heresy," and Complexity

The term "orthodoxy" is the union of two Greek words: *orthos*, which can mean "upright," "straight," "correct," or "true"; and *doxa*, which can mean "opinion," "glory," or "honor."[7] Harold O. J. Brown defined the concept in this way: "Orthodox faith and orthodox doctrines are those that honor God rightly."[8]

For all its significance in Christian history, however, the word "orthodoxy" is not found in the Christian scriptures. According to William Henn, the term was not in wide use until the fourth century. From that time it is found in the writings of Eusebius of Caesarea (d. 339), Julius I (d. 359), Athanasius (d. 373), and Basil the Great (d. 379), as well as the records of the Councils of Ephesus (431) and Chalcedon (451). Henn added, "Thus gradually orthodoxy came to mean not simply right doctrine but the traditional and universal doctrine of the church as defined in opposition to heterodoxy or heresy. In this context it was seen as the pure tradition, handed down in unbroken line from the authentic Gospel of Jesus and his apostles."[9]

Although the term "orthodoxy" does not appear in the New Testament, the term "heresy" (*hairesis*) does. Etymologically, this word and its

---

6. "Schism" in the *New American Encyclopedic Dictionary*, 3572–73. According to David F. Wright, however, "In the early centuries no clear distinction obtained between schism, an offense against unity and love, and heresy, error in doctrine. Heretics were assumed to be, in reality and tendency, outside the church (i.e. schismatics) and vice-versa." (Wright, "Schism").

7. Preisker, "Orthos"; Kittel, "Doxa"; Henn, "Orthodoxy."

8. Brown, *Heresies*, 1.

9. Henn, "Orthodoxy," 732.

derivatives communicated the idea of "choice." In classical Greek usage and in Judaism, this family of words referred to the choosing of doctrines or, especially, of philosophical or religious schools. For example, Josephus viewed the Jewish religious sects—the Essenes, Sadducees, and Pharisees—along the same lines as Greek philosophical schools.[10]

In the book of Acts, the author uses *hairesis* in this neutral way to refer to the sects of the Sadducees and Pharisees (Acts 5:17; 15:5; 26:5) and of the Christians, or Nazarenes (Acts 24:5, 14; 28:22). Elsewhere in the New Testament, *hairesis* and its derivative, *hairetikos*, are used to refer to schismatic impulses among some members of the earliest churches (1 Cor 11:19; Gal 5:20; Tit 3:10; 2 Pet 2:1).

These descriptions of "heresy" paint a picture of factiousness that either led to or was a result of doctrine and behavior that were in opposition to the apostolic teaching presented in the New Testament. The original, neutral nature of the term *haeresis* quickly gave way to its technical, pejorative sense when the threat of these factions became clear. In the early decades of the second century, Ignatius of Antioch warned the Christians at the Trallian church: "I urge you, therefore—yet not I, but the love of Jesus Christ—partake only of Christian food, and keep away from every strange plant, which is heresy. These people, while pretending to be trustworthy, mix Jesus Christ with poison—like those who administer a deadly drug with honeyed wine, which the unsuspecting victim accepts without fear, and so with fatal pleasure drinks down death."[11]

Such references to heresy, however, do not disprove the existence of orthodoxy but, rather, presuppose it. Brown offered this illustration: "Sometimes one catches a glimpse of another person or object in a mirror or a lake before seeing the original. But the original preceded the reflection, and our perception of it. The same we would argue, is true of orthodoxy—the original—and heresy—the reflection. The heresy we frequently see first, but orthodoxy preceded it."[12]

Prior to the linguistic delineation of "orthodoxy" and "heresy," Christian leaders nonetheless possessed and transmitted what they considered to be apostolic teachings and/or traditions, which represented what Arland J. Hultgren identified as "normative Christianity." Hultgren summarized early core teachings in this way:

10. Schleier, "Hairesis." See also Simon, "From Greek *Hairesis* to Christian Heresy," 104.

11. Ign. *Trall.* 6. ET from Holmes, *Apostolic Fathers*, 219.

12. Brown, *Heresies*, 4.

1. The God of Israel can be loved and trusted as the Creator of all that is and as benevolent to humanity.

2. Jesus of Nazareth can be trusted as the one sent by God to reveal God and to redeem humanity.

3. In spite of human failure, which would disqualify one from salvation, trust in God's redemptive work in Christ is the way to salvation, which is begun in this life, but completed beyond it.

4. The person saved by faith in God's redemptive work in Christ is expected to care about, indeed love, others and be worthy of their trust.

5. Those who trust in Jesus as revealer of God and redeemer of humanity are expected to live as disciples in a community whose ethos is congruent with the legacy of his life and teaching.

6. Those who live in communities of faith belong to a fellowship that is larger than that provided by the local community, an extended fellowship.[13]

Although these six affirmations are not exclusive to any one Christian writer, they express the key doctrinal statements of the early church in regard to theology, Christology, soteriology, ethics, and ecclesiology. Furthermore, one church father might have differed from another over certain aspects of doctrine, but, overall, "they stand much closer together than either stands with such figures as Marcion, Valentinus, or Montanus."[14]

Alongside such unity in the early church, however, there existed much diversity. While some of that diversity was regarded as illegitimate heresy, some diversity fell within the range of legitimate orthodoxy.[15] H. E. W. Turner described this diversity as "a symphony composed of varied elements rather than a single melodic theme, or a confluence of many tributaries into a single stream rather than a river which pursues its course to the sea without mingling with other waters."[16] These "flex-

13. Hultgren, *Normative Christianity*, 86.

14. Ibid., 87.

15. For discussions of legitimate and illegitimate diversity in the New Testament, see Köstenberger and Kruger, *Heresy of Orthodoxy*, 81–101; and Köstenberger, "Diversity and Unity in the New Testament," 144–58.

16. Turner, *Pattern of Christian Truth*, 9.

ible elements," as Turner called them, operated within the parameters of normative Christianity.

Having explored the issues involved in heresy and orthodoxy as well as in the unity and diversity within orthodoxy, the complex character of early Christianity becomes obvious. As Alister McGrath has noted, "many of those who came to be regarded as heretics were active and committed participants in Christian communities who were genuinely concerned to enable the gospel to be understood and presented faithfully and effectively."[17]

One of the best examples of the complexity of orthodoxy and heresy in early Christianity is the movement known as Montanism. As enigmatic today as it was in the second and third centuries of the Christian era, Montanism has been characterized as a heresy, a schism, and as a movement of renewal and, therefore, serves well as a case study for the complexity of the issues of orthodoxy and heresy in the early church.

Montanism in Asia

Montanism[18] is named after its founder, Montanus, but the term was intended as a slur by the fourth-century bishop, Cyril of Jerusalem (ca. 315–386), who denied to the Montanists their claims to be Christians.[19] Earlier opponents of Montanism referred to it as the Phrygian heresy[20] and its followers as Cataphrygians.[21] Followers of Montanus referred to their movement as the New Prophecy,[22] or simply the Prophecy,[23] and

17. McGrath, *Heresy*, 58.

18. For an expanded discussion about Montanism, see Butler, *New Prophecy and "New Visions,"* 9–43.

19. "And these Montanists are called, although falsely, by our same name, 'Christian'" (Cyril of Jerusalem, *Cat.* 16.8). Unless otherwise indicated all translations of ancient sources in this section are mine.

20. See, for example, Eusebius's anonymous source, hereafter cited as "Anonymous" (Eusebius, *Hist. eccl.* 5.16.1).

21. See, for example, Anti-Phrygian, cited in Epiphanius, *Haer.* 48.12.4; 51.33.3; and Augustine, *Haer.* 26–27.

22. See Serapion's description: ". . . this false order nicknamed the New Prophecy" (Serapion, cited in Eusebius, *Hist. eccl.* 5.19.2). Tertullian also used the term New Prophecy (*nova prophetia*) repeatedly, for example, *Marc.* 3.24.4, 4.22.4; *Resur.* 63.9; and *Jejun.* 1.3.

23. ". . . the Prophecy, so-called by them" (Anonymous, cited in Eusebius, *Hist. eccl.* 5.16.14).

to themselves as the prophets or prophetesses.[24] This self-designation intended to communicate their desire to present a new, fresh word to the larger Christian community. In its place of origin, Asia Minor, its many adherents enthusiastically received the New Prophecy, but it was condemned as a heresy by multiple gatherings of bishops in that region. At first accepted, then rejected by the Roman papacy, it attracted the allegiance of Tertullian, the leading theologian of the West at the turn of the third century.

Little is known about Montanus, the titular head of the movement since extant information about him and the origins of his movement in Asia Minor consists mostly of what was preserved by his contemporary opponents and later heresiologists, especially Eusebius of Caesarea (ca. 265–ca. 340)[25] and Epiphanius of Salamis (ca. 315–ca. 405).[26] Bauer complained that Eusebius and Epiphanius, as representatives and proponents of orthodoxy, resorted to "defamation of the enemy" rather than "proof from scripture" in their attacks on Montanism.[27] The exaggerations of these heresiologists and others in the early church were woven together with facts about Montanist leaders and doctrines to create a tangled web which the contemporary investigator must address in order to unravel the complexity of heresy and orthodoxy in this movement.

Certainly, Montanus was active in Phrygia during the second half of the second century,[28] exercised prophetic gifts, taught a new revelation,

---

24. Trevett, *Montanism*, 2.

25. Eusebius wrote the first edition of *Historia ecclesiastica*, Books 1–7 about 303, using several sources for his sections on Montanism, including an anonymous source usually referred to as "Anonymous" (who wrote ca. 192), Apollonius (who wrote ca. 205), Serapion (who wrote ca. 210), and others. See Tabbernee, *Fake Prophecy and Polluted Sacrament*, 6–7, 47–48, 53–54, 81–82.

26. Epiphanius began *Panarion omnium haeresium*, or *Medicine Chest against All Heresies*, about 375 and completed the section on Montanism about 377. His main source was an early third-century treatise written by an unknown person often referred to as "Anti-Phrygian." Other sources were unidentified books, documents, and oral reports. See Tabbernee, *Fake Prophecy and Polluted Sacrament*, 264–65.

27. Bauer, *Orthodoxy and Heresy*, 145.

28. The date for the beginning of Montanus's prophetic activity is difficult to determine. Eusebius, *Hist. eccl.* 4.27.1; 5.3.4; 5 *preface*; 1.4 placed the date about 171; Epiphanius, *Haer.* 48.1.2 put the date around 157. Most likely, Montanus began prophesying in 157, and the movement spread to Rome by 171. For a full discussion of the issues and possible resolutions, see Barnes, "Chronology of Montanism," 403–8, especially 404n6–10. See also Knox, *Enthusiasm*, 29.

and gathered disciples, including women.[29] Less likely are the pejorative statements made by his detractors, who did not hesitate to resort to demonizing Montanus with false rumors.[30] Jerome (ca. 342–420), for example, claimed that Montanus was "castrated and emasculated" (*abscisum et semivirum*), suggesting that he had formerly served as a priest of Cybele.[31] Eusebius's anonymous source alleged that Montanus was a recent convert but an ambitious preacher, who used spiritual ecstasy, glossolalia, and prophecy to gain fame and followers. This critic went on to claim, in an attempt to connect Montanus to Judas, that the prophet hanged himself.[32]

Montanus quickly attracted the adherence of two "noble and wealthy women," Priscilla and Maximilla, who left their husbands to follow Montanus and who contributed equally to the prophetic activity and promotion of the movement.[33] These female leaders received criticism and harassment on multiple occasions. Apollonius, another of Eusebius's anti-Montanist sources, complained that the women abandoned their husbands and yet Priscilla was awarded the title "virgin." Furthermore, he criticized both of them for receiving gifts of gold, silver, and costly clothing for their ministry.[34] Eusebius's anonymous source heaped the final indignation upon Maximilla when he gossiped, as he had about Montanus, that she hung herself in the manner of the traitor Judas.[35] This same critic slandered a later Montanist leader, Theodotus, alleging that he died miserably when, in a trance, he was raised up and taken into heaven, having entrusted himself to a deceitful spirit, and was hurled to the ground.[36] Bauer was justly critical of the anonymous source for repeating this scandalous rumor: "Just as in the former instance 'the anonymous'

29. de Soyres, *Montanism and the Primitive Church*, 31.

30. Trevett, *Montanism*, 154.

31. Jerome *Ep.* 41.4. See also Tabbernee, *Montanist Inscriptions and Testimonia*, 18–19; and Frend, "Montanism," 27.

32. Even the anonymous source doubted this particularly sordid rumor (Anonymous, cited in Eusebius, *Hist. eccl.* 5.16.13).

33. Jerome, *Ep.* 133.4; Apollonius, cited in Eusebius, *Hist. eccl.* 5.18.3. See also Jensen, *God's Self-Confident Daughters*, 135–36, 173; and Trevett, *Montanism*, 158–62.

34. Apollonius, cited in Eusebius, *Hist. eccl.* 5.18.3–4.

35. Anonymous, cited in Eusebius, *Hist. eccl.* 5.16.13.

36. Anonymous, cited in Eusebius, *Hist. eccl.* 5.16.14–15. See also Tabbernee, *Montanist Inscriptions and Testimonia*, 52–53.

is reminded of the end of the traitor Judas (EH 5.16.13), so may we, with respect to Theodotus, think of the legend of the death of Simon Magus."[37]

By the end of the second century, as the anonymous anti-Montanist looked back on the few decades of this movement, he saw a history of advance by the Phrygian heresy and rejection by the Asian episcopacy: "Those who were faithful in Asia came together many times and in many places for this purpose: they examined the unfamiliar teachings, declared them blasphemous, and rejected the heresy. Thus, at that point, these persons were ousted from the church and ostracized from communion."[38]

This brief sketch of Montanus, his followers, and their opponents demonstrates the following: First, the movement attracted a number of followers in Asia Minor.[39] Second, the New Prophecy developed an organization intended to maintain the movement past its initial leadership. Third, the established church became alarmed by the encroachment of the movement, and the bishops in the region resisted the New Prophecy and, in some cases, rejected it.[40]

The opponents of Montanism found much in the movement to criticize, not only in the Montanists' message but also in their practice. The accusations of the ecclesiastical leadership against the Montanists can be arranged under the following categories: prophetic activity, new revelation, rigoristic novelties, eschatology, and pneumatology.[41]

Prophetic activity, based upon extensive biblical tradition, thrived in the Christian church through the second century.[42] On the one hand, this tradition facilitated the spread of the new prophets' message and ministry. At the same time, however, the growing influence of the clerical hierarchy marginalized and threatened Christian prophecy through an attempt to subject such activity to episcopal control.[43] In this ecclesias-

---

37. Bauer, *Orthodoxy and Heresy*, 138. In Bauer's usage, EH=Eusebius, *Hist. eccl.*

38. Anonymous, cited in Eusebius, *Hist. eccl.* 5.16.10.

39. Bauer, *Orthodoxy and Heresy*, 133–34.

40. For a list of clerical opponents of the New Prophecy, see Tabbernee, *Fake Prophecy and Polluted Sacraments*, 41–42.

41. Tabbernee, *Fake Prophecy and Polluted Sacraments*, 87.

42. The *Didache* 11–13 (ca. 50–ca. 150), included instructions on testing a genuine prophet. Justin Martyr (ca. 100–ca.165), *Dialogue with Trypho* 82, contended that prophetic gifts manifested by the church testified that Christians were the chosen people. Irenaeus (ca. 130–ca. 200), *Haer.* 2.32.4, also reported that some Christians "have foreknowledge of future events and visions and prophetic utterances."

43. Trevett, *Montanism*, 86; Pelikan, *Emergence of the Catholic Tradition*, 99–100; Ash, "Decline of Ecstatic Prophecy," 227–52.

tical environment, the critics of Montanism brought many complaints against what they considered to be "false prophecy" (*pseudopropheteia*).[44] First, Montanist prophecy was false because it was inspired not by the Holy Spirit but by an evil spirit. The anonymous anti-Montanist reported the reaction of the Phrygians who were opposed to Montanus's ecstatic behavior: "But of those who, at that time, heard those counterfeit utterances,[45] some, being offended by one who was possessed and afflicted by a demon, who was under the influence of a deceiving spirit, and who was disturbing the masses, rebuked him and hindered him from babbling, remembering the Lord's distinction and also his warning to be on guard against coming false prophets." Priscilla and Maximilla also were considered victims of "counterfeit" spirits that were "hazardous to their mental health."[46]

On different occasions, Priscilla and Maximilla were subjected to failed attempts at exorcism—the former at the hands of Bishop Sotas of Anchialus, and the latter by two bishops, Zoticus of Cumane and Julian of Apamea.[47] The opinion of the episcopal church was clearly evident that these women's activities were inspired by demonic spirits.[48]

The second complaint against the Montanists' prophetic activities was the manner in which they were carried out—through ecstasy and glossolalia. When Eusebius's anonymous source first described Montanus's extreme ecstatic behavior (*parekstasis*), he protested that it was "in a manner contrary to the tradition and the succession of the church from the beginning."[49] Miltiades, another anti-Montanist polemicist, insisted that the false prophet was carried away by his ecstasy, "beginning out of voluntary stupidity but terminating in involuntary insanity." In contrast, none of the prophets of the old or new covenant were carried away in this

---

44. Anonymous, cited in Eusebius, *Hist. eccl.* 5.16.4; Apollonius, cited in Eusebius, *Hist. eccl.* 5.18.1; Anti-Phrygian, cited in Epiphanius, *Pan.* 48.1.1—48.13.8. See also Tabbernee, *Fake Prophecy and Polluted Sacraments*, 88.

45. Trevett, *Montanism*, 87, translated this phrase "bastard utterances."

46. Anonymous, cited in Eusebius, *Hist. eccl.* 5.16.8.

47. Eusebius, *Hist. eccl.* 5.19.3; 5.18.12.

48. Trevett, *Montanism*, 157–58.

49. Anonymous, cited in Eusebius, *Hist. eccl.* 5.16.7. Tabbernee, *Fake Prophecy and Polluted Sacraments*, 93, explained that "it was the particular form of the ecstatic state, an abnormal or extraordinary ecstasy, which troubled 'catholics,' such as the Anonymous, about Montanist prophecy."

manner.[50] Epiphanius's anti-Phrygian source described Montanist ecstasy as "madness induced through standing outside of sanity." This critic also insisted that true prophets—such as Abraham, Moses, David, Isaiah, Ezekiel, Daniel, David, Peter, Paul, and Agabus—were inspired by the Spirit of Truth and exercised their gifts with their mental faculties active.[51]

Despite these complaints, however, the early church was accustomed to ecstatic utterances under the influence of the Spirit. As Tabbernee pointed out, "Ignatius of Antioch, half a century earlier, had reminded the Philadelphians that he had spoken to them ecstatically 'in a great voice of God' (Ign. *Phld.* 7.1)."[52] Therefore, it was not the passivity of the Montanists' ecstasy that distressed their opponents but their strange behavior and unintelligible speech.[53] Montanus "was swept away by spiritual enthusiasm and also began suddenly to babble and to speak with strange sounds." The two prophetesses, Priscilla and Maximilla, filled with a counterfeit spirit, also began "to babble senselessly, inappropriately, and outlandishly," just like Montanus.[54]

However, Tabbernee suggested, "there is indeed evidence that (at least some of) the non-intelligible aspects of the prophetic utterances of the New Prophets were 'interpreted' by *interpreters*."[55] When Bishop Sotas attempted to exorcise Priscilla, he was prevented by the *hypokritai*, who, instead of "hypocrites" as they are commonly understood, might have been interpreters of the unintelligible portions of the prophetess's speech. Perhaps Themiso and his companions functioned in the same way for Maximilla, whose exorcism they thwarted. If interpreters were included among the community of New Prophets, they could have legitimized the ecstatic as well as the intelligible prophetic activity of the movement.[56]

These two aspects of New Prophecy—the prophetic pronouncements and the dramatic ways in which they were delivered—attracted many followers, who perceived the movement and the accompanying spiritual gifts to be inspired by the Holy Spirit. The anonymous critic, however, along

---

50. Miltiades, cited in Eusebius, *Hist. eccl.* 5.17.2–3.

51. Anti-Phrygian, cited in Epiphanius, *Haer.* 48.4.6. See also Tabbernee, *Fake Prophecy and Polluted Sacraments*, 99.

52. Tabbernee, *Fake Prophecy and Polluted Sacraments*, 93.

53. Ibid., 92–93.

54. Anonymous, cited in Eusebius, *Hist. eccl.* 5.16.7, 9.

55. Tabbernee, *Fake Prophecy and Polluted Sacraments*, 95–96.

56. Ibid., 96. See also 1 Cor 14:5.

with the clergy whom he represented, attributed both the Montanists' behavior and their followers' responses to the devil's deceptiveness.[57]

The new prophets' messages were recorded, collected, and circulated; and, therefore, another, more serious charge was leveled against
the Montanists: that they revered these writings as authoritative, like
those written by the apostles. Another of Eusebius's sources, Apollonius, reported that Themiso, one of the later Montanist leaders, was
imprisoned; bribed his way out; and, emboldened by his status as a
"confessor," composed a general epistle in imitation of the apostle.[58] By
doing so, Apollonius alleged, Themiso blasphemed against the Lord, the
apostles, and the church.

Previous writings of the New Prophets and the authority granted
to them had attracted criticism also from their opponents in the western
church. During the episcopacy of Zephyrinus of Rome (198–217), Gaius,
representing the Roman church, conducted a debate with Proclus, a
leader of the Montanists in Rome. Gaius charged that the Montanists had
elevated their writings to the status of "new scriptures" (*kainas graphas*).[59]
At about this same time, the author of *Refutatio omnium haeresium*[60]
contended that the Montanists possessed numerous writings and used
them to delude their followers, "asserting that they have learned more
through them than from the Law and the Prophets and the Gospels."[61]

The concern of the Roman church regarding the status of the Montanist writings was also made clear in the fragmentary list known as the
Muratorian Canon.[62] This annotated list of writings was begun in the

57. Anonymous, cited in Eusebius, *Hist. eccl.* 5.16.9.

58. Apollonius, cited in Eusebius, *Hist. eccl.* 5.18.5. Perhaps Apollonius referred to
the Apostle John, whose writings were especially dear to the New Prophets.

59. Eusebius, *Hist. eccl.* 6.20.3. Much of the debate centered on apostolic authority
based upon possession of relics: Gaius appealed to the relics of Peter and Paul; Proclus, to those of the apostle John and Philip's daughters (Eusebius, *Hist. eccl.* 2.25.6–7,
3.31.4, 5.24.2–3). William Tabbernee summarized the tension between West and East
with the title of his article, "'Our Trophies are Better than your Trophies.'"

60. For a discussion of the authorship of the *Refutatio omnium haeresium*, see Tabbernee, *Fake Prophecy and Polluted Sacraments*, 73–74.

61. *Refutatio omnium haeresium* 8.19.1. For another, similar claim from this time
period, see Pseudo-Tertullian, *Haer.* 7.2.

62. For a translation of the Muratorian fragment, see Metzger, *Canon of the New
Testament*, 305–7. The Muratorian fragment has been dated as late as the fourth century by Sundberg, "Canon Muratori," 1–41; and Hahneman, *Muratorian Fragment*,
215–18. These arguments have been countered by Ferguson, "Canon Muratori,"
677–83; and Metzger, *Canon of the New Testament*, 193–94.

latter half of the second century and included Christian books that were considered authoritative for the church as well as other sacred writings that were acceptable for edification. At the end of the extant fragment is a list of writings that were rejected, and these include writings by Miltiades, presumably the leader of the Asian Montanists at that time, and by "the Asian founder of the Cataphrygians," Montanus himself.[63] The author of the Muratorian Canon and the Christian community that endorsed the Canon specifically excluded the writings written by the Montanist leaders and held to be sacred by their followers.

The literary activities of the Montanist leaders in themselves were no more unusual than those of accepted leaders such as Clement of Rome, Ignatius, Polycarp, and others who wrote letters to Christian communities. Montanus, Priscilla, Maximilla, and Themiso did not necessarily claim authority for their own writings, although it seems that, based upon the opposition raised by Gaius and the authors of the *Refutatio* and the Muratorian Canon, their followers did. In the Montanists' estimation, the Paraclete provided new revelations to supplement the older, apostolic writings, but the opposition considered such a view to be blasphemous.[64]

Very little of the offensive content of these Montanist writings is known. In the same section of the *Refutatio*, however, the author reports: "They introduce novel fasts, and feasts, and meals of dry food and cabbages, claiming to have been taught (to do so) by the women."[65] In Phrygia, Apollonius also had commented that Montanus had created laws about fasting.[66]

This new practice of fasting and its condemnation also extended to Carthage, where Tertullian picked up the defense of the New Prophecy in his treatise *De jejunio adversus psychicos*. Tertullian contended that the "Psychics," whom he considered to be carnal Christians, did not reject the New Prophets because of their theological heresy but because they observed extra fasts; extended fast-days into the evenings; practiced the eating of dry foods; fasted from juicy meats, fruits, and wine; and abstained from bathing during fasts "in keeping with our dry diet."[67] The Psychics

---

63. Muratorian Fragment 4, trans. Metzger, *Canon of the New Testament*, 307.

64. Tabbernee, *Fake Prophecy and Polluted Sacraments*, 110.

65. *Refutatio omnium haeresium* 8.19.3, trans. Tabbernee, *Fake Prophecy and Polluted Sacraments*, 111.

66. Apollonius, cited in Eusebius, *Hist. eccl.* 5.18.2.

67. Tertullian, *Jejun.* 1.4, trans. Tabbernee, *Fake Prophecy and Polluted Sacraments*, 111.

accused the New Prophets of promoting novelties, but they could not decide whether these new fasts constituted heresy or pseudo-prophecy, only that, either way, the sentence was anathema.[68]

In spite of the opposition's insistence that these fasting practices were innovations, the New Prophets could have provided scriptural support based on Daniel's practice: "I did not eat any tasty food, nor did meat or wine enter my mouth, nor did I use any ointment at all until the entire three weeks were completed . . . I, Daniel, alone saw the vision . . . I fell into a deep sleep on my face, with my face to the ground" (Dan 10:3–9, NASB). Furthermore, the New Prophets could draw inspiration from 4 Ezra, which detailed Ezra's seven-day fast upon the herbs of Ardat before his vision of New Jerusalem.[69] The *Shepherd of Hermas* also linked humility, fasting, and revelation.[70] The New Prophets' advocacy of fasting, therefore, fit the current prophetic pattern.

For these and other reasons, Origen (ca. 185–ca. 253) debated whether the New Prophets' novel teaching about and practice of fasting was "heretical" or "schismatic."[71] As Christine Trevett pointed out, "At first sight it is hard to see what the fuss was about. But of course 'revelation' from a group considered *pseudo*-prophetic would be suspect and the issue of fasts was one of a number which related to the wider question of the role of the Paraclete in continuing revelation . . . Nor would catholics have liked the reminder that their objections to the Prophecy were based not on issues of wrong doctrine . . . but on reaction to a discipline stricter than their own (*De jej.* 1.3)."[72]

In the same context in which Apollonius accused Montanus of inventing new fasts, he also brought up the charge of teaching the dissolution of marriage.[73] Evidently, this charge, though false, was based upon Apollonius's claim that Priscilla and Maximilla abandoned their husbands in order to follow Montanus. Otherwise, there are no indications that Montanists annulled marriages or rejected the institution of marriage, although they may have encouraged celibacy or sexual abstinence

68. Tertullian, *Jejun.* 1.5.

69 Box, *Ezra-Apocalypse*, 213–14.

70 *Herm. Vis.* 2.2, 3.1. See also Trevett, *Montanism*, 107–8.

71. Origen, *Fr. Tit.*, cited in Tabbernee, *Fake Prophecy and Polluted Sacraments*, 111–12.

72. Trevett, *Montanism*, 108–9.

73. Apollonius, cited in Eusebius, *Hist. eccl.* 5.18.2.

in marriage.[74] Priscilla preached that "the holy minister should know sanctity (*sanctimonium*) in order to serve, for purification (*purificantia*) is in harmony . . . and they see visions, and, furthermore, turning their faces down they hear distinct voices that are as beneficial as they are also secret."[75] Sexual abstinence, however, was not unique to Montanism. For example, women of the apocryphal *Acts*, such as Thecla, embraced celibacy and encouraged other women to do the same.[76] As witnessed by the *Shepherd of Hermas*, "some second-century Christians already maintained a life even of married celibacy."[77]

Although the Montanists' emphasis on sexual abstinence, even within marriage, was not unique to that movement, their prohibition of remarriage after the death of a spouse was a novelty that came under criticism. Tertullian was the major opponent to remarriage, or digamy, and he defended his stance against orthodox objections: "If indeed Christ has nullified what Moses decreed . . . Christ will not be considered to have come from another power; why should the Paraclete not also nullify what Paul conceded . . . ?" He continued, "The new law nullified divorce . . . ; the New Prophecy, second marriage."[78] Tertullian, however, may not have been the only Montanist to argue against digamy. Epiphanius's early anti-Phrygian source implied that digamy was broadly prohibited among Montanists: "For they cast out everyone who has united in a second marriage, and they compel everyone not to become united in a second marriage."[79] Whereas the Montanists rejected extremes of sexual asceticism and did not forbid marriage, they did not condone remarriage. They were aware of Paul's strictures concerning marriage and celibacy now that "the time has been shortened" (1 Cor 7:29, NASB). What Paul had issued as an opinion (1 Cor 7:40), the Paraclete codified.[80]

For Montanus, as for Paul, the motivation for more rigoristic Christian conduct, such as celibacy and fasting, arose from heightened expectation of the *parousia*.[81] The eschatological innovation introduced by Montanus

74. Tabbernee, *Fake Prophecy and Polluted Sacraments*, 113.

75. Priscilla, cited in Tertullian, *Exh. Cast.* 10.5.

76. *Acts of Paul and Thecla* 10.15. See also Bauer, *Orthodoxy and Heresy*, 137.

77. Trevett, *Montanism*, citing *Herm. Man.* 2.2.3; 2.3.1; 4.1.1.

78. Tertullian, *Mon.* 14.3–4.

79. Anti-Phrygian, cited in Epiphanius, *Pan.* 48.9.7. See also Jerome, *Ep.* 41.3.

80. Trevett, *Montanism*, 114. See also Butler, *New Prophecy and "New Visions,"* 40.

81. Trevett, *Montanism*, 104–5. Osborn, *Tertullian, First Theologian of the West*, 177, observed that Tertullian's allegiance to Montanism may have intensified his

was that he "named Pepuza and Tymion 'Jerusalem,'[82] even though they were insignificant towns in Phrygia, intending to gather people from everywhere to that place."[83] Evidently, Montanus expected the New Jerusalem to descend in his region and appealed to his followers to join him there in preparation for what he expected to be an imminent event.[84]

William Tabbernee, Peter Lampe, and an international team of archaeologists discovered what they believe to be the location of Pepuza and Tymion in the Karahalli District, Uşak Province, in western Turkey. According to Tabbernee, these towns were located at the northern and southern boundaries of the "ideal 'landing place' for the New Jerusalem. It was flat enough, level enough, and large enough to accommodate the dimensions of the New Jerusalem as described in Revelation 21."[85] He reported that he stood on a nearby mountain, where he envisioned Montanus, looking out over the plain where the heavenly city would descend. Interestingly, he found Pepuza eighty kilometers east of ancient Philadelphia, where the church received Christ's promise as recorded by John the Revelator: "He who overcomes . . . I will write on him the name of My God, and the name of the city of My God, the new Jerusalem, which comes down out of heaven from My God" (Rev 3:12, NASB).[86]

In support of Montanus's expectation, a prophetess delivered the following *logion*: "Having taken the form of a woman, Christ came to me in a radiant garment and placed in me wisdom and revealed to me this: this place [Pepuza] is holy and in this place Jerusalem will come down from heaven."[87] Epiphanius, who preserved this prophecy, could not specify the identity of the Montanist beyond Priscilla or a later and otherwise

---

eschatological expectation, which in turn emphasized the need for the church to purify itself for Christ's return.

82. Scholars who doubt extraordinary eschatological expectations among Montanists include Powell, "Tertullianists and Cataphrygians," 46; Trevett, *Montanism*, 103–5; Jensen, *God's Self-Confident Daughters*, 166; Poirier, "Montanist Pepuza-Jerusalem," 505–7.

83. Apollonius, cited in Eusebius, *Hist. eccl.* 5.18.2.

84. Louth, *History of the Church from Christ to Constantine*, 223n2. See also de Labriolle, *La Crise Montaniste*, 16–7, 487; de Soyres, *Montanism and the Primitive Church*, 77; Schepelern, *Der Montanismus*, 29–30; and Knox, *Enthusiasm*, 38.

85. Tabbernee, "Portals of the Montanist New Jerusalem," 92–93.

86. Tabbernee, *Fake Prophecy and Polluted Sacraments*, 116. See also Trevett, *Montanism*, 23–24.

87. Epiphanius, *Pan.* 49.1.3.

unknown prophetess named Quintilla.[88] If Priscilla was the source, her vision might have been the inspiration for Montanus's expectation for Pepuza and Tymion.[89] More likely, however, the *logion* should be attributed to Quintilla, who, in that case, might have intended to confirm the view that the New Jerusalem would descend at the Montanists' holy site.[90]

The eschatological innovations introduced by the New Prophecy included not only the descent of New Jerusalem at Pepuza and Tymion but also the immediacy of the event. The differences between the New Prophets and the ecclesiastical establishment were made clear in a fragment from *De ecstasi*, preserved by the heresiologist known as Praedestinatus (ca. 440–450), in which Tertullian stated: "Only in this do we disagree . . . that we do not accept second marriages, and we do not reject Montanus' prophecy about imminent judgment (*futuro judicio*)."[91]

The centrality of eschatology to the New Prophets' theology was such that their movement could be described by Nathanael Bonwetsch as "an effort to mold the whole life of the church in conformity to the expectation of the immediate, impending return of Christ, to define the essence of Christianity from this point of view, and to oppose everything by which ecclesiastical conditions should acquire a more permanent structure for the purpose of entering into a longer, historical generation."[92] The opponents of these eschatological expectations, however, in view of the delay of the parousia, had forecast its date further into the future and had relegated the prophetic era further into the past. Furthermore, these critics of Montanism insisted that John the Revelator had delivered the

---

88. Tabbernee, *Fake Prophecy and Polluted Sacraments*, 118, speculated that Quintilla was a late third- or early fourth-century prophetess, who, in that case, might have been a contemporary to Epiphanius.

89. Jensen, *God's Self-Confident Daughters*, 166; Poirier, "Montanist Pepuza-Jerusalem," 495–96n13.

90. Tabbernee, *Fake Prophecy and Polluted Sacraments*, 118.

91. Tertullian, *Ecst. frag.*, cited in Praedestinatus, *Haer.* 1.26. Tabbernee translated *futuro judicio* as "impending judgment" in his unpublished paper, "Montanist Oracles," 21, presented at the Second Century Seminar, Waco, Texas, on 19 February 2004.

92. Bonwetsch, *Die Geschichte des Montanismus*, 139 (my translation). Other scholars who recognized the eschatological emphases of Montanism were Baur, *Church History of the First Three Centuries*, 1:245–48; de Soyres, *Montanism and the Primitive Church*, 77–78; de Labriolle, *La crise montaniste*, 107–8; Schepelern, *Der Montanismus*, 28–33; Klawiter, "Role of Martyrdom and Persecution," 253; and Frend, "Montanism," 26–27.

final, inspired prophecy and that later pseudo-prophets had no right to claim divine inspiration.[93]

In this case, however, the innovation lay with the episcopacy, not the New Prophecy. According to Wilhelm Schepelern, only "a half-century earlier, such a movement [as the New Prophecy] could reckon on ecclesiastical recognition. Between the preaching of judgment by John and that by Montanus, there extended the decisive period of development in ecclesiastical organization and duties, and the free impulses of the Spirit mounted themselves against this authority in vain."[94]

Montanist theology, in general, was not assailed by the opposition. Even the author of *Refutatio*, who otherwise was critical of Montanists, ascribed to the majority of them an orthodox doctrine of the Trinity: "These [Phrygians], in a similar manner to the church, confess God to be the father of the universe and creator of everything and also as many things concerning Christ as the Gospel testifies."[95] He and Pseudo-Tertullian, however, accused a segment of Roman Montanists with Modalistic Monarchianism, the denial of the distinction between the Father and the Son.[96] Outside of this minority of Montanists in Rome, there is no evidence that other Montanists fell into that heresy, and, indeed, there was no inherent connection between Montanism and Monarchianism.[97] In his treatise *Adversus Praxean*, Tertullian refuted the modalism of any wayward members of his sect.[98]

The pneumatology of the Montanists was suspect, perhaps due to Montanus's claims to have a special relationship to the Paraclete and to receive direct spiritual inspiration:[99] "I am the Father and the Son and the Paraclete;"[100] and, elsewhere, "I am the Lord God, the Almighty dwelling in a human."[101] Instead of arrogation of divinity, however, these formulas

93. Pelikan, *Emergence of the Catholic Tradition*, 106. See also Heine, "Role of the Gospel of John," 15.

94. Schepelern, *Der Montanismus*, 162 (my translation). See also Pelikan, *Emergence of the Catholic Tradition*, 107.

95. *Refutatio omnium haeresium* 8.19.2.

96. *Refutatio omnium haeresium* 8.19.3; Pseudo-Tertullian, *Haer.* 7.2.

97. Tabbernee, *Fake Prophecy and Polluted Sacraments*, 119.

98. Pelikan, "Montanism and Its Trinitarian Significance," 102.

99. de Soyres, *Montanism and the Primitive Church*, 58; Tabbernee, *Fake Prophecy and Polluted Sacraments*, 120—21.

100. Didymus, *Trin.* 3.41.

101. Anti-Phrygian, cited in Epiphanius, *Haer.* 48.11.1.

indicated passive instrumentality as a mouthpiece of God, as was clear when Montanus proclaimed: "Behold, the human being is like a lyre, and I fly over him like a pick."[102] Understood in this way, therefore, "it is virtually impossible to believe that Montanus himself or any of his earliest followers actually equated Montanus with the Paraclete, that is with the *Holy Spirit*."[103] For this reason, the New Prophets' pneumatology seems to modern historians to be completely acceptable for the late second and early third centuries.[104] Furthermore, it has been asserted that the Montanist emphasis on the Spirit helped Tertullian to develop and transmit his Trinitarian formula to the church.[105]

Nevertheless, the Council of Iconium (ca. 230–235) condemned the Cataphrygians and commanded that, should any desire to return to the catholic church, they must be re-baptized. The reasoning of those at the council followed two lines: first, because the Cataphrygians do not hold to the true Holy Spirit, they cannot have the Father and the Son; and, second, when asked what Christ they preach, they answer the one who sent the Spirit who speaks through Montanus and Priscilla.[106] Therefore, "although the adherents of the New Prophecy had been baptized in the name of the Father, Son, and Holy Spirit, their erroneous understanding of the Holy Spirit meant, for those at Iconium, that they had not been baptized in the name of the *true* Holy Spirit and, on the above reasoning, they had not been baptized in the name of the *true* Father and Son either. Consequently, all Montanists were 'heretics,' and any Montanist who wished to join the 'catholic' church had to be baptized by 'orthodox' clergy."[107]

As noted, the Council of Iconium was not the first assembly to oppose the New Prophecy, for, according to Eusebius's anonymous source,

---

102. Anti-Phrygian, cited in Epiphanius, *Haer.* 48.4. See also Tabbernee, "'Will the Real Paraclete Please Speak Forth!,'" 105.

103. Tabbernee, *Fake Prophecy and Polluted Sacraments*, 121.

104. For a thorough discussion and defense of the Montanist pneumatology, see Tabbernee, "Catholic-Montanist Conflict," 97–115.

105. Tertullian, *Prax.* 3. See also Pelikan, *Emergence of the Catholic Tradition*, 105: "The early writings of Tertullian tended to stress the Father and the Son at the expense of the Holy Spirit; those which definitely dated from the Montanist period, on the other hand, did contain a more metaphysical doctrine of the 'Trinity' . . . The emphasis in Montanism on the Spirit is the explanation of this shift that suggests itself most insistently." See also Barnes, *Tertullian*, 142; and McGowan, "Tertullian and the 'Heretical' Origins," 456–57.

106. Firmilian to Cyprian, *Ep.* 75.7.3.

107. Tabbernee, *Fake Prophecy and Polluted Sacraments*, 122.

previous gatherings of bishops in the region already had excommuni-cated adherents of this movement. The Asian bishops charged that the sectarians followed a false prophecy, which was inspired by a false spirit, which was conducted in an unacceptable manner, and which introduced novel teachings and practices.[108]

The New Prophets, however, saw the situation and themselves en-tirely differently. These men and women viewed the increase in ecclesi-astical hierarchy as resignation to the delay of Christ's return, and they condemned the resultant decline in eschatological vision and extraordi-nary manifestations of the Spirit. Their goal was to establish a prophetic movement of eschatological and rigorous renewal led by the Holy Spir-it.[109] The result was not a broadly received renewal, as they had hoped, but rejection by the ecclesiastical establishment, which forced the New Prophets into a situation of schismatic sectarianism, at least, in Asia, where the movement began. When the New Prophecy moved west, to North Africa, however, it found a different kind of reception.

The New Prophecy in North Africa

The New Prophecy arrived in North Africa around the turn of the third century and, by the end of the first decade, had attracted its most famous adherent, Tertullian.[110] Tertullian, however, was not the only well-known representative of the New Prophecy in Carthage. Among the Christians in that community were the key players of the *Passion of Perpetua and Felicitas*, including the martyrs and also the unnamed editor of that document. Written shortly after the events that it chronicles, the *Pas-sion* reported the martyrdom of several catechumens and their teacher in Carthage in 203. The *Passion* includes not only an eyewitness account of these Christians' deaths but also the personal diaries of two of them: Perpetua, a young noblewoman; and Saturus, the teacher. This docu-

108. Anonymous, cited in Eusebius, *Hist. eccl.* 5.16.7–10.

109. Klawiter, "New Prophecy in Early Christianity," 20, saw Montanism as a re-form movement: "prophet against bishop, holiness against catholicity, sect against uni-versalism, the free church of the Spirit against the hierarchical, institutional church, and apocalypticism against the desire to become established." See also de Soyres, *Mon-tanism and Primitive Christianity*, 107–9.

110. For more about Tertullian and North African Christianity, see the essay by Al-exander and Smither in this volume. For the influence of Tertullian on North African Montanism, see Butler, "Tertullianism."

ment is one of the most precious to come out of the patristic period, but among its most intriguing features are its many expressions of Montanist thought, practice, and enthusiasm.[111]

Elsewhere, I have examined the *Passion* and found Montanist tenets expressed throughout the document, in both diaries, the account of the martyrdom, and the editorial framework.[112] "The exaltation of the Spirit was systemic in the *Passion* (1.3, 5; 16.1; 21.11); the validity of continuing revelation was asserted by the editor (1.1–5; 21.11); visions were plentiful and available upon demand by the prophets (4.1; 7.2–3); Perpetua's leadership was promoted unabashedly despite her gender; eschatological expectations were expressed by all the participants (1.4; 4.10; 11–13; 17.2); and rigoristic discipline, although not prominent, was present in Saturus' vision (13.6)."[113] If indeed the *Passion* is the work of Montanists, the diaries, if not the entire document, are the oldest, complete expressions of the New Prophecy, predating the Montanist writings of Tertullian.[114]

The relationship between the New Prophecy and the broader Christian community in Carthage was often tense but never strained to the point of excommunication, at least, not in the time of Tertullian and Perpetua. Many of Tertullian's writings paint a picture in which New Prophets worshipped in regular congregations but gathered separately as well to experience and witness charismatic expressions of the Spirit.[115] Douglas Powell deftly termed this practice an *ecclesiola in ecclesia*[116]—a church within a church[117]—and such an arrangement might have been found in any of the five or six house churches that met in Carthage at the turn of the third century, including Perpetua's congregation.[118]

---

111. Bauer, *Orthodoxy and Heresy*, 177–78.

112. Butler, *New Prophecy and "New Visions,"* 58–96.

113. Ibid., 127–28.

114. According to Barnes, *Tertullian*, 47, Tertullian's adherence to Montanism began about 207 or slightly earlier.

115. Tertullian, *An.* 9.4; *Virg.* 17.3.

116. Powell, "Tertullianists and Cataphrygians," 37–38; Trevett, *Montanism*, 74; Tabbernee, *Montanist Inscriptions and Testimonia*, 55.

117. Examples of similar situations in later history are Puritan conventicles, which met separately from the Church of England during the sixteenth and seventeenth centuries; Pietist private Bible studies in the eighteenth and nineteenth centuries; and twentieth-century charismatics, who maintained their memberships in mainline denominations but gathered in groups outside their churches to practice their *charismata*.

118. Tabbernee, "To Pardon or not to Pardon?," 381. See also Heffernan, *Passion of*

In the *Passion*, there is one scene in Saturus's beatific vision (13.1–8) that may depict the relationships of Perpetua and Saturus to the clergy in Carthage. Having completed their martyrdom and having been carried to the gates of a heavenly place, Saturus and Perpetua saw the bishop Optatus and the presbyter Aspasius, standing apart from each other and looking sad. They prostrated themselves before the martyrs and begged them to make peace between them. Nearby angels chided the clergy and told them to discipline their parishioners, who were quarreling among themselves. As the vision ended, the clergy—whether reconciled or not is uncertain—were outside the gates, which were closing while the martyrs were inside, satisfied and happy.

Saturus's account revealed that, at the time of the martyrdom in 203, a division existed in the Carthaginian church and that the martyrs were believed to have the spiritual prerogatives to effect peace. Tabbernee suggested a possible interpretation of this vision:

> The Montanist coloring of the whole *Passion* and the attitudes and practices of some of the martyrs make it possible that the difference of opinion at Carthage was over the New Prophecy. The presbyter Aspasius, described as standing sadly apart from Optatus (*Pass. Perp.* 13.1), may have been the leader of a pro-New Prophecy faction. Perhaps Aspasius had fallen out with his bishop over the New Prophecy. The evidence, however, is not sufficient for certainty about this.[119]

It seems certain, at least, that Saturus and Perpetua were in relationship with both Optatus and Aspasius: "Are you not our bishop and our presbyter?" (*Non tu es papa noster et tu presbyter*). If indeed the martyrs were affiliated with the New Prophecy, that devotion did not separate them from either the bishop or the presbyter.

The editor of the *Passion* was a New Prophet[120] who witnessed the deaths of the Carthaginian martyrs and then preserved Perpetua's diary and Saturus's account of his vision to create this document. This editor raised points of contention that may provide clues to the cause of the di-

---

Perpetua and Felicity, 10.

119. Tabbernee, *Fake Prophecy and Polluted Sacraments*, 63. See also Heffernan, *Passion of Perpetua and Felicity*, 10–15.

120. Even historians who doubt that Perpetua and Saturus were adherents of the New Prophecy recognize that the editor was a Montanist. See, for example, Tilley, "Passion of Perpetua and Felicity," 832–36; Tabbernee, *Fake Prophecy and Polluted Sacraments*, 64.

vision among the Carthaginian Christians. In the preface to the *Passion*, the editor asserted that the church failed to acknowledge contemporary acts of the Holy Spirit and to accord sufficient honor to "new prophecies and new visions" (1.5).[121] In contrast to the more orthodox view of the traditional canon, the editor proposed an early form of the New Prophecy's openness to charismatic, contemporary revelation.[122] In the conclusion, the editor returned to this theme and exclaimed, "Anyone who magnifies and honors and adores [Jesus Christ], certainly ought to read for the edification of the Church these examples that are no less important than the ancient writings. Furthermore, these new deeds of spiritual power may testify to the one and always the same Holy Spirit, who operates even up to this time, and to the omnipotent God the Father and to his Son, our Lord Jesus Christ, to whom is the glory and immeasurable power to the end of the age" (21.11). The Trinitarian formula included in this doxology is orthodox, yet gives priority to the Holy Spirit, as would be customary among the New Prophecy.

The editor, Perpetua, Saturus, and their companions demonstrated many affinities with the New Prophecy, but their adherence to this movement cannot be demonstrated definitely.[123] A consensus, however, has been achieved recently among historians that, in Carthage, those who followed the New Prophecy never separated from the broader church.[124] This coexistence in North Africa is a striking contrast to the conflict in Asia that led to the condemnation of the "Phrygian heresy" and the excommunication of its followers. One possible reason for the different attitudes is that many Montanist traits were "characteristic of African Christianity generally during the second through the fourth centuries."[125] Taking this idea one step further back, perhaps Montanism found adherents among the earliest generations of Christians in North Africa and left "its mark on the North African theology of the Church, its ideas of the

---

121. Tabbernee, *Montanist Inscriptions and Testimonia*, 59.

122. Heffernan, *Passion of Perpetua and Felicity*, 11. Heffernan added that the editor's framework to the *Passion* is the "first textual expression" of the New Prophecy in North Africa.

123. Tabbernee, *Fake Prophecy and Polluted Sacraments*, 64, graciously recognized my attempt to connect the *Passion* to Montanism: "Butler has recently presented the best case made thus far in favor of Perpetua and the others being 'Montanists,' but, in my view, Butler's work only demonstrates a high likelihood that the martyrs could have been adherents of the New Prophecy."

124. Ibid., 65. See also Heffernan, *Passion of Perpetua and Felicity*, 13.

125. Tilley, "Passion of Perpetua and Felicity," 834.

Christian community, and its relations to society, from the beginning to the end of its existence."[126]

Following their martyrdoms, many tributes were accorded to Perpetua, Felicitas, Saturus, and their companions. They were acclaimed as saints; the date of their martyrdom was celebrated; a basilica as well as inscriptions, mosaics, and murals commemorated the martyrs; and sermons memorializing them were preached by North African bishops such as Augustine and Quodvultdeus.[127]

The *Passion* itself was held in high esteem—too high for Cyprian's secretary and biographer Pontius. In his introduction to the *Vita Cypriani*, Pontius admitted that "our predecessors, in honor of martyrdom itself, paid such a great debt of honor to laypeople and catechumens who had achieved martyrdom that they recorded many things about their sufferings. . . ."[128] In Pontius's opinion, the circulation of the *Passion* and the popularity of the lay martyrs eclipsed the acts and deeds of Bishop Cyprian.

Many scholars cite these honors from the Catholic Church as evidence that Perpetua and her companions were not Montanists.[129] Because of the coexistence of the Montanists within the broader church in Carthage, however, these martyrs may have been adherents of the New Prophecy without separating from what later became known as the Catholic Church.[130] As the fame of the martyrs and the influence of the *Passion* spread throughout the church, the ecclesiastical hierarchy ignored or minimized their connection to Montanism.[131]

126. Frend, *Saints and Sinners in the Early Church*, 70–72.

127. Butler, *New Prophecy and "New Visions,"* 97; for a discussion of the sermons, see 107–11. For a discussion and pictures of the inscriptions, mosaics, and murals, see Tabbernee, *Montanist Inscriptions and Testimonia*, 105–16.

128. Pontius, *Vita Cyp.* 1.2. According to Frend, *Donatist Church*, 126n3, Pontius did not name Perpetua and the other martyrs but obviously referred to them in his comment about "laypeople and catechumens."

129. See, for example, Weinrich, *Spirit and Martyrdom*, 228; and Robeck, *Prophecy in Carthage*, 15.

130. Tabbernee, *Fake Prophecy and Polluted Sacraments*, 65.

131. Butler, *New Prophecy and "New Visions,"* 97–111.

The Complexities of Orthodoxy and Heresy in Asian and North African Montanism

The complexities involved in understanding Montanism are evident in a survey of the evaluations of the movement by historians, who have sifted through the scant evidence to arrive at varying conclusions. Montanism, at least as it was expressed in Asia, has been characterized as, among other things, heresy,[132] synthesis with the Phrygian cult of Attis-Cybele,[133] a Jewish-Christian sect,[134] reclamation of primitive Christianity,[135] and a theologically orthodox movement.[136] Moreover, some have called the movement a "schism" but not a "heresy."[137]

Elsewhere, I have argued that if Montanism were anything other than theologically orthodox, it would not have attracted the adherence of Tertullian, who was a committed Christian apologist and polemicist.[138] The rejection of Montanism, therefore, resulted from other issues—not heterodoxy, but heteropraxy; not incorrect doctrines, but unacceptable practices.

Antti Marjanen offered this list of denounced Montanist practices: "the ecstatic nature of its prophecy, the claim of the Montanist prophecy for greater authority than that of the previous apostolic traditions, the visible role women had in the movement, and the salaries the Montanists paid to their spiritual leaders and teacher in Asia Minor, thus shaking the prevailing church-political power structures."[139] Walter Burkhardt

---

132. de Labriolle, *La crise montaniste*, 129–30, 137; Knox, *Enthusiasm*, 25–49.

133. Neander, *General History of the Christian Religion*, 513; Ramsay, *Church in the Roman Empire*, 438; Schepelern, *Der Montanismus*, 122–30, uncovered several parallels between Montanism and the Phrygian cult but concluded that the differences were more significant and that Montanism was an attempt to reclaim primitive Christianity.

134. Ford, "Was Montanism a Jewish-Christian Heresy?" 145–58.

135. de Soyres, *Montanism and Primitive Christianity*, 107–9; Klawiter, "New Prophecy in Early Christianity," 20.

136. Trevett, *Montanism*, 69, 108–9, 146, 155.

137. See Greenslade, "Heresy and Schism," 5. "Here, though it may not have been originally a reaction from institutionalism, Montanism threatened to disrupt the rather authoritarian pattern which was being designed to meet Gnosticism, and to replace it, not by freedom, but by a different authority." Greenslade surmised, "heresy was not the chief issue in the third century," and he continued, "More concentrated attention was given to problems of discipline and, with them, of schism."

138. Butler, "Tertullianism," 41. See also Trevett, *Montanism*, 69.

139. Marjanen, "Montanism," 210. Doctrine and practice can overlap, of course.

would add eschatological expectations to such a list.[140] Tabbernee characterized Montanism as "an innovative prophetic movement intent on bringing Christianity into line with what it believed to be the ultimate ethical revelation of the Holy Spirit through the New Prophets."[141] Trevett concluded that Montanism was forced out of the established church, or seceded from it, because of "that dangerous entity *prophecy*, and this one of a special kind: inapposite, 'untraditional' and incorporating innovatory discipline."[142]

The strongest opposition to Montanism came from the ecclesiastical establishment in Asia. The clergy there felt threatened by this movement that was capable not only of challenging their prerogatives but also of building an organization of its own. In contrast, the broader church in Carthage coexisted relatively peacefully with the New Prophets, who, instead of organizing rival churches, functioned as a "church within a church." The New Prophecy found a receptive audience in the rigorous North African church, noted both as "a church of the martyrs" and "a church of the Spirit."[143] For these reasons, the New Prophecy, although considered a heresy in Asia, could claim in North Africa the adherence of a theologian of the stature of Tertullian and of the heroic martyrs of the *Passion of Perpetua*.

Conclusion

The complexities of the issues of "orthodoxy" and "heresy" are abundantly evident in the history of Montanism. Although the term "orthodoxy" did not come into use until the fourth century, orthodoxy was a force to be reckoned with much earlier. Bauer claimed that what became known as orthodoxy was authoritatively represented by one party within Christianity, centered in Rome, but the episcopal organization in Asia Minor acted with strength against what it perceived to be a heresy. Here again, the term "heresy" is a complex issue. Montanism was called the "Phrygian heresy," but even its opponents admitted that its theology was orthodox. Furthermore, Montanism was forced outside the Asian church but functioned peaceably within the Carthaginian church—evidently, what

140. Burkhardt, "Primitive Montanism," 339–56.

141. Tabbernee, *Fake Prophecy and Polluted Sacraments*, 424.

142. Trevett, *Montanism*, 147.

143. Ibid., 70. See also Frend, "North African Cult of Martyrs," 154.

was considered a heresy in one community was acceptable in another. The complexities involved in the history of Montanism should not necessarily be construed to support the Bauer Thesis, but they do demonstrate the diversity within normative Christianity during its early centuries.

6

Apostolic Tradition and the Rule of Faith in Light of the Bauer Thesis

Bryan M. Litfin

"Truth always comes before the copy. The imitation comes after the reality. It is absolutely ridiculous for heresy to be considered the earlier doctrine."

—TERTULLIAN OF CARTHAGE, *PRESCRIPTION AGAINST HERETICS* 29.5–6

FOR THOSE WHO DISLIKE the so-called Bauer Thesis, the elephant in the room is that the German lexicographer Walter Bauer was correct in certain ways—and this means contemporary proponents of Bauer's ideas such as Elaine Pagels and Bart Ehrman have a valid historical point to make. What is now called "heresy" did precede "orthodoxy" in certain cities or regions within the Roman Empire. Wide diversity of opinion about Jesus existed in the second and third centuries, and a normative form of Christianity had not yet triumphed.

That being said, the eighty years since the 1934 publication of *Orthodoxy and Heresy in Earliest Christianity* have not been kind to Professor Bauer. Reviewers have repeatedly suggested the author ignored evidence that ran counter to his thesis, engaged in special pleading on behalf of the "heretics," and relied far too much on arguments from silence to buttress his points.[1] Yet beyond such methodological critiques, the very infrastructure of Bauer's argument has been dismantled piece by piece. An appendix to the English translation of *Orthodoxy and Heresy* notes its generally positive initial reception on the Continent, yet with numerous rebuttals of specific points. Then in 1954, H. E. W. Turner leveled a much more damaging indictment in his Bampton Lectures at Oxford.[2] Other severe critiques were soon to follow. Daniel J. Harrington summarized the *status quaestionis* as of 1980 by concluding, "The thesis of early Christian diversity is well established . . . but Bauer's reconstruction of how orthodoxy triumphed remains questionable."[3] Likewise, Thomas A. Robinson's detailed and comprehensive monograph takes *Orthodoxy and Heresy* to task, ending with the damning conclusion, "The Bauer Thesis simply does not work for the area from which we have extensive and relevant data."[4] Bauer's hypothesis is "seriously flawed"; it must be regarded with "suspicion" and "extreme caution"; and it is a "failure" in significant respects.[5] Further studies appearing more recently have continued to uphold this critical assessment—including the present work.[6]

Nevertheless, even if numerous pieces of Bauer's argument have been called into question, the general thesis has been allowed to stand in some scholarly circles. Helmut Koester of Harvard Divinity School is one of the main figures responsible for the wide dissemination of the Bauer Thesis, along with his doctoral student Elaine Pagels, who went on to become a fine scholar in her own right. Pagels's aptitude for popular presentations of the relevant issues (a skill shared by Bart Ehrman) has helped a form of the Bauer Thesis attain the elusive aura of a reigning paradigm, despite the many scholarly critiques leveled against it.

So how does such a widely-criticized hypothesis still have explanatory power? In part it is because, as was noted above, Bauer's general point about diversity was correct. A great variety of what we might call

1. The opening essay of this volume by Rodney Decker adequately surveys the negative scholarly reception of Bauer. Only some of the more significant critiques are mentioned here.

2. Turner, *Pattern of Christian Truth.*

3. Harrington, "Reception," 297–98.

4. Robinson, *Bauer Thesis Examined,* 204.

5. Ibid.

6. Three recent critiques of the Bauer Thesis in its contemporary incarnation are Jenkins, *Hidden Gospels*; Bock, *Missing Gospels*; and Köstenberger and Kruger, *Heresy of Orthodoxy.*

"Jesus-Religions" existed in the second and third centuries. Many groups claimed to own the legacy of Jesus, considering their religious ideas true and their competitors as somehow deficient. The question, then, is not whether numerous competing Jesus-Religions existed in the ancient period, but whether we ought to call *all* these religious perspectives "Christianity." Is expressing an interest in the life and teachings of Jesus sufficient to be designated Christian? Can one simply claim that title for oneself with no regard for what the term originally meant? The present chapter will argue no. Instead, we ought to examine the historical evidence to determine whether any strands among the second or third century Jesus-Religions more faithfully represented the earliest known layers of Christian belief.

To accomplish such a task, two possible approaches could be used. One would be to identify agreement between certain Jesus-Religions and the man Jesus of Nazareth himself. If the teachings of the historical Jesus were taken as a baseline of true Christianity, we could then examine later documents to search for ideas that cohere with his original message. This is not, however, my proposed task. Instead I will investigate what has been called the "apostolic kerygma"—the preaching of the early church. Whether or not the kerygma was a faithful reproduction of Jesus's teaching is beside the point for my present argument. It is still the earliest evidence for any type of Jesus-Religion that followed in the wake of his historical life. When we inquire behind the earliest surviving Christian writings—which most scholars agree are found in the New Testament—what do we discover? What types of ideas circulated among the followers of Jesus in the AD 30s or 40s, to be recorded later by figures such as Paul of Tarsus in the 50s, or the compiler of the sermonic material attributed to Peter in the book of Acts? As we consider this question, we must also ask: Did conflicting ideas exist side-by-side? And if so, were they merely situational expressions of the same basic confession, or were the proclamations fundamentally irreconcilable?

An investigation into the most primitive layer of Christian beginnings is a task Walter Bauer did not take up. The bulk of his evidence comes from the second through fifth centuries. Among the earliest historical documents Bauer mentions are the letters of Ignatius of Antioch, the letter of "Clement" to the Corinthians, and the "anti-heretical" writings in the New Testament (which are, to Bauer, of such unknowable provenance as to be nearly useless).[7] Yet Bauer's approach here is problematic; for even if the provenance and origins of some canonical documents like Jude or 2 Peter are indeed difficult to establish, the accepted writings of Paul surely are not. Solid dating and the historical occasion can be determined for much of the Pauline corpus, and this is generally true for the Synoptics and Acts as well.[8] Taken together, these texts preserve very primitive confessional material. Therefore they are our best sources for teasing out the kerygma that was proclaimed in the decades immediately after Jesus. From an objective historical point of view, this is the most plausible way to establish how "Christianity" should be defined. What was the earliest confession about Jesus of Nazareth?

Bauer was criticized for ignoring the development of primitive Christian creeds.[9] Perhaps the person most acutely aware of this shortcoming was the man who took the time to bridge the gap between the apostolic age and the place where Bauer's evidence begins: James D. G. Dunn in his *Unity and Diversity in the New Testament*. Originally published in 1977, and released in a third edition in 2006, Dunn's book intentionally sets out to determine whether the Bauer Thesis can be applied to the first-century situation.[10] If Dunn concludes that the evidence points to massive and irreconcilable diversity within earliest Christianity, Bauer's hypothesis will not only have been sustained, it will have been taken back to its logical starting point. It would be proven that ever since the beginning, there was no such thing as an "original" Christian message. However, what if a unifying core united the diverse preaching from the outset? Should not that core be taken as the essence of what we mean by the word "Christianity"? As one can immediately determine from Dunn's book title, we discover

7. "As we turn to our task, the New Testament seems to be both too unproductive and too much disputed to be able to serve as a point of departure. The majority of its anti-heretical writings cannot be arranged with confidence either chronologically or geographically; nor can the more precise circumstances of their origin be determined with sufficient precision. It is advisable, therefore, first of all to interrogate other sources concerning the relationship of orthodoxy and heresy . . ." Bauer, *Orthodoxy and Heresy*, xxv.

8. The redactional histories of the Synoptic Gospels and Acts are much debated, of course. Yet most scholars would agree these works record some of the earliest traditions about Jesus available to us today.

9. The editors of the English translation of *Orthodoxy and Heresy* point out that "several reviewers regretted Bauer's failure to discuss the origin and development of the early Christian *regula fidei*, which certainly deserves treatment . . ." (Bauer, *Orthodoxy and Heresy*, 316).

10. Dunn, *Unity and Diversity*, 3–6.

both unity and diversity in the ancient church. Yet the exact meaning of these terms must be unpacked in light of the Bauer Thesis.

In the end, what do I hope to prove? My contention is that when we examine the second- and third-century orthodox *regula fidei*,[11] we find it coheres with the earliest available creedal material to be found in (or discerned behind) the New Testament—which is the most historically-valid baseline for defining the Christian religion, quite apart from any spiritual or canonical value assigned to the Bible. We will discover a set of ideas proclaimed about Jesus of Nazareth that was more widely-accepted, more Judean in provenance, and more likely to be original, than any other set of beliefs about which we have the means to learn. Even if this core confession displayed substantial diversity in its details or modes of expression, the main ideas were recognizably coherent. Given this state of the evidence, it makes the most sense to consider such kerygmatic material as central or normative—while not denying it competed against divergent proclamations about Jesus even in the first century. As we move into the second and third centuries, we find that the orthodox *regula fidei* expresses marked continuity with the reconstructed apostolic preaching.[12] The Rule of Faith proclaimed the same basic message as the earliest kerygma. That being the case, there is no good reason to designate other Jesus-Religions as "Christianity," except by a definition that stretches the word beyond reasonable limits.

In Search of the Apostolic Kerygma

A frequent starting point in the study of the primitive confessional material behind the New Testament is the work of the Welsh scholar Charles H. Dodd (1884–1973) entitled *The Apostolic Preaching and Its Developments*. The book was based on three lectures given at King's College,

11. The term *regula fidei*, or "Rule of Faith" (also known as the "Rule of Truth," the "Ecclesiastical Rule," etc.) refers to abbreviated summaries of Christian doctrine taught to catechumens seeking baptism. Eventually the Rule was incorporated into the baptismal rite as a fixed creed. Polemical writers frequently quoted the Rule when they wanted to define their essential beliefs, and some church fathers also used it as an exegetical norm—a useful synopsis of the overarching Christian story found in the Scriptures. See Hartog, "'Rule of Faith.'"

12. "Not only was the content of [the Rule of Faith], in all essentials, foreshadowed by the 'pattern of teaching' accepted in the apostolic Church, but its characteristic lineaments and outline found their prototypes in the confessions and credal summaries contained in the New Testament documents" (Kelly, *Early Christian Creeds*, 29).

London, in 1935. Dodd begins with the earliest Christian writer whose works are extant, the Apostle Paul. "The Pauline *kerygma*," Dodd claims, "is a proclamation of the facts of the death and resurrection of Christ in an eschatological setting which gives significance to the facts."[13] The Christ-event was the fulfillment of Old Testament prophecy, or in Paul's language, it happened "according to the scriptures."[14] Dodd argues that this message of good news was received by Paul as early as seven years after the death of Jesus.[15] It was not, therefore, a Pauline invention, but reflected the broader proclamation of the Jerusalem church as described in the book of Acts. These two proclamations (Pauline and Jerusalem) are substantially the same,[16] and the terminology of both is squarely lodged in the "traditional eschatology of Judaism."[17] Later on, the primitive confession was adapted by the Johannine community to take on a more mystical tone. Yet Dodd contends there was a "close affinity" between the Fourth Gospel and the apostolic preaching.[18] He concludes that while the New Testament displays an "immense range of variety in the interpretation that is given to the kerygma," nevertheless, "in all such interpretation the essential elements of the original kerygma are steadily kept in view."[19]

For the record, let us list Dodd's reconstruction of the Pauline message:

- The prophecies are fulfilled, and the New Age is inaugurated by the coming of Christ.

- He was born of the seed of David.

- He died according to the Scriptures, to deliver us out of the present evil age.

- He was buried.

- He rose on the third day according to the Scriptures.

---

13. Dodd, *Apostolic Preaching*, 13.

14. 1 Cor 15:3.

15. Dodd, *Apostolic Preaching*, 16.

16. Ibid., 27. Dodd notes Paul did not emphasize the ministry of Jesus like the Jerusalem church did. Furthermore, three items appear in Paul but not the Jerusalem kerygma: Jesus as the Son of God, Jesus's death "for our sins," and the exalted Christ's ministry of intercession (ibid., 25).

17. Ibid., 36.

18. Ibid., 69.

19. Ibid., 74.

- He is exalted at the right hand of God, as Son of God and Lord of the quick and dead.

- He will come again as Judge and Saviour of men.[20]

Similarly, the Jerusalem church proclaimed:

- The age of fulfillment has dawned.

- This has taken place through the ministry, death, and resurrection of Jesus, who is of Davidic descent.

- By virtue of the resurrection, Jesus has been exalted at the right hand of God as Messianic head of the new Israel.

- The Holy Spirit in the Church is the sign of Christ's present power and glory.

- The Messianic Age will shortly reach its consummation in the return of Christ.

- The faithful should repent, receiving forgiveness, the Holy Spirit, and the promise of salvation.[21]

How did Dodd's conclusions fare in subsequent decades? Not a few later scholars identified similar outlines for the apostolic kerygma. One of the finest books ever written about ancient confessional material was J. N. D. Kelly's *Early Christian Creeds*. In this very thorough work, the author praised Dodd's conclusions as "hardly [able to] be bettered."[22] Kelly's only real criticism was that Dodd, with his emphasis on Christ-centered preaching, tended to overlook the early church's confession of the one God as the Father and Creator. This central belief, which was received from Judaism, sometimes appeared alongside Christ-kerygma and the promise of the Spirit to give the primitive confession a triadic or proto-Trinitarian orientation. Yet trifold confessions were not the only type to be found. One-clause (Christological) and two-clause (Father and Lord Jesus) formulations existed alongside the triadic pattern. Bearing this in mind, Kelly concludes: "That the Church in the apostolic age possessed a creed in the broad sense of a recognized body of teaching may be accepted as demonstrated fact. But it is permissible to take a further step. There is plenty of evidence in the New Testament to show that the faith

20. Ibid., 17.

21. Ibid., 21–23.

22. Kelly, *Early Christian Creeds*, 12.

was already beginning to harden into conventional summaries. Creeds in the true meaning of the word were yet to come, but the movement toward formulation and fixity was under way."[23]

Kelly's words "plenty of evidence" are absolutely correct.[24] The sources reveal that in the mid-first century, a Jerusalem-based church (with connections to communities in the Diaspora) possessed a clear and unified set of ideas about Jesus, ideas that were squarely in line with Jewish beliefs and expectations at the time. This primitive confession—centered on the life, death, resurrection, and divine exaltation of the man from Nazareth—is discovered throughout the earliest strata of texts that compose the New Testament (i.e., the undisputed Pauline epistles and the sermonic material in Acts). The core confession is fleshed out even further in the Synoptic Gospels, and can likewise be found in documents such as the Johannine texts, the Pastoral and Petrine Epistles, and Hebrews. This is our earliest secure attestation of any sort of Jesus-Religion in the ancient world.[25]

23. Ibid., 13.

24. For an enumeration of the extensive creedal material in the New Testament, see ibid., 14–23.

25. Some scholars argue that redactional layers within noncanonical Gospels (including second-century gnostic texts) reveal underlying Jesus traditions that are as early as, or earlier than, the material in the canonical Gospels. For example, see John Dominic Crossan, *Four Other Gospels*; or Helmut Koester, *Ancient Christian Gospels* and *From Jesus to the Gospels*. The one document outside the New Testament that is most often said to attest an alternate form of Christian belief in the middle decades of the first century is the Gospel of Thomas. The extant text is from the fourth century, though it probably reproduces a second-century original. Other contenders for early evidence are the *Gospel of Peter*, the *Dialogue of the Savior*, the *Egerton Gospel*, and the *Apocryphon of James*. The final analysis of no less a scholar than N. T. Wright concludes: "Attempts to postulate early (in some cases very early) versions of some of the gnostic texts such as 'Thomas' and 'Peter' have not commanded much general assent outside a vocal North American minority" (Wright, *Judas*, 77). See also Perrin, *Thomas*.

For the purposes of the present study, we will simply point out that the first-century documentary evidence for alternate "Christianities" is theoretical and debatable, rendering it evidentially weak. We possess few relevant texts, and to them we must apply very tenuous and subjective hypotheses about redaction. That is to say, we do not possess any independent versions of Q-Thomas, so whatever is postulated about such materials—or the communities that may have produced them—is highly speculative by default. The apostolic kerygma of the proto-orthodox is far better attested as a historical reality in the most primitive period. As Ehrman acknowledges, "the noncanonical Gospels are of greater importance for understanding the diversity of Christianity in the second and third and later centuries than for knowing about the

At the risk of piling on evidence to prove a point already established, let us note a few other important creedal studies. Oscar Cullmann wrote in 1943 that the essence of the earliest Christian confessions was the proclamation, *Kyrios Christos*. He argues, "the divine Sonship of Jesus Christ and His elevation to the dignity of *Kyrios*, as consequence of His death and resurrection, are the two essential elements in the majority of the confessions of the first century."[26] Similarly, Vernon Neufeld identifies two central elements in the early *homologia*: the naming of Jesus who lived and died in the course of history, and the ascription of a title that identifies his uniqueness, such as Christ, Lord, or Son of God.[27] The disciples' initial conviction that their teacher was the Messiah expanded after the first Easter, so that to confess Jesus as the Christ meant to acclaim the one who suffered death as having experienced resurrection.[28] Although the maturing of theological convictions, as well as conflicts with alternate messages, led to further elaboration upon the primitive confession, the core idea remained constant: the Jesus who lived in history had gained new authority by virtue of his resurrection. Very quickly he came to be accepted as the unique Son of the Father, the only mediator between God and man.[29]

Along these same lines, Frederick Danker, one of the editors of the English edition of Bauer's Greek lexicon, outlines the primitive Christian confession as follows: One God; Jesus is the Christ; Jesus is the Son of God; Jesus is Lord; Jesus Died and Rose; Jesus is Savior. Danker concludes that the earliest church was not characterized by fixed creeds but Spirit-inspired creativity of expression. Nevertheless, "A consistent accent on Jesus Christ lent unity to the greatly varied creedal expression found in the New Testament. And to round out this list of creedal experts, we may consider the monumental work of Jaroslav Pelikan, who suggests the painstaking efforts of New Testament scholars to reproduce the early kerygma has led to the recognition of the following elements:

- The one true God, Creator of heaven and earth;

---

writings of the earliest Christians" (Ehrman, *New Testament*, 192). A rebuttal of the thesis that the gnostic Gospels (and/or the hypothetical layers of a reconstructed Q) provide valid evidence for an alternate history of the earliest Jesus movement has been offered by Philip Jenkins, *Hidden Gospels*.

26. Cullmann, *Earliest Christian Confessions*, 57.

27. Neufeld, *Earliest Christian Confessions*, 140–41.

28. Ibid., 143.

29. Ibid., 143–44.

- His only Son, born of the Virgin Mary, divinely powerful in word and deed, crucified under Pontius Pilate, raised from the dead, and returning to judge the world;

- The Holy Spirit, who inspired the ancient prophets and whose breath is the life of the holy church.[30]

In a sourcebook of virtually all available confessional material, Pelikan joins with Valerie Hotchkiss to offer a list of "Creedal Statements in the New Testament" containing eighteen biblical passages.[31] We are struck once again by the amplitude of the historical evidence that attests to the basic outlines of the first-century Christian proclamation. The original message clearly centered on the death and resurrection of Jesus—the Son of God, the Lord, and the anointed one of Israel.

Interestingly, one of the leading contemporary advocates of the Bauer Thesis has recently come to a similar conclusion. Bart D. Ehrman's latest book, *How Jesus Became God: The Exaltation of a Jewish Preacher from Galilee*, argues that the earliest form of Christian proclamation was grounded in the belief that God had raised Jesus from the dead and elevated him to divine status.[32] Ehrman does not think every Christian group held precisely the same conceptualization of Jesus's divinity.[33] Nevertheless, the core belief of the earliest Christians was that the man Jesus of Nazareth had appeared alive after death and was therefore recognized as the Christ of God who brings salvation to humankind. How early do we find this proclamation about Jesus? Ehrman asserts, "The first who came to this belief were his own remaining disciples—or at least some of them—and possibly others of his followers from Galilee, including Mary

---

30. Pelikan, *Credo*, 377–78.

31. Matt 28:19; Acts 8:36–37; Rom 1:3–4; 4:24; 8:34; 1 Cor 8:6; 15:3–6; 2 Cor 13:13 [*sic*, v. 14]; Eph 4:4–6; Phil 2:5–11; Col 1:12–20; 1 Tim 2:5–6; 3:16; 6:12–16; 2 Tim 4:1–2; Heb 6:1–2; 1 Pet 3:18–22; 1 John 4:2 (Pelikan and Hotchkiss, *Creeds & Confessions*, 33–36).

32. "There can be no doubt, historically, that some of Jesus's followers came to believe he was raised from the dead—no doubt whatsoever. This is how Christianity started" (Ehrman, *How Jesus Became God*, 174).

33. Ehrman stresses, ". . . whenever someone claims that Jesus is God, it is important to ask: God *in what sense*?" (ibid., 210). For his part, Ehrman focuses upon an early "adoptionist" exaltation Christology, and he maintains that the Apostle Paul understood Christ to be an incarnate angel (ibid., 230–82, esp. 232, 252). Contrast Tilling, "Problems"; Tilling, "Misreading Paul's Christology."

Magdalene and some other women."[34] Furthermore, Ehrman professes to know this for precisely the reason I am arguing here: that it was the substance of the pre-Pauline apostolic kerygma as reconstructed from various New Testament documents. Although this is the earliest surviving evidence that attests to the original essence of Christian belief, Ehrman imagines that if a gospel had been written in the years immediately after the life of Jesus, it would have concluded with the "great highlight" that even after his crucifixion by Pontius Pilate, "his story was not yet over."[35] The first and most basic gospel proclamation was that Jesus "had appeared to his disciples, alive again," because "God had raised him, bodily, from the dead,"[36] then "exalted him up to heaven as his own Son, to sit on a throne at God's right hand, to rule as the messiah of Israel and the Lord of all, until he comes back as the cosmic judge of the earth, very soon."[37] Scholars will no doubt want to debate some of Ehrman's conclusions in his new book; indeed, a companion volume offering rebuttal was released at the same time by a subsidiary publisher.[38] Even so, for our present purposes we should not miss that Ehrman is the most recent example in a long list of scholars who understand that the earliest Christian proclamation centered on the resurrection and divine exaltation of the Lord Jesus Christ.

What conclusions, then, can be drawn about the apostolic kerygma? It is an unassailable fact that in the pre-Pauline period, a community of Jews emerged with a specific set of ideas about Jesus of Nazareth.[39] At first

34. Ehrman, *How Jesus Became God*, 213.

35. Ibid., 245–46.

36. Ehrman notes, "It is striking, and frequently overlooked by casual observers of the early Christian tradition, that even though it was a universal belief among the first Christians that Jesus had been raised from the dead, there was not a uniformity of belief concerning what, exactly, 'raised from the dead' meant. In particular, early Christians had long and heated debates about the nature of the resurrection—specifically, the nature of the resurrected body" (ibid., 175). Regarding his own views, Ehrman states, "As an agnostic, I personally do not believe Jesus was raised from the dead" (ibid., 187).

37. Ibid., 246.

38. Bird et al., *How God Became Jesus*.

39. On the subject of Christian beliefs before the Pauline epistles were written, see Hunter, *Paul and His Predecessors*. Hunter claims the *paradosis* recorded in 1 Cor 15:3–5—that Christ died for sins according to the scriptures and was raised on the third day—goes back to the first decade after the crucifixion. As such, it is the oldest Christian "document" we possess (108–9). Hunter's general thesis is that Paul's form of Christianity evidences great continuity with the church that emerged in the immediate

they were centered in Jerusalem, but they soon established connections with other communities that sprang up within the Diaspora. Gentiles also began to be incorporated into this system of belief. Though the core confession of these first believers focused on Jesus, their convictions were sometimes expressed in a binitarian or Trinitarian structure that included the one God and/or his Spirit. Without question, the creator God was understood as the God of Abraham, Isaac, and Jacob—the LORD, the Jewish God described in the Hebrew scriptures. Jesus of Nazareth preached and worked miracles in this God's power, then died on a Roman cross and was buried. When God raised him from the dead, he was recognized or confirmed as "Christ" or "Lord" or "Son of God" in fulfillment of Israel's hopes. He is now exalted to the Father's right hand, and will soon return to judge evil and usher in an age of blessing. Humans everywhere are called to believe in this crucified and resurrected savior, receiving the Spirit of God. This is the gospel of the first Christians.[40]

Nevertheless, while this sort of Christianity undoubtedly existed in the first century AD, we may still ask: Exactly how unified was this religion? Did it manage to proclaim an integrated message? Or did its cacophony of voices produce nothing but evangelistic incoherence? And

---

years after Jesus's life. Yet because the Apostle traveled widely, it is not always clear whether his traditional material was derived from a Jerusalem (Aramaic-speaking) or Diaspora (Greek-speaking) provenance. Another scholar who addresses this issue, John Kloppenborg, concludes from the evidence of 1 Cor 15 that the Christian proclamation originally emerged from the Palestinian church but took its final form in the Jewish-Hellenistic milieu (Kloppenborg, "Analysis of the Pre-Pauline Formula," 351–67). Thus, both of these scholars are in substantial agreement about the unity of the earliest preaching. Despite the Christians' severe differences on matters pertaining to the Jewish law, a central kerygma was shared in common by the Jerusalem church and the Pauline churches of the Diaspora. That is to say, Paul's message was, at its most basic level, the same as what Jesus's own disciples proclaimed after Pentecost: that Jesus died and rose again, becoming Lord and Christ.

40. My conclusions in this chapter cohere with the findings of two important studies of early Christian devotion to Jesus. Larry Hurtado claims that "devotion to Jesus as divine erupted suddenly and quickly, not gradually and late, among first-century circles of followers. More specifically, the origins lie in Jewish Christian circles of the earliest years" (Hurtado, *Lord Jesus Christ*, 650). Likewise, Richard Bauckham writes, "In the earliest Christian [i.e., Palestinian Jewish] community, Jesus was already understood to be risen and exalted to God's right hand in heaven, active in the community by his Spirit, and coming in the future as ruler and judge of the world" (Bauckham, *Jesus and the God of Israel*, 128). Although Hurtado's and Bauckham's investigations do not focus on creeds *per se*, they do support my essential contention that worship of the risen and exalted Jesus in a Jewish context was the first form of Christian proclamation.

perhaps most intriguing of all, we must consider: How early did other forms of Jesus-Religion co-exist with this one?

Unity and Diversity in the First Century

As we noted above, Walter Bauer's book *Orthodoxy and Heresy* does not make any claims about the pre-Pauline period. Occasionally Bauer presents evidence from the very end of the first century, but he never tries to inquire into the immediate decades after Jesus's life.[41] The author contends that widespread "heresy" existed in places such as Edessa, Egypt, Asia Minor, and Greece during the second century and beyond. Eventually the Roman church defeated its competitors by claiming the mantle of original orthodoxy through polemical literature and power politics. In this process, the fourth-century revisionism of Eusebius loomed large. Walter Bauer was primarily interested in showing how the diversity that existed in the second century disappeared (or was vanquished) as one particular type of belief came to predominate.

However, scholars after Bauer sought to apply his thesis to the New Testament period. Helmut Koester attempted this task in a 1965 article in *Harvard Theological Review*.[42] He judged the conclusions of Bauer's "brilliant monograph" to be "convincingly" established and "essentially right."[43] However, since "the apostolic age is seldom considered in Walter Bauer's study," Koester proposed to do so in his essay.[44] His fundamental contention was "Christian movements that were later condemned as heretical can claim genuine apostolic origin."[45] Of course, Koester was obliged to acknowledge that his "sketch must remain both hypothetical and fragmentary."[46] What he basically succeeded in proving is that there was widespread theological warfare happening in the first century. Opponents of the New Testament authors can be discerned everywhere in their writings, and the Gospel of Thomas may provide additional evi-

41. "The essential object of our investigation . . . has been the approximately one hundred years that follow the conclusion of the apostolic age" (Bauer, *Orthodoxy and Heresy*, 130).

42. Koester, "Gnomai Diaphoroi," republished as a contribution to Robinson and Koester, *Trajectories through Early Christianity*.

43. Koester, "Gnomai Diaphoroi," 114.

44. Ibid., 119.

45. Ibid., 115.

46. Ibid., 119.

dence for vigorous early dispute. In other words, the canonical authors of Scripture faced competition for the legacy of Jesus.

About a decade after Koester's article appeared, the full extent of this intellectual wrangling—now going under the friendlier title of "diversity"—became even more clear. James Dunn's *Unity and Diversity in the New Testament* (1977), a seminal work on early Christian origins, provides a comprehensive look at the issues raised by Bauer. For many, Dunn's name is associated with the New Perspective on Paul, a term he is credited with coining in his 1982 Manson Memorial Lecture at Manchester.[47] But in *Unity and Diversity*, Dunn has much more than Pauline theology under his microscope. Several of the book's topics are relevant to the present study: the nature of primitive Christian confessions; early Christological beliefs; and the origins of Gnosticism. Dunn's conclusions about each of these topics will be examined in turn.

In a chapter entitled "Kerygma or Kerygmata?" Dunn argues that the early Christians did not possess one unvarying message, but several versions of a central proclamation.[48] He begins his investigation where our chapter did as well—with C. H. Dodd—but suggests Dodd was too quick to speak of a single kerygma, as if there were one gospel message upon which all believers were agreed. After examining the preaching of Jesus, Acts, the Apostle Paul, and John the evangelist, Dunn concludes we can only speak of primitive *kerygmata* in the plural. And yet, he suggests, a core confession bound the apostolic proclamation together. It contained three elements: the risen, exalted Jesus; the call for faith in this Jesus; and the promise of a benefit offered through him, such as the Holy Spirit, eternal life, forgiveness of sin, union with Christ, etc.[49] While this confession united the earliest believers, they voiced the message in unique ways when the actual moment of proclamation arrived. Differing implications were highlighted as the word was preached. Therefore, situational fluidity characterized the gospel in the act of its announcement.

---

47. Dunn, "New Perspective on Paul." The insights of the New Perspective are beyond the scope of this chapter, yet further investigation would be relevant and illuminating. To the extent that the Apostle Paul's message is understood to be squarely rooted in first-century Palestinian Judaism, it would bolster the argument that the Pauline kerygma bears a tighter connection to the proclamation of Jesus himself, or to Jesus's circle of disciples, than, say, esoteric Gnosticism could claim.

48. Dunn, *Unity and Diversity*, 11–33.

49. Ibid., 30–31.

Building on the notion of situational *kerygmata*, Dunn points out in his chapter on "Primitive Confessional Formulae" that different types of Christians confessed Jesus in different ways. Dunn writes,

> We have uncovered no single, final confession appropriate to all circumstances and times. Any attempt to find a single, primitive confession will almost certainly fail. Our investigation has revealed at least three confessions, all of which deserve the epithet, 'basic and primitive.' . . . [W]e may say that 'Jesus is the Messiah' appears to have been the chief confession of Palestinian Jewish Christians, 'Jesus is the Son of God' of Hellenistic Jewish Christians, 'Jesus is Lord' of Gentile Christians.[50]

Though these three confessions were each meaningful in their respective communities, they made little sense in another setting, so they must be identified as distinct.[51]

What can be said by way of assessment at this point? The above survey of creedal studies has already shown that not everyone shares Dunn's reticence when it comes to identifying a full confessional proclamation in the earliest period. On the contrary, many scholars have felt confident in outlining the basic contours of the apostolic kerygma with more precision and detail than Dunn is willing to acknowledge.[52] But even assuming Dunn is correct that the primitive *kerygmata* varied according to the situation, let us not overlook the fact that the proclamations he has identified—Jesus as Messiah, Son of God, and Lord—all reflect what the catholic Christians will come to embrace as sound doctrine. In other words, these *kerygmata* are compatible with the orthodox view that sees Jesus as the crucified, risen, exalted Christ. Let us grant that

50. Ibid., 61.

51. Dunn certainly highlights the distinctness of the *kerygmata*, even calling them "incompatible" (27, 33). Yet let us keep in mind D. A. Carson's rejoinder to Dunn that the diversity evident in the New Testament often reflects either the "diverse pastoral concerns" or the "diverse personal interests and idiosyncratic styles of the individual writers," with "no implications whatsoever of a different credal structure" (Carson, "Unity and Diversity," 86–90).

52. In addition to the above-mentioned studies, we can note the two-part attempt of Eugene Lemcio to "offer evidence that, contrary to the prevailing view, there is a central, discrete kerygmatic core that integrates the manifold plurality of the New Testament" (Lemcio, "Unifying Kerygma," 1988, 3). Lemcio's summary of the New Testament kerygma is: "God sent or raised Jesus. A response towards God brings benefits" (Lemcio, "Unifying Kerygma," 1990, 3). Though Lemcio disputes Dunn on the issue of unity, he actually ends up settling for a much weaker kerygma than what Dunn himself has offered.

various constituencies within proto-orthodoxy proclaimed Jesus with different shades of meaning. Let us acknowledge that a given title for Jesus in one setting might not have been usable in another. Even so, the New Testament's Jesus is recognizably in view here, albeit through different lenses. When we investigate the initial layer of Christian history, we discover numerous groups of proto-orthodox believers trying to process the meaning of Jesus's death and resurrection in creative ways. While no single community had the full picture yet, that doesn't mean their disparate ideas were incapable of being melded into a unified whole. And as it happened, these concepts eventually congealed into the accepted Christology of the catholics.[53]

Dunn's *Unity and Diversity* directly addresses the topic of primitive Christology. Unlike Bultmann's famous distinction between the Galilean preacher and the church's Christ, Dunn emphasizes a fundamental *unity* between Jesus's ministry and the earliest believers' proclamation of him. The *kerygmata* of the first churches were an expansion on Jesus's own message in light of his resurrection.[54] Nevertheless, though Easter faith remained central, its implications were diverse in the earliest Christian communities. What will later be regarded as a unified "orthodox Christology" is actually "a curious amalgam of different elements taken from different parts of first-century Christianity—personal pre-existence from John, virgin birth from Matthew, the miracle-worker from the so-called 'divine man' christology prevalent among some Hellenistic Christians, his death as atonement from Paul, the character of his resurrection from Luke, his present role from Hebrews, and the hope of his parousia from the earlier decades."[55]

---

53. Dunn considers "early catholicism" to be one strand among several forms of primitive diversity, yet he defines *catholicism* in a different way from how I define it here. "Early catholicism" for Dunn consists of three elements: the fading of imminent eschatological hopes, increasing institutionalization, and crystallization of the faith into set forms (Dunn, *Unity and Diversity*, 377–96). In contrast, when I speak of those who assumed the status of "catholic" in the second century, I use the word with the classic meaning of "universal": those Christians who perceived themselves as bound by a common, worldwide proclamation, and therefore worked to build an intentional network that would safeguard their self-identity. This proclamation centered on the belief that Jesus the Son of God died and rose again for man's salvation. Under this definition, *all* the proto-orthodox could be seen as manifesting "early catholicism."

54. Ibid., 232; cf. 246–47.

55. Ibid., 244.

Yet what ties all these ideas together? Dunn suggests it is "the affirmation of the identity of the man Jesus with the risen Lord."[56] This observation is essential to notice. All the various Christological strands in the New Testament are bound together by the resurrection of the historical Jesus. In light of that transformative event, other things can be claimed about him (his pre-existence, virgin birth, miracles, atoning death, etc.). The development of a full-fledged Christology was no doubt a group project. Many communities contributed different ideas to the entire picture that emerged over several decades. Nevertheless, let us not fail to notice that *all of those communities proclaimed the crucified Jesus as their risen Lord.* The proto-orthodox shared a common confession despite their many differences—and this confession served as the nucleus of an orthodox Christology.

At this point we might wish to ask: What about Christian Gnosticism? Were there any Jesus-Religionists for whom the passion and resurrection were unimportant, or even antithetical to what they wished to say? If so, when did such beliefs emerge? The hotly debated question of the origins of Gnosticism (or "gnosticizing thought") is posed this way by Dunn: "Did first-century Christianity embrace within its acceptable diversity anything that might properly be called *gnostic* Christianity? Or were the boundaries drawn in the latter decades of the second century to separate Christianity and Gnosticism already being drawn in the first century?"[57] Dunn concludes "pre-Gnosticism" did exist in the first century. In fact, there was a decided measure of Hellenistic gnostic speculation circulating in the mid- to late first century. Pre-Gnosticism can be discerned as part of the historical background to some Pauline epistles, and also the sayings source known as Q. Some people clearly wanted to take Paul's ideas or the words of Jesus in a gnosticizing direction. Yet they did so at the expense of the resurrection—the one thing Dunn consistently maintains as the unifying thread in earliest Christianity. "Gnosticism," he writes, "was able to present its message in a sustained way as teaching of Jesus only by separating the risen Christ from the earthly Jesus and by abandoning the attempt to show a continuity between the Jesus of the Jesus-tradition and the heavenly Christ of their faith."[58] Therefore we must see Gnosticism as a *later* development, one which "abandoned" the

56. Ibid., 245.

57. Ibid., 288. See the entirety of chapter 12 for Dunn's discussion of Christian Gnosticism.

58. Ibid., 312.

confession shared by the original believers: that the historical man Jesus of Nazareth rose from the grave as Lord and Christ.

It is obvious from second-century sources that the Apostle Paul was susceptible to gnostic interpretation by his later devotees. Gnosticism is well-attested in that era, and many of the sects took Pauline ideas as their starting point.[59] Nevertheless, any gnosticizing tendencies perceived in Paul's writings do not turn him into a Christian gnostic. Why? Because unlike esoteric religion, Paul always equated the man Jesus with the glorified Christ. Dunn claims that ". . . it is this strong affirmation that Jesus the Lord is Christ the crucified, so consistent in Paul, which cuts at the nerve of Christian Gnosticism. It is this which prevents Paul, for all his openness to Hellenistic thought, from being absorbed into Christian Gnosticism.[60]

And when it comes to the Johannine writings, Dunn affirms something very similar. Though John even more than Paul presented Jesus in a manner congenial to the Gnostics (perhaps as part of an intentional missionary strategy), in the end John's insistence on the resurrection fundamentally separated him from Gnosticism. Belief in the Word who became flesh, who shed his blood and died on the cross, and who is now the glorified Christ in heaven, put John in the same basic camp as his orthodox brethren. The incarnation, passion, and resurrection marked out the encompassing perimeter of "acceptable diversity" in first-century Christianity.[61] Easter faith was inside that boundary, while Gnosticism definitely was not.

To end our investigation of Dunn's masterwork on unity and diversity in the ancient church, let us allow the author to summarize his own conclusions:

> I think it can justly be said that we have discovered *a fairly clear and consistent unifying strand* which from the first both marked out Christianity as something distinctive and different and provided the *integrating centre* for the diverse expressions of Christianity. That unifying element was the unity between the historical Jesus and the exalted Christ, that is to say, the

---

59. Dunn thinks Paul actually embraced certain gnostic ideas himself, but the orthodox church fathers misinterpreted him and obscured his incipient Gnosticism (ibid., 312–18). Though I am skeptical about this particular contention, the present study is not the place for a detailed examination of any perspectives on Paul, whether new or old.

60. Ibid., 320.

61. Ibid., 332.

conviction that the wandering charismatic preacher from Nazareth had ministered, died, and been raised from the dead to bring God and man finally together.[62]

No matter what line of historical evidence was examined,

> . . .the answer came out consistently in more or less the same terms: the cohesive focal point was Jesus, the man, the exalted one. Even when we probed more deeply into the most difficult area of all—the relation between the message of Jesus and the messages of the first Christians—the same answer began to emerge: the continuity between Jesus the man and Jesus the exalted one was not simply assumed or read back as a *post eventum* theological insight, but was rooted in Jesus's own understanding of his relationship with God, with his disciples, and with God's kingdom. So, that there is a fundamental unifying strand running through earliest Christianity in the NT can hardly be doubted, and that unifying strand—Jesus himself.[63]

Of course, the believers who actually proclaimed the exalted Jesus disagreed with one another in many important respects. To complicate matters, the lines between them and the surrounding syncretistic cults were not always clear. This is why Dunn concludes, "there was no single normative form of Christianity in the first century."[64] The statement is true on its face, insofar as the word *single* implies no groups held divergent or competing beliefs, and *normative* implies that a majority view had already triumphed over its competitors. Clearly that was not the case in the first century. Yet Dunn repeatedly points out that a core confession united the early believers. "If anything can claim to run through the NT writings like a golden thread," he asserts, "it is the conviction that God raised Jesus from the dead."[65] In other words, whenever we speak of earliest Christian "diversity," we must not forget to say that such diversity existed underneath the all-encompassing umbrella of the Easter event. Christianity in its first and most basic manifestation proclaimed the message, "He is risen."[66] Anyone whose belief system does not affirm

62. Ibid., 403.

63. Ibid., 403.

64. Ibid., 407.

65. Ibid., 439.

66. The affirmation of the resurrection cannot merely be a reductionist way of saying Jesus's teaching and example stayed alive in the disciples' memory. As Dunn points out, "At the heart of this element of fundamental unity is the claim that something had

this message ought, therefore, to bear a title other than "Christian." Such persons have come to believe something different than the original message—and this judgment is made on historical grounds, not polemical.

How does all this relate to our goal of identifying the type of belief that emerged immediately after Jesus's life? James Dunn's application of the Bauer Thesis to earliest Christian beginnings *does not cohere* with the idea that there were many "Christianities" in the first century, all equally original and valid. To the extent that Dunn highlights a divergence of opinion about Jesus in the apostolic era, his work supports Bauer's argument at the most basic level—that a certain measure of "diversity" existed in the ancient period. Yet Dunn's exhaustive research gives us every reason to distinguish between an initial core confession concerning the exalted Christ and later ideas that were obviously at odds with the original proclamation. Though situational fluidity existed within the message of the proto-orthodox, a unifying truth-claim always bound them: that the Jewish carpenter from Nazareth had risen from the grave by the power of God. Because of this constant and unswerving emphasis, the locus of ideas called Gnosticism—with its rejection of the historical man Jesus, his saving death on a Roman cross, and his bodily resurrection to exalted status—must be viewed as foreign to the apostolic kerygma. By objective historical criteria, gnostic religion (and pre-Gnosticism) ought to be considered as something altogether different from the earliest form of Christian proclamation.[67]

Summarizing what has been said so far in this chapter, I offer the following two points:

1. Many studies of early Christian creeds have identified a full apostolic kerygma that proclaimed the one Creator God of Israel as the Father of Jesus of Nazareth. Jesus was descended from David through Mary, died on a cross, was buried, and was raised by God from the dead to sit at the divine right hand. Soon he would come again to

---

happened to *Jesus* not simply to his disciples, the belief that God had vindicated Jesus, not simply their following of him, and that God now dealt with them '*through*' Jesus and not just 'for his sake'" (ibid., 439–40).

67. N. T. Wright vigorously maintains this view. "These two sets of belief are like oil and water," he writes, "like chalk and cheese. If we cannot see that, we are simply not paying attention to the texts" (Wright, *Judas*, 82). Rodney Stark agrees when he says, "The conflicts between many of these [gnostic] manuscripts and the New Testament are so monumental that no thinking person could embrace both" (Stark, *Cities of God*, 142).

judge evil and usher in an age of blessing. Faith in Jesus would bring benefits such as the outpouring of the Spirit or forgiveness of sins.

2. James Dunn's application of the Bauer Thesis to the first century situation denies that the apostolic kerygma was so thoroughly unified on all these points.[68] Diversity existed in the earliest Christian proclamation—a diversity so radical that a given kerygma could not be transposed from one situation to another. However, the resurrection of the historical Jesus (with the accompanying outpouring of the Spirit) served as the unifying theme of the earliest proclamation. [69] This means, according to Dunn, that while pre-Gnosticism did circulate in the first-century Christian milieu, it remained distinct from those whose confession centered on the risen Christ.

Therefore, even if we grant the legitimacy of Dunn's point about a bare-bones affirmation instead of a fuller apostolic kerygma, we are still left with the historical fact that the Easter event was the original Christian proclamation—which means any type of Jesus-Religion that denied the centrality of the crucifixion and resurrection must be considered as something *later* and something *else*.

The *Regula Fidei* of the Second and Third Centuries

If, as I believe, we can speak of a resurrection-centered message as the core confession of the first-century Christians, and if we can perhaps find good evidence for an even fuller apostolic kerygma—centered on the Jesus who was sent from Israel's God to die, rise, ascend, and return to judge the living and dead—then what remains is to examine the material from the second and third centuries to see which group of Jesus-Religionists advanced this same message. It will not come as a surprise to find that the *regula fidei* of the "orthodox" Christians does in fact encapsulate this particular set of ideas. Let us proceed to the evidence.

---

68. Bart Ehrman also denies two of these points, at least in the very earliest stratum of the kerygma: the birth narrative in which Jesus is virginally conceived by Mary, and the burial or empty tomb traditions. In addition, Ehrman believes the earliest Christians only invested Jesus with the status of divine Sonship after their experience of the resurrection (Ehrman, *How Jesus Became God*, 163–65, 246).

69. Dunn asserts that the ideas "on which all of Christianity was united from the beginning" and which serve as the "historical foundation of Christianity" can be summed up in two words: "Easter" and "Pentecost" (Dunn, *Unity and Diversity*, 437).

It is a simple enough matter to survey the extant creedal material of the ante-Nicene period to determine the general contours of its thought. The texts are well known and in good English translation. Perhaps the only difficulty is determining what constitutes a given instance of the Rule of Faith. Elsewhere I have supplied a list of what I consider to be the thirteen ante-Nicene instances of the Rule—the places within the ancient Christian writings that are full enough to be considered a true *regula fidei* and not just a snippet of confessional material.[70] In the present study, however, we are interested in more than just full-fledged *regulae*. The best recent collection of the relevant texts is that of Pelikan and Hotchkiss, so I have used their sourcebook as my baseline to examine the ideas contained in the Rule, though I have supplemented or re-ordered the list as needed. My study reveals the data in the chart on page 165.[71]

Several observations can be made about the data. First, we should note that the same key ideas keep appearing over and over again (that is to say, the headings of the chart). Even if an author does not cite each and every concept when he mentions the Rule, a wider investigation of his treatise or corpus would reveal them in short order.[72] Therefore the empty boxes do not indicate that the author did not believe the idea. The gaps merely reflect that many writers made passing reference to the Rule in the course of their argumentation—especially in the period prior to Irenaeus.[73] The

70. Litfin, "Learning," 80–94.

71. The sources included in the chart are: Ignatius of Antioch, *Ephesians* 18.2, *Trallians* 9.1–2, and *Smyrnaeans* 1.1–2; Aristides of Athens, *Apology* 1–2; Justin Martyr, *1 Apology* 13, 31, and 61; *Epistle of the Apostles*; Irenaeus *Against Heresies* 1.10.1, 3.4.1–2 and *Proof of the Apostolic Preaching*; Tertullian, *Prescription Against Heretics* 13.1–6, *Against Praxeas* 2.1, and *Veiling of Virgins* 1.3; Hippolytus, *Against Noetus* 17–18 and *Apostolic Tradition* 21; *Didascalia Apostolorum* 26.6.23; Novatian, *On the Trinity*; Origen, *On First Principles* 1.4–8; Cyprian, *Epistle 73, To Jubaianus*; and the baptismal creed of Alexandria (as recovered from Dionysius of Alexandria's *Letter to Pope Stephen*, the *Dêr Balyzeh Papyrus*, a letter of Alexander of Alexandria to the bishop of Constantinople, and the creed of Arius). Other texts from the *Didache*, Polycarp, Irenaeus, Tertullian and Gregory Thaumaturgus appear in Pelikan and Hotchkiss 40–71, but I omit them from the chart as not sufficiently creedal. I have also included additional texts from Justin Martyr, the *Didascalia*, Cyprian, and Dionysius of Alexandria. Because the creedal material is spread throughout some of these texts, I have recorded data from all of the *Epistle of the Apostles*, Irenaeus's *Proof*, Hippolytus's *Against Noetus* 17–18, and Novatian's *On the Trinity*—not just the portions quoted in Pelikan and Hotchkiss.

72. For example, Tertullian does not make reference to the apostles in his quintessential quotation of the Rule at *Prescription against Heretics* 13—yet if any work from the patristic age argues for the importance of the apostolic lineage, it is this one!

73. Bishop Irenaeus marks a boundary of sorts. After his era, the fathers became

church fathers may not have had a reason to quote every detail of the Rule on every occasion. However, when we find authors who are intentionally reproducing the baptismal creed, we get a much fuller recitation of the Rule's theology, in which most or all of the central ideas appear.

Second, a close study of the Rule of Faith reveals that a few additional ideas occasionally show up beyond what is mentioned in the chart. These would include the church's baptism, Jesus's actual burial, and holy living or Christian ethics. Among the church fathers, Origen's *regula fidei* stands out as containing extra ideas that rarely appear elsewhere, such as allegorical exegesis or various speculations about the soul. I simply note this fact here without having space to comment further, except to remark that Origen does record the traditional ideas alongside his unique elements.[74]

Third, certain ideas within the Rule seem to be of special importance. The one almighty God appears consistently, and likewise the death and resurrection of Jesus are affirmed by every author (though not in every single text). Jesus is uniformly referred to as "Christ," and faith in him is emphasized. The Holy Spirit also receives prominent mention in the Rule.

In summary, then, I offer nine dramatic actions to be found in the patristic Rule of Faith:[75]

1. The act of Creation by the Father God

2. The act of Prediction through the Spirit in the Old Testament

3. The act of Incarnation by the Holy Spirit of the Virgin Mary

4. The act of Ministration in which Jesus serves the world, preaches, and works miracles

5. The act of Crucifixion for the purpose of salvation

6. The act of Resurrection in triumph

7. The act of Exaltation to the Father's right hand

8. The act of Proclamation by the Spirit's power in the apostolic church

---

aware that the church's catechetical summary could be employed as a theological framework or an exegetical guidepost. This is the beginning of the great age of the *regula fidei*.

74. For more on Origen's Rule, see Hanson, *Origen's Doctrine of Tradition*, and Outler, "Origen and the *Regula Fidei*."

75. These concepts are adapted from Litfin, "Learning," 96.

9. The act of Consummation when Christ returns to raise the dead for judgment or reward

These nine points can be taken as describing a cohesive type of Jesus-Religion that existed in the second and third centuries. When we compare these points with the earliest Christian kerygma, we find remarkable similarity. Even if we take a more skeptical stance as does Dunn, restricting our sense of unity to the core confession that Jesus of Nazareth died and rose again to power, we still have a much stronger reason to equate the catholic Christians with the original message than anyone else. The historical evidence reveals a straight line of continuity (admittedly with some expansion[76]) from the earliest apostolic preaching to the message confessed by the orthodox church fathers of later centuries. The original believers were united in their proclamation that death has been overcome by the empty tomb of the Lord Jesus Christ. This is the gospel, the good news of what ought to be called "Christianity." Although Walter Bauer has helpfully reminded us of the many diverse opinions about Jesus in the ancient period, we should discriminate carefully between them all, remembering that only one type was there at the beginning.[77]

---

76. Several ideas in the Rule of Faith represent an advancement from the most primitive layer of the apostolic preaching: Jesus's birth from the Virgin Mary; the specific name of Pontius Pilate; and the future resurrection of the flesh. While these concepts are not known to be part of the pre-Pauline kerygma, they are found either in Paul himself or in the Synoptics. We should view their integration as a slightly later development of the original proclamation about Jesus's life, death, resurrection, and exaltation.

77. Contemporary Bauer Thesis advocates frequently obscure the historical situation by insisting on using the word *Christian* to describe any individual or group that claimed to follow Jesus, no matter what their beliefs. Perhaps this is intended as generosity toward the variety of ancient viewpoints. Even so, the practice is at best confusing, and at worst misleading. Ehrman, for example, recognizes that the earliest Christians proclaimed the resurrection of Jesus, as the messiah of Israel and exalted Son of God. Yet having said so, he still portrays "Christian" diversity in the second and third centuries as including people who believed in 365 gods, or that the God of Israel was not the God of Jesus, or that Jesus was not a true human being, or that the creation of the cosmos was the work of an evil god (Ehrman, *How Jesus Became God*, 286–89). He also suggests that the diversity of early Christian writings leaves all of these options open, as if all ancient texts that speak about Jesus have equal historical value. According to Ehrman, one particular type of Christianity managed to emerge as triumphant, thus permitting it to define the term. But who can really say which form is "right"? In reply to this modern version of the Bauer Thesis, let us remember: No one is asking the historian to pass judgment on which view represents ultimate religious truth. However, it is certainly possible to define the basic contours of a religion as it first emerged, then to assess which later groups most closely adhere to what was proclaimed at the outset. The refusal to distinguish between the original message of Christianity and the

Content of the Ante-Nicene *Regula Fidei*

	God	Creator	OT /Jews/David	Birth (from Mary)	Life of Jesus	Pilate	Passion/Cross/Death	Resurrection	Exaltation	Church	Holy Spirit	Future Resurrection	Judgment/Rewards	Faith/Obedience	"Christ"	"Son" ("Father") God	"Lord"	Apostles/Tradition
Ign *Eph*	X		X	X			X				X				X			
Ign *Tral*	X		X	X	X	X	X	X				X		X	X	X		
Ign *Smyr*	X		X	X		X	X	X		X				X	X	X	X	X
Arist *Apol*	X		X	X	X		X	X	X						X	X		
Just *1Ap 13*	X	X		X		X	X				X			X	X	X		X
Just *1 Ap 31*	X		X	X	X		X	X	X		X			X	X	X		X
Just *1 Ap 61*	X		X			X	X				X			X	X			X
Ep Apost	X	X	X	X	X	X	X	X	X	X	X	X	X	X	X	X	X	X
Ir *AH 1.10*	X	X	X	X			X	X	X	X	X	X	X	X	X	X	X	X
Ir *AH 3.4*	X	X		X		X	X	X	X	X	X			X	X	X		X
Ir *Proof*	X	X	X	X	X	X	X	X	X	X	X	X	X	X	X	X	X	X
Ter *Prescr*	X	X	X	X	X		X	X	X			X	X	X	X	X	X	
Ter *AgPrax*	X			X			X	X	X		X			X	X	X	X	
Ter *VeilVir*	X	X		X		X	X	X	X			X	X	X	X	X		
Hip *AgNoe*	X	X	X	X	X	X	X	X	X	X	X		X	X		X		X
Hip *ApTrad*	X			X		X	X	X	X	X	X	X	X	X	X			
Did *Apost*	X		X			X	X	X	X			X	X	X	X	X	X	
Nov *Trin*	X	X	X	X	X		X	X	X	X	X	X	X	X	X	X	X	X
Or *FirstPr*	X	X	X	X			X	X	X	X	X	X	X	X	X	X	X	X
Cyp *Ep73*	X	X		X			X	X		X	X			X	X	X	X	X
Alex *Creed*	X		X	X			X	X	X	X	X	X	X	X	X	X	X	X

later, recognizably different alternatives to it—even if they did include Jesus in their belief systems—creates a false impression of early Christian origins that should be rectified by greater terminological clarity.

7

Bauer's Forgotten Region: North African Christianity

David C. Alexander and Edward L. Smither

CHRISTIANITY IN NORTH AFRICA (as distinct from Egypt) did not emerge until late in the second century—a region and period generally outside the "earliest Christianity" considered by Walter Bauer in his famous research.[1] The story of North African Christianity, including the thought of its leading Christian theologians (Tertullian, Cyprian, and Augustine), was apparently regarded by Bauer as too late and thus inadmissible evidence for the debate on the emergence of orthodoxy and heresy. Nevertheless, North Africa is an area of early Christianity with well-documented character, conflicts and rapid emergence. As Robert A. Kraft acknowledged in the 1971 English edition of *Orthodoxy and Heresy*, "a fresh approach to the origins of Christianity in North Africa" was among the important explorations "still lacking" from Bauer's line of research.[2] This chapter is designed

---

1. Bauer drew on Tertullian, as discussed below, and extended his discussion in a number of locations to the end of the second century and beyond. However, his treatment mostly centered on developments before 180. Moreover, unlike most areas Bauer considered, there are no clear candidates for a first-century Christianity in Roman North Africa (which in this essay excludes Egypt and its surrounding areas). While North African Christianity has a bearing on elements of Bauer's thesis, this area is not an example of "earliest Christianity."

2. Bauer, *Orthodoxy and Heresy*, 315; for Koch's critique of this lacuna, see ibid., 289.

as a first step in just such an approach. In positively answering whether the emergence and development of North African Christianity is of any relevance to the Bauer Thesis we hope to point toward a more general "fresh approach" for understanding the unity and diversity of Christian origins and early Christian orthodoxy itself.

In fact, the character and development of early North African Christianity provides a useful case study, or parallel test, on a number of fronts for elements and implications of Bauer's proposal. We ask whether the interpretative assumptions, methods and conclusions Bauer and others have applied to areas with sparser evidence of Christian origins would prove historically viable if they were brought to bear on the Christian origins in North Africa. Such an examination reveals weaknesses in several key implications of Bauer's view (and its more recent presentations). In this connection the case of Tertullian, whom Bauer does appropriate for his arguments, is particularly relevant.

Beyond Tertullian, a number of unique aspects of the emergence of Christianity in North Africa, which likely would have been grist in the mill of Bauer's arguments had they appeared fifty to seventy-five years earlier in abstracted form, when viewed in context actually illuminate that "orthodoxy" was something conceived too narrowly by Bauer and that an orthodox penumbra allowed for considerable diversity and even competition. Beginning with a consideration of origins we will first show that this was a case in point where a "later" development of orthodoxy occurred without any preceding heresy, counter to Bauer's pattern. The local flavors of Christianity which emerged in Roman Africa were not different entities or segments of a broader group competing in terms of essential authority and doctrine.

Second, we will demonstrate that North African distinctives and internal conflicts did not derive from pluriform or repressed origins. Seen *in situ* such developments manifest that strongly distinctive regional Christianity (singular) and even competition between distinctive regional groups need not imply the existence of different or "lost" Christianities. The distinctive nature of North African Christianity is clear from its earliest moments right through to Augustine.[3] Yet, as our analysis of Tertullian and third-century developments will show, it was not superseded by

---

3. Cf. Wright, "Latin Fathers," 148–50; and Sider, "Africa," 15.

an authentically different "orthodox"[4] Christianity over time.[5] In sum, Christian emergence in Roman Africa manifested considerable diversity within a core unity; successful resistance to an established church at Rome precisely on the issue of right beliefs; and a broad commitment to a Christian experience which centered on the action of the Spirit in the world and both "apostolic" and Jewish Scriptures. That is, it seems to be a microcosm of many characteristics that stand in contrast to Bauer's reconstructions of "earliest Christianity."

The Origins of North African Christianity

How, when, and in what form(s) did Christianity come to Roman North Africa? The region of modern day Tunisia and portions of Algeria and Libya had been part of the empire since the conclusion of the Punic Wars (146 BC). The first undisputed evidence for Christianity in North Africa comes as an account of the martyrdom, on July 17, AD 180, of a group of Christians brought to Carthage from the small village of Scilli/um—so small that we are not certain of its location.

The account is unusual for several reasons. First, it gives a specific date and specific names (including uniquely African names), and the martyrs display some sophistication in their faith. Second, the account is in Latin and the martyrs evidence a Latin Bible (representing an indigenous Latin Christianity). Third, it represents rural Christians, and since early Christian expansion was uniform in spreading first to urban areas and only later penetrating the countryside, for Christianity to have

4. Terminology is key in this discussion. When Robert A. Kraft introduces a citation of Hans Dieter Betz by stating: "Clearly there was no 'pure' form of Christianity that existed in the beginning and can be called 'orthodox'" (in Bauer, *Orthodoxy and Heresy*, 309), we get an illustration of how essential defining terms is to avoiding extremes. Three levels of meaning for "orthodox" are used in this chapter. 1. Conscious connection or perceived dependence on connections to Jesus as Messiah and risen Lord through apostolic Christianity as it was broadly received. 2. Teachings which were held to be consistent with the open, general teaching of the Scriptures in the broader ("catholic") church. 3. "True" as opposed to "false" teachings labeled as "heresy" in contemporary sources. All three aspects, not just a narrow focus on the last, are important to retain within a full consideration of unity and diversity within Christian origins.

5. Although the fourth-century requirement from Rome to support Caecillian's party only if they renounced the African practice of rebaptism did represent loss of an aspect of African tradition and a portion of Cyprian's theology, it did not constitute a loss of the legacy of Cyprianic theology; cf. Burns, *Cyprian the Bishop*, 166–77.

reached a village the size of Scili/um and to have a number of obvious, informed, and devout converts from there suggests that Christianity preceded this date in North Africa by some time (perhaps even decades).

After this account, Christian evidence in North Africa virtually explodes from 190–220 with accounts of multiple martyrdoms in Carthage—most notably the *Passion of Perpetua*, perhaps the earliest extant writing by a Christian woman[6]—and numerous Christian discourses from Tertullian, beginning ca. 195. Though the "brilliant Carthaginian" has been considered the "creator of Christian Latin," Tertullian also wrote in Greek.[7] As a baseline, therefore, a large and indigenous bilingual Christian community, both urban and rural, existed by 200. Christianity in North Africa appeared later than in other areas, displayed clear distinctives, and began in the second century, lacking first-century evidence or a tradition of evangelization.[8]

From what location did Christianity come to North Africa? The various possible geographic sources naturally consist of Rome/Italy, Asia Minor, Syria, Egypt, and Gaul. Of these, Italy and Asia Minor are the most likely candidates in terms of frequency of contact and similarities in Christian focus and observance. In antiquity, Africa did not include Egypt—they were quite separate—and there was relatively little interaction between Carthage and Alexandria.[9] If preference be given to one source, the idea that Christianity came to Africa from Asia Minor is probably most cor-

---

6. Perpetua represents the aristocratic class as well as Greek-speaking Christians at Carthage and perhaps more broadly.

7. Wright, "Latin Fathers," 148–50.

8. A helpful broad chronology of "early" Christianity in North Africa might break down as follows:
Late first century–mid-second century: Possible first Christian contacts;
(170s–) 180s: Clear origins;
190–230: Dramatic, vibrant growth and development;
240–280s: Organization and consolidation;
280–330: Division from politics following persecution;
330–412: Internal battle over who or what constituted "authentic" Christianity in North Africa;
413–500: Theological legacy amidst growing political unrest.

9. Especially between their Christian communities. There is debate about the role of Judaism as a conduit because details about the North African community are unclear and the evidence is minimal. Depending upon one's perspective, some anti-Jewish comments in early North African Christian writings may indicate that Christianity did or did not spread through this group to North Africa (cf. Tertullian, *Against the Jews*, chaps. 1-8; Decret, *Early Christianity in North Africa*, 13-15).

rect.[10] With the amount of commercial traffic between Carthage and Rome, and the proximity to Italy, that might seem the logical choice; however, the characteristics of earliest North African Christianity are not as reflective of Rome as they are of Asia Minor. In all of the possible source areas, including Rome, Greek was the language of the church for some time. While a Greek component of early Christianity in Africa is clear from the earliest writings of Tertullian as well as the language of the *Passio* of Perpetua and her colleagues, North African Christianity would be dominated by Latin from the very beginning. Decret's assertion that "the Gospel converged on Africa" from both Roman Italy and the East at around the same time seems likely, even if in the end we cannot draw strong conclusions about the precise details, timeframe, and order of its arrival.[11]

What is clear is that North African Christianity emerged quickly from 180 onward as a demographically and linguistically diverse entity. This young church quickly began to relate to the broader church in Asia Minor, the East, and Rome in ways both confidently connected and independent. Moreover, it did so from a perspective that was enthusiastic and self-consciously "orthodox." As it relates to Bauer's thesis, it is worth noting that the multiple potential sources for Christianity in North Africa did not lead to multiple emergences or competing entities. That is to say, our earliest testimonies to Christianity in North Africa (180–202/3) represent clearly distinct communities:

- Perpetua and companions—urban, Greek, aristocratic classes and servants;

10. One may note, in particular, the "New Prophecy" (Montanist) connection that is apparent in some of the earliest evidence we have from Carthaginian Christians as well as the lack of deference accorded to Rome by the young North African church, e.g. under Cyprian. Moreover, commercial contact was very strong between North Africa and Asia Minor, and the Asian churches seem to have been a little more expansive in this connection than churches in other areas—with Lyon and Irenaeus providing a case in point.

11. The tendency of Bauer to argue from silence will not be attempted here for the hypothetical aspects of earlier second- or even first-century Christianity in Africa for which Decret envisages the most important conduit being Italian immigrants. Saxer ("Africa," 13) notes the contesting views that Christianity came to Africa from either Rome or through Libya/Egypt. Sider ("Africa," 14), noting the early Greek elements of the Christian community there, gives the nod to Greek-speaking eastern merchants as the likely source. Decret, (*Early Christianity in North Africa*, 12–13), hypothesizes a late first-/early second-century process whereby "the Gospel converged on Africa from both [Roman Italy and the East] at the same time" with the most important conduit being Italian immigrants (also attended by some Jewish connections).

- Tertullian—urban, Latin, educated classes, bilingual;
- Scillitan martyrs – rural, Latin, indigenous.

Yet the general character (tenor, foci, and emphases) from all three groups are largely indistinguishable. Such a result would not be anticipated by Bauer's assumptions and has been underappreciated. One implication is that the various sources of North African Christianity shared a core unity evidenced by the diverse groups that comprised this early regional church.

North African Christianity's Distinctive Character

Regardless of its provenance, the distinctive features of early North African Christianity are well-known, illustrating that a locale can and often does introduce one or more distinctive flavors to Christianity.[12] Robert D. Sider is not unique when he lists characteristics such as:

1. Literary vigor and creativity;
2. A profound focus on martyrdom;
3. A tendency to be "factious and schismatic;" and
4. A focus on conciliar decision making.[13]

To these other aspects of this early regional Christianity may be added: rural penetration; a rigorous approach to Christian observance; apologetic against the world (in contrast, for example, to apologetic from Alexandria or Justin which engaged the world and philosophy more positively); a charismatic stress on the Spirit; and a somewhat self-sufficient originality and theological inventiveness. Several of these distinctives are important in our assessment of Bauer.

Rural Penetration, Martyrdom, Rigor, and Latin

We have noted the rural penetration of early North African Christianity, but it is significant that vibrant rural Christianity would endure as a shaping influence in the African church perhaps more than in any other

12. Celtic Christianity would be another, later case in point.
13. Sider, "Africa," 15.

region of the empire. The Donatist schism in the early fourth century was only made viable with the support of rural Numidian bishops, who were wary of the influence of Carthage.

Even more distinctive of African Christianity was its focus on martyrdom. It is not by accident that the first evidence of Christianity in North Africa is a martyrdom account. From this seminal point, the regional church glorified martyrdom, was characterized by rigor, took a more detached or opposing view of the world (paganism, false religion, corruption, etc.), and tended to view life as a conflict with demonic forces. The earlier *Acts of the Scillitan Martyrs* is followed by the famous martyrdom of Perpetua and Felicitas (203/204), a vivid group account which, as David F. Wright notes, "displays astonishing feminine sensitivity, incorporating Perpetua's prison diary, the earliest writing by a Christian woman."[14]

This emphasis on martyrdom connected directly to an emphasis on the Holy Spirit.[15] The charismatic influence of martyrs and *confessors* so dramatic in this account is also visible in the later controversy surrounding the restoration of the lapsed in 253 during the Decian persecution wherein the response to persecution and avoidance of martyrdom nearly undermined Cyprian's episcopacy in Carthage.[16] The role of the faithful during the great persecution was at the core of the Donatist schism, and even in Augustine's day festivals surrounding martyrs' anniversaries were more enthusiastic and strongly emphasized than in the broader church.[17]

Perhaps the best single word to describe North African Christianity is "rigorous." The emphasis was on one's *religio* (a "duty of observance") and related to the Roman ideal of *pietas* (or "piety"). Behavior ought to be consistent with conviction, as Tertullian states in *On Repentance*: "It is utterly vain to say, 'I willed, but yet I did not.' Rather you ought to carry the thing through because you will; or else not will at all, since you do not carry it through" (*On Repentance* 4). For North African Christians like Tertullian there was a tendency to allow few, if any, exceptions to

---

14. Wright, "Latin Fathers," 148.

15. Not unlike what appears in the account of the martyrs at Lyon (ca. 177), or Phrygian Montanism, or the *Martyrdom of Polycarp* (in Asia Minor).

16. An avoidance that Cyprian proved did not derive solely from fear when he was martyred on 14 September, 258.

17. Cf. Augustine, *Confessions* 5.8.15 (see also the note in Henry Chadwick's translation: Chadwick, *Saint Augustine*, 82n12) and *Confessions* 6.2.2, regarding Monica's observance of the martyrs' anniversaries.

those who lapsed.[18] The critiques by Perpetua of the laxity of her church leaders, or by Tertullian towards laxity anywhere, or his progression from allowances of very few post-baptismal lapses in his early writings to no post-baptismal lapses in his later "Montanist" writings, are but a few of the most obvious manifestations of this rigorous Christianity.

Good order and organization were not far behind, as represented in the person of Cyprian and his many pioneering administrative initiatives. Yet this feature is already visible in ecclesiastical structure and clerical ministry in North Africa in Perpetua's and Tertullian's time.[19] The significance of the striking emphasis on *plurality* in decision making and leadership structures would have been worth Bauer's consideration.

North African rigor also translated into a distinctive apologetic directed against the "world." Tertullian again is a prime example and provided the best defense of Christianity against persecution and misinformation, though his apologetic style reads in stark contrast to Greek apologists such as Alexandrian apologists like Clement and Origin, Justin in Asia Minor and Rome, or Irenaeus in Gaul.[20]

Lastly, it was in Africa that specifically Latin Christianity found its real home. The Roman church was still using Greek at this time and the first Latin-speaking bishop of Rome, Victor (d. 196), was a North African. North Africa, not Rome or Italy, would be the vibrant locus of Latin Christianity in the pre-Constantinian period. Here the church, partially from necessity, developed original and theologically inventive terms and concepts to convey and understand the Christian message. Tertullian, the author of some thirty or so books from 195–215, was the most significant figure in this and other developments (as will be seen below). In him Latin theology began and Latin Christianity gained a forceful personality.[21] The Old Latin Bible glimpsed in the *Acta* of the Scillitan martyrs was the central text for the church in North Africa up to Augustine's day.

---

18. E.g. Tertullian's earlier *On Repentance* and his later *On Purity*.

19. See, for example, the clerical structure and significant role of the council of *seniores* (community "elders") in Tabbernee, "Perpetua, Montanism, and Christian Ministry," 435–38.

20. Wright, "Latin Fathers,"149. Decret's note that Tertullian "represented an entire people" is nowhere more true than in the apologist's statement: "We want no curious disputation after possessing Christ Jesus, no inquisition after enjoying the gospel" (Tertullian, *Praescr.* 7.12; Decret, *Christianity in North Africa*, 34).

21. E.g., coinage of the term "Trinity" for the Godhead and describing its meaning in the typically concise Latin expression of "one nature in three persons."

The preceding more than demonstrate how Christianity in a new locale (here late second-century North Africa) could develop, marked by characteristics and distinctives from Christianity practiced elsewhere and from which it derived. It is equally clear that it would be a mistake to ascribe to this North African local and particular manifestation the status of a new "competitor" Christianity in the religious arena of the time. Ascription of such local varieties to unknown earlier versions of Christianity is invalid in the North African case since the distinctive features are reflected *within* diverse communities. Additionally, these diverse communities shared a conscious affinity to unity and assumed apostolic continuity. The identity of North African Christians with the catholic church—and a sense of possession of "authentic" Christianity—is visible in Cyprian's conciliar initiatives and theory. It is also apparent in Tertullian's appeals to witnesses of the universal church and its Scriptures in his apologetic, and in his considered attraction to the "New Prophecy" that originated in Asia Minor. Indeed, this combination of unique character and commitment to broader orthodoxy in North Africa is perhaps best illustrated by Tertullian.

Why Tertullian Matters to Bauer

Though Bauer did not deal with North Africa in his geographical survey of early Christianities, he seems to contradict his own method by finding support for his arguments on more than a few occasions from Tertullian of Carthage (ca. 160–220). It was for this reason that Walther Völker's critique in 1935 concluded that Bauer "arrives at these astonishing conclusions by . . . inferences from later periods."[22] This focused section will first show briefly how Bauer presents Tertullian in light of his broader argument. Second, because Bauer has opened the door to "later" early Christian thought, we will show why Tertullian's theology and example of a second- and third-century African Christian may indeed challenge Bauer's core thesis on three specific fronts. Put another way, we will show why Tertullian matters to Bauer and then argue why Tertullian ought to matter more to him.

It should interest the reader to know that Bauer refers to the Carthaginian father no less than ten times throughout his work. Also, in the

22. Völker, "Walter Bauer's *Rechtgläubigkeit*," 404.

appendix to the 1971 English edition, George Strecker makes mention of him.[23] Bauer presents Tertullian as a known heresy-fighter,[24] one who was familiar with the Ebionite teachings,[25] and one who also ridiculed the theology of Melito of Sardis (died ca. 180).[26] In his remaining interaction with Tertullian, Bauer limits his discussion to the topic of Tertullian and Montanism.

Bauer identifies Tertullian as one who collected Montanist writings[27] and who served to interpret the movement for the church and for historians.[28] Bauer notes that Tertullian refers to Montanism simply as the "New Prophecy"[29] and that he acknowledged the presence of one woman in his congregation who participated in the liturgical assembly by offering charismatic utterances.[30] Bauer adds that Tertullian regarded himself as one enabled by the Holy Spirit to speak correctly about the movement, not unlike those empowered by the Spirit to interpret Scripture.[31] Hence, for Bauer, Tertullian was a thoroughgoing Montanist—a member of a New Prophecy congregation that had physically split from the great church in Carthage.[32]

Throughout the course of his argument, Bauer interacts with a number of Tertullian's writings, including *Against Praxeas, Against Marcion, On the Resurrection of the Flesh,* and *On the Soul.*[33] However, he concludes that Tertullian's Montanist-related polemics—his defense of the movement—cannot be trusted and he largely dismisses Tertullian's contributions by stating, "Tertullian is only able to teach us that even 'the church' has become the object of violent and unjust attacks."[34]

In short, Bauer depicts Tertullian as an unreliable polemicist who resides completely within a separatist community. Surely, Tertullian is of interest to Bauer because of his apparent simultaneous commitment to

23. Bauer, *Orthodoxy and Heresy,* 312.

24. Ibid., 99.

25. Bauer, *Orthodoxy and Heresy,* 281.

26. Ibid., 154, basing this on Jerome's account in *Vir. ill.* 24.

27. Bauer, *Orthodoxy and Heresy,* 142.

28. Ibid., 177.

29. Ibid., 180.

30. Ibid., 178.

31. Ibid., 180.

32. Ibid., 177, 211.

33. Ibid., 180.

34. Ibid., 144.

"heresy" and "orthodoxy." Tertullian has, of course, troubled many historians and theologians because of his alleged dabbling in heresy while also being remembered as a key contributor to Christian orthodoxy. In the appendix of Bauer's work, Strecker raises this very question: "What happens when we find a person who is clearly a predecessor of 'orthodoxy' in one sense but not in another? How do we handle a Tertullian, with his Montanist sympathies?"[35]

Why Tertullian Should Matter More to Bauer

Given that Bauer has opened the door and referenced this African church father in support of his thesis, it is fair to cross-examine Bauer and to raise some pertinent points about Tertullian's contribution that may in fact call into question some aspects of Bauer's general proposals. In fact, Gerald Bray asserts that Tertullian did not merely represent his own private thoughts, but that his life and thought offer a window into the everyday life of second- and third-century North African Christianity.[36] Similarly, François Decret adds:

> Tertullian's prominent place in the history of the church is due to the fact that he . . . aptly represented his context and provided great evidence for the African Christianity of his day.
> . . . Through his genius and weaknesses, boldness in the midst of battles, revolt in the face of injustices, excesses, affinity for provocation, preference for paradox, quibbling spirit, and appetite for brilliant and subtle formulas, Tertullian represented an entire people.[37]

For the sake of space, our cross-examination will be confined to three areas.

Roman Ecclesiastical Dominance?

A key part of Bauer's argument is that Christian orthodoxy is really the belief system of the church at Rome—"the center and chief source of

---

35. Strecker, "Reception of the Book," 312.

36. Bray, "Tertullian," 65.

37. Decret, *Early Christianity in North Africa,* 34.

power for the 'orthodox' movement within Christianity."[38] That is, since the episcopate of Clement of Rome (ca. 88–97), when the Roman church wrote to and instructed the Corinthian church, the Roman church effectively bullied the broader church, through coercion and manipulation, toward its version of orthodoxy. It seems, however, that Tertullian's orthodox actions, especially toward the leadership of the Roman church, provide a healthy challenge to Bauer's presupposition.

We should remember that *Against Praxeas*, Tertullian's greatest theological work that anticipated the Council of Nicaea more than a century later, was leveled at the teaching of a heretical bishop of Rome—probably Callistus (ca. 217–222).[39] Tertullian challenged this insufficient articulation of the Godhead (monarchianism) that was held not only by Callistus but also by at least one other second-century Roman bishop, Zephyrinus (ca. 198–217). In forging a vocabulary and framework for describing the Trinity, Tertullian made orthodox Christian arguments that have largely endured. Yet, in doing so, he openly challenged the authority of the Roman church leadership.

Tertullian's theological activity in this encounter not only showed Trinitarian concerns, but it also revealed his ecclesiology, especially concerning the office of bishop or overseer. Challenging the notion that Peter's alleged Roman episcopate perpetually endowed his successors with authority, Tertullian argued that every church pastor is in reality a Peter for his church. Pastoral authority is given to leaders of *congregations*, not simply to the leader of the Roman congregation.[40] This African perspective toward Rome (and African influence over against Rome) would continue through the following centuries as Cyprian of Carthage (248–258) challenged Stephen of Rome (254–257) over rebaptism, or when Augustine of Hippo (395–430) engaged the Roman bishops Innocent (401–417) and Zosimus (417–418) over the Pelagian controversy.[41]

38. Bauer, *Orthodoxy and Heresy*, 229.

39. McGowan, "Tertullian and the 'Heretical' Origins," 438.

40. Tertullian, *On Modesty*, 21.9–10, 16–17; Decret, *Early Christianity in North Africa*, 40.

41. Cyprian, *Ep.* 74; Augustine, *Ep.* 176–77; also Smither, *Augustine as Mentor*, 29, 32–33, 38, 172–74, 201–204.

What about His Montanism?

Bauer refers to the early African father as the "Montanist Tertullian."[42] As noted, Bauer works from the premise that Tertullian officially broke with the catholic church and embraced a Montanist doctrine that was incompatible with Christian orthodoxy. At first glance, Tertullian's Montanist attachment seems to lend credence to the overall Bauer framework on heresy and orthodoxy. However, let us revisit Tertullian's Montanist journey and explore what this meant for his relationship to the "great church," and for his theological development.

Bauer is correct in asserting that Tertullian described the Montanist movement as the New Prophecy.[43] While Tertullian's interest in the group was both theological and ethical, it seems that he was mostly driven by the latter. As Bray asserts, Tertullian's Montanist leanings are most apparent in his pastoral and ethical treatises.[44] Jaroslav Pelikan adds that for Tertullian, "the central content of these visions, revelations, prophecies, and dreams was not doctrinal but ethical. Tertullian insisted that the Paraclete had come to establish a new discipline, not a new teaching."[45] Indeed, in *Against Praxeas,* Tertullian distinguishes between average and rather lax Christians (*psychici*) and those that are following the Paraclete and living fully the intended Christian experience.[46] In a related way, he envisioned the church as a "spirit church" led by prophets instead of priests who had bought into a worldly hierarchical system. Also regarding worship, Tertullian noted that some participants in liturgical assemblies offered charismatic utterances. While this may seem distinctive of second- and third-century Montanism, Justin (Ephesus and Rome, died ca. 165), Irenaeus (Gaul, d. 202), and later Cyprian (Carthage, d. 258) also described a similar phenomenon in their contexts.[47]

Given that Tertullian was interested in the rigorous lifestyle and worship of the so-called Montanists, how did he regard their eschatological claims—namely that Christ would return to Pepuza in Asia Minor? In his work *Against Marcion,* Tertullian has Christ returning to Jerusalem and

---

42. Bauer, *Orthodoxy and Heresy,* 211.

43. Tertullian, *Marc.* 3.24.4, 4.22.4; *Res.* 63.3; also Trevett, *Montanism,* 67.

44. Bray, "Tertullian," 70.

45. Pelikan, *Emergence of the Catholic Tradition,* 100.

46. Tertullian, *Prax.* 1.7; McGowan, "Tertullian and the 'Heretical' Origins," 442.

47. Pelikan, *Emergence of the Catholic Tradition,* 99–100.

not Pepuza. It may be that Tertullian rejected these Montanist teachings or, as Christine Trevett has argued, perhaps he was completely unaware of these Montanist ideas that were present in Asia Minor and even Rome.[48]

Bauer's assertion that Tertullian was a Montanist who officially split with the great church has been largely dismissed by the consensus of scholarship of the last generation. It seems that Bauer and others who have insisted on a schismatic Tertullian have largely depended upon Jerome's questionable depiction of the African father.[49] Bray, representing the thoughts of Decret, Trevett, and Powell, asserts: "to say that [Tertullian] broke with the mainline church at Carthage and joined the sect is taking the evidence we have too far."[50] Trevett adds that since the New Prophecy had already been condemned in Asia Minor, the form that arrived in Africa in the late second century was much more orthodox. Trevett continues: "We should not assume that a *schismatic* prophetic community was formed apart from the catholics in Carthage. Tertullian the catholic Christian remained catholic in his thinking."[51]

What then can we conclude about Tertullian's theological development in light of his relationship to the New Prophecy? First, it seems that Tertullian's involvement with the group helped to clarify his Trinitarian thinking, especially regarding the person of the Holy Spirit.[52] As noted, his articulations of the Trinity were quite innovative and anticipated Nicene thinking. On the other hand, it should be noted that Tertullian, through his strength and individualism, probably shaped African Montanism by causing it to look different than its counterpart in Asia Minor, especially on the doctrines of the Holy Spirit and eschatology.[53] Second, as we will argue shortly, Tertullian's most cherished theological value and method was following the Rule of Faith (*regula fidei*). Hence, the thought and practice associated with the New Prophecy had to be filtered through the

---

48. Tertullian, *Marc.* 3.24.3–4; also Powell, "Tertullianists and Cataphrygians"; Trevett, *Montanism*, 75.

49. Jerome, *Vir. ill.* 53.4; also McGowan, "Tertullian and the 'Heretical' Origins," 438.

50. Bray, "Tertullian," 64; also Decret, *Early Christianity in North Africa*, 37; Powell, "Tertullianists and Cataphrygians," 33–36; and Trevett, *Montanism*, 67–69.

51. Trevett, *Montanism*, 68–69.

52. A good example of this development is found in comparing Tertullian's thoughts in *Apol.* 21.11–14 with *Prax.* 3.1. McGowan, "Tertullian and the 'Heretical' Origins," 440–45; also Pelikan, *Emergence of the Catholic Tradition*, 105–6.

53. Powell, "Tertullianists and Cataphrygians," 50; also Pelikan, *Emergence of the Catholic Tradition*, 101.

Rule. In short, Decret argues that Tertullian's theology was not actually altered by his Montanist journey, and Trevett concludes that "Tertullian the Montanist" was always "Tertullian the Montanist catholic."[54]

In conclusion, Tertullian's Montanism was not so much a story of heresy and orthodoxy as it was one of diversity within an otherwise orthodox Christianity.[55] Again, Tertullian represents the passionate and, at times, uncooperative spirit of early African Christianity. In this sense, the New Prophecy gatherings could be regarded as special meetings within the "great church" or, as Trevett has concluded, "enthusiasts of the New Prophecy were *not* so separated, but were more probably an *ecclesiola in ecclesia*."[56]

His Concern for the Rule of Faith?

Concerning Tertullian's Montanist leanings and orthodoxy, Decret has argued that Tertullian's highest priority was to uphold the Rule of Faith rather than to promote new ideas on ecclesiology or prophecy.[57] In *On Monogamy*, Tertullian asserts that the Paraclete is a "restorer more than an innovator."[58] Therefore, in this final line of questioning, let us consider Tertullian's understanding of the Rule of Faith, how it connected him to the broader early Christian church, and why this is a significant rebuttal to Bauer's thesis.

Bryan Litfin defines the Rule of Faith as "a confessional formula (fixed neither in wording nor in content, yet following the same general pattern) that summarized orthodox beliefs about the actions of God and Christ in the world" and as "a convenient summary of catholic orthodoxy."[59] Articulations of the Rule appear at least three times in Tertullian's writings with the clearest occurring in his *Prescription against Heretics* where he writes:

---

54. Decret, *Early Christianity in North Africa*, 38; Trevett, *Montanism*, 69.

55. Indeed, this is what some of Bauer's early critics said about his thesis. See a summary of these in Köstenberger and Kruger, *Heresy of Orthodoxy*, 35–38.

56. Trevett, *Montanism*, 74; also Powell, "Tertullianists and Cataphrygians," 37–38.

57. Decret, *Early Christianity in North Africa*, 39.

58. Tertullian, *On Monogamy* 4.1 cited in McGowan, "Tertullian and the 'Heretical' Origins," 454.

59. Litfin, "Learning from Patristic Use," 79; see also Köstenberger and Kruger, *Heresy of Orthodoxy*, 54.

This rule of faith . . . there is one only God, and that He is none other than the Creator of the world, who produced all things out of nothing through His own Word, first of all sent forth; that this Word is called His Son, *and*, under the name of God, was seen "in diverse manners" by the patriarchs, heard at all times in the prophets, at last brought down by the Spirit and Power of the Father into the Virgin Mary, was made flesh in her womb, and, being born of her, went forth as Jesus Christ; thenceforth He preached the new law and the new promise of the kingdom of heaven, worked miracles; having been crucified, He rose again the third day; [then] having ascended into the heavens, He sat at the right hand of the Father; sent instead of Himself the Power of the Holy Ghost to lead such as believe; will come with glory to take the saints to the enjoyment of everlasting life and of the heavenly promises, and to condemn the wicked to everlasting fire, after the resurrection of both these classes shall have happened, together with the restoration of their flesh. This rule, as it will be proved, was taught by Christ, and raises amongst ourselves no other questions than those which heresies introduce, and which make men heretics.[60]

Contemporary Patristic scholars such as John Behr, Larry Hurtado, and Gerald Bray see the Rule of Faith as an effective bridge between the apostles, New Testament writings, and the early Christian creeds.[61] Köstenberger and Kruger assert that the content of the Rule of Faith was largely expressed in the eventual Nicene Creed.[62] It should be noted that one role of the church fathers was to hand over and pass down the apostolic teaching. For this reason, Hippolytus (ca. 170–ca. 236) referred to the Rule as the "tradition of the apostles" (*paradosis tōn apostolōn*).[63] Litfin carefully asserts that the Rule of Faith was in process and that the most developed expression of it does not appear until the works of Irenaeus. Still, Litfin, Köstenberger, and Kruger effectively argue that the Rule of Faith establishes a basic theological connection between Tertullian (ca. 160–ca. 220) and Clement of Rome (died ca. 99), Ignatius of Antioch (died ca. 110), Aristides (died ca. 133/140), Justin (100–165), Clement of

60. Tertullian, *Praescr.* 13; see also *Virg.* 1; *Prax.* 2; cf. Bray, "Tertullian," 75–76.

61. See Behr's general argument for the progression of orthodoxy in Behr, *Way to Nicaea*. See also Hurtado, *Lord Jesus Christ*; Bray and Oden, *We Believe in One God*, vol. 1, xxxvi.

62. Köstenberger and Kruger, *Heresy of Orthodoxy*, 56–57.

63. Hippolytus, *Noet.* 17–18; also Irenaeus, *Haer.* 3.3.3; Litfin, "Learning from Patristic Use," 88; Köstenberger and Kruger, *Heresy of Orthodoxy*, 55.

Alexandria (ca. 150–ca. 215), Origen (185–254), Hippolytus (170–236), Novatian (200–258), Cyprian (died 258), Dionysius (died 265), Athanasius (ca. 295–373), and Augustine (354–430).[64]

In short, Tertullian's conviction about and use of the Rule of Faith to summarize salvation history, interpret Scripture, and ultimately make sense of Christian experiences and practice such as the New Prophecy placed him in a large community of Christian theologians from the first three centuries who were from diverse geographic and cultural backgrounds.[65] Professor Bauer would have done well to reflect more on Tertullian and the noted father's concern for the Rule of Faith (and orthodoxy). In fact, H. E. W. Turner offered this same critique of Bauer in his 1954 work, *The Pattern of Christian Truth*.[66]

Summary Impact

Though Bauer regarded Tertullian as generally too late and thus largely irrelevant for discussion, he nevertheless appealed to Tertullian when it was convenient. We have seen how Bauer perceived and appropriated Tertullian. However, in doing so, he opened the door to fresh considerations for how Tertullian's life, actions, and theology could actually pose a challenge to his overall thesis. Specifically:

1. Tertullian did not passively submit to the church at Rome; rather, he openly challenged the Roman church when monarchianism was held by its leadership.

2. Tertullian was more orthodox in his Montanism than Bauer recognized. Also, as more recent scholarship has maintained, his Montanist leanings probably did not lead him to break from the "great church."

3. Tertullian's concern for the Rule of Faith places him in the geographically and culturally diverse orthodox company of church fathers who lived from the first to the fifth centuries.

---

64. Litfin, "Learning from Patristic Use," 80–94; Köstenberger and Kruger, *Heresy of Orthodoxy*, 54.

65. See Hartog, "'Rule of Faith.'"

66. Turner, *Pattern of Christian Truth*, 28–31; also Köstenberger and Kruger, *Heresy of Orthodoxy*, 34.

Tertullian's story within the landscape of North African Christianity seems to run counter to Bauer's proposal that heresy eventually developed into or was forced into orthodoxy. However, what it does show is a church movement that was consciously clinging to the essentials of the apostolic teaching while exhibiting development and diversity within a "catholic" unity.

Diversity, Competition, and Conflict within Christian North Africa

The same conscious affinity for right belief and practice visible in Tertullian highlights other, broader implications of North African Christian development for Bauer's thesis. The following discussion outlines several of these. The fact that Tertullian was later labeled as heretical or schismatic has often obscured a proper historical understanding of his position in and relative to the church at large and has prevented appreciation of his representative character of broader North African Christianity— something of which Bauer himself was guilty. In drawing too polarized and uniform a demarcation between "orthodoxy" and "heresy," might not similar confusion have been unintentionally promoted by Bauer and his followers in their assessment and interpretation of other "heretics" and conflicts? A suspect judgment based on suspect sources (e.g., here of Jerome's account) can lead to a hasty yet unwarranted appropriation of later material and labels to one's arguments about "earliest" Christianity. One is also warned against a truncated or polarizing understanding of the orthodox-heretical spectrum of early Christian development.[67]

Bauer's view of competing "Christianities" involving "orthodox" perspectives generally assumes an external force which subjects or supplants an "earlier" original, regional Christianity.[68] In North Africa, however, diverse (even competing) Christian groups emerged in the same locale within a consciously "orthodox" and "catholic" matrix. That is, the various flavors which Christianity took on there stimulated competition of sorts between Christians in the area. If anything, the measured, significant embrace of the "New Prophecy" in North Africa represented by (not only) Tertullian, shows that relatively recent, distinctive, regional Chris-

---

67. A spectrum which was "catholic" as defined by Bryan Litfin's essay in this volume.

68. Bauer, *Orthodoxy and Heresy*, 229–30.

tianity was capable of adopting an emphasis from the church beyond its borders on its doctrinal merits and in a way that reflected continuity with the apostolic scriptures (e.g. predictions regarding the Paraclete) and the apostolic *regula fidei*.

Early evidence in North Africa does reveal considerable conflict within the church. We have already referenced criticism of local clergy by Perpetua and Tertullian. And while the view that Tertullian was excommunicated from or broke with the church at Carthage has now been rightly rejected,[69] such a *possibility* still clearly indicates the level reached by voices of critical protest raised in Carthage.[70] Yet the conflicts in North Africa occurred between constituents who considered themselves affiliated, not between groups which saw each other as *essentially* different—as the incidences of schism and potential schism confirm.

On a number of occasions schism did occur precisely because of an emphasis typical of Christianity in North Africa. Following the onset of the first truly empire-wide persecution under Decius (250), many Christians lapsed under the pressure. This created a large-scale problem out of what had been a long-term but localized nagging issue for the church. Such *lapsi* were universally viewed as apostates who had put themselves at risk outside the communion of the church—but how were they to be reconciled, if at all?[71] The issue was difficult for Cyprian to handle because he went into hiding during the onset of the persecution so that the church in Carthage would not be left leaderless during the crisis. Meanwhile some *confessors*—Christians who had suffered persecution and torture but not to the point of death and who had often been assigned with a certain charismatic authority—began to restore the lapsed. Cyprian regarded this as the bishop's business and ordered that the lapsed should wait for peace and then let the episcopate collectively address the issue. The ensuing controversy was sharp, but eventual compromise was reached wherein the gravity of the lapse would determine the severity of

---

69. As noted above, Tertullian remained in the church as part of an internal holiness movement centered on the Spirit within the church at Carthage (see also Powell, "Tertullianists and Cataphrygians," 33–54). Moreover, he may well have retained his role on the council of lay-elders, or *seniores*, which played a significant role in the churches of North Africa (Tabbernee, "To Pardon or not to Pardon?," 375–76 and 380–86).

70. Though particularly true after he adopted the "New Prophecy" of the Paraclete derived from Montanus, Maxilla, and Priscilla in Phrygia, it was also true of Tertullian before he entered his "Montanist" phase.

71. Bonner, "Schism and Church Unity," 222–23.

the penance, following which the bishop would accept the lapsed back into communion. Some thought this too strict, some not strict enough, and both in Rome and in North Africa schisms resulted.[72]

Several points deserve note here. The first is that the dialogue in the midst of controversy implies a desire for overall unity; the parties tried to correct each other for the sake of (their view of) the whole.

Second is the obvious spectrum of belief and practice within the entire church in Carthage (and based on Cyprian's appeal to conciliar approach, we may say North Africa). Occasions of division reinforce the existence of prior diversity within an overarching unity. Many lapsed, good numbers were later martyred and "confessed" Christ, and committed Christians such as Cyprian went into hiding, as no doubt did many of varying levels of commitment. So the fractures in the North African church revealed by general persecution testify to a breadth of diversity still held within unified confines in the mid-third century that are consistent with what has already been demonstrated about earliest known North African Christianity (ca. 180–215).

Third, as did Tertullian's, Cyprian's writings reflect the assumed authority of apostolic connection and accepted Scriptures (*passim*, e.g. *On Unity* 4–5; 14–17). Cyprian was quite able to describe a schismatic as violating the Scriptures, but he never argued as if his opponents had rejected his Scriptures, nor that they held to other Scriptures. He assumed a broadly and deeply ordered and integrated community.[73] All sides in this controversy appear to share common depictions of commitment to orthodoxy and unity as well as a claim to represent aspects of African traditional emphasis.[74] Finally, it is significant that Cyprian sought for an ordered response to the issue through conciliar methods based on the plurality of churches in the North African province.[75] Appeal to the broader church in

---

72. The backdrop of separate laxist and rigorist congregations at Carthage helps frame Cyprian's most famous work, *On the Unity*.

73. See e.g. Burns, *Cyprian the Bishop*, 13.

74. Tertullian's views are particularly reflected in his rigorous responses, and he viewed flight from persecution as a form of apostasy. However, his respect for the work of the Spirit also finds a place in both Cyprian and certain "laxist" positions (whether in Cyprian's claimed dream vision or through the martyrs/confessors).

75. Something anticipated by Tertullian's ecclesiology; see the discussion of his Montanism above.

an area characterized by strong opinions and diversity reflects a confidence in and commitment to authority beyond one's control.[76]

The potential for internal division as Christianity developed in North Africa is clear. What is significant *contra* Bauer is that divisions were emergent, not original; they are factious and sometimes even schismatic, but not reflective of competing "orthodoxies." African regional Christianity shows that competitors emerged from shared origins to represent various strands along the same essential trajectory, not initially different species. This holds true whether considering Tertullian and local or broader church leadership, Perpetua and local clergy,[77] Cyprian and the confessors of the Decian persecution, or the split between Donatists and Catholics. The arguments in North Africa were most often over who was being true or more true to an agreed-upon, authentic Christian authority.[78]

We do not see a willingness to explore new Christian variations that are outside the frame of these "authentic" connections.[79] In fact new movements in the church, such as asceticism and monasticism, were often slow to reach and take off in North Africa.[80] The view that the Paraclete was restoring rather than innovating through the "New Prophecy" bears repeating. It was a movement that was driven by engagement with the apostolic writings and the expectations of the apostolic generations, and was expected to be consistent with the *regula fidei*. Doctrinal similarities almost always outweighed doctrinal differences in North African conflicts.

---

76. In this we also see what Tilley calls African "collegial" Christianity in the face of confrontations; cf. Tilley, "North Africa," 392–95 (esp. 394); cf. Tilley, "Collapse of a Collegial Church," 7–9.

77. Moreschini and Norelli observe that "opposition between martyrs and the ecclesiastical hierarchy was common in Tertullian's time due to the tension between the spiritual authority to grant reconciliation to the lapsed that was seen to reside both with the martyrs and with the bishop (Moreschini and Norelli, *Early Christian Greek and Latin Literature*, vol. 1, 358).

78. Also significant, relative to Bauer, is that such authority is not geographically dependent but is tied to the Rule of Faith, the Apostles, the Scriptures, and the Holy Spirit.

79. "Authentic" here applies to the perception of these connections by the figures at the time, not as it relates to some objective or modern perspective. Tertullian's ability to embrace "Montanism" within the framework of the Rule of Faith and "apostolic" Scriptures is a prime example.

80. Cf. Alexander, *Augustine's Early Ecclesiology*, 227–28.

"Lost Christianities," the Retention of the Ideas, and the Influence of Dissenters

Our early North African case study shows that when certain Christian aspects or groups were "lost" in an area, their evidence was not necessarily eliminated nor their influence discarded. Tertullian was not "lost" even though his name (and maybe some like-minded prophetic believers) went "missing" from North African Christianity for a time. Indeed, the reconciliation of a small *Tertullianistae* sect into the broader church in the fifth century illustrates this.[81] Though he may have been posthumously *persona non grata* in name for some official church circles, Tertullian was still clearly influential for Cyprian. The bishop never referred to the great theologian by name, but he had read him thoroughly and likely considered him as his doctrinal "master."[82] The broader church also retained Tertullian's *corpus*, apologetic arguments, theological formulations and terminology; and the North African church continued to be characterized by his earnestness and rigor. That is, both locally and universally, even when Tertullian came to be painted with the brush of "schism" or "heresy" (his "name" was "lost"), the majority of his Christianity was retained by the church with nearly all of its distinctives.

Similarly, was the charismatic emphasis of Perpetua "lost" when Catholic editors dropped the original (arguably "Montanist") introduction in later editions of her *Passio*?[83] The almost canonical legacy of her account in Augustine's day as well as the original manuscript tradition attest otherwise,[84] as does the Spirit-focus of Cyprian's *corpus* and correspondence. Nor were Cyprian or even Donatism "lost," even though Augustine and the eventually triumphant "Catholic" church rejected their ideas of rebaptism or sacramental holiness.[85] Though each of these was in some way repudiated (even as extensions of Augustine's thought were

81. Bonner, "Schism and Church Unity," 221. Cf. Augustine, *On Heresies* 86. Even when certain followers of Tertullian did break with the broader church, their existence some 200 years later and their appearance in the context of being welcomed back into the broader church at a council in Carthage shows that they had not been "lost."

82. Decret, *Early Christianity in North Africa*, 70–71.

83. Cf. Tabbernee, "Perpetua, Montanism, and Christian Ministry," 432.

84. Cf. Moreschini and Norelli, *Early Christian Greek and Latin Literature*, vol. 1, 358.

85. On the broad legacy of Cyprianic theology, see "Cyprian's African Heritage," in Burns, *Cyprian the Bishop*, 166–77. The ongoing openness to Donatist baptism in the Catholic church in the controversy is important.

tempered with the Synod of Orange), it must be recognized that the flavor they represent was preserved and assimilated into the DNA of this
regional Christianity in an identifiable and enduring way that remained
distinctive *and* orthodox.[86] Their legacy certainly does not correspond to
silence.[87]

More importantly, in their own times, all of these considered themselves and were treated as "orthodox" in the important sense of apostolic
connection, reliance on catholic Scriptures, and even catholic desire for
unity. Competition of various sorts, not untainted by politics, did result
in "losers" that in some cases were subject to repression or negative labeling (e.g. Donatism being officially pronounced as a "heresy" in 405). But
the retention of essentially orthodox doctrine and Scriptures by figures
such as Tertullian, Cyprian, and the Donatists cannot be ignored. North
Africa shows that the inevitable grey area between what is considered
reconcilable and irreconcilable with authentic Christian parameters
must be acknowledged.

Rome and the Church in North Africa

We conclude by returning to Bauer's key tenet that "orthodoxy" was a
later superimposition on originally pluriform regional churches by particular, powerful churches and especially Rome. The very absence of a
tradition about the gospel's arrival in North Africa is significant here.
Neither external source nor indigenous character are cited by North African Christians in their internal competition or with external figures and
churches. So upon what did these regional Christians base their confident
actions relative to areas older in the faith? This lack of concern would
seem to result from the general assumption that they were effectively tied
to the Christianity of the Christ, Paraclete, and apostles by connections
independent of geography or lineage and confirmed by their participation in the Church of the martyrs. As discussed for Tertullian, our study

86. Indeed, one could do an entire study profitably considering Tertullian, Cyprian, and Augustine as transmitters of "authentic" North African Christianity.

87. In Ehrman's phrase "reformed or repressed, their traces covered over, until
scholars in the modern period . . . rediscovere[d] . . . anew the rich diversity and importance of these lost Christianities" (Ehrman, *Lost Christianities*, 11). Instead, from
Tertullian and Perpetua to Cyprian or Tyconius and beyond, the distinctive character
of African Christianity was not silenced until swept away by Islamic expansion, and
was well preserved in the literary tradition.

displays clear cases of North African influence upon the Roman church (e.g. in terms of Latin, theological vocabulary, and ideas—both doctrinal and administrative).[88] Evidence to 215 did not show influence from Rome on North Africa. Indeed, early Christianity in the province showed a willingness to criticize Rome on explicit theological lines. In this case influence flowed not from Rome; rather, we observe influence flowing *from* North African regional Christianity *upon* Rome. One would not expect to see this inversion based on Bauer's view of standard practice in emerging Christianity.[89]

In addition to this inversion of influence, the resistance of the regional church to attempts by external forces to exercise their influence in North Africa is remarkable. North African Christianity's self-sufficiency, even when embracing external influences by making them its own, is clear in Tertullian's time and Cyprian's, as this "younger" church fended off claims for control from Rome, for example.

Perhaps nothing epitomizes this more than the conflict (ca. 255–257) between Cyprian and Stephen of Rome. In the context of dealing with the lapsed following widespread persecution, questions arose regarding the administration of baptism outside the Catholic Church. Namely, if one received baptism in schism and then came to the Catholic Church, did the prior baptism count or was (re)baptism necessary? In the North African tradition, not surprisingly, such baptism was not viewed as valid and its recipients needed to be baptized *de nova*.

Stephen took a different line by stating that the traditional practice at Rome of laying on of hands in a rite of reconciliation was sufficient to validate previous non-Catholic baptism and condemned the North African practice of (re)baptism. Cyprian was not impressed by Roman tradition *per se* and such a directive flew in the face of Cyprian's ideal of the equality of all bishops and the unity of the church resting on the unity of its episcopate.

The two went head-to-head over this issue and it was in this conflict that Stephen made the first use of the Matthew 16:18 passage ("you are Peter, and on this *Petrus*, I will build my church . . . ") to claim specific authority for the Roman see over all other bishops. Even so, Cyprian would

---

88. Cf. also receipt of Cyprian's *On the Lapsed* by followers of the Novatianist schism at Rome.

89. Regarding creativity and theological exposition, James Moffatt's comment within his review of Bauer that "The real thinking upon vital Christianity for centuries was done outside the Roman Church" (Bauer, *Orthodoxy and Heresy*, 292) remains generally valid and specifically so for Latin Christianity.

not agree or back down, acknowledging only that the apostolic authority was given to Peter first as a symbol of the unity that was given to all the apostles and thus to all the bishops of the church.[90]

Things reached a fever pitch, and Stephen threatened to excommunicate Cyprian, who returned the favor unfazed. It is significant that Cyprian received support and agreement against Stephen from Antioch and other major sees.[91] Moreover, Cyprian's conciliar initiatives and his theory of the *collegium* of bishops were affirmed by several correspondents in the East. The rift with Rome was not fought out to a bitter end since Cyprian was martyred in 258, and Stephen died soon after that (not as a martyr).

The whole episode clearly shows that North African Christianity's resistance to external pressure, even conflict with the Bishop of Rome, was much greater than Bauer assumed for earlier contexts. North Africans were quite ready to defend their beliefs against Rome or others, and the primate of Carthage was quite comfortable taking on the bishop of Rome directly. None of these phenomena would be expected by Bauer's thesis. More importantly, on Bauer's view they should be *less* likely by the time of our test case.

Conclusions

It is clear that early North African Christianity is of value for examining the Bauer Thesis and its implications. The same kind of developmental material from the province, if selectively available from 50 to 75 years earlier, might have been claimed by proponents of the Bauer Thesis as evidence of another distinctive regional Christianity later subjugated to external "orthodoxy." Yet, solid contextual information shows that on issues of the nature and location of authority, on issues of the canon, and in general doctrine and the Rule of Faith, earliest North African Christianity does not line up with Bauer.

The presence of early, strong distinctives here do not suggest unknown or counter-orthodox Christian antecedents. Conflict in the region did not require or evidence external meddling—rather local distinctives themselves may be taken to different conclusions and provide all the fodder needed for conflict and even competition. Opponents in situations

---

90. I.e., it indicated priority not primacy. Cf. Cyprian, *Ep.* 68.

91. Cf. *Ep.* 75, from Firmillian.

such as North Africa may well have derived from the same origins. In any case, their origins manifest diversity within initial unity along with antecedents sharing catholic and orthodox claims to apostolic teaching and the Scriptures. Thus this study supports the view of emergent/evolving local competition against the assumption of competing origins or the superimposition of external "orthodoxy."

The enduring character of early Christianity in regions such as North Africa is quite dramatic, even when certain persons or groups "typical" of the region are condemned or marginalized. Moreover, the North African character was confident in judging external input for orthodoxy and proved resistant to external pressures, showing that Rome in particular was not necessarily capable of enforcing its "orthodoxy" on other areas in the periods prior to Constantine. More than a century later than the supposed Roman oppression of Christianity in Egypt (based on Mark's gospel),[92] Rome proved quite incapable of bringing the upstart Carthaginian church into line.

In terms of theological doctrine, early Christianity in North Africa constitutes one of the clearest examples that the understanding of the core Christian message (Christ as risen Savior and Lord) continued to develop in the light of reflections on generally accepted Christian Scriptures and the essential elements of Christian belief, as illustrated in the *regula fidei*. Issues of practice were still acknowledged as fluid, yet within certain, established parameters.[93] From North Africa, Tertullian's contribution to Trinitarian thought and vocabulary is the most dramatic example, but Cyprian's sacramental and ecclesiastical practical theology could also be cited. That no neatly encapsulated (i.e. completely formulated or completely canonized) Christianity or systematic theology came from first-generation Christians does not appear to undermine the concept of "orthodoxy" in the late second- or early third-century church.[94] Rather, the development and diversity we observe within parameters for unity suggest a pattern that had long since been the case.

For all the significant feuds within the family, including those that resulted in separation, North African Christianity embodied many such

92. Bauer, *Orthodoxy and Heresy*, 116–17.

93. One could cite as evidence the grudging view Tertullian took of infant baptism, or the arguments for a younger African "tradition" of (re)baptism of heretics/schismatics against the older Roman tradition (see above).

94. That is, a normative Christianity in the sense of developing "apostolic" parameters for "true" doctrine.

instructive and distinctive reflections of a unified body of Christ and unified reliance on the Spirit in the face of hostility and persecution. As occurred in the other regions where Christianity emerged, this established a legacy of "early orthodoxy" that was of benefit to the larger church of its time and to the broader church down through the centuries. In North Africa, a uniform gospel message and set of core beliefs appear in the midst of a diverse, expanding, and evolving context of structure, doctrinal understanding, practice, liturgy, and mission. It is this evolutionary development in light of core teachings that are believed to be essential for experiencing the work of Christ (salvation) that births North Africa's orthodoxy. Such phenomena may, despite Bauer's protests, help to frame a new, more comprehensive, and more balanced appreciation of orthodoxy in earliest Christianity in its diverse contexts.

8

Patristic Heresiology: The Difficulties of Reliability and Legitimacy

W. Brian Shelton

The second and third centuries of Christianity witnessed a significant surge in aggressive writings against what the "great church" perceived to be false doctrine. This era evidences heightened polemical treatises against the theology, culture, and morality of the heretics, their communities, and their writings. This genre of writings is known as "heresiology." Contemporary views of these works range from recognizing them as valid church writings against heresy to aggressive constrictions of doctrinal definition against its own constituents. Therefore, these polemical treatises pose a problem for historical interpretation, to the extent that some scholars regard them as unreliable and illegitimate. This essay seeks to better understand and appreciate these writings.

In various regions of the empire, writers targeted sundry types of organized theological threats. From first hand exposure travelling across the ancient world, Hegesippus offered one of the earliest rebuttals that targeted all forms of developed heresy. From Lyons, Irenaeus's *Against Heresies* addressed multiple heresies, while focusing on the gnostic movements. From Rome, Hippolytus sought to address all heresies by linking them thematically and causally in his *Refutation of All Heresies*. From

Carthage, Tertullian assaulted the late heretical writers and leaders individually in works like *Against Marcion* and corporately in *Prescription against Heretics*. From Corinth, Dionysius wrote several pastoral epistles to Greek churches cautioning them about heretical ideologies in their ranks. From Cyprus, Epiphanius designed a "medicine chest" against the dangerous teaching of Origen and Arius. The traditional Christian reading of these writers has been one of implicit support, an appreciation that the early church managed to suppress the erroneous and even harmful doctrines that competed with the development of orthodoxy.

For critical historians like Walter Bauer, however, these writings triumphed through socio-political and geographical influence, and thus unduly shaped the development of church history and the self-understanding of the "great church." In this manner, these writings simply reflect privileged viewpoints.[1] The triumphant voices are "the vote of but *one* party" whose favorable circumstances promoted their theological preferences, not permitting a fair development of Christian ideas. "The 'church' is clearly in a privileged position insofar as it became "an authoritative bearer and custodian of the tradition."[2] These triumphant voices are the more prevalent "only because the chorus of others has been muted."[3] The heresiologists are the loudest of these dominant voices, the great bullies of momentum against the marginalized voices. In this way, they supposedly embody the power establishment of authoritarian and repressive marginalization. The issue of the legitimacy of such heresiologists thus joins the topics of other essays in this book as a challenge to the so-called Bauer Thesis, named after the early twentieth-century German scholar, Walter Bauer.

This essay will address the issue of the legitimacy and credibility of these orthodox writers. Because even a summary review of each significant heresiologist would prove to be too lengthy, this essay will provide only a small sampling of several of their works and methodologies. This sampling, however, will be sufficient to analyze the passionate discourse and ideological bents that characterized the heresiologists and their role in the development of Christian doctrine. With appropriate nuances, this essay

---

1. Bauer, *Orthodoxy and Heresy*, xi.

2. Ibid., 169.

3. Ibid., xxi. For a basic summary of Bauer's most important historical elements and the scholarship surrounding the Bauer era, see Bingham, "Development and Diversity," 45–66. The Evangelical Theological Society dedicated a national conference in 2005 to constructive responses to the Bauer Thesis.

will establish the legitimacy of the heresiological treatises and the relative reliability of the writings as historical sources and as theological milestones, worthy of critical evaluation yet not to be dismissed as mere vitriolic works.

Corpus and Problem

The difficulties of heresiological writing center on the issue of partiality. Voices like those of the patristic authors mentioned above shouted against perceived heresy as part of their overall strategy to defend the faith. Their boisterous declarations were part individual personality, part protection of their congregations, and part hatred for the errors that were viewed as threatening the theological or practical welfare of the church. Behind these motives, though, are other factors that may have been at play: socio-religious incentives, manipulation of truth, exaggerated explanations of scriptures that favored their views, falsification of practices among the heretical churches, and rewritings of history.[4] The historian's task entails the discernment of fact, perspective, and influential motive. An introduction to the characters and their works can guide us to a greater discernment of their claims.

Authors and Heresies

Hegesippus (d. 180) is among the early ecclesiastical pioneers who accused proponents of false doctrine. He provided the first list of Roman bishops that allowed for a continuity of authority and tradition over against schismatic heretics. He first identified the beginning of all heretical thought as rooted in one Thebuthis who "made a beginning secretly to corrupt the virgin church" when he was overlooked for a bishopric position. Similar sects—seven, in fact—arose of Jewish origin, that in turn produced doctrines of false Christs, prophets, and apostles that divided the unity of the church.[5]

Irenaeus (d. 202) addressed multiple opponents in *Against Heresies*, focusing upon the gnostic movements affecting the church. Irenaeus

---

4. As a polemical summary of the polemicists, Bart Ehrman offers two chapters of the orthodox "arsenal of conflicts," with numerous examples of patristic polemics against heresies (Ehrman, *Lost Christianities*, 181–227).

5. Eusebius, *Hist. eccl.* 4.22.4–6; ET from Cruse, *Eusebius' Ecclesiastical History*, 134.

seemed most interested in disciples of Valentinus, a gnostic figure with Western residence and influence. About the gnostic system he wrote: "The very fathers of this fable . . . [seem] inspired by different spirits of error. This very fact forms an *a priori* proof that the truth proclaimed by the Church is immovable, and that the theories of these men are but a tissue of falsehoods."[6] The structuring of *Against Heresies* and its possible inclusion of previous heresiological materials continue to spur fruitful scholarly endeavors.[7]

Hippolytus (d. 235) sought to reveal all heresies by linking them thematically and causally in *Refutation of All Heresies*. His idea of all heresies finding a source in Simon Magus resembles the claims of Justin Martyr.[8] Hippolytus provided a compendium of polemical opposition to pagan philosophies and practices, as well as divergent Christian beliefs. He even targeted Callistus, a contemporary bishop, who was accused of maintaining modal monarchianism, later named Sabellianism, and Hippolytus claimed that Bishop Callistus "perverted Sabellius himself."[9]

Tertullian (d. 220) assaulted the late heretical writers and leaders individually in works like *Against Marcion* and corporately in *Prescription against Heretics*. Tertullian believed that heretics were providentially used to keep proper Christian belief moving along its divinely appointed course.[10] Heretics "existed by virtue of God's desire to bring revelation to completion and discipline to perfection."[11] To this day, Tertullian is known for his sharp and biting rhetoric.[12] In his treatise against Marcion, he declared: "You may, I assure you, more easily find a man born without a heart or without brains, like Marcion himself, than without a body, like Marcion's Christ."[13] Similarly Tertullian charged: "To men of diseased vision even one lamp looks like many."[14]

---

6. Irenaeus, *Against Heresies* 1.9.5 (ANF: 1:330).

7. Kalvesmaki, "Original Sequence"; Hill, "Polycarp *contra* Marcion"; Moll, "Man with No Name"; Hill, "Reply"; Hill, "Man Who Needed No Introduction."

8. Wisse, "Nag Hammadi Library," 218. The origin in Simon Magus became a common motif (see Cohen, "Virgin Defiled," 8). On Justin's own rhetoric of heresy, see Royalty, "Justin's Conversion."

9. Hippolytus, *Refutation* 9.6 (ANF 5:128).

10. Kaufman, "Tertullian on Heresy," 168.

11. Ibid., 178.

12. For a full examination of Tertullian's rhetoric, see Sider, *Ancient Rhetoric*.

13. Tertullian, *Against Marcion* 4.10 (ANF 3:360).

14. Tertullian, *Against Marcion* 1.2 (ANF 3:272).

Dionysius (d. 176), bishop of Corinth, insisted that "the apostles of the devil have filled [the church] with tares, exchanging some things, and adding others . . . some have adulterated the sacred writings of the Lord."[15] Thus, he claimed, the brethren asked him to write his epistles, training congregations to beware of heresies.

Epiphanius (d. 403), bishop of Salamis, viewed "heresies" as "opinions" to be differentiated from true "dogma," and as distortions that reflected the fragmentation of the unity of humanity. For him, "heresies" included not only Christian deviations, but also Hellenism and its sects, Judaism and its sects, and other groupings.[16] In fact, Epiphanius believed that eighty heresies existed as an allegory to the eighty concubines referenced in Song of Songs 6:8–9, demonstrating how "alien the heretical tradition is to the faith of the church and [how] firmly it must be opposed."[17] Gérard Vallée insists, "Epiphanius has no equal in the history of heresiology for the art of insulting. His descriptions of heretical sects give much room to slander, insinuations, calumny, and ambiguities."[18]

Such heresiological voices have historically been the best sources for scholars to reconstruct the history of conflicts surrounding the development of doctrine. Not until the discovery of the manuscripts at Nag Hammadi that secured a collection of the gnostic legacy did primary source access to the purported heretics become available to us. Those targeted by early Christian polemics were defeated and their voices seemed drowned out of history, except in the select quotes that are dispensed at the mercy of the heresiologists. Therefore, much of modern scholarship has petitioned for the limitation of orthodox voices and for historical reconstructions more favorable to the marginalized communities. Averil Cameron sums up this position: "The extent to which early Christian heresy can be objectified in modern scholarship is limited indeed."[19] In fact, he even charges the traditional thinker: "Traditionalist Christians and true believers might look to an unchanging core of Christian belief, but most scholars will reject that as a satisfactory methodology, and even were it to be accepted, the problem remains of agreeing what that core

---

15. Eusebius, *Hist. eccl.* 4.23.12 (ET from Cruse, *Eusebius' Ecclesiastical History*, 137).

16. See Young, "Did Epiphanius Know."

17. Vallée, *Study in Anti-Gnostic Polemics*, vol. 1, 72.

18. Ibid., 73.

19. Cameron, "Violence of Orthodoxy," 103.

actually is or on what it is based."[20] The work of Walter Bauer is both a model and an impetus for contemporary scholarship to reconstruct the role of heresiologists and their validity in the development of doctrine.

Nevertheless, the historical critic Walter Bauer does not directly address heresiologists as frequently as one might expect in his classic work *Orthodoxy and Heresy in Earliest Christianity*. His work seems to avoid Hippolytus and Epiphanius, although it otherwise would happily identify the prejudice of ancient ecclesiastical authors, even as Elaine Pagels and Bart Ehrman do today. This surprise tactic of not directly attacking heresiologists holds true in this classic work—except for one exception. Walter Bauer treats Eusebius like a heresiologist.

The great historian of the church reported on orthodox activities against heresies in the era leading up to his time. Eusebius has been well noted among scholars as lacking objectivity in favor of the orthodox position.[21] Some of Bauer's comments offer a snapshot of his doubt about the historicity of the Eusebian *Ecclesiastical History*: "How can we believe that Eusebius actually has read these books?" "What Eusebius intends by piling up superlatives is quite clear. . . . He wants to show that the general rejection of false belief can be found from earliest times in Christian literature." "I cannot hide my suspicion that in my opinion these words [from Melito], especially their conclusion, could hardly have stood in Melito's work." "Eusebius tosses off the kind of statement with which we are already familiar in one form or another." "Eusebius' phrase 'still extant at the present time' is suspicious because of its monotonous repetition."[22] Bauer is right that Eusebius has an orthodox preference and is not above polemical statements himself, as the ancient historian's intent is to applaud his ecclesiastical predecessors for their legacy and influence.

Polemics, Tone, and Unreliability

Heresiological authors wrote in an argumentative style that deserves closer examination. Their works discuss the doctrinal errors of heresies in a polemical fashion. At times, this in itself leads to questionable results, all the more so because orthodox truth claims are assumed over against other metaphysical claims to truth. These heresiological figures employ

20. Ibid., 104.

21. Heyne, "Devious Eusebius?," 325–31.

22. Bauer, *Orthodoxy and Heresy*, 149, 150, 153, 156, 158, respectively.

ad hominem attacks when they accuse and demean their opponents, as if their sins made the doctrines guilty by association or show the logical consequence of false belief.[23] Heresy and heretics are assigned to an empowered category that is different, foreign, and threatening to a significant part of the "established" church. Alain Le Boullec rightly points out the power ploy of categorically transforming another into a "heretic" whose expulsion from the church seems all the more reasonable.[24] Thus the polemical works cannot be trusted, or so the Bauer Thesis goes. Frederick Wisse remarks, "The evidence presented by the heresiologists does not inspire the present-day historian to great confidence. . . . To prove such a point, a passionate polemicist, even if he was a saintly bishop, would not be above playing fast and loose with the evidence."[25]

Yet not all scholars agree that the polemics are so detrimental that the works lack historical legitimacy. For example, did Epiphanius draw fairly from heretical sources? Vallée could say, "We have no reason to reject *a priori* the information he is providing."[26] In fact, Epiphanius separates out his exposition, his refutation, and his invective materials in a pattern fashion that allows for a more objective consideration of the subjects of attack.[27] Darrell Bock also finds the polemics plenty salvageable, although willingly admitting that two methodological points by Bauer have stood the test of time: the place of geography and the exaggeration of the heresiologists. "In their desire to refute these views, the church fathers overstated their own case and sometimes were inaccurate about what was taking place." [28] Bauer's obvious example is the patristic claim that all heresies stemmed from the same root cause. Yet Bock argues that this observation about the heresiologists should not be overstated. "A check of Irenaeus against the sources of views he challenged reveals that he described those views accurately. Many of the details of views noted in other fathers also stand corroborated. The implications are important."[29]

In fact, the general accuracy of the heresiological claims about gnostic theology—our essential source of such thought until Nag

23. Grant, "Charges of 'Immorality.'"

24. Le Boulluec, "La réflexion d'Origène," 297, 307.

25. Wisse, "Nag Hammadi Library," 206–7.

26. Vallée, *Study in Anti-Gnostic Polemics*, 64, 69.

27. On Epiphanius's rhetoric, see Kim, "Bad Bishops."

28. Bock, *Missing Gospels*, 48.

29. Ibid. This claim comes not merely in the context of one particular source, but as a general description of Irenaeus's methodology in light of Bauer's theory.

Hammadi—has commonly been accepted as quite impressively reliable by many scholars. As Thomas Ferguson remarks, "Did Irenaeus represent his foes faithfully, or was he only concerned with proving his point? The general consensus now is that Irenaeus was fairly reliable in his transmission of Gnosticism."[30] Ferguson explains, "Asking whether Irenaeus is a systematic theologian or an accurate historical source is inherently flawed, for he aspired to be neither in composing *Against Heresies*. The debates surrounding Irenaeus's accuracy have failed to take into account the internal rhetorical argument, use of language, and intricate structural composition which have been recognized as hallmarks of his method."[31]

Mary Ann Donovan's guidebook to Irenaeus ends with an appendix addressing "The Question of Irenaeus's Reliability."[32] She acknowledges "two major discrepancies" between the Nag Hammadi library and the heresiologists. First, there is a "lack of significant overlapping in material and detail."[33] Second, the question is raised "whether the sects were indeed as differentiated by doctrine as the ancient Church writers indicated."[34] Nevertheless, Donovan concludes as follows: "If read with attention to his goal and methodology the work of Irenaeus can yield a fair appreciation of the Valentinians. Study of the Nag Hammadi material has not thus far raised substantial challenges to this opinion."[35] Of course, "The issue remains controverted,"[36] and not all heresologists were as dependable as Irenaeus.

Critics like Karen King can rightly bring out specific details of inaccuracy, but the larger picture painted by heresiologists is accepted as generally faithful to the gnostic position.[37] Frederik Wisse points out that

---

30. Ferguson, "Rule of Truth," 358. Elaine Pagels has attacked Irenaeus's reliability. See such critiques as found in Pagels, *Gnostic Gospels*; and in response, Grant, "Review." Note how John D. Turner was able to weave together Irenaeus, *Haer.* 1.29 with six Nag Hammadi tractates (Turner, "Gnostic Threefold Path").

31. Ferguson, "Rule of Truth," 358. On Irenaeus's rhetoric, see Perkins, "Irenaeus and the Gnostics"; Sullivan, "Identification and Dissociation."

32. Donovan, *One Right Reading?*, 175–77. Apart from the concluding paragraph, the same material was previously published as "Irenaeus" in *ABD* 3:457–61.

33. Donovan, *One Right Reading?*, 175.

34. Ibid.

35. Ibid., 176.

36. Ibid.

37. King analyzes Irenaeus's references to the *Secret Revelation of John* to draw out many similarities between them, but she notes that matters like the gnostic view of the body faced misrepresentation. "To say that *SRJ* considers the body to be evil by

much of what is contained in the polemical fathers is not present in the Nag Hammadi library, and he expends great energy in discrediting the classifications of gnostic groups employed by the fathers.[38] Despite pointing out some interesting details of error among the patristic writers, such contemporary studies tend to be so technical that ancient cases against heresies can lose their situated context in the rhetoric of the period.[39] Does a mislabeling of a gnostic sect as "Sethites" rather than "Shemites" completely discredit an ancient discussion within a culture of writing in which accuracy was commonly a lower value than rhetorical effect?[40]

Most recently, gnostic thought has received much attention in both scholarly and popular circles, and has come to epitomize the battle of orthodoxy vs. heresy. The words of Jaroslav Pelikan three decades ago still reflect Gnosticism in the early church context: "Mythology as well as philosophy, speculation combined with magic, were all intertwined in a bizarre and bewildering variety of forms."[41] Pelikan continued by describing Gnosticism's relationship to the rest of the church: "Gnostics delighted in these as ritual, and orthodox Christians delighted in them as proof of the absurdity of heresy and of its demonic origin."[42]

Reliability and Legitimacy

This understanding of the larger conflict leads to a consideration of how best to handle the reliability of the heresiologists. Without fully engaging the significant historical critical scholarship about the era and influence

---

nature misses the complexity of the text's presentation of the human body as both map and territory, as both revelation and battleground, as the soul's ally and the demiurgic weapon against which it must struggle" (King, "Social and Theological Effects," 43). Perhaps this is a fair charge of one point of one author about one text, but it seems to miss the larger point that Irenaeus and other anti-gnostic writers were making charges of the system itself—such as the very existence of a demiurge—often in a broad-stroke fashion.

38. Wisse, "Nag Hammadi Library," 208–11. Wisse offers a brief and helpful history of sympathetic and unsympathetic readings of the heresiologists (201–9).

39. On Irenaeus's rhetoric in particular, see Perkins, "Irenaeus and the Gnostics"; Sullivan, "Identification and Dissociation."

40. Irenaeus, likes some other classical authors, actually used the common perspective as an opposing paradigm in his own rhetoric (see Schoedel, "Philosophy and Rhetoric," 22).

41. Pelikan, *Emergence of the Catholic Tradition*, 83.

42. Ibid.

of these writers, below are several ways to address the credibility problem of the patristic heresiologists. These are lines of thinking, efforts towards understanding and even appreciating the heresiological claims. Critical scrutiny of these writers and their works must continue, and this list and its contents should not be viewed as a blind endorsement of the "winning side." The question of reliability and legitimacy is a real one, but not an insurmountable one nor a disqualifying one.

Reality of Theological Exploitation

Scholars of an orthodox position should not be afraid to concede the reality of exaggerative treatments of heretics and heretical thought by heresiologists. The dual context of the ancient world and passionate faith help explain the exploitive rhetoric of these writers as they encountered obstacles and threats to their belief system.[43] At the center of heresiological accusation remains a question of truth—a challenge to the orthodox deposit of the faith.

Polemical expression was a natural tactic in the classical rhetorical tradition, which was inevitably utilized by the orthodox heresiologists.[44] Pheme Perkins has shown that Irenaeus employs the expected approach of attacking an opponent by using specific methods of refutation, allegorical features, exaggerations, moral confrontations, and claims to humility—a virtual rhetorical handbook as one would expect in the ancient world.[45] Given the expected contextualization of the works, latitude of style and passion should be granted to the writers without accusing them of illegitimacy. The historian cannot expect the accuracy of these writers to be an automatic litmus test of legitimacy, when a partially inaccurate caricaturization was the accepted tactic of the day.

Hippolytus's writing about Callistus, his contemporary and bishop of Rome, is an excellent example of obvious inflation. In a work entitled

43. Cf. Shaye Cohen's comparison of the similar theorization and polemic in the patristic and rabbinic approaches to self-definition and authentication (Cohen, "Virgin Defiled").

44. Schoedel argues that the "general structure" and "method of argumentation" of Irenaeus's *Against Heresies* indicate "the influence of rhetorical principles" (Schoedel, "Philosophy and Rhetoric," 28). Irenaeus's use of dilemmas (and even rhetorical questions) tends to have a polarizing effect (Schoedel, "Philosophy and Rhetoric," 29–31). See also Donovan, *One Right Reading?*

45. Perkins, "Irenaeus and the Gnostics," 193–200.

Refutation of All Heresies, Hippolytus accused the Roman bishops Zephyrinus and Callistus of maintaining a monarchial position on the Trinity. With Callistus seemingly in view, Hippolytus charged: "He maintains that the Father is not one person and the Son another, but that they are one and the same; and that all things are full of the Divine Spirit, both those above."[46] Hippolytus insisted that Callistus maintained the position which he calls "Noetianism," but that he was cunning enough to speak in an orthodox fashion to the people. This deceitful bishop shirked "the ability of rectifying this heretic's error."[47] The attacks against the Roman bishop were not exclusively Trinitarian in impetus, however. In the face of persecution, Callistus's response to the lapsed seemed more lenient than that of Hippolytus, leading the latter to accuse the former of extreme laxity in church discipline by allowing rebaptism. Additionally, the work *Philosophoumena* included a criticism of Callistus's relaxing of the marital policy for clergy, all of which seemingly led to some schismatic commotion in the Roman community.[48] The variety of accusations grants an opportunity to infer political or ecclesiastical motivations in Hippolytus—not just theological.

Yet the reality of conflict does not necessarily warrant a reading of unscrupulous prejudice and exploitation. Walter Bauer, as both the focus of two chapters and as a theme supporting his overall thesis, posited how "the Roman church toward the close of the second century feels inclined and able to extend further the boundaries of her influence."[49] But Robert Williams has shown that Hippolytus rejected Montanist influence in Rome for more developed, theological reasons. The church in Rome did not merely reject Montanism because it fit the category of "heresy," or because it granted too much privilege to women, or because its spiritual gifts were threatening the liturgy, but Hippolytan writers "subordinated prophetic succession to apostolic succession in order to establish the superiority of scripture to subsequent prophecy, and notably without suppressing women's ordination."[50] The reasons were more theologically epistemological than politico-geographical: The written scriptures and

46. Hippolytus, *Refutation* 9.7 (ANF 5:130). He seems to have shared with Tertullian an animosity toward Callistus, but there is room for possibility that he is not the target of criticism here. Cf. Tertullian, *On Purity* 1.

47. Hippolytus, *Refutation* 9.6 (ANF 5:128).

48. Shelton, *Martyrdom from Exegesis*, 26–32

49. Bauer, *Orthodoxy and Heresy*, 129.

50. Williams, "'Hippolytan' Reactions," 136.

204 ORTHODOXY AND HERESY IN EARLY CHRISTIAN CONTEXTS

the oral prophecies should correlate. However, after this initial claim, Williams posits that "such tendencies would jeopardize the Roman church's growing stature and legitimacy" as a secondary consequence. Williams theologically contextualizes the issues, and thus he does not reduce heresiological motivation to political maneuvering.[51] The inevitability of conflict for these writers stemmed from the question of truth.

In the end, this reality of conflict does not stem merely from a desire to marginalize heresies and establish a power structure for orthodoxy.[52] Its motive is to confront the threat of error, the potential and actual harm to ecclesiastical congregations and the tradition inherited from the past. It stems first and foremost from a passionate protection of faith. Terry Tiessen says that for Irenaeus, "The Gnostic teachings and writings were not historical artifacts but living and dangerous realities" that threatened the faith that each side surely held dear.[53]

Truth Claims among Pre-Modern Thinkers

Truth claims by the "great church" about the faith were the epicenter around which the heresiological conflicts rumbled. The agenda of the contemporary Bauer approach seems unwilling to allow genuinely theological debates within the early church, preferring matters to be eclipsed by political and socio-geographical techniques of suppression. The criticism of this came as early as Walther Völker, who tackled several examples of Bauer's claim to political maneuvering in the texts of the *Edessene Chronicle*, *Diatessaron*, *Barnabas*, the Ignatian epistles, and *1 Clement*: "Unfortunately the author [Bauer] has made rich use of his imagination, and the result is that in many passages his evidence cannot stand up in the face of careful scrutiny."[54]

Accusations of ulterior motives distract from the nature of the battles between pre-modern thinkers. They were driven by an insistence upon the religious truth of Christ himself because they thought that the faith itself was at stake. Bauer and other descendants of the Enlightenment offer

---

51. Ibid., 137.

52. Elaine Pagels remarks that Irenaeus's motive was to "'subvert and destroy' the theology of those he considers a threat to the church" ("Conflicting Versions," 53).

53. Tiessen, "Gnosticism as Heresy," 31. See also the earlier version: Tiessen, "Gnosticism and Heresy."

54. Völker, "Walter Bauer's *Rechtgläubigkeit*," 400.

important critical evaluations of history, theology, and numerous other disciplines that come as an inheritance from a pre-modern world. However, the inevitable conclusion to such thought has birthed twentieth-century alternative responses as well: Fundamentalism, Evangelicalism, and Neo-Orthodoxy, just to name a few. And scholars themselves have not unanimously accepted the indictment that orthodoxy and heresy are relative to early church power shifts, as some insist that pertinent claims of truth can, in fact, be more or less true.

Cameron asserts: "Late antique Christians shared the belief that there was indeed such a thing as 'true' faith, and believed that their version corresponded to it."[55] As a result, he insists that historians must avoid the view that orthodoxy is an actual matter of truth. In response, Gerald Bray reflects on Tertullian's legacy and remarks: "Modern Christians tend to discount the importance of doctrine, or regard it as the concern of a few somewhat eccentric specialists, but it is the foundation of our common life and witness. Orthodoxy is not just one opinion among many; it is the cornerstone of the church which must not be shifted or weakened."[56] In this way, we are reminded as contemporary believers that in fact orthodoxy and heresy are real and not relative, and we partner with the core tenets of patristic heresiology. The question of objectivity is judged somewhat differently.

This is further brought out by the significant discontinuity between orthodox belief and many of the heretical systems, most notably Gnosticism. Bernard Green captures the point: "Lost gospels, secret teaching, hidden mysteries: these all sound intoxicating to the modern reader but when the myths are written out in cold prose they sound banal and absurd. This is precisely the technique used by Irenaeus to ridicule them."[57] The very Christ of these systems—as well as the anthropology, soteriology, and cosmology—is not merely a nuance of truth but a significant religious paradigm shift.[58]

---

55. Cameron, "Violence of Orthodoxy," 107.

56. Bray, "Tertullian," 105.

57. Green, *Christianity in Ancient Rome*, 7.

58. Köstenberger and Kruger, *Heresy of Orthodoxy*, 65.

Imposing Defense from Continuity

The apostolic tradition, the scriptures, the practices of the church, and other components of the orthodox movement offered a comprehensive and universal case against the theology of several heresies. Congregations that came to be called "orthodox" displayed certain uses of scripture, views of God and humanity, and a shared understanding of the effective work of Christ in salvation, mainly in the physical resurrection. Green comments: "Mutual recognition of church leadership and participation in the eucharistic communion were ways of aligning the orthodox against the heretics."[59] The dictum of Vincent of Lérins—*quod ubique, quod semper, quod ab omnibus creditum est*—that which is maintained commonly in all parts of the empire, always, and in all the churches where the apostles have tread—in fact do unite against certain heresies at certain times.[60] In his essay in this volume, Bryan Litfin demonstrates the related significance of the role of the Rule of Faith.

Irenaeus lands on a three-part epistemological argument against gnostic thinking that illustrates this. For him, apostolic tradition, scripture, and a common rejection of certain heresies combine to solidify the true revelation of Christ. His method of refutation against his primary target, the gnostics, is straightforwardly based on logic, scripture, and theology. The effect of ideological continuity exposed gnostic doctrines in the West and potentially throughout the empire because their theological position was subordinate. There was no place for esoteric visions and gnostic salvation in Christian belief.[61] Similarly, Ephiphanius, in his *Panarion* posited a corresponding *successio haereticorum*—formally linking the chain of heresies seen in Irenaeus and Hippolytus—even assigning the phenomenon its own name. The chaining of heretical movements formed a *traditio haereticorum*. [62]

---

59. Green, *Christianity in Ancient Rome*, 95.

60. Vincent of Lérins, *Commonitory* 2.6 (NPNF2 11:132). He explicates, "We hold that faith which has been believed everywhere, always, by all. For that is truly and in the strictest sense 'Catholic,' which, as the name itself and the reason of the thing declare, comprehends all universally. This rule we shall observe if we follow universality, antiquity, consent."

61. Shelton, "Irenaeus," 26–27. Gérard Vallée notes how Irenaeus's "engaging" approach is coupled and contrasted by Hippolytus's "uncovering" approach against heresies (Vallée, *Study in Anti-Gnostic Polemics*, 51–54).

62. Epiphanius, *Pan.* 9.1.1; See Vallée, *Study in Anti-Gnostic Polemics*, 70.

Historical Value of Intentions

The debate reveals the value struggles of the time that remained crucial for the process of the development of doctrine. Gerard Vallée has argued that we should not expect to gain the exact truth of the heretic or a ready-made account of historical interaction between opposing groups. Yet he thinks that a clear portrait of the system that the heresiologist would *like* to portray can be uncovered. From polemical works, we can also see what key tenets were preferred by the orthodox to characterize the core doctrines of the church. He says, "The essential content and motive of such polemics might emerge in a fuller light; for what each heresiologist sadly misses in the combated doctrines is very likely to stand close to what he holds to be the backbone of Christianity."[63] And if the heresiologist believes it so, then he probably represents a church that does, and perhaps a larger geographic persuasion within Christianity as well.

Vallée provides an example of how "normative Christianity"[64] developed in the debate surrounding Epiphanius. When Epiphanius wrote against Origen and his followers, he could not conceal his own inflated view of himself. "Epiphanius seems to be more interested in crushing his opponents than in persuading them."[65] This creates room for power techniques against heretical thinkers that become clearer by the fourth century. Compared with Irenaeus's day, such maneuvering had become more power-based, through the progressive empowering of the monarchical bishopric with all its prestige and influence.

Yet in the midst of such sociological insights about the heresiologist, there remains a perspectival theme with a call for a "universal" position rather than a "centrist" position. The call for a pure theology agreed upon among churches does not necessitate the call for a particular power of conformity—a distinction that seems lost upon many Bauer supporters who skew the role and significance of power. The art of separating an author's passion from the inclusion of facts is essential, and Karen King is right: "It does not seem good to base historical reliability on authorial intention."[66]

---

63. Vallée, *Study in Anti-Gnostic Polemics*, 7.

64. His term for the orthodox tradition (ibid., 1–8).

65. Ibid., 98.

66. King, "Social and Theological Effects," 29.

Persecution as a Challenge to Political Charges

The methods and arguments of Walter Bauer have been recognized as inadequate by many scholars, and this book highlights several of those weaknesses in order to offer a more accurate understanding of the era. Bauer does not adequately supply textual data to evidence facets of his theory, and his defense of marginalized communities is often characterized by arguments from silence. Many of the details of his geographical claims have been challenged, as well as the belief that heresy precedes orthodoxy as a regular early church pattern.[67]

However, the charge of political abuse by heresiologists over against Gnosticism deserves due consideration. The claim is that the established church, mainly what came to be known as "orthodoxy," used its hegemony to marginalize the gnostic movement. Nevertheless, although there is merit to the claim—both in motive and in effect—it is worth noting that this claim does not reflect the marginalization and even persecution that orthodoxy itself experienced.

Nicholas Perrin has suggested that the context of persecution in the early church further validates the claims of heresiologists. If orthodoxy were so focused on self-preservation and solidifying power and authority over Gnosticism, it would not have adopted a position so counter-cultural to Roman culture and would not have suffered persecution—unlike a Gnosticism that was compatible with established power.[68] This line of reasoning is employed by Thomas Robinson in his response to Bauer: "From a docetic perspective, a person could escape persecution and martyrdom without, at the same time, blatantly forsaking Christ. This docetic perspective would have been a powerfully attractive option under the Christian rubric."[69]

Religious Bias Affirmed

Finally, the problem of partiality for a religious writer is nothing new and has even been argued as a *sine qua non* of effective religious writing.

---

67. The literature critical of Bauer's thesis is prolific, but both a brief and an extensive summary are worth mentioning: Ayres, "Question of Orthodoxy," 395–98; and Robinson, *Bauer Thesis Examined*.

68. Perrin, *Lost in Translation*, 160–61.

69. Robinson, *Bauer Thesis Examined*, 216–17.

Augustine asserted what has become dictum, *Crede ut intelligas*, "Believe that you may understand," a posture that keeps faith tentative yet continually seeking. Faith remains confident while its knowledge and understanding change, even when encountering ideas seemingly opposed to itself. Augustine inherited the second-century writings and seems familiar with the earlier conflicts against heresy. He remarked, "Unless we walk by faith, we shall not attain to sight which does not pass away, but abides, our understanding being purified by holding to the truth."[70] Green warns how "this—like virtually all shorthand summaries of theological insights and convictions—is prone to misunderstanding,"[71] but for us it demonstrates the legitimacy of patristic heresiologists, even with their limitations.

While any hope of a more objective treatment by the heresiologists themselves is long past, the actuality of subjectivity and struggle in the doctrinal processes should be acknowledged fearlessly and confidently. The polemical components and rhetorical manipulation do not invalidate their particular contributions. Likewise, our ability to study and learn from the texts and traditions that contain such subjectivity or prejudice persists. The pre-modern writers simply wrote with a bias towards the version of faith that transformed both their personal lives and eventually the empire itself. Therefore, for a work like Irenaeus's *Against Heresies* to be properly comprehended, one must approach it as "rooted in a biblical theological logic that can be appreciated only by first appreciating the bishop on his own terms."[72]

Ironically, here we can actually appropriate the model of Elaine Pagels in her approach to understanding gnostic adherents. Her appeal to empathy, to appreciate the gnostic heart-felt seeking of truth in the midst of uncertainty,[73] should find a corollary in a parallel empathy for the polemical tone of heresiologists, who were so passionate at times

70. Augustine, *On Christian Doctrine* 2.17 (NPNF1 1:540). The "sight" here refers to 2 Cor 5:7.

71. Green, "Augustine," 272.

72. Perrin, "Irenaeus and Lyotard," 127. In original context, Perrin was speaking of Irenaeus's comparison of the four Gospels to the four winds and four earthly directions. Cf. Mary Ann Donovan, who described Irenaeus's style as functioning "with assumptions alien to contemporary readers," and who declared that "my first intention is to present his thought on its own terms" (Donovan, *One Right Reading?*, 3–4).

73. In her narrative introduction to the Gospel of Thomas, Pagels adopts a human element of her own suffering and journey of reflection that parallels the confusion and struggle of the gnostic cause in antiquity (Pagels, *Beyond Belief*).

that they left no room for speculation or uncertainty.[74] Yet within the orthodox writers are variations of doctrine reflecting their own limited efforts to land on what they perceived as the truth of Christianity. For example, concerning the early grappling with Trinitarian notions even among authors perceived to be "orthodox," Bertrand de Margerie defends imperfect positions, remarking: "We can understand how the pre-Nicene Fathers without exception left us expressions that could be interpreted in a subordinationist sense, but which do not always need to be understood that way. A correct exegesis of their writings is often difficult."[75]

The dictum "faith seeks understanding" becomes a hallmark principle of the Augustinian legacy, and the pastoral spirit that these writers modeled for their own churches might have profited their theological enemies if they would have been appropriated differently. For example, Hippolytus employs a martyrdom motif in the book of Daniel to encourage his beleaguered congregations under persecution to stand strong in the faith, but he blasts church members of a neighboring church community under his rubric of heresy.[76] There remains a "black and white" view of truth and error among those who championed their churches against heresies, which is better understood by appreciating their keen pastoral motivations and intentions.

Conclusion

Several patristic writers in the traditional category of "heresiologists" confronted what they perceived as threatening heresies through means of writing treatises for the wider church to understand the imminent dangers. These writings employ both general and specific doctrinal and historical details in a polemical tone. The claims made by heresiologists have been challenged by modern historians in the nineteenth and twentieth centuries by exposing patristic biases and exaggerations in a manner

74. In 1949, Robert M. Grant lamented, "Too often we are content with a picture of Irenaeus as orthodox but rather stupid" (Grant, "Irenaeus and Hellenistic Culture," 223). Subsequent scholarship, including the rhetorical analysis of *Against Heresies*, has rehabilitated the image of Irenaeus (Ferguson, "Rule of Truth," 357). See also Donovan, "Irenaeus in Recent Scholarship."

75. de Margerie, *Christian Trinity in History*, 75.

76. Shelton, *Martyrdom from Exegesis*, 143–59. This contrast of purposes seems so great at times that scholars deliberate about the possibility of two different historical figures contributing to the corpus of Hippolytus, but not yet with agreement.

that has undermined the credibility of their specific claims about the heresies and has raised questions of authorial credibility. Chief among these critics has been Walter Bauer, who used the polemics of such heresiological writers to assert that the success of their doctrinal claims was political, power-based, and exaggerative. He accordingly critiqued their suppression of the heresies and the resultant triumph of the collective consciousness of one part of the church over other parts. The victimized opponents included adherents of gnostic Christianity.

Concessions to challenges of legitimacy are fitting today. Polemical heresiologists at times employed false accusations, guilt by association, and slanted claims concerning particular theologies, systems, groups, and persons.[77] Bauer teaches us to weigh the nature and place of polemics, but he is not right to construct a theory of developing orthodoxy that overplays the misrepresentations by the heresiologists or that overemphasizes the role of ecclesiastical power structures in the ante-Nicene churches. Matters of doctrinal development and theological truth require more nuance. Scholars must filter out the certain exaggerations, temper the possible exaggerations, and show appropriate confidence in the remaining reliable material.

This essay explored the nature of rhetorical exploitation, the nature of truth claims among pre-modern thinkers, the power of continuity displayed in phenomena like the Rule of Faith, the discernment of authorial intention, the disclosure of catholic persecution, and the inevitability of religious bias. These factors must be acknowledged, and they combine to challenge the Bauer Thesis as simplistic, at times unfair, and even biased in its own venture.

In the end, modern scholars must sagaciously scrutinize and evaluate the heresiologists and their opinionated treatises. However, the heresiologists cannot and should not be ignored, discarded, or dismissed as merely prejudiced. Even their theological preferences can evidence significant facets of the thinking of early churches, including the sustained resistance against gnostic Christianity. Heresiologists, even with their flawed methodology or their theological and philosophical inclinations, cannot be the basis for theoretical reconstructions of Christian origins that misleadingly validate "heretical" opponents.[78]

77. Cf. Efroymson, "Tertullian's Anti-Jewish Rhetoric."

78. On the relationship between Irenaeus's philosophical perspectives and his rhetoric, see Schoedel, "Philosophy and Rhetoric." "I am more interested at this point in discussing Irenaeus's attitude towards philosophy and his more obvious acquaintance

The case for alternative Christianities requires more evidence for the validity of these sects, and not solely an assault upon the credibility of the heresiological writers. The united voice of the heresiologists reflects a powerful case that gnostic systems and scriptures were too inferior, exclusive, and inconsistent with the scriptures that Jews and apostolic Christians had used. Carl Smith remarks: "The clear impression that the early heresiologists gave to later historians was that Gnosticism was an aberration of apostolic Christianity."[79] Legitimate criticisms of the heresiologists must be accompanied by evidence from gnostic writings themselves that invalidate orthodox claims to apostolicity. In so doing, however, scholars must come to terms with the irreconcilable contrast between orthodox and gnostic thought which proved detrimental to gnostic claims to apostolic faith.

---

with it. It will be seen that on this level Irenaeus's knowledge and use of philosophy is somewhat superficial. It will also be seen that whatever evidence there may be of ordered thought in the *Adversus haereses*, it can more often be traced to rhetorical training" (ibid., 22). "This would suggest, then, that Irenaeus had at some time been exposed to the fundamentals of Hellenistic education, grammar, and rhetoric, but that his acquaintance with the higher discipline of philosophy had remained somewhat elementary in character" (ibid., 31).

79. Smith, *No Longer Jews*, 20.

9

Bauer's Early Christian Rome and the Development of "Orthodoxy"

Glen L. Thompson

AS SEVERAL EARLIER ARTICLES in this collection have mentioned, the church in Rome is pivotal to Walter Bauer's reconstruction of early church history. His theory can be summarized as follows: Rome developed for a century or more in a virtual theological vacuum, unbothered by Gnosticism and other competing forms of Christianity. This allowed the church there to develop a unity of vision and purpose unmatched in other areas of the Mediterranean. As a result, it was able actively to intervene and influence the teachings of the churches in Corinth, Alexandria, and other eastern areas, and eventually it succeeded in foisting its version of Christianity on much of the rest of the church. In the process, the Roman version of Christian teaching and practice became orthodoxy, while all other varieties came to be labeled heresies.[1] In the following

1. Bauer gave a succinct summary of his thesis in a short article published the same year as his book and with the same title: "Rechtgläubigkeit und Ketzerei im ältesten Christentum," *Forschungen und Fortschritte* 10 (1934), 99–101; reprinted in Bauer, *Aufsätze und Kleine Schriften*, 229–33. Concerning the Roman church, he concludes with the following statements (p. 231): "Rom war von Anfang an Mittelpunkt und Hauptkraftquelle der „rechtgläubigen" Bewegung in der Christenheit, die zu Beginn des zweiten Jahrhunderts noch als Ganzes „katholische Kirche" heißt, um am Ende des gleichen Jahrhunderts für das römische oder rombeeinflußte Bewußtsein in die „katholische" oder „große" Kirche einerseits und die massa perditionis der Ketzer

pages we will try to determine whether the last half-century of scholarship on the church at Rome supports the assumptions, evidence, and logic used by Bauer and thus whether his main tenets and conclusions are defensible today.

One major challenge to such an evaluation is Bauer's own presentation. When introducing the English edition of Bauer's work, Robert Kraft commented:

> Bauer writes in a dynamic and highly sophisticated manner, mixing precision with irony and even insinuation, pictorial language with careful presentation of the historical evidence, hypotheses and caveats with the subtle use of overstatement and understatement in cleverly nuanced expressions. His German is literary but not necessarily formal. Long sentences with closely interrelated parts appear alongside brief, sometimes cryptic or oblique comments couched in clever, often scholarly German idiom. Frequently the presentation flows along rapidly in an exciting manner, despite the difficulties of the subject matter—but its flow is such that the motion is difficult to capture in translation, and is sometimes even difficult to follow in the original, unless one is already completely steeped in the evidence being discussed and in Bauer's general orientation toward it![2]

As a result, while Bauer's frequent use of insinuation, overstatement and understatement, and cryptic and oblique comments painted a colorful and dynamic picture of the early church, these same characteristics, combined with his extremely broad historical generalizations, make the examination of specific geographical and chronological areas within his work especially challenging. And when one looks closely, it appears that

---

andererseits auseinanderzufallen. Oder etwas anders ausgedrückt: die Form, die das Christentum in Rom angenommen hat, ist von ihm zum Sieg geführt und dadurch als Rechtgläubigkeit bewährt worden." ET [my translation]: "From the beginning Rome was the center and the primary driving force for the 'orthodox' movement within Christianity, which at the beginning of the second century already as a whole was called the 'catholic church,' and which by the end of that same century separated the Roman and Roman-influenced consciousness within the 'catholic' or 'great' church on the one side from the *massa perditionis* of the heretics on the other side. Or to put it a bit differently, Rome saw its version of Christianity through to victory, and as a result that form was established as orthodoxy."

2. Bauer, *Orthodoxy and Heresy*, xiv–xv. In his recent *Making of Paul*, Richard Pervo makes few references to Bauer except in a few footnotes with comments such as "[Bauer] may, not for the first time, overstate the case" (286n35) and "his thesis drove him to incorrect conclusions" (348n74).

Bauer often lumps together ancient hearsay and tradition, the theories of his own day, and the more substantial ancient evidence, not attempting to distinguish them when they are used to support his theory. The result was clearly a tour de force of innovative thinking. Below this veneer, however, his reconstruction has a rather flimsy framework of anecdotal evidence to support it, and this also makes it difficult to examine in a systematic way.

Our immediate subject is further complicated by the paradoxical fact that, despite Rome's central position in his larger theory, Bauer's book actually devotes very little space to any substantive discussion of the early Roman church. Most of what he says about Rome comes in the form of presupposition, mere background to his discussion of other areas. This makes his views on Rome itself even more difficult to evaluate on their own terms. There are few quotable quotes, no close reading of the evidence, and therefore no reasoned argumentation about such evidence. In other words, Bauer presents *ab initio* a picture of the Roman church which he assumes as valid for the sake of his larger argument concerning orthodoxy and heresy.

Yet Bauer's picture of the early church quickly became the accepted one, the illustration on the jig-saw puzzle box of early Christian studies. Scholars ever since have attempted to interpret the scattered literary and archaeological "pieces" of that period in such a way as to see that overarching picture. Yet only a small percentage of the pieces have survived, and thus there is room for competing reconstructions. And since there is no prima facie reason that Bauer's box-cover illustration is any more accurate than any other, we must construct our picture, and evaluate all others, based on the pieces themselves and the logic of how they can best be inter-related.[3]

The Role of Rome in Bauer's Thesis

Although Bauer devotes chapters four and five of his book to Rome's influence on the rest of the church, these pages do not offer a complete account of his conception of the internal history of the Roman church. This we must piece together from comments interwoven in his description of Rome's larger program of external interference. Bauer's simultaneously

3. Andreas Köstenberger and Michael Kruger include a section examining Bauer's theory about the early congregation in Rome (Köstenberger and Kruger, *Heresy of Orthodoxy*, 50–52), but in fact they merely summarize the earlier critique of Bock, *Missing Gospels*, 50–51.

complimentary and critical picture of the congregation at Rome can be broken down into the following three component parts: 1) Compared with all other early Christian communities, Rome's had unmatched unity, focus, and vision. 2) This unity was formed around a belief system and ecclesiastical practice that differed fundamentally from that of most, if not all, other Christian communities. 3) This unity allowed the Christ-followers in the city of Rome from its first decades to actively plan, plot and eventually spread its version of doctrine and practice to all the other areas of the Mediterranean that claimed allegiance to Christ.[4]

Note that if this theory had been propounded in the seventeenth or eighteenth century, many Protestant church historians might have been reluctant to accept it because it so boldly proclaims the church at Rome as the "mother of orthodoxy."[5] On the other hand, if this schema had been propounded by a 1920s fundamentalist, it would have been summarily dismissed as merely emanating from some innate bias against the Roman Catholic church, some sort of "Romanist-Papist-phobia." But instead it was propounded by a noted twentieth-century German scholar, and so it has been accepted by much of the scholarly community since then as ground-breaking. Bauer's visionary reconstruction has in turn helped solidify two important historical theses which have become foundational for many of the current models of the early church. First of all, it confirms that there was not a single initial Gospel message effectively propounded by a historical Christ to a historically concrete group of disciples; rather there existed numerous groups of competing first-century Jesus-communities with widely divergent understandings of who Jesus was and what his church should be, each spreading very distinctive and often contradictory theologies. Secondly, it elaborated an explanation of how orthodoxy came to dominate and seemingly eliminate its competitors.[6] As a result, in the era leading up to and following World War II, few

---

4. Again, these points are implied rather than clearly stated in Bauer's *Orthodoxy and Heresy*. Pages 95–129 contain his most thorough discussion of the situation in Rome, but they too are not overt in stating his theory. Reviews of Bauer's book, both positive and negative, however, have agreed that this is Bauer's reconstruction.

5. On the other hand, Protestant historians might have merely co-opted this theory as further evidence of how far the post-Constantinian Roman church later "fell" into superstition and false practice.

6. This tenet can be found in recent readings which see the tyrannical behavior of the post-Constantinian orthodox church as the dominant factor in the success of the Trinitarian theology which has a core shared by Orthodox, Catholic, and Protestant adherents alike.

saw Bauer as overtly anti-Roman in a negative way, or, if they did, they were not brave enough to say so.[7]

We have also been reminded in the previous contributions that there are, as in most dangerous and misleading theories, core elements of truth in Bauer's book. Some pictures of the early church have under-reported the diversity among early Christians. Others have intimated that the theological details which later distinguished the orthodox from the heterodox were more clearly understood and enunciated by second-century Christians than was really the case. Still others do not accurately see that the lines between one early Christian community and its neighbor group were not always clearly understood or defined by those within the groups (although we should note that the question of amorphous boundaries applied to all supposedly Christian groups, not just the "orthodox"; self-identity and boundaries were a concern on every side).

Finally, we must also grant that in many areas orthodoxy was often engaged in a life and death struggle with heresy, and that the outcome would have often seemed uncertain to contemporary observers or participants. In other words, orthodoxy did "emerge" more and more clearly, both propositionally and numerically as time passed.[8] This, however, does not in and of itself commend the view of Bauer that has since become so widespread in our post-modern and post-post-modern times, i.e. that there was no single body of teaching about Jesus that was accurately passed down to his disciples, and that, therefore, all early claims to "hand down" the Nazarene's words and ideas were and are equally valid.[9] Bauer's theory, like others that are evaluated and found wanting, can be valuable in that it leads us to nuance more carefully our own pictures of

7. For some of the earlier critics of Bauer's reconstruction, see Rodney Decker's essay in this volume. Cf. also the review of scholarship by Harrington, "Review." While Harrington notes many scholarly points of critique, he finds none which attacked Bauer for being anti-Catholic.

8. Cf. Carl B. Smith, "Post-Bauer Scholarship," 87 pt. 7 (in this volume).

9. This logical fallacy has now crept into textual studies as well, with the idea becoming more and more widespread that since some of the early canonical texts may have been redacted by their original authors or other early readers, therefore there was no single original text for any New Testament document, and therefore the textual critic should abandon his search for such a text and concentrate on elucidating the textual history of any given document.

We should also remind ourselves that such a view contradicts another common picture of Jesus—that he was a great teacher. Great teachers know their subject matter and communicate their message accurately to their students. If there was so much diversity of belief in the earliest church, Jesus could not have been a master teacher.

early Christianity—and that is what my essay tries to do with the early congregation in the city of Rome, examining the three components of Bauer's Rome hypothesis as summarized earlier.

Did the Roman Church Have Unity, Focus, and One Vision from the Start?

Bauer's foundational contention is that the church in Rome's first century environment had two main characteristics: 1) It was heavily impacted by the persecutions of Nero and Domitian. The former cut short its active association with its two apostolic founders, while the latter continued to thin the ranks of its leadership. 2) Yet it was spared the effects of serious rivals in the form of heresies and as a result achieved a homogeneity unknown in the rest of the early church. Thus Bauer says, "The whole environment spurred the Christians on toward the creation of stable forms for life in the community" (120). This led the Roman church at a very early stage in its development to a united vision and purpose not just for itself but for the rest of the church, a virtual "foreign policy" which led it to interfere with churches in other regions, such as Corinth (as seen in *1 Clement*). Thus, while Bauer only speaks of a monepiscopate as being in place by the time of Soter (died ca. 174), he still conceives of a Roman church which already at a much earlier date was seeking to strengthen the monepiscopate elsewhere in order to fight Gnosticism and other heresies. Thus, the Roman church is assumed by Bauer to be functioning with one mind and vision long before Soter, though how this happened without a monepiscopate is never stated. Bauer finds evidence for this position by claiming that the Pastoral Epistles, the so-called Third Epistle to the Corinthians, and the Second Epistle of Peter were all creations of the Roman church which propagandized for this Roman position (182–83). The church also highly valued Luke and the Synoptics, while ignoring John's Gospel (and Revelation) for decades, considering it a forgery by Cerinthus. It treasured only a limited group of Paul's letters until Marcion introduced the expanded collection in the mid-second century. The Roman church helped establish Paul as an apostle more widely, and created the Pastorals to counterbalance the forgeries of the heretics.[10]

---

10. It should also be noted that many of Bauer's component ideas about the early Roman church were not original to him. Much of this picture was already part of B. H. Streeter's reconstruction as seen in his Hewett Lectures for 1928, published as Streeter,

The publication of Peter Lampe's comprehensive study *From Paul to Valentinus: Christians at Rome in the First Two Centuries* opened a new chapter in the study of the first two centuries of the church in Rome.[11] According to Lampe, Christianity entered Rome mostly along the Puteoli-Rome land trade route which dominated Rome until the Flavians developed the port of Ostia in the later first century. At first the church grew in association with the multiple synagogues, but the number of Jewish Christians was lessened by the expulsion in AD 49. However, by the time of the Great Fire of AD 64 the authorities had come to distinguish Christians from Jews. From early on Christians met in multiple groupings, with lower class members gathering in the areas of Trastevere and along the Via Appia outside the Porta Capena; groups which included more prosperous members were to be found in the areas bordering the Aventine and in the Campus Martius. The majority of early Christians in Rome were easterners or of eastern descent. The groups were socially mixed, from slaves to highly placed elites.

During these early centuries the majority of the adherents were Greek-speaking, as we find that the Christian writings originating in second-century Italy were mostly written in Greek (*1 Clement*, Hermas, Justin's works) or were poor translations from the Greek (the Muratorian Fragment) that do not measure up to Latin Christian materials produced in North Africa. Although Lampe sees the Vatican as the most probable site for Peter's gravesite, he notes that the first evidence comes from the small *edicula* erected a full century later, probably built and tended by the poorer Christians of Trastevere. The picture he creates points to a situation in which there was still no organized community structure even in the mid-second century. Yet by the time of the *Traditio Apostolica* which "reflects Roman conditions from at least the period around 200" we find deacons caring for the poor and indigent, assisted by subdeacons.[12]

Primitive Church. More recently, Markus Vinzent has revived and taken aspects of this theory to new lengths in his *Christ's Resurrection in Early Christianity.*

11. Lampe's work began as a 1983 doctoral dissertation at the University of Bern, and was first published in German as *Die stadtrömischen Christen in den ersten beiden Jahrhunderten* in 1987, with a second expanded German edition appearing already in 1989. An English version first came out in London (Continuum) in 2002, but we will cite from the more accessible American edition (Lampe, *From Paul to Valentinus*).

12. The citation is from Lampe, *From Paul to Valentinus*, 127. For the regions of the city where Christians live, see chapter 3; on Nero's persecution, chapter 7; on the social classes of Christians, chapters 4, 10–11, and 13; on the Vatican cemetery, chapter 12. It may have been the ongoing connection to the Greek-speaking communities of Asia

Numerous subsequent studies have refined and built on Lampe's general picture. Roger Gehring argued for at least seven different Christian fellowships in first-century Rome. Noting that in the Letter to the Romans Paul never uses *ekklesia* in the singular when referring to Rome, he sees no united or "physical center" for the Roman house churches at that time (Rom 16:23).[13] Similarly, Allen Brent sees little evidence of a highly centralized church structure while the episcopate was slow in developing. Even in the early third century, at the time of Callistus (r. 217–222), Brent still argued that in Rome the bishop:

> presided over a group of house churches with loose bonds of intercommunion between the presiding *episkopos/presbyteros* of each individual community. The presbyters, like their counterparts in the Jewish synagogue, did meet formally for discussions. . . . They did have at their head a chairman-secretary, who . . . supervised the distribution of letters from external Churches amongst the house churches, and who was responsible for writing replies where necessary on behalf of all the groups. Clement of Rome had been such a figure, and, if not identical with him, also the Clement of Herm. *Vis.* II. 4, 2–3, who had such a function entrusted to him (*epitetraptai*) as his ministry.[14]

Michael Borgolte's study of early episcopal gravesites also lends no support to either an early monepiscopate or a more centralized church structure in Rome. The earliest evidence of an episcopal funerary monument was the structure on the Vatican associated with Peter, which, as noted earlier, was no earlier than 160, and must have been the apostolic *tropaion* mentioned two decades later by Gaius. He concludes that the early Christians may have been prevented by the Neronian persecution, or by a lack of resources, from caring for Peter's remains. The other likelihood is that because they thought the parousia was imminent they just did not bother with an elaborate memorial. This would account for the fact that there is no specific notice of a date of his death in early Roman tradition, and it would be in line with evidence elsewhere that it is only around 300 that we start seeing the burials of saints and martyrs receiving consistent special attention. Gaius also indicates that Peter and Paul

---

Minor that prompted the high emotions in the Easter controversy in the later second century (cf. n. 26 below).

13. Gehring, *House Church and Mission*, 146. This argument is strengthened by the fact that in Rom 16:23 Paul refers to "the whole church" in Corinth sending greetings.

14. Brent, "Imperial Cult," 313–14.

were jointly reverenced at Rome, and only from the time of Constantine on was Peter singled out as founder of the congregation and first bishop. This would fit better with an early multi-episcopate.[15]

In his study of leadership development in the early Roman church, Mario Ziegler agrees with this same general picture, saying that we can know little about second-century bishops beyond their names. He adds that until the middle of the century, there must have been "eine kollegiale Leitung" in Rome. He concludes that it took nearly a hundred years for the monepiscopate to develop, and "it is very likely that some of the people named in the list held office simultaneously." His timeline is even more extended, citing Victor (ca. 190) as the first to act as a spokesman (*Wortführer*) for the entire Christian congregation.[16]

Most recently Bernard Green has surveyed this period anew. While he too does not reference Bauer directly, his assessment is not amenable to a view of a Roman congregation as a sheltered and focused unity by the end of the first century. He states that: "Roman Christians in the second and early third centuries struggled not only to work out how their community should live and worship but what they should believe. An astonishing variety of proposals for the construction and definition of Christianity could be heard in Rome in the middle decades of the second century . . ."[17]

Green cites Epiphanius's story about Marcion debating with the Roman presbyters as credible evidence that the Roman church of the mid-second century still had multiple leaders rather than a single doctrinal or administrative leader.[18] He further notes that Cerdo was disturbing the church a decade earlier and Valentinus a decade after Marcion. Green further stresses that these men all were members of the Roman congregation before leaving and/or being expelled from the fellowship, citing Irenaeus's description of Valentinus as being a "fellow disciple and fellow deserter" with Marcion. This must surely be further evidence of a time when multiple fellowships made it possible for people and teachings to

15. Borgolte, *Petrusnachfolge und Kaiserimitation*, esp. 17–21.

16. " . . . daß einige der in den Listen genannten Personen zeitgleich amtierten" (Ziegler, *Successio*). The citations are from pp. 296 and 297 respectively. It has long been recognized that this is the best way to make sense of the early episcopal lists.

17. Green, *Christianity in Ancient Rome*, 60.

18. "Epiphanius does give an account of Marcion debating with the presbyters and arguing about the interpretation of the Gospel which has the ring of authenticity, largely because Epiphanius could scarcely have invented a scene that fitted so well the situation of the Roman church in the 140s but not the church of his own day over two centuries later" (Green, *Christianity in Ancient* Rome, 63).

be accepted in parts of the city while being rejected in other parts, and yet ultimately some sort of group action was required for each leader and his group to be accepted, rejected, or expelled.

Green does question whether scholars have enough evidence definitively to hypothesize "a loose federation of independent groups which gradually came together in the late second century to form a united church under one leader; in other words, a bishop emerged in Rome at a fairly late stage . . . " Yet he acknowledges that "the Roman Christians must have had multiple assemblies at quite an early stage . . . " and that "the author of 1 Clement writes on behalf of the church rather than in his own name." Only about AD 170 with Dionysius's letter to Soter does he envision the church as having an *episkopos* who is "sole authoritative representative of the church in dealings with other churches and organizer of aid." He further thinks that it was about this time that the earliest list of Roman bishops was compiled, probably to link the Roman church's anti-gnostic and anti-Marcionite doctrinal position directly with Peter and Paul. That same situation caused the senior presbyter/president/bishop to now become something resembling a monarchical bishop.[19]

Most telling, however, is Einar Thomassen's 2004 study "Orthodoxy and Heresy in Second-Century Rome." Thomassen argues that until the late second century, the church at Rome was fragmented and unorganized, and that the various groups were either not organizationally capable of or interested in enforcing a unified belief system until late in the second century. He argues that Marcion and Valentinus were not expelled from the church but were rather forced to break away and set up their own organizational structures because, unlike the other Christians in Rome, they saw the need to enforce doctrinal unity among their followers. "Only towards the end of the century, and most clearly during the episcopate of Victor, is there evidence that other Christian communities in Rome had joined to form a somewhat more unified organization, one that began to issue warnings about heresy and to excommunicate heretics."[20] The aura of Bauer and his hypothesis led Thomassen to mention him only directly in a footnote, but there he says clearly, ". . . we cannot accept this view of early Roman orthodoxy and uniformity."[21]

---

19. Green, *Christianity in Ancient Rome*; 65 on Cerdo; 73–74 on Valentinus; 92–95 on Dionysius; and 95–96 on the earliest bishops lists.

20. Thomassen, "Orthodoxy and Heresy," 241–56; the quotation is from 255.

21. Ibid., 250n38.

Thus, while differing in emphasis, modern scholars of every stripe who have made detailed examinations of the archaeological and literary evidence of the Roman church of the first two centuries paint the same general picture of a church that was not centralized administrationally or otherwise. It was made up of numerous groups that had a common identity as brothers and sisters in the faith, normally functioning quite independently of each other, yet also consulting and acting as a group when issues of common concern arose. The collective Christian *ekkēsia* of Rome had a reputation for caring for those in need, at home and abroad, and did not shirk from involvement with other churches when problem areas came to its attention. We see this in *1 Clement*, in Polycarp's visit with Anicetus in the mid-second century, and in the Roman church's involvement in the ransoming of imprisoned Christians. However, there is no evidence whatsoever that in the century from AD 50–150, the Roman church possessed a leadership structure which could have hammered out the common vision or the plan for attacking heresy abroad which would have been necessary in Bauer's reconstruction.

In fact, Bauer himself spoke of the fragility of the Roman leadership structure. He noted that it had the two apostles in its midst for but a short time; the leaders who succeeded them were forced to tread cautiously after the Neronian persecution; the leaders that did emerge were literally not very memorable, as we know their names and almost nothing else of them, and there are questions about the accuracy of even that sparse information. Collegial leadership would have brought more long-term stability, but would have made a bold plan of "outreach" against the heretics more difficult to mount.[22] All of this makes it difficult to imagine that the congregation in Rome as a unit devised a vision and strategy and then remained united behind it for over a century. It also remains difficult to accept that despite the suspicions and persecutions the Roman church faced locally, and an ever-growing local ministry of preaching and charitable activity, it was able to have the time, manpower, and financial resources to carry out a program involving regular long-distance communication and activity across the Mediterranean. In fact, there are few congregations, ancient or modern, which have formulated and carried out such a unified plan over several centuries and over such a large geographical area.

22. One might also postulate that Christians in the city of Rome would have likely followed the ancient Roman tradition of always having collegial oversight of its institutions, supposedly a reaction to its period under the rule of kings.

In other words, Bauer's theory does not really account in a substantive way for how such a strong and long-lasting focus and vision could be created and maintained without a strong centralized administration—in effect a papacy—for over a century after the death of the two apostles. As we have seen, scholars, Catholic as well as Protestant, are increasingly pushing the monepiscopate at Rome into the mid-to-late second century.[23] When a strong leader does finally come along in the person of Victor, Bauer attributes his actions to the church of Rome's attitudes rather than to his own personal character, claiming that in the Easter dispute "Rome shows itself to be controlled and motivated more by a strong desire for power than by the sense of brotherly love . . . " (97). Bauer ignores the inconvenient truth that the earlier consultation of Polycarp with Anicetus was carried out in a loving and brotherly fashion with the two sides agreeing to disagree (Eusebius, *Hist. eccl.* 5.24.16–17). He speaks similarly about the third century controversy on second repentance and rebaptism: "Rome also was not in favor of forcing the issue and demanding the impossible" and "official Rome was prepared to make significant concessions" (127). The truth is that there was no "official" Christian Rome until much later than Bauer hypothesizes.

Not only is there little evidence to support Bauer's hypothesis of an early organizing vision to further Rome's unique doctrine and practice, it is simply nonsensical to speak of a Rome shielded from Gnosticism and the other varieties of teaching which were impacting the church elsewhere. In fact, this is the exact opposite of everything we know about ancient Rome. We need only recall Juvenal who, along with his contemporaries, was convinced that "the Syrian Orontes has long since poured into the Tiber, bringing with it its lingo and its manners, its flutes and its slanting harp-strings" (Juvenal, *Satire* 3).[24] Christian students from Tatian to Jerome came to the capital city just as traders, philosophers, and hucksters did century after century. Cultural influences went in both directions, but Rome was never immune from the styles and trends across the empire. To postulate that the Roman Christians of the first century, made up largely of immigrants from the East, were somehow ignorant of

23. Kimberly Bowes is even more extreme, describing the Rome of Hippolytus and Callistus as "a city jostling with individual churches and schools, but as yet no church writ-large" (Bowes, *Private Worship*, 52). According to Bowes, the fourth-century struggles of Liberius and Damasus were part of the Roman bishops' ongoing struggle to solidify their authority within Rome itself.

24. ET from Ramsay, *Sixteen Satires of Juvenal*, 14.

or impervious to all such influences is a hypothesis that needs more than theoretical support to be taken seriously.

Did Rome's Belief System and Ecclesiastical Practice Differ Fundamentally from that of Other Christian Communities?

Several essays in this volume have joined earlier critiques in showing that Bauer's study was wrong in claiming that in the first two centuries those teachings and practices which later came to be called "orthodox" did not exist in most other parts of the empire.[25] Even if there is no total agreement on whether the orthodox or the various other groups were dominant in a particular area, one can no longer seriously argue that during this period orthodox teaching was predominantly limited to Rome. It is now clear that it was found virtually everywhere the Gospel was preached. Thus I will not re-survey that evidence yet again. However, there are several other points of comparison between the early Roman church and those elsewhere that can be profitably drawn.

First of all, it is a just observation that from the beginning the Christians at Rome were not in any sense a "typical" congregation. The Roman church must have been considerably larger and more diverse than most other congregations. Because so many immigrants came to the city, Christianity arrived at a very early stage, and both evangelistic activity and further immigration constantly swelled the ranks of the faithful, despite the temporary setback of the Jewish expulsion by Claudius in AD 49. That Paul could name twenty-six individuals before he had even visited the city in the late-50s indicates a substantial size for the congregation. This number was again thinned by the Neronian persecution following the Great Fire of 64, but the witness of the martyrs caused the numbers to quickly be replaced. Ethnicity, geographical heritage and kinship were all factors that played into the groupings which developed in Rome. For example, it can plausibly be inferred that there were still groups with roots in the province of Asia in the mid-second century, and it was their use of the Asian method of calculating Easter that led to Polycarp's visit and discussions with Anicetus (Eusebius, *Hist. eccl.* 5.24.16–17).[26]

25. Harrington, "Reception," 294–95, gives Davids, "Irrtum und Häresie" and Norris, "Ignatius, Polycarp, and I Clement" as examples of this critique.

26. George La Piana seems to be the first to make this connection between

While most early Roman converts were middle and lower class Greek-speakers, there is persistent evidence of a few middle and upper class Latin converts in Rome itself. While Lampe doubts that T. Flavius Clemens, consul in 95 and a close relation to Emperor Domitian, was a Christian, he thinks that Domitilla (Clemens's wife or niece) was. Irenaeus further mentions Christians as being present among the slaves and freedpersons of the imperial household.[27] Ignatius also implies that the Roman congregation had highly-placed contacts that might (against his will!) be used to achieve his release (Ign. *Rom.* 2–6). As the decades passed, the number (if not the percentage) of influential and wealthy Christians in Rome must have slowly increased, giving the church a very different relationship to the imperial government than most other Christian congregations. At the same time, no other group's activities were more under the imperial microscope than that of the Roman church. There also is evidence that the congregation was quite wealthy compared to fellowships in other cities and regions. It had a growing reputation for frequent and widespread charitable activities—helping the poor, orphans, and widows, and ransoming imprisoned and captive Christians.[28] And, not least of all, they were able to claim as founding figures not one but two apostles, and the two that were arguably the most important pillars of the early church outside Palestine.

Yet, while the Roman church was clearly atypical, in other ways it was unexceptional. Except for Victor's attempt to solve the Quartodeciman controversy, Rome is never singled out in the extant sources for imposing on others any of its own practices or innovations in doctrine. Although we have little information on the last decades of the first century, by the mid-second century Rome also is troubled by the usual

---

Polycarp's visit and one or more groups of Asian Christians in Rome (La Piana, "Roman Church," esp. 215–20). This incident again confirms the picture sketched in the previous section that in the mid-second century worship groups within the city of Rome were still semi-independent but regularly interacted with each other (thus the question arose as to the proper date for celebrating Easter), treating each other as brothers while still considering themselves free to follow their own worship customs.

27. On T. Flavius Clemens and his family, cf. Lampe, *From Paul to Valentinus*, 198–205 (citing Cassius Dio, *Roman History* 67.14; Suetonius, *Domitian* 15; Eusebius, *Hist. eccl.* 3.18.4); on Christians in the *familia Caesaris*, cf. Irenaeus, *Haer.* 4.30.2 and Tertullian, *Apol.* 37.4.

28. On the Roman church's help for the poor, cf. *1 Clem.* 38.2, 55.2 and 59.4; Herm. *Sim.* 9.26.2; Justin, *1 Apol.* 1.13.1, 1.67; Dionysius of Corinth in Eusebius, *Hist. eccl.* 4.23.10.

heresies found elsewhere—competing varieties of Gnosticism, Marcion and his followers, Carpocratians, Quartodecimans, etc. At the end of the century we read of two Roman presbyters, Florinus and Blastus who, in seemingly separate incidents, were both recognized as teaching new doctrine ("innovations") and were forced from the fellowship of the church together with their numerous followers.[29] About the same time one of the most educated and well-to-do believers, a man named Apollonius, was martyred after a malcontent slave accused him to the authorities of being a Christian (Eusebius, *Hist. eccl.* 5.21).

The Roman congregation was also not monolithic in its teaching and outlook. The Quartodeciman question lived on in Rome throughout the second century. The *Shepherd of Hermas* with it Hebraic visions and similitudes, and the later Clementine corpus and *Didascalia Apostolorum*, were probably all produced or edited by Roman Christians and seemingly were quite popular in the capital and its surroundings. Immigrants such as Marcion and Justin (Martyr) with his Samaritan background, brought new vitality to the congregation, but also challenges. As La Piana pointed out nearly a century ago, "the constant influx of eastern immigration continued to bring to Rome from the various Christian centres of the East individuals and groups which . . . introduced into it the various peculiar practices and traditions developed by Christianity in the churches of Syria, Asia Minor, and Egypt."[30] At the same time, local Roman converts, especially those from the upper classes, would have experienced stresses when joining local fellowships whose culture was still very Greek and eastern. And all the while the Roman church was being watched by the government more carefully than any other congregation in the empire. It is highly unlikely that such a church would have had the luxury of a highly-organized bureaucracy with either the ability or motivation to develop a unified vision and plan such as Bauer supposed.

---

29. They are mentioned in Eusebius, *Hist. eccl.* 5.15, 20, who says that Irenaeus wrote works against both of them. Pseudo-Tertullian says Blastus was a Judaizer and Quartodeciman (Pseudo-Tertullian, *Haer.* 8) while Pacianus states that he was a Montanist (*Ep.* 1 *ad Sympronianus* 2.1); cf. the translation of Hanson, *Iberian Fathers*, vol. 3, 18. Florinus seems to have been teaching a variety of Gnosticism in Rome at the time when Victor was bishop of Rome (AD 189–198/199).

30. La Piana, "Roman Church," 207.

Did the Christians of Rome Actively Plan and Successfully Spread its Brand of Doctrine and Practice throughout the Mediterranean?

The contribution in this volume by Smither and Alexander has argued forcefully that in the North African context of the early third century one can show that in matters of both doctrine and practice "influence flowed not from Rome, but from this regional Christianity [i.e., North Africa] back towards Rome." They further note that Tertullian saw no problem in challenging the perceived modalism of two Roman bishops—Zephyrinus and Callistus—and "in doing so, he openly challenged the authority of the Roman church leadership." Similarly Cyprian challenged Stephen a half century later over rebaptism.[31] We can further note that the North African church did not make any attempts to produce evidence that it could claim descent from either an Apostle or Rome, but simply claimed spiritual descent from the true apostolic doctrine. Why did Rome not give it a proper apostolic legend, as Bauer postulates it gave Mark to Alexandria? Why was Tertullian's challenge to the Roman church and its authorities not suppressed by Rome? This would have been important to do if the Roman church did indeed have a monolithic hierarchical structure and the long-range vision and goals that Bauer attributes to it. Rome certainly would have been as interested in co-opting Latin North Africa for its own purposes as Bauer claims it did in Greek Egypt.

Furthermore, Bauer's claim that Rome imposed a connection with Mark, whether historical or legendary, upon the Alexandrian church has found little support in the scholarship of the past half century. While most scholars are dubious about the historical Mark having ever been present in Alexandria, others have held out the possibility of a connection, even a strong one, between Mark and the congregations in the two largest cities of the empire. For instance, in a 1964 article entitled "St. Mark and Alexandria," L. W. Barnard argued that a historical connection between Mark and Egypt should not be summarily dismissed. He cited approvingly C. H. Roberts's theory that the Roman church was the source behind the Alexandrian church's early adoption of the codex for Christian texts. He saw further evidence in the relationship between some Sahidic and Old Latin variant readings, as well as the constant contact between the

---

31. Cf. also Dunn, *Cyprian and the Bishops of Rome*, chap. 4 and especially pp. 179–80.

two cities caused by the grain trade.[32] More recently, Thomas Oden has championed a more Afrocentric view of African Christianity in general, and now more specifically the role of Mark in the foundational legends which formed the African church's self-identity for almost two millennia.[33] He states that "the most fundamental insight we derive from the early sources regarding Mark (Papias, Irenaeus, Clement and Eusebius) is the presumed strong connection between the founding of the church of Rome and the church of Alexandria."[34] Yet Oden, like Barnard, never identifies Mark's role in Alexandria, or more broadly in Libya and Egypt, as a conscious plan or vision of the Roman church. Here again scholarship has lent no support to Bauer's hypothesis.[35]

Two Apostles, One Plan

One final claim of Bauer is that Rome understood "from the outset" the advantage of its dual apostolic foundation, a view which he bases on Ignatius (Ign. *Rom.* 4.3) and Dionysius of Corinth (Eusebius, *Hist. eccl.* 2.25.8).[36] His theory can be summarized as follows. In the early second century Rome cherished Paul and a small collection of his letters. According to Bauer, much of the rest of the church wanted to exclude Paul and his letters and rely solely on the twelve apostles, but:

> Rome (together with the "church," which it led) had already accepted too much from the Apostle to the Gentiles, had appealed to him too often, suddenly to recognize him no longer. He had become a martyr-apostle of Rome—had helped it to develop the popular slogan "Peter and Paul;" and even if Rome did not really know how to begin to put to use Paul's letter to the Romans,

32. Barnard, "St. Mark and Alexandria," 145–50. H. L. Swete's critical summary of the Mark traditions is still useful (Swete, "St. Mark in Early Tradition," 268–77). He notes that Epiphanius is the first to claim Peter as the person behind Mark's trip to Egypt (*Pan.* 51.6).

33. Thomas Oden's Afrocentric picture was first encapsulated in Oden, *How Africa Shaped the Christian Mind*. More recently he has concentrated on Mark in Oden, *African Memory of Mark*.

34. Oden, *African Memory of Mark*, 134.

35. In his *Studies in the Gospel of Mark*, Martin Hengel pointedly cites his agreement with Bauer that Mark did have a close association with Peter (151n58), but he says nothing about the rest of Bauer's reading of the Roman church's relationship with its Egyptian counterpart.

36. Bauer, *Orthodoxy and Heresy*, 12.

> 1 Corinthians had proved itself to be extremely productive
> for purposes of church politics in the hands of Rome. By that
> means, Paul and his letter came to have permanent claims on
> the "church." (225)

It was Rome that put 1 Corinthians "at the disposal of the orthodox communities in Smyrna and Antioch . . . about the year 100" (221). It was almost a half century later when in the Roman church the smaller group of Pauline letters "were then surpassed and replaced by Marcion's more complete collection."[37] But since the heretics also had co-opted Paul for their own use by forging the letters to Laodicea and Alexandria, the orthodox in turn forged the Pastoral Letters to counteract them (226). So by around the year 180 "the apostle Paul with his collection of letters must have stood alongside the Old Testament and the Lord" [i.e., the Gospels] as fully authoritative (213–14). However, at the end of the second century, Rome eliminated its emphasis on the two apostles in order instead to emphasize Peter as its founder and first bishop. This was because it felt threatened by Valentinus and Marcion, and thus needed to emphasize its own monarchial episcopate. The decision was made in favor of Peter because "only Peter provides the close tie to Jesus which alone guarantees the purity of church teaching" and "Paul . . . was no longer of any help in the battle against Marcion" (114).

In his assumption that both Peter and Paul were present, executed, and buried in Rome, Bauer is taking the more traditional position still held by the majority of those who have written on this subject. There are a few exceptions, such as Otto Zwierlein, who would contend that the earliest evidence for Peter ever visiting Rome comes from the mid-second century and thus implies that his presence and death in the city was a much later invention.[38] Yet the Acts of the Apostles clearly depicts Paul imprisoned in Rome, and there is no competing tradition to conflict

---

37. Ibid., 221. Bauer also goes out of his way specifically to argue this contra Adolf Harnack whom he quotes in support of a Pauline corpus of thirteen letters with a *terminus ad quem* ca. AD 100 (ibid., 223). Again, Vinzent's recent *Christ's Resurrection in Early Christianity* goes still further in positing that Marcion not only popularized the larger Pauline corpus but added to it the first written Gospel, Q.

38. Zwierlein, *Petrus in Rom*. Zwierlein's main hypothesis is that the later story of Peter confronting Simon Magus was the impetus for all other accounts of Peter's presence in Rome. The opposite is the more natural scenario. Zwierlein's minimalist use of the evidence (dating 1 *Clement* to ca. 125, and considering the references in the Ignatian letters to be later interpolations) has little to commend it.

with Peter's presence there as well.[39] The majority of writers still see *1 Clement* as emanating from the church at Rome at the turn of the first century and agree that it shows a firm belief that both Apostles had been martyred (5.3–6.1), and this is echoed by Ignatius (Ign. *Rom.* 4.3).[40] The fact that Ignatius discusses this in his letter to the Romans implies that their martyrdoms took place in Rome. Eusebius cites two sources from the later second century that are more clear about the latter—a writing by a certain Gaius who speaks of the "trophies" of Peter on the Vatican and of Paul on the Via Ostiensis, and a letter of Dionysius of Corinth to the Romans which says the two apostles both "planted" at Rome, and "suffered martyrdom there at the same time" (*Hist. eccl.* 2.25.7–8). So in this respect, Bauer's assumption that there was in fact a historical basis for the two apostles' association with Rome does have ancient support.

Bauer's further theorizing about the two apostles in Rome, however, is almost pure speculation. We are simply lacking evidence about what Roman Christians in the century after Nero's persecution thought about Peter and Paul in relation to their own congregation. Tacitus confirms the fact that an "immense multitude" of Christians were arrested and executed because they were part of this "destructive superstition" who were known for their "hatred towards mankind."[41] Because of the intensity of this persecution in the mid-60s, the Christian community in Rome, even more than their brothers and sisters elsewhere, must have expected the parousia to be imminent. Living in constant fear of renewed outbreaks of violence, they were unlikely to have been thinking in terms of any long-range vision much less the one which Bauer has espoused. In addition, this situation accounts for the lack of interest Rome showed in commemorating its relationship with the two apostles martyred in its midst or in their burial sites.

None of the first- or second-century documents originating from the Roman community make more than oblique references to any of the local martyrs. Our earliest archaeological evidence for formal

39. Though see Zwierlein, *Petrus in Rom*.

40. In the long version of Ignatius's *Letter to the Trallians* 7.3 the author associates Linus as a disciple of Paul and Clement as a disciple of Peter. While this passage is seen as a later interpolation by most, it still shows that the association of these two apostles with Rome was widespread.

41. Tacitus, *Ann.* 15.44: *exitiabilis superstitio . . . multitudo ingens . . . odio humani generis*. Tajra notes that Tacitus's description of the fire and Nero's response comes in his section on the good deeds of the emperor! See Tajra, *Martyrdom of St. Paul*, 27–32.

commemoration comes from the Vatican funerary memorial in the second half of the second century.[42] The local church may well have felt its situation to be constantly threatened until that period and only then, when the parousia seemed to be delayed indefinitely, would they have felt it possible or appropriate to remember more publicly its connection with the two men—men who were revered as martyrs by Christians, but by their neighbors were seen as rebels implicated in causing the greatest disaster and loss of life and property in the history of the city.[43] Thus it is not until the later second century that one can even conceive of the church officials in Rome as wanting to "use" the congregation's connection with the two apostles for their own ecclesiastical agenda.

Bauer further hypothesizes that in the late second century Rome's emphasis on the monepiscopate forced church leaders to choose one of the two apostles to be remembered as their founding father figure. At that juncture Peter, who had had more direct contact with Jesus, was chosen. Paul, whose writings were being used by gnostics (who had only in mid-century become a problem at Rome), was relegated to a distant secondary position in the congregation's history. Again, archaeological and literary evidence provide little information about this formative period, and so Bauer's reconstruction, while not impossible, also has little concrete support. Peter obviously does gain a primacy within the church's traditions, but it is difficult to see this as a late second-century development. Irenaeus's genealogical list of Roman founders does put Peter, rather than Paul, at the head of its list of *episkopoi*, but the fact that Irenaeus was literally just two generations removed from the founding of the Roman congregation, makes it just as likely that his selection was based either on testimony about Peter's historical presence in Rome or was influenced by the combination of the words of Jesus as recorded in the Gospels of Matthew and John.[44] Finally, it is also significant that the writings emanating from Rome do not stress the two canonical letters of Peter over

---

42. Cf. note 6 above.

43 John C. O'Neil argues that Peter and Paul were probably buried by devout Jews (who were not Christian!) since the Christians would have been afraid to do so. They were probably buried together in the catacombs of San Sebastiano where there were other nearby Jewish catacombs, and only reburied on the Via Ostiensis and on the Vatican respectively in the fourth century during the episcopate of Damasus. Thus while the *tropaia* existed since the second century, they were not tombs but just memorials. See O'Neil, "Who Buried Peter and Paul," 103–7.

44. Matt 16:16–18 and John 21:17–19.

Paul's epistles.[45] In other words, there is little evidence to support this prioritization occurring at the time and for the reasons that Bauer states.

In the fourth century, the legalization of Christianity allowed for a more open expression of the faith for the first time. Previous catacomb art did not often depict the two saints, although their remains were a destination of pilgrimage together with those of other martyrs at the catacomb of San Sebastiano. While dates and reasons are still debated, it seems most likely that their remains were transferred there for safe-keeping during one of the persecutions and remained there until the mid-fourth century. By that time Constantine and/or one of his sons had nearly completed construction of the large basilica of St. Peter which covered the Apostle's supposed grave-site on the Vatican. A much smaller memorial basilica over St. Paul's supposed burial site on the Via Ostien-sis was also constructed at this time. The calendar of martyr festivals in the so-called Chronograph of 354 lists the two apostles' festival on the third day before the kalends of July (June 29), but lists Peter's festival as taking place in the Catacombs, and Paul's on the road to Ostia.[46] About this time catacomb paintings, sarcophagus reliefs, mosaic decorations in basilicas, and gold-glass images on cups begin to frequently picture the two Apostles—at times together, and at times separately.[47] Thus, although by the later fourth century the bishop of Rome is being referred to as the

45. Echoes of 1 Peter are found in Clement of Rome and Hermas; and Irenaeus and Tertullian regard it as Petrine. Thus, even if in the later second century 2 Peter was not known or considered apostolic at Rome, at least the former must have been available for some apologetic use there.

46. Cf. the edition of Mommsen, *Gestorum Pontificum Romanorum*, vol. 1, 71–72. The entry reads: *Petri in Catacumbas. et Pauli Ostense, Tusco et Basso cons.* The consular date given is 258. This would be the last—and worst—year of the persecution under Valerian which led to the execution of Bishop Sixtus along with the seven deacons of the city. Gallienus, who had been appointed by his father to rule in Italy as Caesar, halted the persecution in Rome towards the end of the year, perhaps after the death of his son, Valerian II (Eusebius, *Hist. eccl.* 7.13). Thus the entry could in a garbled way be referring to the relics being transferred to the Catacombs that year (at this period *Catacombs* referred to a specific area along the Via Appia); or, if not, to the restoration of Paul's bones to the memorial on the Via Ostiensis after the persecution ended late in the year.

47. For the archaeological remains of the early memorials as well as samples of the other early epigraphical and iconographical evidence, cf. Donati, *Pietro e Paolo*. For the development of the Pauline tradition, cf. Eastman, *Paul the Martyr*.

occupant of "The See [or Seat] of Peter," we still see Paul represented and revered alongside of Peter.[48]

Conclusion

While our picture remains fragmentary, recent scholarship has done nothing to bolster any aspect of Bauer's thesis concerning the early Roman church. The Roman congregation(s) continued to grow during a long period of overt and covert persecution, and their steadfast witness and Christian charity continued to impress the rest of the church. By the third century the Roman church was playing an increasingly important role in the Christian west, and in the fourth century in the East. Its reputation may have even been strengthened by the fact that it did not overtly interfere in the life of other congregations on a regular basis. We have no evidence that the brotherly letter sent to the Corinthians by "Clement" was followed up by attempts to implement the will of Rome in the matter. Interference at other times and in other places is also purely hypothetical. Bauer was not the first or the last to read later Roman papal policies and attitudes back into the congregation's first two or three centuries.[49] For the most part, the Roman church was absorbed in its own local affairs, building up its own members, witnessing to non-Christians residents, and struggling to define and delimit its own doctrine and practice. Evidence of a wider self-definition or a more comprehensive vision of its relationship with the rest of the church is not found in the first two centuries before Victor.[50]

---

48. Cf. Stephen Andrew Cooper's study of Paul in Christian art in his *Marius Victorinus' Commentary*, esp. 49–87.

49. The first glimmerings of the power politics of the medieval papacy can be seen no earlier than the time of Damasus I (366–384), although many have incorrectly adduced such ideas from Julius I's letter to the eastern bishops in 341 (cf. my introduction to the letter in Thompson, *Correspondence of Julius I*).

50. See also the very recent study of Novatian by James Papandrea (Papandrea, *Novatian of Rome*). When tracing the historical situation at Rome previous to and at the time of Novatian, he finds no need to discuss Bauer, and his own reconstruction lends no support to any of Bauer's theories about the Roman congregation.

10

From Völker to this Volume: A Trajectory of Critiques and a Final Reflection

Paul A. Hartog

BORROWING A WORD MADE famous by twentieth-century research into developments within early Christianity, this concluding essay will trace the "trajectory" of scholarly critiques of Bauer.[1] First, the study will begin with a comparison between the present volume and the early critique of Walter Bauer written by Walther Völker (1935).[2] Second, this closing essay will orient a future possible trajectory by highlighting a topic for further reflection: the pertinent role of philosophical/theological "horizons" in historiography.

A Comparison of the Critiques of Völker (1935) and This Collected Volume

In the years following Bauer's 1934 study, more than twenty-four book reviews were published in six different languages.[3] Most of the reviews

1. Cf. Marshall, "Orthodoxy and Heresy," 6–7.
2. The review was first published in *ZNW* 54 (1935) 628–31.
3. Köstenberger and Kruger, *Heresy of Orthodoxy*, 33; drawing from Strecker,

found positive elements in Bauer's proposal (and rightfully praised various creative insights), and some of them were highly appreciative of his work.[4] Some properly pointed out various weaknesses in the framework, assumptions, arguments, and underlying methodologies of Bauer's proposal.

One review was a sharp critique written by Walther Völker, a German church historian. An English language translation of Völker's 1935 review came at the hand of Thomas Scheck and appeared in the *Journal of Early Christian Studies* in 2006. Just as the 1971 English translation of Bauer's original work fully introduced the Anglophone world to his historical reconstructions, so this translation introduced the Anglophone world to Völker's pointed criticisms.[5] Decker's helpful review of the critical literature in this present volume did not interact with the relatively recent appearance of this translation, so I will summarize Völker's evaluation here.

Völker highlighted Bauer's admittance that he was "forced to rely heavily on conjectures" and that "some degree of imagination should be necessary," while pinpointing the repetitive language of "perhaps" and "probably" that underscored Bauer's "brilliantly witty conjectures" (400–401). Völker countered, "Unfortunately the author has made rich use of his imagination, and the result is that in many passages his evidence cannot stand up in the face of careful scrutiny" (400). Völker's sharp pen critiqued Bauer's work as being "riddled with the argument from silence" (401), neglecting possible counter-examples (402), failing to supply sufficient evidence (402), making logical leaps (403), and interpreting "all isolated occurrences in a way that is consistent with this fundamentally new point of view" (404).[6]

Völker concluded, "The author [Bauer] arrives at these astonishing conclusions by repeated use of the arguments from silence, by bold combinations of unrelated passages, by unprovable conjectures which themselves are reused as a precarious foundation for further conjectures, by inferences drawn from later periods, and finally by the arrangement of all isolated facts into the schema orthodoxy/heresy, whereby the variegated

---

"Reception of the Book."

4. These reviews are not discussed in Decker's essay but are summarized in Strecker, "Reception of the Book."

5. On a sidenote, I observe that several important German articles pertaining to "orthodoxy" and "heresy" did not appear in the essays of this volume, including but not limited to: Koester, "Häretiker im Urchristentum"; Elze, "Häresie und Orthodoxie"; Blank, "Zum Problem."

6. Others have added charges of special pleading, anachronisms, and red herrings.

historical events are robbed of the full richness of their causes and motivations" (404).[7] Völker closed with his own conjecture: that Bauer's
reconstruction of history would not be accepted by scholars but would
inevitably occasion "just as extreme a reaction" as Gottfried Arnold's rehabilitation of the heretics around the year 1700 (405).[8]

Such was the critique of Walther Völker, written the year after
the appearance of Walter Bauer's first German edition of *Rechtgläubigkeit und Ketzerei*. A lot of water has gone under the bridge of relevant
scholarship in the last eighty years. What noticeable differences does one
detect between Völker's evaluations and the discussions of this collected
volume?[9] Where has the "trajectory" of critical analysis led over the
last eight decades?

First, and most obviously, the essays of this volume recognize the
ongoing influence of Bauer's work, both in contemporary scholarship
and in the projected future. Völker consigned Bauer to the ash heap of
history, a specimen of an academic oddity that would not survive the
rigor of critique. Perhaps Völker was reading his own "extreme" reaction
into the projected responses of others, but he definitely underestimated
the future acceptance of Bauer's overall "approach to church history"
(405).[10] One could contrast Bart Ehrman's assessment that ". . . the *opinio
communis* that has emerged is that despite the clear shortcomings of his
study, Bauer's intuitions are right *in nuce*."[11] Contra Völker's prediction,
Bauer's framework has taken up permanent residence, within both aca-
demia and the popular imagination.

7. "Throughout the book Bauer argues extensively from silence. This is always
a difficult argument, since one must be able to establish that the silence is significant
and not just accidental, that there ought to be something there which is missing. An
argument from silence, to be persuasive, must present us with an absence that needs
explaining and that can only be explained in a particular way. But quite often, Bauer
simply uses silence as a space within which to create history out of whole cloth" (Mc-
Cue, "Bauer's *Rechtgläubigkeit und Ketzerei*," 31).

8. Arnold, *Unparteiische Kirchen- und Ketzerhistorie*. See Roberts, "Gottfried
Arnold."

9. Of course, the essays of this volume do not always agree among themselves.
One notices even small differences, such as assumptions regarding the authorship of
the *Refutatio omnium haeresium* and the appropriateness of the terms "proto-orthodoxy" and "Christianities," etc.

10. For a listing of early works influenced by Bauer, see Koester, "Häretiker im
Urchristentum," 17–21.

11. Ehrman, *Orthodox Corruption of Scripture*, 8.

Köstenberger and Kruger assert, "It is no exaggeration to say that the Bauer-Ehrman thesis is the prevailing paradigm with regard to the nature of early Christianity in popular American culture today."[12] They comment, "Bauer's thesis has been largely discredited in the details, but, miraculously, the corpse still lives—in fact, it seems stronger than ever!"[13] They add, "What is beyond dispute is Bauer's influence, which extends to virtually every discipline related to Christian studies."[14] Most recently, a 2012 session at the annual North American meeting of the Society of Biblical Literature was dedicated to Walter Bauer's legacy.[15] And his influence remains international, as witnessed by another thesis examining Bauer's proposal appearing in 2012—in Spanish.[16] The essays of this contribution, therefore, readily recognize the influential contribution and ongoing impact of the Bauer Thesis, even in the midst of critical evaluation.

Second, Völker was so withering in his criticism that he seemed to lack even faint praise for any facet of Bauer's work. While the essays of this volume have weighed the Bauer Thesis and found it wanting in particulars, four positive threads have also weaved their way throughout the critiques: (1) an appreciation for Bauer's recognition of the diversity indicated by the materials relevant to the study of early Christianity; (2) an appreciaton for the insight "that the theological reflection of the writers of antiquity cannot be divorced, as pure dogmatic speculation, from the ecclesial, social and political situations and struggles in which they were immersed";[17] (3) an appreciation for a critical reading (along a spectrum) of the heresiologists and other orthodox authors;[18] (4) an ap-

---

12. Köstenberger and Kruger, *Heresy of Orthodoxy*, 23.

13. Ibid., 18.

14. Ibid., 38.

15. "Orthodoxy and Heresy: the Legacy of Walter Bauer," Chicago, IL, Nov. 17, 2012.

16. Martín Domínguez, "La relación entre ortodoxia y herejía."

17. Behr, *Way to Nicaea*, vol. 1, 4. Behr does add further clarifications and caveats, agreeing with Jon Elster: "There is no reason to suppose that beliefs that serve certain interests are also to be explained by those interests" (Elster, "Belief, Bias, and Ideology," 143). "There is no denying that, however elevated, theology is only ever undertaken within the 'real world,' that there were many other agendas operative in the various controversies, and in our modern interpretations of them, but to assume that these other agendas *explain* the theological points made is to overlook deliberately what are the stated concerns of the subjects under investigation and to presume to know them better" (Behr, *Way to Nicaea*, vol. 1, 5).

18. See Heron, "Interpretation of I Clement," 544. Even those who support the

preciation for Bauer's geographical methodology, by which he examined specific phenomena and data related to particular historical locales. In fact, these essays demonstrate that Bauer's own methodology (his focus upon geographical specificities) can easily turn upon him at times, as when Alexander and Smither focus upon the particularities of the North African context and come to conclusions contesting Bauer's proposal.

Therefore, while Völker now seems rather one-sided in his scathing critiques, these essays have found Bauer's pioneering work to be a launching point not only for pointed criticism (of which there has been plenty) but also some positive construction, although more could be done. One is reminded of a parallel in Lewis Ayres's comment upon the role of Adolf von Harnack, that "the best studies of the last fifty years have found the rejection of his views to be a stimulus for good scholarship."[19]

Third, Völker's work seems characterized by a certain binary mindset. While the overall perspective of this volume has definitely been critical of Bauer, one notes the presence of appropriate nuances and the acknowledgment of multiple complexities. Butler's entire essay demonstrates the simplicity of "orthodoxy vs. heresy" by inserting a *tertium quid* into the mix: a schismatic movement.[20] While the Patristic authors castigated the "Phrygian heresy," Butler's assessment of the "New Prophecy" is more nuanced.[21] And Shelton's chapter on the heresiologists acknowledges certain shortcomings in their partisan (and "prejudiced") writings, even while espousing an empathetic reading of their materials (cf. Smith's similar second point in his concluding remarks).[22] No doubt, many of the heresiological writings are "emotionally charged" and some of them are "vitriolic."[23]

---

heresiological materials by-and-large would acknowledge discrepancies, mischaracterizations, and *ad hoc* arguments—i.e., not all heretical movements stemmed from Simon Magus, although a repeated claim. For one assessment of Irenaeus's "reductionist" tendencies, see Benoit, "Irénée et l'hérésie."

19. Ayres, "Question of Orthodoxy," 396.

20. One also thinks of the spectrum of personal disagreements, at times rooted in theological differences (cf. Acts 15:37–40; Gal 2:11–14; 3 John 9–10).

21. See also Lawlor, "Heresy of the Phrygians."

22. As a concrete example, note the differences in the descriptions of Basilides as found in Irenaeus, *Haer.* 1.24.3–7 and Hippolytus, *Refutation* 7.7–15. For a recent "empathetic" reading of the heresiologists, see Hill, "Exclusive Reading."

23. Ehrman, *Orthodox Corruption*, 18. For evaluations beyond those mentioned in Shelton's essay, see Koschorke, *Hippolyt's Ketzerbekämpfung*; Greer, "Dog and the Mushrooms."

One could add further examples of complexity, such as the eventual marginalization of Quartodecimanism in the early churches (as reflected in the synodal letter of the First Council of Nicaea in AD 325), even though key leaders such as Polycarp, Polycrates, and Irenaeus had previously defended it as apostolic.[24] And Tertullian propagated doctrines and coined terms greatly influential in the developing orthodox cause, although he was later viewed as a schismatic (as noted by Alexander and Smither).[25] Similarly, Origenianism faced a roller-coaster-ride of acceptance and non-acceptance in the patristic period.[26] The "orthodox" (normative) vs. "heretical" binary can be too reductionist, by not taking such complexities and later narrowings into account (even as Smith has warned against reading fully developed orthodoxy back into earlier writings).

Fourth, although Völker was an accomplished church historian in his own right, his review largely (but not entirely) focused upon some counter-evidences from the New Testament and multiple counter-evidences from the Apostolic Fathers.[27] While one essay in this collection centered upon Polycarp and *1 Clement* (my own chapter), the remaining materials extended far and wide within various literary, geographical, socio-cultural, and theological contexts.[28] In fact, Varner's essay discusses a field entirely bypassed by Bauer (Jewish Christianity). The patristic focus of this collected volume reflects the academic acumen of the majority of contributors, many of whom are primarily patristic scholars rather than New Testament scholars.[29] The various second- and third-century foci of this volume actually align it with Bauer's original work (which skipped

24. Cullen, "Question of Time."

25. See McGowan, "Tertullian and the 'Heretical' Origins."

26. Kannengiesser and Petersen, *Origen of Alexandria.*

27. "The significance of Völker's devastating critique of Walter Bauer's thesis and historical method is that it stemmed from a scholar whose stature in the field of patristic studies was not negligible and whose expertise was precisely focused on the material and time period covered in Bauer's work" (Scheck in Völker, "Walter Bauer's *Rechtgläubigkeit und Ketzerei,*" 399).

28. Although more could be done further afield. Cf. H. J. W. Drijvers's work in Syriac Christianity (Drijvers, "Rechtgläubigkeit und Ketzerei"). See also Jones, "Were Ancient Heresies."

29. Although Decker's primary research field was New Testament Greek, and Hartog, Smith, Varner, and Thompson have regularly taught both New Testament and patristic studies. Tellingly, the original context of this volume's research was a consultation of a Patristics and Medieval History Section.

past most of the first century),[30] and differentiates it from many others appraisals of his book, including the opening chapters of the recent critique by Köstenberger and Kruger, who are both New Testament scholars (*The Heresy of Orthodoxy*, 2010).

Fifth, the essays in this collection have interacted with primary source discoveries that were not available to Bauer or Völker. Here one thinks especially of Smith's essay on Gnosticism(s), which appropriately included the adjective of "post-Bauer" in its title. One cannot fault Bauer's 1934 work for not being conversant with the Nag Hammadi library, after all.[31] And without the Nag Hammadi primary sources, discovered in 1945, Shelton's comparison of the heresiologists with their opponents' own literature would not be possible. More could be mentioned, however, such as the fact that there are less than twenty extant second- or third-century papyri from Egypt, and only one reflects gnostic-like material.[32] Statistically, the manuscript evidence does not support a gnostic preponderance in second-century Egypt. Nevertheless, "In fairness to Bauer, these manuscripts were not discovered until after he published his work."[33]

Sixth, new fields of study have burgeoned since Bauer and Völker, and the impact of these disciplines is evident in this volume. One thinks of Varner's essay on Jewish Christianit(ies), which interacts with decades of post-Bauer scholarship on the notion of "the parting of the ways." Jewish Christianity was a non-player in Bauer's work (although it entered as a bench-warmer in Strecker's supplemental addendum). But the study of Jewish Christianity has blossomed in recent decades, and Varner appropriately highlights the current status of the field. One also thinks of the rise of rhetorical studies, and how rhetorical criticism affects the study of the heresiologists (as reflected in Shelton's essay). Rhetorical criticism even influences the interpretation of specific idioms, such as the *hoi polloi* of anti-heretical denunciations (as noted in my own essay).

---

30. "It is certainly interesting to observe that the highest praise for Bauer's thesis has come from New Testament scholars, such as Bultmann and Koester; yet Bauer's work does not deal with the New Testament, but with second and third century Christianity" (Scheck, in Völker, "Walter Bauer's *Rechtgläubigkeit und Ketzerei*," 399).

31. Attridge, *Nag Hammadi*; Pearson, *Roots of Egyptian Christianity*; Pearson, *Gnosticism, Judaism, and Egyptian Christianity*; Pearson, *Gnosticism and Christianity*; Roberts, *Manuscript, Society, and Belief*.

32. Roberts, *Manuscript, Society and Belief*, 12–14; Pearson, "Earliest Christianity in Egypt," 132–33.

33. Köstenberger and Kruger, *Heresy of Orthodoxy*, 47.

"Intensity of rhetoric does not translate to any particular estimate of numerical preponderance."[34]

Seventh, (and more specifically) two contemporary scholars recurrently reappear in the pages of this collected volume. I am thinking of the work of Peter Lampe on early Christianity in Rome and the work of Larry Hurtado on the early proclamation of Jesus as the divine, risen Lord.[35] Although Thomas Robinson's focused monograph *The Bauer Thesis Examined* is worthy of specific mention as well, these works by Lampe and Hurtado have influenced the conversation without targeting Bauer in particular. The former effectively undermines Bauer's reconstruction of a powerful, united Roman church enforcing its will abroad in the late first and early second centuries (as explained in Thompson's essay). And the latter roots the proclamation of the risen Lord in the pre-Pauline kerygma of the church (as developed in Litfin's work on the *regula fidei*).

Early devotion to Jesus is reflected in the alteration of traditional Jewish theology evident in 1 Corinthians 8:4–6, the pre-Pauline materials reflected in Philippians 2:6–11, the "functional overlap" of Jesus and God, the prayer of *maranatha* (1 Cor 16:22), the proclamation of "Jesus is Lord" (2 Cor 12:3), and the focus upon Jesus as the risen, exalted Messiah and Savior (1 Cor 15:3–6; Phil 2:6–11). A level of theological continuity stretches from such materials to the *regula fidei* of the early theologians, as argued by a fourth book of profound influence, the *Pattern of Truth* by H. E. W. Turner.[36] Litfin's essay in this volume enriches this discussion.

Precedence, Plurality, and Normativity

Walter Bauer insisted that "heresy" was regularly the first form of Christianity in most locales of the ancient world. And he accentuated a diversity of movements claiming the banner of early "Christianity." Therefore, "heresy" was not secondary, nor was it a derivative off-shoot entailing a minority status.[37] Critics of Bauer often mount a full attack upon his reconstructions

---

34. Rodney J. Decker, as quoted in ibid., 62.

35. Contrast Bousset, *Kyrios Christos*.

36. Turner, *Pattern of Truth*. Besides the studies found in Litfin's essay, see also: Ammundsen, "Rule of Truth"; Countryman, "Tertullian and the *Regula Fidei*"; Osborn, "Reason and Rule of Faith"; Blowers, "*Regula Fidei*"; Rombs and Hwang, *Tradition and the Rule of Faith*.

37. Ehrman, *Orthodox Corruption*, 6–7.

of chronology (the precedence of heresy in given locations).[38] While not disagreeing with the gist of many such examinations of particular geographical locations, one does wonder if scholars with a traditional penchant have sometimes over-reacted to the notion of Christianity's first arrival in a given locale being non-orthodox in form.

As Scheck rightly notes, "The traditional view, that orthodoxy preceded heresy, does not require that orthodoxy existed in every conceivable place prior to heresy."[39] We know in Late Antiquity, for example, that Arian missionaries were the first to enter some eastern European regions and that various Germanic tribes converted to Arianism before later conversion to Nicene Christianity.[40] Ehrman is undoubtedly correct that "In some regions, what was later to be termed 'heresy' was in fact the original and only form of Christianity."[41]

Scholars oriented toward the more traditionalist segments of the spectrum should think carefully about their insistence upon the

38. Consider the conclusions of Köstenberger and Kruger in their assessments found in *Orthodoxy and Heresy*: "In light of the available evidence from Asia Minor, there is no reason to suppose that heresy preceded orthodoxy in this region" (45). "The five responses detailed above combine to suggest that Bauer's argument fails to obtain also with regard to Egypt. Rather than support the notion that Gnosticism preceded orthodoxy, the available evidence from Alexandria instead suggests that orthodox Christianity preceded Gnosticism also in that locale" (48). "Evidence is lacking, therefore, that heresy preceded orthodoxy in Edessa" (50). "Although Roman control certainly solidified in subsequent centuries, it is erroneous to suggest, as Bauer did, that early orthodoxy did not exist elsewhere" (52). "The above examination of the extant evidence has shown that in all the major urban centers investigated by Bauer, orthodoxy most likely preceded heresy or the second-century data by itself is inconclusive" (52). In the minds of Köstenberger and Kruger, the "inconclusive" case involves Edessa. The point in this present essay is that critics of Bauer's thesis should not feel compelled to prove that orthodoxy preceded heresy in such a location as Edessa—that the notion of normativity can be distinguished from both precedence and plurality.

39. Scheck, in Völker, "Walter Bauer's *Rechtgläubigkeit und Ketzerei*," 401n1. See also McCue, "Bauer's *Rechtgläubigkeit und Ketzerei*." Contra Origen's remark that "All heretics are at first believers; then later they swerve from the rule of faith" (*Commentary on the Song of Songs* 3; ET from Ehrman, *Orthodox Corruption*, 37).

40. Jones, "Were Ancient Heresies," 293–94.

41. Ehrman, *Orthodox Corruption*, 7. If heresy (of any sort) preceded orthodoxy in Edessa, what would or should change in more traditionalist reconstructions of early Christian history as a whole? Köstenberger and Kruger argue that if the Antiochene Jewish community had contact with Jerusalem (750 miles away), they would have had contact with Edessa (ca. 250 miles away). But, of course, the Jewish community in Antioch would have had religious foci in Jerusalem not present in Edessa. See Köstenberger and Kruger, *Heresy of Orthodoxy*, 49.

chronological priority of orthodoxy over heresy (on multiple levels).[42] A nuanced understanding of this issue is already suggested by first-century Christian texts that came later to be called "orthodox." For instance, the Gospel of Matthew does not end with the crucifixion of Jesus but includes a resurrection narrative. Clearly, the author believed that the resurrection was a singular event—a unique working of God in human history.[43] Yet the narrative portrays a diversity of responses existing *ab initio*, from the founding events of the Jesus movement (whether denial as in vv. 11–15 or doubt as in v. 17).[44] At the same time, the text assumes that a proper understanding of the apostolic kerygma was integrated with the authority of the risen Lord, and that the diversity of responses reflected a multiplicity of subjective reactions to the singularity of an objective occurrence.[45]

On a historiographical level (and not just in early Christian studies), one may distinguish between event, interpretation, and evaluation of interpretation. The basic and particular point at this immediate juncture is not an argument concerning whether the resurrection happened as a demonstrably historical event (nor the historical reliability of the Gospel narratives), but simply that pertinent early Christian traditions *themselves* allow for a singularity of event *immediately* followed by a plurality of response.[46] In fact, the Gospel of Matthew portrays the religious leaders'

42. Köstenberger, "Diversity and Unity," 158.

43. Cf. the singularity of the Christ event in Ign. *Eph.* 7.2.

44. The Greek for "doubted" could be translated as "hesitated." Cf. Ehrman, *When Jesus Became God*, 189–90.

45. Various essays in this volume could have dealt more fully with the issue of rival claims of apostolicity. Many discussions seemed merely to assume that "apostolicity" could be easily equated with "orthodoxy" without making a case. Ehrman declares, "In point of fact, the Gnostics claimed authorization for their views by appealing to the apostles, and through them to Jesus, as the guarantors of their doctrines. After his resurrection, Christ had allegedly revealed the secrets of true religion to his apostles, who in turn transmitted them orally to those they deemed worthy. This secret knowledge comprised both the mystical doctrines of the (Christian-) Gnostic religion and the hermeneutical keys needed to find these teachings in the sacred texts that the majority of church people errantly insisted on construing literally. Interestingly enough, the Gnostic Christians could make plausible claims for the apostolicity of their views" (Ehrman, *Orthodox Corruption*, 25). Interestingly enough, those "deemed worthy" implies a minority status, and as noted the "majority of church people" assumed a literal interpretation.

46. Two recent scholarly examinations which defend the historicity of the resurrection are Wright, *Resurrection of the Son of God*; and Licona, *Resurrection of Jesus*. In passing, Ehrman refers to "the recent, and very large, books by Christian apologist Mike Licona and by renowned New Testament scholar N. T. Wright" (Ehrman, *How*

unbelief as a continuation of their pre-Easter opposition (and thus as an orientation preceding the resurrection, the linchpin event in orthodox belief). The descriptive statement that multiple interpretive communities and perspectives claimed to be early responses to the figure of Jesus or his ministry does not logically necessitate that all were equally valid.

The ultimate question is not the chronological precedence in a particular locale, nor the diverse plurality of religious communities arising from similar roots, but the nature and possibility of normed unity—whether a focused normativity is available. Those early followers who believed that Jesus had risen from the dead would naturally be inclined to think that such a norm was available, that only perspectives rooted in the risen Lord (whom they proclaimed) would possess the proper, derivative authority.[47] In other words, their belief in Jesus's resurrection unsurprisingly issued forth a complementary understanding of authority.[48]

As a result, a foundational outlook regarding the reality or possibility or dismissal (as well as the knowability and unknowability) of Jesus's resurrection greatly affects one's scholarly reconstruction of early Christianity.[49] If one believes that Jesus rose from the dead, this commitment would naturally affect one's approach to the historical materials of the early Jesus movement(s), at least in "horizon."[50] The principle is true,

---

God Became Man, 188).

47. Consider the lack of the resurrection in Helmut Koester's position: "Christianity did not begin with a particular belief, dogma, or creed . . . Rather, Christianity started with a particular historical person, his works and words, his life and death: Jesus of Nazareth. Creed and faith, symbol and dogma are merely the expressions of responses to this Jesus of history. . . . The diversifications of this response were caused, and still today are caused, by two factors: first, by the several different religious and cultural conditions and traditions of the people who became Christians; and, second, by the bewildering though challenging impact of Jesus's own life, works, words, and death" (Koester, "Structure and Criteria," 205). For his part, Ehrman emphasizes *belief* in Christ's resurrection as the pivotal fulcrum: "No, what made Jesus different from all the others teaching a similar message was the claim that he had been raised from the dead. Belief in Jesus' resurrection changed absolutely everything" (Ehrman, *How Jesus Became God*, 131).

48. "Even though historians cannot prove or disprove the historicity of Jesus's resurrection, it is certain that some of the followers of Jesus came to *believe* in his resurrection. This is the turning point in Christology. . . . belief in the resurrection changed everything Christologically" (Ehrman, *How Man Became God*, 204).

49. Svigel, "You Got to Know When to Hold' em."

50. Wright, *Resurrection of the Son of God*, 712; cf. 717. On "horizons" in historiography, see also Licona, *Resurrection of Jesus*, 38–50. Ehrman lists "the appropriate presuppositions" he believes are relevant to historians *qua* historians, including the indemonstrability of miracles (Ehrman, *How Jesus Became God*, 144–46). "The first

mutatis mutandis, if one denies or doubts that Jesus rose from the dead.[51] Every scholar necessarily approaches the historical inquiry with commitments or "horizons" that inform and frame his or her historiography and hermeneutic.[52]

For example, if one accepted the claim of Jesus's resurrection, then one would naturally believe that it could function as a benchmark of normativity. But if one believes that Jesus did not rise from the dead, then one would not believe that the purported event (since it never happened) could serve as a criterion of normativity. And if one believes that one cannot *know* whether or not the resurrection occurred, then one could not land firmly upon the claim as a point of reference in discussions of normativity, nor could one firmly dismiss the same possibility.[53] One would naturally avoid assessing which Christologies of the era were proper, but would only note which Christologies prevailed.[54]

I. Howard Marshall remarks that Bauer's work proves that "there was a variety of belief in the first century," but does not prove the lack of

---

thing to stress is that everyone has presuppositions, and it is impossible to live life, think deep thoughts, have religious experiences, or engage in historical inquiry *without* having presuppositions. The life of the mind cannot proceed without presuppositions. The question, though, is always this: What are the appropriate presuppositions for the task at hand?" (ibid., 144).

51. This sentence comes from Svigel, "You Got to Know When to Hold 'em," reworded to fit this context.

52. Ehrman states, "Most historians, of course, can trace their own lineage back through a tradition that claims the triumph of Christian orthodoxy as one of its historical roots. And so it is scarcely surprising to see that many historians find this form of Christianity essentially compatible with the teaching of Jesus and his followers. We should not allow this consensus to blind our eyes to the impossibility of disinterested evaluation in the hands of contextually situated investigators; the postmodern world has seen in this modernist quest for objectivity a myth of its own. This applies, of course, to *all* investigators: even those who repudiate the consensus" (Ehrman, *Orthodox Corruption,* 43n40). Some would differentiate between "disinterested," "neutral," and "objective." While historians should *strive* for objectivity, the human-personal nature of investigation usually is motivated by personal interest and is not sustained by bare neutrality.

53. Ehrman declares that ". . . as a historian, I do not think we can show—historically—that Jesus was in fact raised from the dead. To be clear, I am not saying the opposite either—that historians can use the historical disciplines in order to demonstrate that Jesus was *not* raised from the dead. I argue that when it comes to miracles such as the resurrection, historical sciences simply are of not help in establishing exactly what happened" (Ehrman, *How Jesus Became God,* 132; cf. 143).

54. Ibid., 287–88.

normative teaching in "earliest" Christianity.[55] The New Testament authors "often seem quite clear where the lines of what is compatible with
the gospel and what is not compatible are to be drawn."[56] It seems, therefore, that the foundational issue is ultimately neither precedence (whether orthodoxy or heresy was the first to arrive in a particular locale) nor
plurality (as all agree that various groups claimed ties to the figure and/
or teachings of Jesus). Rather, a basic question regarding "diversity and
unity" concerns normativity (and specifically the possibility and knowability of a resurrection), and therefore the scope of historical events and
the "horizoning" of historiography.[57]

Although the earliest writers of the "great church" differed in idiom,
in backgrounds of thought, and in individual characteristics, they shared
a common set of core beliefs.[58] Litfin's essay in this volume demonstrates
this phenomenon, as substantiated by other scholars such as C. H. Dodd,
J. N. D. Kelly, and James Dunn.[59] Butler's contribution to this volume
includes Arland Hultgren's full listing of the core beliefs of the "normative tradition."[60] Hultgren argued that the unifying elements of earliest
Christianity included not only doctrinal tenets, but also the ethos, fellowship, and community of the church. Andreas Köstenberger has focused
upon three integrating motifs of apostolic Christianity: (1) monotheism,

55. Marshall, "Orthodoxy and Heresy," 13.

56. Ibid.

57. For example, Gerd Lüdemann resolutely denies the bodily resurrection of Jesus. "We can no longer take the statements about the resurrection of Jesus literally"
(Lüdemann, *What Really Happened to Jesus*, 134). "Jesus decayed and did not rise
bodily" (Lüdemann, *Unholy in Holy Scripture*, 133). "The resurrection appearances
to his disciples are to be derived from visions which can be explained in purely psy-
chological terms" (Lüdemann, *Unholy in Holy Scripture*, 133). Lüdemann sums up his
opinion of the "hoax of the resurrection" in these words: "So let us say quite specifically: the tomb of Jesus was not empty, but full, and his body did not disappear, but
rotted away" (Lüdemann, *What Really Happened to Jesus*, 135). "There is no such thing
as the 'Risen Christ'" (Lüdemann, *Great Deception*, 110). As a logical consequence,
would not this mindset impact Lüdemann's understanding of orthodoxy and heresy
(as reflected in Lüdemann, *Heretics*)? And would not the same be true in an analogous
manner for a historian who believes Jesus rose from the dead?

58. Köstenberger and Kruger, *Heresy of Orthodoxy*, 34; following the work of
Turner, *Pattern of Christian Truth*.

59. Dunn, *Unity and Diversity*, 403.

60. On "tradition" in the early church, see Cullmann, "Tradition"; Florovsky,
"Function of Tradition"; Mitros, "Norm of Faith"; Hanson, *Tradition in the Early
Church*.

that is, belief in the one God, Yahweh, as revealed in the Old Testament; (2) Jesus as the Christ and the exalted Lord; and (3) the saving message of the gospel."[61] The recent, jointly authored volume of Köstenberger and Kruger similarly advocates that the earliest normative Christianity "centered on Jesus's death, burial, and resurrection for the forgiveness of sin."[62] This belief in a risen Lord naturally served as a benchmark of applicable normativity for those who espoused the tenet.

In a closing reflection for future trajectories of inquiry, the decisive issue does not seem to entail a historical discernment of precedence (which could theoretically vary by locale) or of plurality (which all scholars acknowledge in some form or manner) but of the possibility and nature of a focused normativity. In discussions of normativity, a full inquiry cannot avoid cognitive consonance with one's assessment (whether positive or negative or undecided) of the *significant* claims of the kerygma.[63] Would not one's approach to matters of unity, diversity, and normativity within early Christianity(ies) inevitably be influenced by one's commitment to a view of history that either accepts or does not accept the possibility and/or knowability of a risen Lord?[64]

---

61. As summarized in Köstenberger and Kruger, *Heresy of Orthodoxy*, 38; see Köstenberger, "Diversity and Unity," 154–57.

62. Köstenberger and Kruger, *Heresy of Orthodoxy*, 55.

63. Ehrman states, "I do not think it would be a historical sin at all to leave the matter of external stimuli—were the visions veridical or not—undecided, so that believers and unbelievers can reach common ground on the *significance* of these experiences. That is my ultimate concern" (Ehrman, *How Jesus Became God*, 189). But can the full *significance* of the experiences be agreed upon without assessment of their veridicality?

64. See Hartog, "Blondel Remembered," 12–14.

Bibliography

Aland, Barbara. "Gnosis und Kirchenväter: ihre Auseinandersetzung um die Interpretation des Evangeliums." In *Gnosis*, edited by Barbara Aland, 158–215. Göttingen: Vandenhoeck & Ruprecht, 1978.

Alexander, David C. *Augustine's Early Theology of the Church: Emergence and Implications. 386–391*, Patristic Studies 9. New York: Lang, 2008.

Altaner, Berthold, "Der 1. Clemensbrief und der römische Primat." In *Kleine patristische Schriften*, edited by Günter Clockmann, 534–39. TU 83. Berlin: Akademie Verlag, 1967.

Altendorf, Hans-Dietrich. "Zum Stichwort: *Rechtgläubigkeit und Ketzerei im ältesten Christentum.*" *ZKG* 80 (1969) 64.

Ammundsen, Valdemar. "The Rule of Truth in Irenaeus." *JTS* 13 (1912) 574–80.

Arnold, Gottfried. *Unparteiische Kirchen- und Ketzerhistorie von Anfang des neuen Testaments bis auff das Jahr 1688.* Frankfurt am Main, 1699.

Ash, James L., Jr. "The Decline of Ecstatic Prophecy in the Early Church." *TS* 37 (1976) 227–52.

Attridge, Harold. "Valentinian and Sethian Apocalyptic Traditions." *JECS* 8 (2000) 173–211.

Attridge, Harold W., et al. *Nag Hammadi, Gnosticism, & Early Christianity.* Peabody, MA: Hendrickson, 1986.

Ayres, Lewis. "The Question of Orthodoxy." *JECS* 14 (2006) 395–98.

Baird, William. *History of New Testament Research.* Vol. 1: *From Deism to Tübingen.* Minneapolis: Augsburg Fortress, 1992.

Bakke, Odd Magne. *"Concord and Peace": A Rhetorical Analysis of the First Letter of Clement with an Emphasis on the Language of Unity and Sedition.* WUNT 2.143. Tübingen: Mohr Siebeck, 2001.

Barnard, Leslie W. "The Early Roman Church, Judaism, and Jewish Christianity." *ATR* 49 (1967) 371–84.

———. "St. Mark and Alexandria." *HTR* 57 (1964) 145–50.

Barnes, Timothy David. "The Chronology of Montanism," *JTS* 21 (1970) 403–8.

———. *Tertullian: A Historical and Literary Study.* Rev. ed. Oxford: Clarendon, 1985.

Barns, John W. B., et al. *Nag Hammadi Codices: Greek and Coptic Papyri from the Cartonnage of the Covers.* NHS 16. Leiden: Brill, 1981.

Batluck, Mark. "Ehrman and Irenaeus: A Comparison of their Views on the Ebionites." *Scottish Bulletin of Evangelical Theology* 27 (2009) 155–63.

Bauckham, Richard. "The Early Jerusalem Church, Qumran and the Essenes." In *The Dead Sea Scrolls as Background to Postbiblical Judaism and Early Christianity*, edited by James R. Davila, 63–89. STDJ 46. Leiden: Brill, 2003.

———. "James and the Gentiles (Acts 15, 13–21)." In *History, Literature and Society in the Book of Acts*, edited by Ben Witherington III, 154–84. Cambridge: Cambridge University Press, 1996.

———. "James and the Jerusalem Church." In *The Book of Acts in Its First Century Setting*, edited by Bruce W. Winter, vol. 4: *The Book of Acts in Its Palestinian Setting*, edited by Richard Bauckham, 417–80. Grand Rapids: Eerdmans, 1995.

———. "James at the Centre." *EPTA Bulletin* 14 (1995) 23–33.

———. *Jesus and the God of Israel: God Crucified and Other Studies on the New Testament's Christology of Divine Identity*. Grand Rapids: Eerdmans, 2008.

———. *Jewish World Around the New Testament*. Grand Rapids: Baker Academic, 2008.

———. "Jews and Jewish Christians in the Land of Israel at the Time of the Bar Kochba War, with Special Reference to the Apocalypse of Peter." In *Tolerance and Intolerance in Early Judaism and Christianity*, edited by Graham N. Stanton and Guy G. Stroumsma, 228–38. Cambridge: Cambridge University Press, 1998.

———. *Jude and the Relatives of Jesus in the Early Church*. Edinburgh: T&T Clark, 1990.

———. "The Origin of the Ebionites." In *The Image of the Judaeo-Christians in Ancient Jewish and Christian Literature*, edited by Peter J. Tomson and Doris Lambers-Petry, 162–81. WUNT 158. Tübingen: Mohr Siebeck, 2003.

———. "The Relatives of Jesus." *Them* 21 (1996) 18–21.

———. "Why Were Early Christians Called Nazarenes?" *Mishkan* 38 (2003) 80–85.

Bauer, Johannes Baptist. *Die Polykarpbriefe*. Kommentar zu den Apostolischen Vätern 5. Göttingen: Vandenhoeck & Ruprecht, 1995.

Bauer, Walter. *Der Apostolos der Syrer in der Zeit von der Mitte des vierten Jahrhunderts bis zur Spaltung der Syrischen Kirche*. Giessen: Ricker/Töpelmann, 1903.

———. *Das Leben Jesu im Zeitalter der neutestamentlichen Apokryphen*. Darmstadt: Wissenschaftliche Buchgesellschaft, 1967.

———. *Orthodoxie et hérésie aux débuts du christianisme*. 2nd ed. Translated by Philippe Vuagnat. Revised by Christina Mimouri and Simon C. Mimouni. Patrimoines—christianisme. Paris: Cerf, 2009.

———. *Orthodoxy and Heresy in Earliest Christianity*. 2nd ed. Edited by Robert A. Kraft and Gerhard Krodel. Philadelphia: Fortress, 1971.

———. *Rechtgläubigkeit und Ketzerei im ältesten Christentum*. Beiträge zur historischen Theologie 10. Tübingen: Mohr Siebeck, 1934.

———. "Rechtgläubigkeit und Ketzerei im ältesten Christentum." In *Aufsätze und kleine Schriften*, edited by Georg Strecker, 229–33. Tübingen: Mohr Siebeck, 1967.

Bauer, Walter, and Frederick William Danker, with W. F. Arndt and F. W. Gingrich. *Greek-English Lexicon of the New Testament and Other Early Christian Literature*. 3rd ed. Chicago: University of Chicago Press, 2000.

Bauer, Walter, and Georg Strecker. *Rechtgläubigkeit und Ketzerei im ältesten Christentum*. Beiträge zur historischen Theologie 10. 2nd ed. Tübingen: Mohr Siebeck, 1964.

Baur, Ferdinand Christian. *The Church History of the First Three Centuries*. 2 vols. Translated by Allan Menzies. 3rd ed. Theological Translation Fund Library 16, 20. Edinburgh: Williams & Norgate, 1879.

Becker, Adam H. and Annette Yoshiko Reed, editors. *The Ways That Never Parted: Jews and Christians in Late Antiquity and the Early Middle Ages*. Texte und Studien zum antiken Judentum 95. Tübingen: Mohr Siebeck, 2003.

Behr, John. *The Way to Nicaea. The Formation of Christian Theology*, vol. 1. Crestwood, NY: St. Vladimir's Seminary Press, 2001.

Benoit, A. "Irénée et l'hérésie: Les conceptions hérésiologiques de l'évêque de Lyon." *Augustinianum* 20 (1980) 55–67.

Berding, Kenneth. "John or Paul? Who Was Polycarp's Mentor?" *TynBul* 59 (2008) 135–43.

———. *Polycarp and Paul: An Analysis of their Literary & Theological Relationship in Light of Polycarp's Use of Biblical & Extra-Biblical Literature*. VCSup 62. Leiden: Brill, 2002.

———. "Polycarp's Use of 1 Clement: An Assumption Reconsidered." *JECS* 19 (2011) 127–39.

Betz, Hans Dieter. "Orthodoxy and Heresy in Primitive Christianity." *Int* 19 (1965) 299–311.

Beyschlag, Karlmann. *Clemens Romanus und der Frühkatholizismus: Untersuchungen zu I Clemens 1-7*. BHT 35. Tübingen: Mohr Siebeck, 1966.

Bianchi, Ugo, editor. *Le origini dello gnosticismo*. SHR 12. Leiden: Brill, 1970.

Bingham, D. Jeffrey. "Development and Diversity in Early Christianity." *JETS* 49 (2006) 45–66.

Bird, Michael F., et al. *How God Became Jesus: The Real Origins of Belief in Jesus' Divine Nature*. Grand Rapids: Zondervan, 2014.

Blaising, Craig. "Faithfulness: A Prescription for Theology." *JETS* 49 (2006) 6–9.

Blank, Josef. "Zum Problem 'Häresie und Orthodoxie' im Urchristentum." In *Zur Geschichte des Urchristentum*, edited by Gerhard Dautzenberg, 142–60. Freiburg im Breisgau: Herder, 1979.

Blowers, Paul. "The *Regula Fidei* and the Narrative Character of Early Christian Faith." *ProEccl* 6 (1997) 199–228.

Bobichon, Philippe. "Persécutions, calomnies, 'Birkat ha-minim' et émissaires juifs de propagande antichrétienne das les écrits de Justin Martyr." *REJ* 162 (2003) 403–19.

Bock, Darrell L. *The Missing Gospels: Unearthing the Truth Behind Alternative Christianities*. Nashville: Nelson, 2006.

———. *Studying the Historical Jesus: A Guide to Sources and Methods*. Grand Rapids: Baker, 2002.

Boer, Martinus C. de. "The Nazoreans: Living at the Boundary of Judaism and Christianity." In *Tolerance and Intolerance in Early Judaism and Christianity*, edited by Graham N. Stanton and Guy G. Stroumsa, 239–62. Cambridge: Cambridge University Press, 1998.

Bonner, Gerald. "Schism and Church Unity." In *Early Christianity: Origins and Evolution to AD 600*, edited by Ian Hazlett, 218–28. London: SPCK, 1991.

Bonwetsch, G. Nathaniel. *Die Geschichte des Montanismus*. Erlangen: Deichert, 1881.

Borgolte, Michael. *Petrusnachfolge und Kaiserimitation: die Grablegen der Päpste, ihre Genese und Traditionsbildung*. Göttingen: Vandenhoeck & Ruprecht, 1989.

Bousset, Wilhelm. *Kyrios Christos: A History of the Belief in Christ from the Beginnings of Christianity to Irenaeus*. Translated by John E. Steely. Nashville: Abingdon, 1970.

Bovon-Thurneysen, Annegreth. "Ethik und Eschatologie im Philipperbrief des Polycarp von Smyrna." *TZ* 29 (1973) 241–56.

Box, George Herbert, editor. *The Ezra-Apocalypse*. London: Pitman, 1912.

Bowe, Barbara E. *A Church in Crisis: Ecclesiology and Paraenesis in Clement of Rome.* Philadelphia: Fortress, 1988.

Bowes, Kimberly. *Private Worship, Public Values, and Religious Change in Late Antiquity.* Cambridge: Cambridge University Press, 2008.

Boyarin, Daniel. *Border Lines: The Partition of Judaeo-Christianity.* Divinations: Rereading Late Ancient Religion. Philadelphia: University of Pennsylvania Press, 2004.

———. *The Jewish Gospels: The Story of the Jewish Christ.* New York: New Press, 2011.

Boyd, Gregory A. *Cynic Sage or Son of God? Recovering the Real Jesus in an Age of Revisionist Replies.* Wheaton, IL: Victor, 1995.

Brakke, David. *The Gnostics: Myth, Ritual, and Diversity in Early Christianity.* Cambridge, MA: Harvard University Press, 2010.

Brandon, Samuel G. F. *The Fall of Jerusalem and the Christian Church: A Study of the Effects of the Jewish Overthrow of A.D. 70 on Christianity.* 2nd ed. London: SPCK, 1957.

Bray, Gerald L. "Tertullian." In *Shapers of Christian Orthodoxy*, edited by Bradley G. Green, 64–107. Downers Grove, IL: InterVarsity, 2010.

Bray, Gerald L. and Thomas C. Oden, editors. *We Believe in One God: Ancient Christian Doctrine*, vol. 1. Downers Grove, IL: InterVarsity, 2009.

Brent, Allen. *Ignatius of Antioch: A Martyr Bishop and the Origin of Episcopacy.* T. & T. Clark Theology. London: T. & T. Clark, 2007.

———. *The Imperial Cult and the Development of Church Order: Concepts and Images of Authority in Paganism and Early Christianity before the Age of Cyprian.* VCSup 45. Leiden: Brill, 1999.

Broadhead, Edwin Keith. *Jewish Ways of Following Jesus: Redrawing the Religious Map of Antiquity.* WUNT 266. Tübingen: Mohr Siebeck, 2010.

Broek, Roelof van den. "The Present State of Gnostic Studies." *VC* 37 (1983) 41–71.

Brox, Norberg. "Häresie." *RAC*, vol. 13, cols. 248–97.

Brown, Harold O. J. *Heresies: Heresy and Orthodoxy in the History of the Church.* Peabody, MA: Hendrickson Publishers, 1998.

———. *Heresies: The Image of Christ in the Mirror of Heresy and Orthodoxy from the Apostles to the Present.* Grand Rapids: Baker, 1984.

Brown, Raymond E. "Not Jewish Christianity and Gentile Christianity but Types of Jewish/Gentile Christianity." *CBQ* 45 (1983) 74–79.

Brown, Raymond E. and John P. Meier. *Antioch and Rome: New Testament Cradles of Catholic Christianity.* Mahwah, NJ: Paulist, 1983.

Burke, Gary T. "Celsus and Late Second-Century Christianity." PhD diss., University of Iowa, 1981.

———. "Walter Bauer and Celsus: The Shape of Late Second-Century Christianity." *JECS* 4 (1984) 1–7.

Burkhardt, Walter. "Primitive Montanism: Why Condemned?" In *From Faith to Faith: Essays in Honor of Donald G. Miller*, edited by Dikran Hadidian, 339–56. Pittsburgh: Pickwick, 1979.

Burns, Dylan M. *Apocalypse of the Alien God: Platonism and the Exile of Sethian Gnosticism.* Divinations: Rereading Late Ancient Religion. Philadelphia: University of Pennsylvania Press, 2014.

Burns, J. Patout. *Cyprian the Bishop.* London: Routledge, 2002.

Butler, Rex D. *The New Prophecy and "New Visions": Evidence of Montanism in the Passion of Perpetua and Felicitas.* Washington, DC: Catholic University of America Press, 2006.

———. "Tertullianism: Tertullian's Vision of the New Prophecy in North Africa." *Journal of Baptist Theology and Ministry* 8 (2011) 40–58.

Cambe, Michel. *Kerygma Petri: textus et commentarius.* Turnhout: Brepols, 2003.

Cameron, Averil. "The Violence of Orthodoxy." In *Heresy and Identity in Late Antiquity*, edited by Eduard Iricinschi and Holger M. Zellentin. Tübingen: Mohr Siebeck, 2008.

Campenhausen, Hans von. *Kirchliches Amt und geistliche Vollmacht in den ersten drei Jahrhunderten.* 2nd edition. BHT 14. Tübingen: Mohr Siebeck, 1963.

Carlson, Stephen C. *The Gospel Hoax: Morton Smith's Invention of Secret Mark.* Waco, TX: Baylor University Press, 2005.

Carson, D. A. "Unity and Diversity in the New Testament: The Possibility of a Systematic Theology." In *Scripture and Truth*, edited by D. A. Carson and John D. Woodbridge, 65–100. Grand Rapids: Zondervan, 1983.

Chadwick, Henry. *Saint Augustine: Confessions.* London: Oxford University Press, 1991.

Chapa, Juan. "The Fortunes and Misfortunes of the Gospel of John in Egypt." *VC* 64 (2010) 327–52.

Chapman, G. Clarke. "Some Theological Reflections on Walter Bauer's *Rechtgläubigkeit und Ketzerei im ältesten Christentum*: A Review Article." *JES* 7 (1970) 564–74.

Chesnut, Glenn F. "Radicalism and Orthodoxy: The Unresolved Problem of the First Christian Histories." *AThR* 65 (1983) 292–305.

Chilton, Bruce and Jacob Neusner. *The Brother of Jesus: James the Just and His Mission.* Louisville: Westminster John Knox Press, 2001.

Cohen, Shaye J. D. "A Virgin Defiled: Some Rabbinic and Christian Views on the Origins of Heresy." *USQR* 36 (1980) 1–11.

Cohick, Lynn. "Jews and Christians." In *The Routledge Companion to Early Christian Thought*, edited by D. Jeffrey Bingham, 68–86. New York: Routledge, 2010.

Cooper, Stephen Andrew. *Marius Victorinus' Commentary on Galatians: Introduction, Translation, and Notes.* Oxford Early Christian Studies. Oxford: Oxford University Press, 2005.

Cooper, Tim. "Gnosticism Then and Now." *Stimulus* 14 (2006) 17–21.

Couliano, Ioan P. *The Tree of Gnosis: Gnostic Mythology from Early Christianity to Modern Nihilism.* Translated by H. S. Wiesner and Ioan P. Couliano. San Francisco: HarperSanFrancisco, 1992.

Countryman, L. William. "Tertullian and the *Regula Fidei*." *SecCent* 2 (1982) 208–27.

Corrigan, Kevin, et al. *Gnosticism, Platonism and the Late Ancient World: Essays in Honour of John D. Turner.* Nag Hammadi and Manichaean Studies. Leiden: Brill, 2013.

Crossan, John Dominic. *Four Other Gospels: Shadows on the Contour of the Canon.* Minneapolis: Winston, 1985.

Cullen, Olive M. "A Question of Time or a Question of Theology: A Study of the Easter Controversy in the Insular Church." PhD diss., Pontifical University, St. Patrick's College, 2007.

Cullmann, Oscar. *The Earliest Christian Confessions.* Translated by J. K. S. Reid. London: Lutterworth, 1949.

———. "The Tradition." In *The Early Church: Studies in Early Christian History and Theology*, edited by A. J. B. Higgins, 59–99. Philadelphia: Westminster, 1956.

Daniélou, Jean. *A History of Early Christian Doctrine Before the Council of Nicea*, vol. 1: *The Theology of Jewish Christianity*. Translated and edited by John A. Baker. London: Darton, Longman & Todd, 1964.

Danker, Frederick W. *Creeds in the Bible*. St. Louis: Concordia, 1966.

Dart, John. *The Jesus of Heresy and History*. San Francisco: Harper & Row, 1988.

Davids, Adelbert. "Irrtum und Häresie: 1 Clem.-Ignatius von Antiochien-Justinus." *Kairos* 15 (1973) 165–87.

Davidson, Ivor J. *The Birth of the Church: From Jesus to Constantine, A.D. 30–312*. Baker History of the Church 1. Grand Rapids: Baker, 2004.

Davies, Stevan L. *The Gospel of Thomas and Christian Wisdom*. 2nd ed. Dublin: Bardic Press, 2005.

de Labriolle, Pierre. *La crise montaniste*. Paris: Leroux, 1913.

de Soyres, John. *Montanism and the Primitive Church: A Study in the Ecclesiastical History of the Second Century*. Cambridge: Deighton, 1878.

Decker, Rodney. "The Rehabilitation of Heresy: 'Misquoting' Earliest Christianity." *Journal of Ministry and Theology* 13 (2009) 30–63; 56–95.

———. "Using BDAG." In *Koine Greek Reader: Selections from the New Testament, Septuagint, and Early Christian Writers*, 245–62. Grand Rapids: Kregel, 2007.

DeConick, April D., editor. *The Codex Judas Papers: Proceedings of the International Congress on the Tchacos Codex Held at Rice University, Houston Texas, March 13–16, 2008*. NHMS 71. Leiden: Brill, 2009.

———. *The Original Gospel of Thomas in Translation: With a Commentary and New English Translation of the Complete Gospel*. New York: T. & T. Clark, 2006.

———. *The Thirteenth Apostle: What the Gospel of Judas Really Says*. New York: Continuum, 2007.

Decret, François. *Early Christianity in North Africa*. Translated by Edward L. Smither. Eugene, OR: Cascade, 2009.

Dehandschutter, Boudewijn. "Polycarp's Epistle to the Philippians: An Early Example of 'Reception.'" In *The New Testament in Early Christianity: la réception des écrits néotestamentaires dans le christianisme primitif*, edited by Jean-Marie Sevrin, 275–91. BETL 86. Leuven: Peeters, 1989.

Desjardins, Michel. "Bauer and Beyond: On Recent Scholarly Discussions of Αἵρεσις in the Early Christian Era." *SecCent* 8 (1991) 65–82.

Dodd, C. H. *The Apostolic Preaching and Its Developments*. London: Hodder & Stoughton, 1936.

Donati, Angela, editor. *Pietro e Paolo*. La storia, il culto, la memoria nei primi secoli. Milano: Electa, 2000.

Donovan, Mary Ann. "Irenaeus." In *ABD*, vol. 3, 457–61.

———. "Irenaeus in Recent Scholarship." *SecCent* 4 (1984) 219–41.

———. *One Right Reading? A Guide to Irenaeus*. Collegeville: Liturgical Press, 1997.

Drijvers, H. W. "The Origins of Gnosticism as a Religious and Historical Problem." *NedTTs* 22 (1968) 321–51.

———. "Rechtgläubigkeit und Ketzerei im ältesten syrischen Christentum." *OCA* (1974) 291–310.

Dunderberg, Ismo. "The School of Valentinus." In *A Companion to Second-Century Christian "Heretics,"* edited by Antti Marjanen and Petri Luomanen, 64–99. *VCSup* 76. Leiden: Brill, 2005.

Dunn, Geoffrey D. *Cyprian and the Bishops of Rome: Questions of Papal Primacy in the Early Church.* Strathfield: St Pauls, 2007.

Dunn, James. "The New Perspective on Paul." *BJRL* (1983) 95–122.

———. *Unity and Diversity in the New Testament: An Inquiry into the Character of Earliest Christianity.* 3rd ed. London: SCM, 2006.

Dunn, James D. G., editor. *Jews and Christians: The Parting of the Ways, A.D. 70 to 135.* Grand Rapids: Eerdmans, 1999.

Eastman, David. *Paul the Martyr: The Cult of the Apostle in the Latin West,* SBL Writings from the Greco-Roman World Supplements 4. Atlanta: SBL, 2011.

Efroymson, David P. "Tertullian's Anti-Jewish Rhetoric: Guilt by Association." *USQR* 36 (1980) 25–37.

Ehrhardt, Arnold. "Christianity before the Apostles' Creed." *HTR* 55 (1962): 73–119.

Ehrlich, Uri and Ruth Langer. "The Earliest Texts of the Birkat ha-Minim." *HUCA* 76 (2005) 63–112.

Ehrman, Bart D. *Apostolic Fathers,* vol. 1: *1 Clement, 2 Clement, Ignatius, Polycarp, Didache.* LCL. Cambridge, MA: Harvard University Press, 2003.

———. *Forged: Writing in the Name of God, Why the Bible's Authors Are Not Who We Think They Are.* New York: HarperOne, 2011.

———. *God's Problem: How the Bible Fails to Answer Our Most Important Question—Why We Suffer.* New York: HarperOne, 2008.

———. *How Jesus Became God: The Exaltation of a Jewish Preacher from Galilee.* New York: HarperOne, 2014.

———. *Jesus Interrupted: Revealing the Hidden Contradictions in the Bible (and Why We Don't Know about Them).* New York: HarperOne, 2009.

———. *Lost Christianities: The Battles for Scripture and the Faiths We Never Knew.* New York: Oxford University Press, 2003.

———. *The Lost Gospel of Judas: A New Look at Betrayer and Betrayed.* New York: Oxford University Press, 2006.

———. *Lost Scriptures: Books that Did Not Make It into the New Testament.* New York: Oxford University Press, 2003.

———. *Misquoting Jesus: The Story Behind Who Changed the Bible and Why.* New York: HarperSanFrancisco, 2005.

———. *The New Testament: A Historical Introduction to the Early Christian Writings.* New York: Oxford University Press, 2000.

———. *The Orthodox Corruption of Scripture: The Effect of Early Christological Controversies on the Text of the New Testament.* New York: Oxford University Press, 1993.

———. *Truth and Fiction in "The Da Vinci Code."* New York: Oxford University Press, 2004.

Eisenman, Robert H. *James the Brother of Jesus.* New York: Penguin, 1996.

Elster, Jon. "Bias, Belief, and Ideology." In *Rationality and Relativism,* edited by Martin Hollis and Steven Lukes, 123–48. Oxford: Blackwell, 1982.

Elze, Martin. "Häresie und Einheit der Kirche im 2.Jahrhundert." *ZThK* 71 (1974) 389–409.

Eusebius. *Eusebius: The History of the Church from Christ to Constantine.* Translated by G. A. Williamson. Minneapolis: Augsburg Publishing House, 1965.

Evans, Craig A. *From Jesus to the Church: The First Christian Generation.* Louisville: Westminster John Knox, 2014.

———. "The Jewish Christian Gospel Tradition." In *Jewish Believers in Jesus: The Early Centuries,* edited by Oskar Skarsaune and Reidar Hvalvik, 241–77. Peabody, MA: Hendrickson, 2007.

Evans, Craig A., et al., editors. *Nag Hammadi Texts and the Bible: A Synopsis and Index.* New York: Brill, 1993.

Evans, G. R. *A Brief History of Heresy.* Blackwell Brief Histories of Religion. Malden, MA: Blackwell, 2002.

Faivre, Alexandre. "Des adversaires vus de Rome: l'art de gérer un conflit en proposant de novelles frontiers pour L'Ekklèsia." *RevScRel* 84 (2010) 373–85.

Farkasfalvy, Denis M., "'Prophets and Apostles': The Conjunction of the Two Terms before Irenaeus." In *Texts and Testaments: Critical Essays on the Bible and Early Church Fathers,* edited by W. Eugene March, 109–34. San Antonio: Trinity University Press, 1980.

Fascher, Erich. "Walter Bauer als Kommentator." *NTS* 9 (1962) 23–38.

Ferguson, Everett. "Canon Muratori: Date and Provenance." *StPatr* 17 (1982) 677–83.

Ferguson, Everett, editor. *Orthodoxy, Heresy, and Schism in Early Christianity.* Studies in Early Christianity 4. New York: Garland, 1993.

Ferguson, Thomas C. "The Rule of Truth and Irenaean Rhetoric in Book 1 of *Against Heresies.*" *VC* 55 (2001) 356–75.

Filoramo, Giovanni. *A History of Gnosticism.* Cambridge: Blackwell, 1990.

Fitzmyer, Joseph A. *The Dead Sea Scrolls and Christian Origins: Studies in the Dead Sea Scrolls and Related Literature.* Grand Rapids: Eerdmans, 2000.

Flora, Jerry. "A Critical Analysis of Walter Bauer's Theory of Early Christian Orthodoxy and Heresy." ThD diss., The Southern Baptist Theological Seminary, 1972.

Florovsky, Geore. "The Function of Tradition in the Ancient Church." *Greek Orthodox Theological Review* 9 (1963) 181–200.

Frend, W. H. C. *The Donatist Church: A Movement of Protest in Roman North Africa.* Oxford: Clarendon, 1952.

———. "Montanism: A Movement of Prophecy and Regional Identity in the Early Church." *BJRL* 70 (1988) 25–34.

———. "The North African Cult of Martyrs: From Apocalyptic to Hero-Worship." In *Jenseitsvorstellungen in Antike und Christentum: Gedenkschrift für Alfred Stuiber,* 154–67. JAC 9. Münster: Aschendorff, 1982.

———. *Saints and Sinners in the Early Church: Differing and Conflicting Traditions in the First Six Centuries.* Theology and Life 11. Wilmington, DE: Glazier, 1985.

Fuellenbach, John. *Ecclesiastical Office and the Primacy of Rome: An Evaluation of Recent Theological Discussion of First Clement.* SCA 20. Washington, DC: 1980.

Funk, Robert W. *Honest to Jesus.* San Francisco: HarperSanFrancisco, 1996.

Garland, David E. *1 Corinthians.* BECNT. Grand Rapids: Baker Academic, 2003.

Gehring, Roger W. *House Church and Mission: The Importance of Household Structures in Early Christianity.* Peabody, MA: Hendrickson, 2004.

Gerke, Friedrich. *Die Stellung des ersten Clemensbriefes innerhalb der Entwicklung der altchristlichen Gemeindeverfassung und des Kirchenrechts.* TU 47.1. Leipzig: Hinrichs, 1931.

Gero, Stephen. "With Walter Bauer on the Tigris: Encratite Orthodoxy and Libertine Heresy in Syro-Mesopotamian Christianity." In *Nag Hammadi, Gnosticism and Early Christianity*, edited by Charles W. Hedrick and Robert Hodgson, Jr., 287–307. Peabody, MA: Hendrickson, 1986.

Gingrich, F. Wilbur. "Walter Bauer, 1877–1960." *NTS* 9 (1962) 1–2.

Grant, Robert M. *The Apostolic Fathers: A Translation and Commentary*, vol. 1: *An Introduction*. New York: Nelson, 1964.

———. "Charges of 'Immorality' Against Various Religious Groups in Antiquity." In *Studies in Gnosticism and Hellenistic Religions*, edited by R. van den Boek and M. J. Vermaseren, 161–70. Leiden: Brill, 1981.

———. *Gnosticism and Early Christianity*. Rev. ed. New York: Harper & Row, 1966.

———. "Irenaeus and Hellenistic Culture." *HTR* 43 (1949) 41–51.

———. "Review of *The Johannine Gospel in Gnostic Exegesis* and *The Gnostic Paul*, by Elaine Pagels." *RelSRev* 3 (1977) 30–34.

Grant, Robert M. and Holt H. Graham. *First and Second Clement*. The Apostolic Fathers: A New Translation and Commentary 2. New York: Nelson, 1965.

Green, Bernard. *Christianity in Ancient Rome: The First Three Centuries*. New York: T. & T. Clark, 2010.

Green, Bradley G. "Augustine." In *Shapers of Christian Orthodoxy*, edited by Bradley G. Green, 235–92. Downers Grove, IL: InterVarsity, 2010.

Greenslade, S. L. "Heresy and Schism in the Later Roman Empire." In *Schism, Heresy, and Religious Protest*, edited by Derek Baker, 1–20. Studies in Church History 9. Cambridge: Cambridge University Press, 1972.

Greer, Rowan. "The Dog and the Mushrooms: Irenaeus's View of the Valentinians Assessed." In *Rediscovery of Gnosticism*, vol. 1, edited by Bentley Layton, 146–71. Studies in the History of Religion. Leiden: Brill, 1980.

Gregory, Andrew. "Disturbing Trajectories: 1 Clement, the Shepherd of Hermas and the Development of Early Roman Christianity." In *Rome in the Bible and the Early Church*, edited by Peter Oakes, 142–66. Grand Rapids: Baker Academic, 2002.

———. "1 Clement: An Introduction." In *The Writings of the Apostolic Fathers*, edited by Paul Foster, 21–31. London: T. & T. Clark, 2007.

———. "1 Clement and the Writings that Later Formed the New Testament." In *The Reception of the New Testament in the Apostolic Fathers*, edited by Andrew F. Gregory and Christopher M. Tuckett, 129–57. Oxford: Oxford University Press, 129–57.

———. "Hindrance or Help: Does the Modern Category of 'Jewish-Christian Gospel' Distort our Understanding of the Texts to Which it Refers?" *JSNT* 28 (2006) 387–413.

———. "Jewish-Christian Gospels." In *Non-Canonical Gospels*, edited by Paul Foster, 54–67. London: T. & T. Clark, 2008.

Guillaumont, Antoine, et al. *The Gospel According to Thomas*. Leiden: Brill, 1959.

Hagner, Donald A. *The Use of the Old and New Testaments in Clement of Rome*. Leiden: Brill, 1979.

Hahneman, Geoffrey Mark. *The Muratorian Fragment and the Development of the Canon*. Oxford: Clarendon, 1992.

Häkkinen, Sakari. "Ebionites." In *A Companion to Second-Century Christian "Heretics,"* edited by Antti Marjanen and Petri Luomanen, 247–78. VCSup 76. Leiden: Brill, 2005.

Hanson, Craig L., editor. *Iberian Fathers*, vol. 3: *Pacian of Barcelona and Orosius of Braga*. FC 99. Washington, DC: Catholic University of America Press, 1999.

Hanson, R. P. C. *Origen's Doctrine of Tradition*. London: SPCK, 1954.

———. *Tradition in the Early Church*. London: SCM, 1962.

Harnack, Adolph von. *The Mission and Expansion of Christianity in the First Three Centuries*, 2 vols. 2nd ed. Translated by James Moffatt. Theological Translation Library 19–20. New York: Putnam, 1908.

Harrington, Daniel J. "The Reception of Walter Bauer's *Orthodoxy and Heresy in Earliest Christianity* during the Last Decade." *HTR* 73 (1980) 289–98.

Hartog, Paul. "1 Corinthians 2:9 in the Apostolic Fathers." In a forthcoming volume on the reception of the New Testament in the second century, edited by D. Jeffrey Bingham and Clayton N. Jefford. Leiden: Brill, forthcoming.

———. "Blondel Remembered: His Philosophical Analysis of the 'Quest for the Historical Jesus." *Them* 33 (2008) 5–15.

———. "The Implications of Paul as Epistolary Author and Church Planter in *1 Clement* and Polycarp's *Philippians*." In *the Apostolic Fathers and Paul*, edited by Todd D. Still and David E. Wilhite. New York: T. & T. Clark, forthcoming.

———. "The Opponents in Polycarp, *Philippians*, and 1 John." In *Trajectories through the New Testament and the Apostolic Fathers*, edited by Andrew F. Gregory and Christopher M. Tuckett, 375–91. Oxford: Oxford University Press, 2005.

———. "Peter in Paul's Churches: The Early Reception of Peter in *1 Clement* and in Polycarp's *Philippians*." In a forthcoming volume on the reception of Peter in the early church, edited by Larry W. Hurtado. Grand Rapids: Eerdmans, forthcoming.

———. "Polycarp, Ephesians, and 'Scripture.'" *WTJ* 70 (2008) 255–75.

———. *Polycarp's Epistle to the Philippians and the Martyrdom of Polycarp: Introduction, Text, and Commentary*. Oxford Apostolic Fathers. Oxford: Oxford University Press, 2013.

———. *Polycarp and the New Testament: The Occasion, Rhetoric, Theme, and Unity of the Epistle to the Philippians and Its Allusion to New Testament Literature*. WUNT 2.134. Tübingen: Mohr Siebeck, 2002.

———. "The Relationship between *Paraenesis* and Polemic in Polycarp, *Philippians*." *StPatr* 65 (2013) 27–37.

———. "The 'Rule of Faith' and Patristic Biblical Exegesis." *TrinJ* 28 (2007) 65–86.

Headlam, Arthur C. "The Epistle of Polycarp to the Philippians." *CQR* 141 (1945) 1–25.

Heffernan, Thomas J. *The Passion of Perpetua and Felicity*. Oxford: Oxford University Press, 2012.

Heine, Ronald. "The Role of the Gospel of John in the Montanist Controversy." *SecCent* 6 (1987) 1–19.

Hengel, Martin. "Early Christianity as a Jewish-Messianic, Universalist Movement." In *Conflicts and Challenges in Early Christianity*, edited by Donald A. Hagner et al., 1–41. Harrisville, PA: Trinity, 1999.

———. *Studies in the Gospel of Mark*. Philadelphia: Fortress, 1985.

Henn, William. "Orthodoxy." In *The New Dictionary of Theology*, edited by Joseph A. Komonchak et al., 731–33. Wilmington, DE: Glazier, 1987.

Henne, Philippe. "L'Évangile des Ebionites: Une fausse harmonie: Une vraie supercherie." In *Peregrina curiositas Eine Reise durch den orbis antiques: zu Ehren von Dirk van Damme*, edited by Andreas Kessler, Thomas Ricklin, and Gregor Wurst, 57–75. Göttingen: Vandenhoeck & Ruprecht, 1994.

Henry, Patrick. "Why Is Contemporary Scholarship So Enamored of Ancient Heresies?" *StPatr* 17 (1982) 123–26.

Hernando, James Daniel. "Irenaeus and the Apostolic Fathers: An Inquiry into the Development of the New Testament Canon." PhD diss., Drew University, 1990.

Heron, A. I. C. "The Interpretation of I Clement in Walter Bauer's *Rechtgläubigkeit und Ketzerei im ältesten Christentum.*" *Ekklesiastikos Pharos* 55 (1973) 517–45.

Heyne, Thomas. "The Devious Eusebius? An Evaluation of the *Ecclesiastical History* and its Critics." *StPatr* 46 (2010) 325–31.

Hill, Charles E. "An Exclusive Religion: Orthodoxy and Heresy, Inclusion and Exclusion." In *How God Became Jesus: The Real Origins of Belief in Jesus' Divine Nature*, edited by Michael F. Bird, 151–67. Grand Rapids: Zondervan, 2014.

———. *From the Lost Teaching of Polycarp*. WUNT 186. Tübingen: Mohr Siebeck, 2006.

———. "Ignatius, 'the Gospel', and the Gospels." In *Trajectories through the New Testament and the Apostolic Fathers*, edited by Andrew F. Gregory and Christopher M. Tuckett, 267–85. Oxford: Oxford University Press, 2005.

———. *The Johannine Corpus in the Early Church*. Oxford: Oxford University Press, 2006.

———. "The Man Who Needed No Introduction: A Response to Sebastian Moll." In *Irenaeus: Life, Scripture, Legacy*, edited by Sara Parvis and Paul Foster, 95–104. Minneapolis: Fortress, 2012.

———. "Polycarp *contra* Marcion. Irenaeus' Presbyteral Source in *AH* 4.27–32." *StPatr* 40 (2006) 399–412.

Hoffman, Daniel H. *The Status of Women and Gnosticism in Irenaeus and Tertullian.* Studies in Women and Religion 36. Lewiston, NY: Mellen, 1995.

Holmes, Michael W. *The Apostolic Fathers: Greek Texts and English Translations.* 3rd ed. Grand Rapids: Baker Academic, 2007.

———. "Paul and the Letter of Polycarp." In *Paul and the Second Century*, edited by Michael F. Bird and Joseph R. Dodson, 57–69. LNTS 412. London: Continuum, 2011.

———. "Polycarp of Smyrna." In *DLNT*, 934–38.

———. "Polycarp's *Letter to the Philippians* and the Writings that Later Formed the New Testament." In *The Reception of the New Testament in the Apostolic Fathers*, edited by Andrew F. Gregory and Christopher M. Tuckett, 187–227. Oxford: Oxford University Press, 2005.

Hopkins, Keith. *A World Full of Gods.* New York: Free Press, 2000.

Horbury, William. *Jews and Christians in Contact and Controversy.* Edinburgh: T. & T. Clark, 1998.

Horrell, David G. *The Social Ethos of the Corinthians Correspondence: Interests and Ideology from 1 Corinthians to 1 Clement.* Studies of the New Testament and Its World. Edinburgh: T. & T. Clark, 1996.

Hort, Fenton John Anthony. *Judaistic Christianity.* London: Macmillan, 1904.

Hultgren, Arland. *The Rise of Normative Christianity.* Minneapolis: Fortress Press, 1994.

Hunter, Archibald M. *Paul and His Predecessors.* Philadelphia: Westminster, 1961.

Hurtado, Larry. *Lord Jesus Christ: Devotion to Jesus in Earliest Christianity.* Grand Rapids: Eerdmans, 2003.

Instone-Brewer, David. "The Eighteen Benedictions and the Minim before 70 CE." *JTS* 1 (2003) 25–44.

Iricinschi, Eduard, and Holger M. Zellentin, editors. *Heresy and Identity in Late Antiquity.* Texts and Studies in Ancient Judaism 119. Tübingen: Mohr Siebeck, 2008.

Jakab, Attila. *Ecclesia Alexandria.* 2nd ed. Bern: Lang, 2004.

Jaubert, Annie. *Clément de Rome: Épitre aux Corinthiens.* 2nd ed. Sources chrétiennes 167. Paris: Cerf, 2000.

Jeffers, James S. *Conflict at Rome: Social Order and Hierarchy in Early Christianity.* Minneapolis: Fortress, 1991.

Jeffery, Peter. *The Secret Gospel of Mark Unveiled: Imagined Rituals of Sex, Death, and Madness in a Biblical Forgery.* New Haven: Yale University Press, 2006.

Jefford, Clayton N. *The Apostolic Fathers: An Essential Guide.* Nashville: Abingdon, 2005.

———. *The Apostolic Fathers and the New Testament.* Peabody, MA: Hendrickson, 2006.

———. *Reading the Apostolic Fathers: A Student's Introduction.* 2nd ed. Grand Rapids: Baker Academic, 2012.

Jenkins, Philip. *Hidden Gospels: How the Search for Jesus Lost its Way.* Oxford: Oxford University Press, 2001.

Jensen, Anne. *God's Self-Confident Daughters: Early Christianity and the Liberation of Women.* Translated by O. C. Dean, Jr. Louisville: Westminster John Knox Press, 1996.

Jocz, Jacob. *The Jewish People and Jesus Christ: A Study in the Relationship between the Jewish People and Jesus Christ.* 3rd ed. Grand Rapids: Baker, 1979.

Johnson, Luke Timothy. *The Real Jesus: The Misguided Quest for the Historical Jesus and the Truth of the Traditional Gospels.* San Francisco: HarperSanFrancisco, 1996.

Jonas, Hans. "The Delimitation of the Gnostic Phenomenon—Typological and Historical." In *Le origini dello gnosticismo,* edited by Ugo Bianchi, 90–108. Leiden: Brill, 1970.

———. *The Gnostic Religion.* 2nd rev. ed. Boston: Beacon, 1963.

Jones, A. H. M. "Were Ancient Heresies National or Social Movements in Disguise?" *JTS* 10 (1959) 280–98.

Jones, F. Stanley. *An Ancient Jewish Christian Source on the History of Christianity: Pseudo-Clementine Recognitions 1.27–71.* Christian Apocrypha Series 2, Texts and Translations 37. Atlanta: Scholars, 1995.

Kalvesmaki, Joel. "The Original Sequence of Irenaeus, *Against Heresies* 1: Another Suggestion." *JECS* 15 (2007) 407–17.

Kannengiesser, Charles and William Lawrence Petersen, editors. *Origen of Alexandria: His World and His Legacy,* Notre Dame, IN: University of Notre Dame Press, 1988.

Kasser, Rudolphe, et al. *The Gospel of Judas, Critical Edition: Together with the Letter of Peter to Philip, James, and a Book of Allogenes from Codex Tchacos.* Washington, DC: National Geographic, 2007.

———. *The Gospel of Judas: From Codex Tchacos.* Washington, DC: National Geographic, 2006.

Katz, Steven T. "Issues in the Separation of Judaism and Christianity after 70 C.E.: A Reconsideration." *JBL* 103 (1984) 43–76.

Kaufman, Peter Iver. "Tertullian on Heresy, History, and the Reappropriation of History." *CH* 60 (1991) 167–79.

Kelly, J. N. D. *Early Christian Creeds.* 3rd ed. New York: Longman, 1972.

Kessler, Edward. "The Writings of the Church Fathers." In *An Introduction to Jewish-Christian Relations*, 45–64. Cambridge: Cambridge University Press, 2010.

Kim, Young Richard. "Bad Bishops Corrupt Good Emperors: Ecclesiastical Authority and the Rhetoric of Heresy in the *Panarion* of Epiphanius of Salamis." *StPatr* 47 (2010) 161–66.

Kimelman, Reuven. "Birkat ha-Minim and the Lack of Evidence for an Anti-Christian Jewish Prayer in Late Antiquity." In *Jewish and Christian Self-Definition*, vol. 2: *Aspects of Judaism in the Graeco-Roman Period*, edited by E. P. Sanders et al., 226–44. Philadelphia: Fortress, 1981.

King, Karen L. *The Gospel of Mary of Magdala: Jesus and the First Woman Apostle*. Santa Rosa, CA: Polebridge, 2003.

————. "'Jesus said to them, 'My wife . . .': A New Coptic Papyrus Fragment." *HTR* 107 (2014) 131–59.

————. "The Origins of Gnosticism and the Identity of Christianity." In *Was There a Gnostic Religion?*, edited by Antti Marjanen, 103–20. Göttingen: Vandenhoeck & Ruprecht, 2005.

————. "Social and Theological Effects of Heresiological Discourse." In *Heresy and Identity in Late Antiquity*, edited by Eduard Iricinschi and Holger M. Zellentin. Tübingen: Mohr Siebeck, 2008.

————. *What Is Gnosticism?* Cambridge, MA: Belknap, 2003.

Kittel, Gerhard. "Doxa." In *TDNT*, vol. 2, 233–53.

Klawiter, Frederick C. "The New Prophecy in Early Christianity: The Origin, Nature and Development of Montanism, A.D. 165–220." PhD diss., University of Chicago, 1975.

————. "The Role of Martyrdom and Persecution in Developing the Priestly Authority of Women in Early Christianity: A Case Study of Montanism." *CH* 49 (1980) 251–61.

Kleist, James A. *The Didache; the Epistle of Barnabas; the Epistles and the Martyrdom of St. Polycarp; the Fragments of Papias; the Epistle to Diognetus*. ACW 6. Westminster: Newman, 1948.

————. *The Epistles of St. Clement of Rome and St. Ignatius of Antioch*. ACW 1. New York: Paulist, 1946.

Klijn, Albertus Frederik Johannes. *Seth in Jewish, Christian and Gnostic Literature*. Leiden: Brill, 1977.

Klijn, A. F. J. and G. J. Reinink. *Patristic Evidence for Jewish-Christian Sects*. NovTSup 36. Leiden: Brill, 1973.

Kloppenborg, John. "An Analysis of the Pre-Pauline Formula 1 Cor 15:3b–5 in Light of Some Recent Literature." *CBQ* 40 (1978) 351–67.

Knox, Ronald Arbuthnott *Enthusiasm: A Chapter in the History of Religion*. Oxford: Clarendon, 1950.

Koester, Craig. "The Origin and Significance of the Flight to Pella Tradition." *CBQ* 51 (1989) 90–106.

Koester, Helmut. *Ancient Christian Gospels: Their History and Development*. Philadelphia: Trinity Press International, 1990.

————. "Apocryphal and Canonical Gospels." *HTR* 73 (1980) 105–30.

————. *From Jesus to the Gospels: Interpreting the New Testament in Its Context*. Minneapolis: Fortress, 2007.

———. "Gnomai Diaphoroi: The Origin and Nature of Diversification in the History of Early Christianity." *HTR* 58 (1965) 279–318. Reprinted in *Trajectories through Early Christianity*, edited by James M. Robinson and Helmut Koester, 114–57. Philadelphia: Fortress Press, 1971.

———. "Häretiker im Christentum." In *RGG*. 3rd edition, vol. 3, 17–21.

———. "Häretiker im Christentum als theologisches Problem." In *Zeit und Geschichte*, edited by Erich Dinkler and Hartwig Thyen, 61–76. Tübingen: Mohr Siebeck, 1964.

———. "History and Development of Mark's Gospel: From Mark to Secret Mark and 'Canonical' Mark." In *Colloquy on New Testament Studies: A Time for Reappraisal and Fresh Approaches*, edited by Bruce C. Corley, 35–58. Macon, GA: Mercer University Press, 1983.

———. "The Structure and Criteria of Early Christian Beliefs." In *Trajectories through Early Christianity*, edited by James M. Robinson and Helmut Koester, 205–31. Philadelphia: Fortress Press, 1971.

Köhler, Wolf-Dietrich. *Die Rezeption des Matthäusevangeliums in der Zeit vor Irenäus*. WUNT 2.24. Tübingen: Mohr Siebeck, 1987.

Körtner, Ulrich H. J. *Papias von Hierapolis: Ein Beitrag zur Geschichte des frühen Christentums*. Göttingen: Vandenhoeck & Ruprecht, 1983.

Koschorke, Klaus. *Hippolyt's Ketzerbekämpfung und Polemik gegen die Gnostiker*. Wiesbaden: Harrassowitz, 1975.

———. *Die Polemik der Gnostiker gegen das kirchliche Christentum*. Leiden: Brill, 1978.

Köstenberger, Andreas J. "Diversity and Unity in the New Testament." In *Biblical Theology: Retrospect and Prospect*, edited by Scott J. Hafemann, 144–58. Downers Grove, IL: InterVarsity, 2002.

Köstenberger, Andreas J., and Michael J. Kruger. *The Heresy of Orthodoxy: How Contemporary Culture's Fascination with Diversity Has Reshaped our Understanding of Early Christianity*. Wheaton, IL: Crossway, 2010.

Kruger, Michael J. *Canon Revisited: Establishing the Origins and Authority of the New Testament Books*. Wheaton, IL: Crossway, 2012.

———. *The Question of Canon: Challenging the Status Quo in the New Testament Debate*. Downers Grove, IL: IVP Academic, 2013.

Kurt, Barbara Aland, and Victor Reichmann. *Griechisch-Deutsches Wöterbuch zu den Schriften des Neuen Testaments und der frühchristlichen Literatur*. 6th ed. Berlin: De Gruyter, 1988.

La Piana, George. "The Roman Church at the End of the Second Century." *HTR* 18 (1925) 201–77.

Lake, Kirsopp. *The Apostolic Fathers*, vol. 1: *I Clement, II Clement, Ignatius, Polycarp, Didache, Barnabas*. LCL. London: Heinemann, 1912.

———. *Eusebius: The Ecclesiastical History*. LCL. Cambridge, MA: Harvard University Press, 1965.

Lampe, Peter. *From Paul to Valentinus: Christians at Rome in the First Two Centuries*, edited by Marshall D. Johnson, translated by Michael Steinhauser. Minneapolis: Fortress, 2003.

Lange, Nicholas R. *Origin and the Jews: Studies in Jewish-Christian Relations in Third Century Palestine*. University of Cambridge Oriental Publications 25. Cambridge: University of Cambridge Press, 1976.

Langton, Daniel R. *The Apostle Paul in the Jewish Imagination: A Study in Modern Jewish-Christian Relations.* Cambridge: Cambridge University Press, 2010.

Lansing, Carol. "Popular Belief and Heresy." In *A Companion to the Medieval World,* edited by Carol Lansing and Edward D. English, 276–92. Blackwell Companions to European History. Chichester: Wiley-Blackwell, 2009.

Lawlor, H. J. "The Heresy of the Phrygians." *JTS* 9 (1908) 481–99.

Lawson, John. *A Theological and Historical Introduction to the Apostolic Fathers.* New York: Macmillan, 1961.

Layton, Bentley. *The Gnostic Scriptures: A New Translation with Annotations and Introductions.* New York: Doubleday, 1987.

———. "Prolegomena to the Study of Ancient Gnosticism." In *The Social World of the First Christians: Essays in Honor of Wayne A. Meeks,* edited by L. Michael White and O. Larry Yarbrough, 334–50. Minneapolis: Fortress, 1995.

———. ed. *The Rediscovery of Gnosticism,* 2 vols. Studies in the History of Religions 41. Leiden: Brill, 1981.

Le Boulluec, Alain. "La Bible chez les marginaux de l'orthodoxie." In *Monde grec ancient et la Bible,* 153–70. Paris: Éditions Beauchesne, 1984.

———. *La notion d'hérésie dans la littérature grecque IIe–IIIe siècles.* Paris: Études Augustiniennes, 1985.

———. "La réflexion d'Origène sur le discours hérésiologique." *RTP* 116 (1984) 297–308.

Leloup, Jean-Yves. *The Gospel of Mary Magdalene.* Rochester, VT: Inner Traditions, 2002.

Lemcio, Eugene. "The Unifying Kerygma of the New Testament." *JSNT* (1988) 3–17 and (1990) 3–11.

Lewis, Nicola Denzey. *Introduction to "Gnosticism": Ancient Voices, Christian Worlds.* New York: Oxford University Press, 2013.

Licona, Michael R. *The Resurrection of Jesus: A New Historiographical Approach.* Downers Grove, IL: IVP Academic, 2010.

Lieu, Judith M. *Image and Reality: The Jews in the World of the Christians in the Second Century.* Edinburgh: T. & T. Clark, 1996.

———. *Neither Jew nor Greek: Constructing Early Christianity.* Edinburgh: T. & T. Clark, 2002.

———. "'The Parting of the Ways': Theological Construct or Historical Reality." *JSNT* 56 (1994) 101–19. Reprinted in Judith Lieu, *Neither Jew Nor Greek? Constructing Early Christianity,* 1–29. London: T. & T. Clark, 2002.

Lightfoot, J. B. *The Apostolic Fathers: Clement, Ignatius, and Polycarp,* vol. II.3. 2nd ed. London: Macmillan, 1889.

Lindemann, Andreas. *Die Clemensbriefe.* HNT 17. Tübingen: Mohr Siebeck, 1992.

———. *Paulus im ältesten Christentum: Das Bild des Apostels und die Rezeption der paulinischen Theologie in der frühchristlichen Literatur bis Marcion.* BHT 58. Tübingen: Mohr Siebeck, 1979.

Litfin, Bryan M. "Learning from Patristic Use of the Rule of Faith." In *The Contemporary Church and the Early Church: Case Studies in Resourcement,* edited by Paul A. Hartog, 76–99. ETS Monographs 9. Eugene, OR: Pickwick, 2010.

Logan, Alistair H. B. *Gnostic Truth and Christian Heresy: A Study in the History of Gnosticism.* Peabody, MA: Hendrickson, 1996.

Lohmann, Hans. *Drohung und Verheißung: Exegetische Untersuchungen zur Eschatologie bei den Apostolischen Vätern.* BZNW 5. Berlin: De Gruyter, 1989.

Lohse, Bernhard. *Das Passafest der Quartadecimaner.* Beiträge zur Förderung christlicher Theologie 2.54. Gütersloh: Bertelsmann, 1953.

Lona, Horacio E. *Der erste Clemensbrief.* Kommentar zu den Apostolischen Vätern 2. Göttingen: Vandenhoeck & Ruprecht, 1998.

Louth, Andrew, editor. *Eusebius: The History of the Church from Christ to Constantine.* Translated by G. A. Williamson. Rev. ed. Penguin Classics. New York: Penguin, 1989.

Lüdemann, Gerd. *The Great Deception: And What Jesus Really Said and Did.* Translated by John Bowden. Amherst: Prometheus Press, 1999.

———. *Heretics: The Other Side of Early Christianity.* Translated by John Bowden. Louisville: Westminster John Knox, 1996.

———. *Opposition to Paul in Jewish Christianity.* Translated by M. Eugene Boring. Minneapolis: Fortress, 1989.

———. "The Successors of Pre-70 Jerusalem Christianity: A Critical Evaluation of the Pella-Tradition." In *Jewish and Christian Self-Definition,* vol. 1: *The Shaping of Christianity in the Second and Third Centuries,* edited by E. P. Sanders, 161–73. Philadelphia: Fortress, 1980.

———. *The Unholy in Scripture: The Dark Side of the Bible.* Translated by John Bowden. Louisville: Westminster John Knox, 1997.

———. *What Really Happened to Jesus: A Historical Approach to the Resurrection.* Translated by John Bowden. Louisville: Westminster John Knox, 1995.

———. "Zur Geschichte des ältesten Christentums in Rom. I. Valentin und Marcion; II. Ptolemäus und Justin." *ZNW* 70 (1979) 86–114.

Luomanen, Petri. "Nazarenes." In *A Companion to Second-Century Christian "Heretics,"* edited by Antti Marjanen and Petri Luomanen, 279–314. VCSup 76. Leiden: Brill, 2005.

Lyman Rebecca. "Hellenism and Heresy." *JECS* 11 (2003) 209–22.

———. "Reckonings in Heresy and Orthodoxy, Ancient and Modern." *AThR* 74 (1992) 125–32.

MacRae, George W. "Seth in Gnostic Texts and Traditions." In *SBLSP* 11 (1977) 17–24.

Mahé, Jean-Pierre. "Hermetic Religion." In *The Nag Hammadi Scriptures: The International Edition,* edited by Marvin Meyer, 795–98. New York: HarperOne, 2007.

Maier, Harry O. "The Politics and Rhetoric of Discord and Concord in Paul and Ignatius." In *Trajectories through the New Testament and the Apostolic Fathers,* edited by Andrew F. Gregory and Christopher M. Tuckett, 307–34. Oxford: Oxford University Press, 2005.

Malina, Bruce. "Jewish Christianity or Christian Judaism? Toward a Hypothetical Definition." *JSJ* 7 (1976) 46–57.

Marcus, Joel. "Birkat ha-Minim Revisited." *NTS* 55 (2009) 523–51.

de Margerie, Bertrand. *The Christian Trinity in History.* Still River, MA: St. Bede's Publications, 1975.

Marjanen, Antti. "Gnosticism." In *Oxford Handbook of Early Christian Studies,* edited by Susan Ashbrook Harvey and David G. Hunter, 203–20. New York: Oxford University Press, 2008.

———. "Montanism: Egalitarian Ecstatic 'New Prophecy.'" In *A Companion to Second-Century Christian "Heretics,"* edited by Antti Marjanen and Petri Loumanen. VCSup 76. Leiden: Brill, 2005.

Marjanen, Antti, editor. *Was There a Gnostic Religion?* Göttingen: Vandenhoeck & Ruprecht, 2005.

Marjanen, Antti, and Petri Luomanen, editors. *A Companion to Second-Century Christian "Heretics."* VCSup 76. Boston: Brill, 2005.

Markschies, Christoph. *Gnosis: An Introduction.* Translated by John Bowden. New York: T. & T. Clark, 2003.

———. *Valentinus Gnosticus?: Untersuchungen zur valentinianischen Gnosis mit einem Kommentar zu den Fragmenten Valentins.* WUNT 65. Tübingen: Mohr Siebeck, 1992.

Markus, Robert Austin. "The Problem of Self-Definition: From Sect to Church." In *Jewish and Christian Self-Definition*, vol. 1: *The Shaping of Christianity in the Second and Third Centuries*, edited by E. P. Sanders, 1–15. Minneapolis: Fortress, 1980.

Marshall, I. Howard. "Orthodoxy and Heresy in Earlier Christianity." *Them* 2 (1976) 5–14.

Martín Domínguez, María del Mar. "La relación entre ortodoxia y herejía: el valor de la tesis de Walter Bauer a principios del siglo XXI." MA thesis, Universidad Complutense de Madrid, 2012.

Martin, Brice L. "Some Reflections on the Unity of the New Testament." *SR* 8 (1979) 143–52.

Martin, Vincent. *A House Divided: The Parting of the Ways Between Synagogue and Church.* Stimulus Books. New York: Paulist, 1995.

McCabe, Matthew. *Jewish Christianity Reconsidered: Rethinking Ancient Groups and Texts.* Minneapolis: Fortress, 2007.

McCue, James F. "Bauer's *Rechtgläubigkeit und Ketzerei.*" In *Orthodoxy and Heterodoxy*, edited by Johannes Baptist Metz, 28–35. Concilium 192. Edinburgh: T. & T. Clark, 1987.

———. "Orthodoxy and Heresy: Walter Bauer and the Valentinians." *VC* 33 (1979) 118–30.

McDonald, Lee Martin. *The Biblical Canon: Its Origin, Transmission, and Authority.* Peabody, MA: Hendrickson, 2007.

McGowan, Andrew B., "Tertullian and the 'Heretical' Origins of the 'Orthodox' Trinity." *JECS* 14 (2006) 437–57.

McGrath, Alister E. *Heresy: A History of Defending the Truth.* New York: HarperOne, 2009.

Meagher, John Carney. "The Constitution of Normative Understanding in Earliest Christianity, Especially as Evidenced in Pauline, Lucan-Synoptic, and Johannine Writings." PhD diss., McMaster University, 1975.

Metzger, Bruce Manning. *The Canon of the New Testament: Its Origin, Development, and Significance.* Oxford: Oxford University Press, 1987.

———. *The Text of the New Testament: Its Transmission, Corruption, and Restoration.* 4th ed. New York: Oxford University Press, 2005.

Meyer, Marvin. *The Gnostic Discoveries: The Impact of the Nag Hammadi Library.* San Francisco: HarperSanFrancisco, 2005.

———. *The Gnostic Gospels of Jesus: The Definitive Collection of Mystical Gospels and Secret Books about Jesus of Nazareth.* New York: HarperCollins, 2005.

———. *The Gospel of Thomas: The Hidden Sayings of Jesus.* 2nd ed. New York: HarperCollins, 1992.

———. "Thomas Christianity." In *The Nag Hammadi Scriptures*, 779–83.

Meyer, Marvin, editor. *The Nag Hammadi Scriptures: The International Edition.* New York: HarperCollins, 2007.

Miller, Robert J., editor. *The Complete Gospels.* 4th ed. Salem, OR: Polebridge, 2010.

Mimouni, Simon Claude. "Étude critique: la question de l'hérésie ou de l'orthodoxie et de l'hétérodoxie." *Apocrypha* 20 (2009) 265–79.

———. "La 'Birkat ha-minim': une prière juive contre les judéo-chrétiens." *RevScRel* 71 (1997) 275–98.

———. *Le judéo-christianisme ancien: essais historiques.* Paris: Cerf, 1999.

———. *Les chrétiens d'origine juive dans l'antiquité.* Présence du Judaïsme poche 29. Paris: Michel, 2004.

Mimouni, Simon Claude, and F. Stanley Jones, editors. *Le judéo-christianisme dans tous ses états.* Paris: Cerf, 2001.

Mitros, Joseph F. "The Norm of Faith in the Patristic Age." *TS* 29 (1968) 444–71.

Moffat, James. "Review of Professor Bauer's *Rechtgläubigkeit und Ketzerei im ältesten Christentum.*" *ExpTim* 45 (1933–1934) 475.

Moll, Sebastian. "The Man with No Name: Who Is the Elder in Irenaeus's *Adversus Haereses IV?*" In *Irenaeus: Life, Scripture, Legacy*, edited by Sara Parvis and Paul Foster, 89–93. Minneapolis: Fortress, 2012.

Mommsen, Theodor, editor. *Gestorum Pontificum Romanorum*, vol. 1: *Monumenta Germaniae historica inde ab anno Christi quingentesimo usque ad annum millesimum et quingentesimum.* Berlin: Weidmannos, 1898.

Moreschini, Claudio and Enrico Norelli. *Early Christian Greek and Latin Literature: A Literary History*, vol. 1: *From Paul to the Age of Constantine.* Translated by Matthew J. O'Connell. Peabody, MA: Hendrickson, 2005.

Munck, Johannes. "Jewish Christianity in Post-Apostolic Times." *NTS* 6 (1960) 103–16.

Murray, Robert. "Defining Judaeo-Christianity." *Heythrop Journal* 15 (1974) 303–07.

Myllykoski, Matti. "Cerinthus." In *A Companion to Second-Century Christian "Heretics,"* edited by Antti Marjanen and Petri Luomanen, 213–46. VCSup 76. Leiden: Brill, 2005.

———. "James the Just in History and Tradition: Perspectives of Past and Present Scholarship." Parts I and II. *CBR* 5.1 (2006) 73–122; 6.1 (2007) 11–98.

Neander, Augustus. *General History of the Christian Religion and Church*, vol. 1. 11th ed. New York: Hurd & Houghton, 1871.

Neufeld, Vernon. *The Earliest Christian Confessions.* Grand Rapids: Eerdmans, 1963.

Nock, Arthur Darby and A. J. Festugière, editors. *Corpus Hermeticum.* 4 vols. Paris: Les Belles Lettres, 1954.

Norris, Frederick W. "Asia Minor before Ignatius: Walter Bauer Reconsidered." In *Studia Evangelica VII*, edited by E. A. Livingstone, 365–77. Berlin: Akademie-Verlag, 1982.

———. "Ignatius, Polycarp, and I Clement: Walter Bauer Reconsidered." *VC* 30 (1976) 23–44.

Oden, Thomas C. *The African Memory of Mark: Reassessing Early Church Tradition.* Downers Grove, IL: IVP Academic, 2011.

————. *How Africa Shaped the Christian Mind : Rediscovering the African Seedbed of Western Christianity.* Downers Grove, IL: InterVarsity, 2007.

————. *Early Libyan Christianity: Uncovering a North Africa Tradition.* Downers Grove, IL: IVP Academic, 2011.

O'Neill, John Cochrane. "Who Buried Peter and Paul?" In *Christians as a Religious Minority in a Multicultural City,* edited by Jürgen Zangenberg and Michael Labahn, 103–7. *JSNT*Sup 243. London: T. & T. Clark, 2004.

Opitz, Helmut. *Ursprünge frühkatholischer Pneumatologie: Ein Beitrag zur Entsehung der Lehre vom Heiligen Geist in der römischen Gemeinde unter Zugrundlegung des I. Clemensbriefes und des 'Hirten' des Hermas.* ThA 15. Berlin: 1960.

Osborn, Eric. "Reason and Rule of Faith in the Second Century AD." In *The Making of Orthodoxy,* edited by Rowan Williams, 40–61. Cambridge: Cambridge University Press, 1989.

————. *Tertullian, First Theologian of the West.* Cambridge: Cambridge University Press, 1997.

Outler, Albert C. "Origen and the *Regulae Fidei.*" *SecCent* 4 (1985) 133–41.

Oxford Society of Historical Theology. *The New Testament in the Apostolic Fathers.* Oxford: Clarendon, 1905.

Pagels, Elaine. *Beyond Belief: The Secret Gospel of Thomas.* New York: Vintage, 2003.

————. "Conflicting Versions of Valentinian Eschatology: Irenaeus's *Treatise* vs. *Excerpts from Theodosius.*" *HTR* 67 (1974) 35–53.

————. *The Gnostic Gospels.* New York: Random House, 1979.

Pagels, Elaine, and Karen King. *Reading Judas: The Gospel of Judas and the Shaping of Christianity.* New York: Viking, 2007.

Paget, James Carleton. "Jewish Christianity." In *The Cambridge History of Judaism,* vol. 3, edited by William Horbury et al., 731–75. Cambridge: Cambridge University Press, 1999.

Painter, John. *Just James: The Brother of Jesus in History and Tradition.* Columbia, SC: University of South Carolina Press, 1997.

Papandrea, James L. *Novatian of Rome and the Culmination of Pre-Nicene Orthodoxy.* Princeton Theological Monograph Series. Eugene, OR: Pickwick, 2012.

Pattengale, Jerry. "How the 'Jesus' Wife' Hoax Fell Apart." *Wall Street Journal,* May 1, 2014.

Paulsen, Henning. *Die Briefe des Ignatius von Antiochia und der Brief des Polykarp von Smyrna.* HNT 18. Tübingen: Mohr Siebeck, 1985.

Pearson, Birger A. *Ancient Gnosticism: Traditions and Literature.* Minneapolis: Fortress, 2007.

————. "Anti-Heretical Warnings in Codex IX from Nag Hammadi." In *Gnosticism, Judaism, and Egyptian Christianity,* 183–93. Studies in Antiquity and Christianity. Minneapolis: Fortress, 1990.

————. "Basilides the Gnostic." In *A Companion to Second-Century Christian "Heretics,"* edited by Antti Marjanen and Petri Luomanen, 1–31. VCSup 76. Leiden: Brill, 2005.

————. "Earliest Christianity in Egypt: Some Observations." In *The Roots of Egyptian Christianity,* edited by Birger A. Pearson and James E. Goehring, 132–59. Studies in Antiquity and Christianity. Philadelphia: Fortress, 1986.

———. "The Figure of Seth in Gnostic Literature." In *Gnosticism, Judaism, and Egyptian Christianity*, 52–83. Studies in Antiquity and Christianity. Minneapolis: Fortress, 1990.

———. "Friedländer Revisited: Alexandrian Judaism and Gnostic Origins." In *Gnosticism, Judaism, and Egyptian Christianity*, 10–28. Studies in Antiquity and Christianity. Minneapolis: Fortress, 1990.

———. *Gnosticism and Christianity in Roman and Coptic Egypt*. Studies in Antiquity and Christianity. New York: T. & T. Clark, 2004.

———. *Gnosticism, Judaism, and Egyptian Christianity*. Studies in Antiquity and Christianity. Minneapolis: Fortress, 1990.

———. "Gnosticism as a Religion." In *Was There a Gnostic Religion?*, edited by Antti Marjanen, 81–101. Göttingen: Vandenhoeck & Ruprecht, 2005

———. "Jewish Elements in Gnosticism and the Development of Gnostic Self-Definition." In *Gnosticism, Judaism, and Egyptian Christianity*, 124–35. Studies in Antiquity and Christianity. Minneapolis: Fortress, 1990.

———. "Nag Hammadi Codices." In *ABD*, vol. 4, 984–91.

———. *The Roots of Egyptian Christianity*. Philadelphia: Fortress, 1986.

Pelikan, Jaroslav. *The Christian Tradition: A History of the Development of Doctrine*, vol. 1: *The Emergence of the Catholic Tradition, 100–600*. Chicago: University of Chicago Press, 1975.

———. *Credo: Historical and Theological Guide to Creeds and Confessions of Faith in the Christian Tradition*, vol. 4. New Haven: Yale University Press, 2003.

———. "Montanism and Its Trinitarian Significance." *CH* 25 (1956) 99–109.

Pelikan, Jaroslav and Valerie Hotchkiss. *Creeds & Confessions of Faith in the Christian Tradition*, vol. 1. New Haven: Yale University Press, 2003.

Perkins, Pheme. *Gnosticism and the New Testament*. Minneapolis: Fortress, 1993.

———. "Irenaeus and the Gnostics: Rhetoric and Composition in *Adversus Haereses* Book One." *VC* 30 (1976) 193–200.

Perrin, Nicholas. "Irenaeus and Lytoard Against Heresies, Ancient and Modern." In *Ancient Faith for the Church's Future*, edited by Mark Husbands and Jeffrey P. Greenman, 126–40. Downers Grove, IL: IVP Academic, 2008.

———. *Lost in Translation: What We Can Know About the Words of Jesus*. Nashville: Nelson, 2007.

———. *Thomas, the Other Gospel*. Louisville: Westminster John Knox, 2007.

Pervo, Richard I. *The Making of Paul: Constructions of the Apostle in Early Christianity*. Minneapolis: Fortress, 2010.

Pétrement, Simone. *A Separate God: The Origins and Teachings of Gnosticism*. Translated by Carol Harrison. San Francisco: HarperSanFrancisco, 1990.

Pines, Shlomo. "The Jewish Christians of the Early Centuries of Christianity According to a New Source." *Proceedings of the Israel Academy of Sciences and Humanities* 2 (1968) 237–309.

Poirier, John C. "Montanist Pepuza-Jerusalem and the Dwelling Place of Wisdom." *JECS* 7 (1999) 491–97.

Powell, Douglas. "Tertullianists and Cataphrygians." *VC* 29 (1975) 33–54.

———. "Tertullianists and Cataphrygians." *VC* 41 (1987) 139–53.

Power, Owen. *Hugh Schonfield: A Case Study of Complex Jewish Identities*. Eugene, OR: Wipf & Stock, 2013.

Preisker, Herbert. "Orthos." In *TDNT*, vol. 5, 449–51.

Pritz, Ray A. *Nazarene Jewish Christianity: From the End of the New Testament Period until its Disappearance in the Fourth Century.* SPB 37. Leiden: Brill, 1988.

Prümm, Karl. *Gnosis an der Wurzel des Christentums? Grundlagenkritik d. Entmythologisierung.* Müller: Salzburg, 1972.

Räisänen, Heikki. "Marcion." In *A Companion to Second Century Christian "Heretics,"* edited by Antti Marjanen and Petri Loumanen, 100–24. VCSup 76. Leiden: Brill, 2005.

———. "'Werkgerechtichkeit'—eine 'frühkatholische' Lehre? Überlegungen zum 1. Klemensbrief." *ST* 37 (1983) 79–99.

Ramsay, G. G. *The Sixteen Satires of Juvenal.* New York: Digireads.com, 2011.

Ramsay, William Mitchell. *The Church in the Roman Empire before A.D. 170.* New York: Putnam's, 1893.

Rensberger, David K. "As the Apostle Teaches: The Development of the Use of Paul's Letters in Second-Century Christianity." PhD diss., Yale University, 1981.

Riley, Gregory J. *One Jesus, Many Christs: How Jesus Inspired Not One True Christianity, But Many.* San Francisco: HarperSanFrancisco, 1997.

Ritter, Adolf Martin. "De Polycarpe à Clément: Aux origines d'Alexandrie chrétienne." In *ΑΛΕΞΑΝΔΡΙΝΑ: Hellénisme, judaïsme et christianisme à Alexandrie,* edited by P. Claude Mondésert, 151–72. Paris: Cerf, 1987.

Robeck, Cecil M., Jr. *Prophecy in Carthage: Perpetua, Tertullian, and Cyprian.* Cleveland: Pilgrim, 1992.

Roberts, Colin H. *Manuscript, Society, and Belief in Early Egypt.* SchL 1977. London: Oxford University Press, 1979.

Roberts, Frank Carl. "Gottfried Arnold as a Historian of Christianity: A Reappraisal of the Unparteiische Kirchen- und Ketzer-historie." PhD diss., Vanderbilt University, 1973.

Robinson, James M. "From *The Nag Hammadi Codices* to *The Gospel of Mary* and *The Gospel of Judas.*" Occasional Papers of the Institute for Antiquity and Christianity 48. Claremont, CA: Institute for Antiquity and Christianity, 2006.

Robinson, James M., editor. *The Nag Hammadi Library in English.* 3rd ed. San Francisco: Harper & Row, 1988.

Robinson, James M. and Helmut Koester. *Trajectories through Early Christianity.* Minneapolis: Fortress, 1971.

Robinson, Thomas A. *The Bauer Thesis Examined: The Geography of Heresy in the Early Christian Church.* Studies in the Bible and Early Christianity 11. Lewiston, NY: Mellen, 1988.

———. *Ignatius of Antioch and the Parting of the Ways: Early Jewish-Christian Relations.* Peabody, MA: Hendrickson, 2009.

———. "Orthodoxy and Heresy in Western Asia Minor in the First Christian Century: A Dialogical Response to Walter Bauer." PhD diss., McMaster University, 1985.

Rohde, Joachim. "Häresie und Schisma im ersten Clemensbrief und in den Ignatiusbriefen." *NT* 10 (1968) 216–33.

Rombs, Ronnie J., and Alexander Y. Hwang, editors. *Tradition and the Rule of Faith in the Early Church: Essays in Honor of Joseph T. Lienhard.* Washington, DC: Catholic University of America Press, 2010.

Roukema, Riemer. *Gnosis and Faith in Early Christianity: An Introduction to Gnosticism.* Translated by John Bowden. Harrisburg, PA: Trinity Press International, 1999.

———. *Jesus, Gnosis and Dogma.* New York: T. & T. Clark, 2010.

Royalty, Robert M. "Justin's Conversion and the Rhetoric of Heresy." *StPatr* 40 (2006) 509–14.

Rudolph, Kurt. *Gnosis: The Nature and History of Gnosticism*. Edited and translated by R. McL. Wilson. San Francisco: Harper & Row, 1983.

Ruether, Rosemary Radford. *Women and Redemption*. Minneapolis: Fortress, 1998.

Saliba, Issa A. "The Bishop of Antioch and the Heretics: A Study of a Primitive Christology." *EvQ* 54 (1982) 65–76.

Saxer, Victor. "Africa." In *Encyclopedia of the Early Church*, edited by Angelo Di Berardino, translated by Adrian Walford, 13–14. New York: Oxford University Press, 1991.

Schenke, H. M. "Das sethianische System nach Nag-Hammadi-Handschriften." In *Studia Coptica*, edited by Peter Nagel, 165–74. Berliner Byzantinische Arbeiten 45. Berlin: Akademie-Verlag, 1974.

————. "The Phenomenon and Significance of Gnostic Sethianism." In *The Rediscovery of Gnosticism*, vol. 2, edited by B. Layton, 588–616. Studies in the Histories of Religion 41. Leiden: Brill, 1981.

Schepelern, Wilhelm. *Der Montanismus und die phrygischen Kulte: Eine religionsgeschichtliche Untersuchung*. Tubingen: Mohr Siebeck, 1929.

"Schism." In the *New American Encyclopedic Dictionary*, edited by Edward Thomas Roe et al., 3572–73. New York: Hill, 1907.

Schleier, Heinrich. "Hairesis." In *TDNT*, vol 1, 180–85.

Schmithals, Walter. *Gnosticism in Corinth: An Investigation of the Letters to the Corinthians*. Translated by John E. Steely. Nashville: Abingdon, 1971.

Schneemelcher, Wilhelm. "Walter Bauer als Kirchenhistoriker." *NTS* 9 (1962) 11–22.

Schoedel, William R. *Ignatius of Antioch: A Commentary on the Letters of Ignatius of Antioch*. Philadelphia: Fortress, 1985.

————. "Philosophy and Rhetoric in the *Adversus Haereses* of Irenaeus." *VC* 13 (1959) 22–32.

————. *Polycarp, Martyrdom of Polycarp, Fragments of Papias*. The Apostolic Fathers: A New Translation and Commentary 5. New York: Nelson, 1967.

————. "Theological Norms and Social Perspectives in Ignatius of Antioch." In *Jewish and Christian Self-Definition*, vol. 1: *The Shaping of Christianity in the Second and Third Centuries*, edited by E. P. Sanders, 30–56. Philadelphia: Fortress, 1980.

Schoeps, Hans Joachim. *Jewish Christianity: Factional Disputes in the Early Church*. Philadelphia: Fortress, 1969.

Scholer, David M. "Gnosis, Gnosticism." In *Dictionary of the Later New Testament & Its Development*, edited by Ralph P. Martin and Peter H. Davids, 400–12. Downers Grove, IL: InterVarsity, 1997.

————. *Nag Hammadi Bibliography 1948–1969*. Nag Hammadi Studies 1. Leiden: Brill, 1971.

————. *Nag Hammadi Bibliography 1970–1994*. Nag Hammadi and Manichaean Studies 32. Leiden: Brill, 1997.

————. *Nag Hammadi Bibliography 1995–2006*. Nag Hammadi and Manichaean Studies 65. Leiden: Brill, 2009.

Schonfield, Hugh J. *According to the Hebrews: A New Translation of the Jewish Life of Jesus (the Toldoth Jeshu)*. London: Duckworth, 1937.

————. *The History of Jewish Christianity: From the First to the Twentieth Century*. London: Duckworth, 1936.

Schweitzer, Albert. *Geschichte der Leben-Jesu-Forschung.* 2nd ed. Tübingen: Mohr Siebeck, 1913.

———. *The Quest of the Historical Jesus: A Critical Study of Its Progress from Reimarus to Wrede.* Translated by William Montgomery. 2nd ed. London: Black, 1911.

Segal, Alan F. "Jewish Christianity." In *Eusebius, Christianity, and Judaism,* edited by Harold W. Attridge and Gōhei Hata, 327–51. SPB 42. Leiden: Brill, 1987.

———. *Rebecca's Children: Judaism and Christianity in the Roman World.* Cambridge, MA: Harvard University Press, 1986.

———. *Two Powers in Heaven: Early Rabbinic Reports about Christianity and Gnosticism.* Leiden: Brill, 2002.

Selby, Andrew M. "Bishops, Elders, and Deacons in the Philippian Church: Evidence of Plurality from Paul and Polycarp." *PRSt* 39 (2012) 79–94.

Semler, Johann and Edmund S. Whitman. *Abhandlung von freier Untersuchung des Canons.* Halle: Hemmerde, 1776.

Setzer, Claudia. *Jewish Responses to Early Christianity: History and Polemics, 30–150 C.E.* Minneapolis: Fortress, 1994.

Shelton, W. Brian. "Irenaeus." In *Shapers of Christian Orthodoxy,* edited by Bradley G. Green, 15–63. Downers Grove, IL: InterVarsity, 2010.

———. *Martyrdom from Exegesis in Hippolytus: An Early Church Presbyter's Commentary on Daniel.* Milton Keynes: Paternoster, 2008.

———. "Africa." In *Encyclopedia of Early Christianity,* edited by Everett Ferguson, 14–15. New York: Garland, 1990.

Sider, Robert D. *Ancient Rhetoric and the Art of Tertullian.* London: Oxford University Press, 1971.

Simon, Marcel. "From Greek *Hairesis* to Christian Heresy." In *Early Christian Literature and the Classical Intellectual Tradition,* edited by William R. Schoedel and Robert Louis Wilken, 101–16. *Théologie historique* 53. Paris: Éditions Beauchesne, 1979.

———. *Versus Israel: étude sur les relations entre chrétiens et juifs dans l'empire romain (135–425).* 2nd ed. Paris: Édition-Diffusion de Boccard, 1983.

Skarsaune, Oskar. *In the Shadow of the Temple: Jewish Influences on Early Christianity.* Downers Grove, IL: InterVarsity, 2002.

———. *The Proof from Prophecy: A Study in Justin Martyr's Proof-Text Tradition: Text-type, Provenance, Theological Profile. NovT*Sup 56. Leiden: Brill, 1987.

Skarsaune, Oskar, and Riedar Hvalvik, editors. *Jewish Believers in Jesus: The Early Centuries.* Peabody, MA: Hendrickson Publishers, 2007.

Smalley, Stephen S. "Diversity and Development in John." *NTS* 17 (1971) 276–92.

Smith, Carl B., II. "Is the Maker of Heaven and Earth the Father of Jesus?" In *The Light of Discovery: Studies in Honor of Edwin Yamauchi,* edited by John D. Wineland, 25–63. ETS Monograph Series 6. Eugene, OR: Pickwick, 2007.

———. *No Longer Jews: The Search for Gnostic Origins.* Peabody, MA: Hendrickson, 2004.

Smith, D. Moody. "The Epistles of John: What's New since Brooke's *ICC* in 1912?" *ExpTim* 120 (2009) 373–84.

Smith, Morton. *Clement of Alexandria and a Secret Gospel of Mark.* Cambridge, MA: Harvard University Press, 1973.

———. *The Secret Gospel: The Discovery and Interpretation of the Secret Gospel According to Mark.* New York: Harper & Row, 1973.

Smither, Edward L. *Augustine as Mentor: A Model for Preparing Spiritual Leaders.* Nashville: B & H Academic, 2008.

Staats, Reinhart. "Die Katholische Kirche des Ignatius von Antiochien und das Problem ihrer Normativität im zweiten Jahrhundert." *ZNW* 77 (1986) 126–45, 242–54.

Stanton, Graham N., and Guy G. Stroumsa, editors. *Tolerance and Intolerance in Early Judaism and Christianity.* Cambridge: Cambridge University Press, 1998.

Stark, Rodney. *Cities of God: The Real Story of How Christianity Became an Urban Movement and Conquered Rome.* New York: HarperOne, 2006.

———. *The Rise of Christianity: How the Obscure, Marginal Jesus Movement Became the Dominant Religious Force in the Western World in a Few Centuries.* Princeton: Princeton University Press, 1996.

Staten, Stephen Francis. "Was There Unity in the Sub-Apostolic Church? An Investigation of the Tunnel Period (A.D. 62–150)." MA thesis, Wheaton College, 1996.

Steinmetz, Peter. "Polykarp von Smyrna über die Gerechtigkeit." *Hermes* 100 (1972) 63–75.

Stemberger, Günter. *Jews and Christians in the Holy Land: Palestine in the Fourth Century.* Translated by Ruth Tuschling. Edinburgh: T. & T. Clark, 2000.

Strecker, Georg. *Das Judenchristentum in den Pseudoklementinen.* 2nd ed. Texte und Untersuchungen 70. Berlin: Akademie-Verlag, 1981.

———. "The Reception of the Book." In *Orthodoxy and Heresy in Earliest Christianity,* by Walter Bauer, 2nd ed., edited by Robert A. Kraft and Gerhard Krodel, 286–316. Philadelphia: Fortress, 1971.

———. "Walter Bauer: Exeget, Philologe, und Historiker: Zum 100 Geburtstag am 8/8/1977." *NovT* 20 (1978) 75–80.

Streeter, Burnett Hillman. *The Primitive Church: Studied with Special Reference to the Origins of the Christian Ministry.* New York: Macmillan, 1929.

Strickland, Michael. "Revising the Ancient Faith: Primitivism, the Gospel of Thomas, and Christian Beginnings." *ResQ* 49 (2007) 217–27.

Stroker, William Dettwiller. "The Formation of Secondary Sayings of Jesus." PhD diss., Yale University, 1970.

Stroumsa, Guy G. *Another Seed: Studies in Gnostic Mythology.* Nag Hammadi Studies 24. Leiden: Brill, 1984.

Stuckwisch, David R. "Saint Polycarp of Smyrna: Johannine or Pauline Figure?" *CTQ* 61 (1997) 113–25.

Sullivan, Dale. "Identification and Dissociation in Rhetorical Exposé: An Analysis of St. Irenaeus' *Against Heresies.*" *Rhetorical Society Quarterly* 29 (1999) 49–76.

Svigel, Michael J. "You Got to Know When to Hold 'em: Trumping the Bauer Thesis." Available at bible.org/article/"you-got-know-when-hold-'em"-trumping-bauer-thesis.

Swete, Henry. "St. Mark in Early Tradition." *Expositor* 5 (1897) 268–77.

Tabbernee, William. *Fake Prophecy and Polluted Sacraments: Ecclesiastical and Imperial Reactions to Montanism.* VCSup 84. Leiden: Brill, 2007.

———. "The Montanist Oracles: A New Classification." Paper presented at the Second Century Seminar, Waco, Texas, on 19 February 2004.

———. "'Our Trophies Are Better Than Your Trophies': The Appeal to Tombs and Reliquaries in Montanist-Orthodox Relations." In *StPatr* 31 (1997) 206–17.

———. "Perpetua, Montanism, and Christian Ministry in Carthage c. 203 C.E." *Perspectives in Religious Studies* 32 (2005) 421–41.

———. "To Pardon or Not to Pardon?: North-African Montanism and the Forgiveness of Sins." *StPatr* 36 (2001) 375–86.

———. "'Will the Real Paraclete Please Speak Forth!': The Catholic-Montanist Conflict over Pneumatology." In *Advents of the Spirit: An Introduction to the Current Study of Pneumatology*, edited by Bradford E. Hinze and D. Lyle Dabney, 97–115. Marquette Studies in Theology 30. Milwaukee: Marquette University Press, 2001.

Tabbernee, William, editor. *Montanist Inscriptions and Testimonia: Epigraphic Sources Illustrating the History of Montanism*. Patristic Monographs 16. Macon, GA: Mercer University Press, 1997.

Tabor, James D. *The Jesus Dynasty: The Hidden History of Jesus, His Royal Family, and the Birth of Christianity*. New York: Simon and Schuster, 2006.

Tajra, Harry W. *The Martyrdom of St. Paul: Historical and Judicial Context, Traditions, and Legends*. WUNT 2.67. Tübingen: Mohr Siebeck, 1994.

Taylor, Joan E. *Christians and Holy Places: The Myth of Jewish Christian Origins*. New York: Oxford University Press, 1993.

———. "The Phenomenon of Early Jewish Christian Christianity: Reality or Scholarly Invention?" *VC* 44 (1990) 313–34.

Teppler, Yaakov Y. *Birkat haMinim: Jews and Christians in Conflict in the Ancient World*. Texts and Studies in Ancient Judaism 120. Tübingen: Mohr Siebeck, 2007.

Theobald, Michael. "Paulus und Polykarp an die Philipper: Schlaglichter auf die frühe Rezeption des Basissatzes von der Rechtfertigung." In *Lutherische und Neue Paulusperspektive*, edited by Michael Bachmann, 349–88. WUNT 182. Tübingen: Mohr Siebeck, 2005.

Thomassen, Einar. "Orthodoxy and Heresy in Second-Century Rome." *HTR* 97 (2004) 241–56.

———. *The Spiritual Seed: The Church of the "Valentinians."* Nag Hammadi and Manichaean Studies 60. Leiden: Brill, 2008.

Thompson, Glen L. *The Correspondence of Julius I*. Library of Early Christianity. Washington, DC: Catholic University of America Press, 2014.

Thompson, Michael B. "The Holy Internet: Communication between Churches in the First Christian Generation." In *The Gospels for All Christians: Rethinking the Gospel Audiences*, edited by Richard Baukham, 49–70. Grand Rapids: Eerdmans, 1998.

Tiessen, Terrance L. "Gnosticism as Heresy: The Response of Irenaeus." In *Hellenization Revisited: Shaping a Christian Response within the Greco-Roman World*, edited by Wendy E. Hellerman, 339–56. Lanham: University Press of America, 1994. Reprinted as "Gnosticism as Heresy: The Response of Irenaeus." *Didaskalia* 18 (2007) 31–48.

Tilley, Maureen, "The Collapse of a Collegial Church: North African Christianity on the Eve of Islam." *TS* 62 (2001) 3–22.

———. "North Africa." In *The Cambridge History of Christianity*, vol. 1: *Origins to Constantine*, edited by Margaret M. Mitchell and Frances M. Young, 381–96. Cambridge: Cambridge University Press, 2006.

———. "The Passion of Perpetua and Felicity." In *Searching the Scriptures*, vol. 2: *A Feminist Commentary*, edited by Elisabeth Schüssler Fiorenza, 829–58. London: SCM, 1995.

Tilling, Chris. "Misreading Paul's Christology: Problems with Ehrman's Exegesis." In *How God Became Jesus: The Real Origins of Belief in Jesus' Divine Nature*, edited by Michael F. Bird, 134–50. Grand Rapids: Zondervan, 2014.

————. "Problems with Ehrman's Interpretive Categories." In *How God Became Jesus: The Real Origins of Belief in Jesus' Divine Nature*, edited by Michael F. Bird, 117–33. Grand Rapids: Zondervan, 2014.

Tomson, Peter J., and Doris Lambers-Petry, editors. *The Image of the Judaeo-Christians in Ancient Jewish and Christian Literature.* WUNT 158. Tübingen: Mohr Siebeck, 2003.

Trebilco, Paul. "Christian Communities in Western Asia Minor into the Early Second Century: Ignatius and Others as Witnesses Against Bauer." *JETS* 49 (2006) 17–44.

————. "Christians in the Lycus Valley: The View from Ephesus and from Asia Minor." In *Colossae in Space and Time: Linking to an Ancient City*, edited by Alan H. Cadwallader and Michael Trainor, 180–211. Göttingen: Vandenhoeck & Ruprecht, 2011.

————. *The Early Christians in Ephesus from Paul to Ignatius.* WUNT 166. Tübingen: Mohr Siebeck, 2004.

Trevett, Christine. *Montanism: Gender, Authority and the New Prophecy.* Cambridge: Cambridge University Press, 1996.

Turner, H. E. W. *The Pattern of Christian Truth: A Study in the Relations between Orthodoxy and Heresy in the Early Church.* London: Mowbray, 1954.

Turner, John D. "The Gnostic Threefold Path to Enlightenment: The Ascent of Mind and the Descent of Wisdom." *NovT* 22 (1980) 324–51.

————. "Sethian Gnosticism: A Literary History." In *Nag Hammadi, Gnosticism, and Early Christianity*, edited by Harold W. Attridge et al., 55–86. Peabody, MA: Hendrickson, 1986.

————. *Sethian Gnosticism and the Platonic Tradition.* Bibliothèque Copte de Nag Hammadi 6. Quebec: Les Presses de L'Université Laval, 2001.

————. "The Sethian School of Thought." In *The Nag Hammadi Scriptures*, edited by Marvin Meyer, 784–89.

Unnik, Willem Cornelius van. "*The Gospel of Truth* and the New Testament." In *The Jung Codex*, edited by Frank Leslie Cross et al., 79–129. London: Mowbray, 1955.

Uro, Risto. *Thomas: Seeking the Historical Context of the Gospel of Thomas.* New York: T. & T. Clark, 2003.

Vallée, Gérard. *A Study in Anti-Gnostic Polemics: Irenaeus, Hippolytus, and Epiphanius*, vol 1. Studies in Christianity and Judaism. Ontario: Wilfrid Laurier University Press, 1981.

Van Cauwelaert, R. "L'intervention de l'église de Rome à Corinthe vers l'an 96." *RHE* 31 (1935) 267–306, 765–68.

Van der Horst, Pieter W. "The Birkat ha-Minim in Recent Research." *ExpTim* 105 (1994) 363–68.

Van Elderen, Bastiaan. "Early Christianity in Transjordan." *TynBul* 45 (1994) 97–117.

Van Voorst, Robert E. *The Ascents of James: History and Theology of a Jewish-Christian Community.* SBLDS 112. Atlanta: Scholars, 1989.

Varner, William. *Ancient Jewish-Christian Dialogues: Athanasius and Zacchaeus, Simon and Theophilus, Timothy and Aquila.* Lampeter: Mellen, 2005.

————. "In the Wake of Trypho: Jewish-Christian Dialogues in the Third to Sixth Centuries." *EvQ* 80 (2008) 219–36.

Verheyden, Joseph. "Epiphanius on the Ebionites." In *The Image of the Judaeo-Christians in Ancient Jewish and Christian Literature*, edited by Peter J. Tomson and Doris Lambers-Petry, 182–208. WUNT 158. Tübingen: Mohr Siebeck, 2003.

———. "The Flight of the Christians to Pella." *ETL* 66 (1990) 368–84.

Vinzent, Markus. *Christ's Resurrection in Early Christianity and the Making of the New Testament*. Burlington, VT: Ashgate, 2011.

Visotzky, Burton L. *Fathers of the World: Essays in Rabbinic and Patristic Literature*. WUNT 80. Tübingen: Mohr Siebeck, 1995.

Völker, Walther. "Walter Bauer's *Rechtgläubigkeit und Ketzerei im ältesten Christentum*." Translated by Thomas P. Scheck, *JECS* 14 (2006) 399–405.

Weinrich, William C. *Spirit and Martyrdom: A Study of the Works of the Holy Spirit in Contexts of Persecution and Martyrdoms in the New Testament and Early Christian Literature*. Washington, DC: University Press of America, 1981.

Welborn, L. L. "Clement, First Epistle of." In *ABD*, vol. 1, 1055–60.

Wilhite, David E. "Polycarp's Reception of Paul and Rhetorical Structure: Can One Inform the Other?" In *The Apostolic Fathers and Paul*, edited by Todd D. Still and David E. Wilhite. London: T. & T. Clark, forthcoming

Wilken, Robert L. "Diversity and Unity in Early Christianity." *SecCent* 1 (1981) 101–10.

Wilkins, Michael J., and J. P. Moreland, editors. *Jesus Under Fire: Modern Scholarship Reinvents the Historical Jesus*. Grand Rapids: Zondervan, 1995.

Williams, A. Lukyn. *Adversus Judaeos: A Bird's-eye View of Christian Apologiae until the Renaissance*. Cambridge: Cambridge University Press, 1935.

Williams, Michael A. *Rethinking "Gnosticism": An Argument for Dismantling a Dubious Category*. Princeton: Princeton University Press, 1996.

———. "Was There a Gnostic Religion? Strategies for a Clearer Analysis." In *Was There a Gnostic Religion?*, edited by Antti Marjanen, 55–79. Göttingen: Vandenhoeck & Ruprecht, 2005

Williams, Robert Lee. "'Hippolytan' Reactions to Montanism: Tensions in the Churches of Rome in the Early Third Century." *StPatr* 39 (2006) 131–37.

Williams, Rowan. "Does It Make Sense to Speak of Pre-Nicene Orthodoxy?" In *The Making of Orthodoxy: Essays in Honour of Henry Chadwick*, edited by Rowan Williams, 1–23. Cambridge: Cambridge University Press, 1989.

Willitts, Joel. "Paul and Jewish Christianity in the Second Century." In *Paul and the Second Century*, edited by Michael F. Bird and Joseph R. Dodson, 140–68. LNTS 412. London: T. & T. Clark, 2011.

Wilson, R. McL. *Gnosis and the New Testament*. Philadelphia: Fortress, 1968.

Wilson, Stephen. *Related Strangers: Jews and Christians, 70–170 C.E.* Minneapolis: Fortress, 1995.

Wise, Michael O. "Nazarene." In *Dictionary of Jesus and the Gospels*, edited by Joel B. Green et al., 571–74. Downers Grove, IL: InterVarsity, 1992.

Wisse, Frederik. "The Epistle of Jude in the History of Heresiology." In *Essays on the Nag Hammadi Texts*, edited by Martin Krause, 133–43. Leiden: Brill, 1972.

———. "The Nag Hammadi Library and the Heresiologists." *VC* 25 (1971) 205–23.

———. "Die Sextus-Sprüche und das Probleme der gnostischen Ethik." In *Zum Hellenismus in den Schriften von Nag Hammadi*, edited by Alexander Böhlig and Frederik Wisse, 55–86. Wiesbaden: Harrassowitz, 1975.

———. "Stalking Those Elusive Sethians." In *The Rediscovery of Gnosticism*, vol. 2, edited by Bentley Layton, 563–78. Studies in the History of Religions 41. Leiden: Brill, 1981.

———. "The Use of Early Christian Literature as Evidence for Inner Diversity and Conflict." In *Nag Hammadi, Gnosticism, & Early Christianity*, edited by Charles W. Hedrick and Robert Hodgson, Jr., 177–90. Peabody, MA: Hendrickson, 1986.

Witherington, Ben, III. *The Jesus Quest: The Third Search for the Jew of Nazareth*. 2nd ed. Downers Grove, IL: IVP, 1997.

———. *What Have They Done with Jesus? Beyond Strange Theories and Bad History— Why We Can Trust the Bible*. San Francisco: HarperSanFrancisco, 2006.

Wright, David F. "The Latin Fathers." In *Early Christianity: Origins and Evolution to AD 600*, edited by Ian Hazlett, 148–62. London: SPCK, 1991.

———. "Schism." In *The New Dictionary of Theology*, edited by David F. Wright and Sinclair B. Ferguson, 619. Downers Grove, IL: InterVarsity, 1988.

Wright, N. T. *Judas and the Gospel of Jesus: Have We Missed the Truth about Christianity?* Grand Rapids: Baker, 2006.

———. *The Resurrection of the Son of God*. Christian Origins and the Question of God 3. Minneapolis: Fortress, 2003.

Yamauchi, Edwin M. "The Crucifixion and Docetic Christology." *Concordia Theological Quarterly* 46 (1982) 1–20.

———. "Hermetic Literature." In *Interpreter's Dictionary of the Bible, Supplementary Volume*, edited by Keith Crim et al., 48. Nashville: Abingdon, 1976.

———. "History-of-Religions School." In *New Dictionary of Theology*, edited by S. B. Ferguson et al., 308–9. Downers Grove, IL: InterVarsity, 1988.

———. "The Issue of Pre-Christian Gnosticism Reviewed in Light of the Nag Hammadi Texts." In *The Nag Hammadi Library after Fifty Years: Proceedings of the 1995 Society of Biblical Literature Commemoration*, edited by John Douglas Turner and Anne Marie McGuire, 72–88. Nag Hammadi and Manichaean Studies 44. Leiden: Brill, 1997.

———. *Pre-Christian Gnosticism: A Survey of the Proposed Evidences*. 2nd ed. Grand Rapids: Baker, 1983.

Yarbrough, Robert W. "The Date of Papias: A Reassessment." *JETS* 26 (1983) 181–91.

Young, Frances M. "Did Epiphanius Know What He Meant by Heresy?" *SP* 17 (1982) 199–205.

Young, Stephen E. *The Jesus Tradition in the Apostolic Fathers*. WUNT 2.311. Tübingen: Mohr Siebeck, 2011.

Zetterholm, Magnus. *The Foundation of Christianity in Antioch: A Social-Scientific Approach to the Separation between Judaism and Christianity*. New York: Routledge, 2003.

Ziegler, Mario. *Successio: die Vorsteher der stadtrömischen Christengemeinde in den ersten beiden Jahrhunderten*. Bonn: Habelt, 2007.

Zwierlein, Otto. *Petrus in Rom, die literarischen Zeugnisse: mit einer kritischen Edition der Martyrien des Petrus und Paulus auf neuer handschriftlicher Grundlage*. Berlin: De Gruyter, 2009.